THE TASTEMAKERS

The Shaping of American Popular Taste

Russell Lynes

With a new Afterword

Dover Publications, Inc.
New York

To Adelaide Sparkman Lynes

Published in Canada by General Publishing Company, Ltd., 30 Lesmill Road, Don Mills, Toronto, Ontario.

Published in the United Kingdom by Constable and Company, Ltd., 10 Orange Street, London WC2H 7EG.

This Dover edition, first published in 1980, is an unabridged republication of the work originally published by Harper & Brothers, New York, in 1955. The author has written an Afterword especially for the present edition.

International Standard Book Number: 0-486-23993-4
Library of Congress Catalog Card Number: 80-65770

Manufactured in the United States of America
Dover Publications, Inc.
180 Varick Street
New York, N.Y. 10014

CONTENTS

Part One: The Public Taste

I.   Enter the Lawyer's Wife   3

II.   Every Man a Connoisseur   8

III.   Smiling Lawns and Tasteful Cottages   21

IV.   The Art Missionaries   37

V.   Art and Fashion—Cheap and Popular   65

VI.   Palaces for the People   81

VII.   Packaged Taste   97

Part Two: The Private Taste

VIII.   Stately Homes   121

IX.   Societies for Truth and Beauty   147

X.   The Peacock on the Newel Post   163

XI.   Suitability!   180

XII.   Whirlwind on Twenty-Sixth Street   196

Part Three: The Corporate Taste

XIII.   Taste on Wheels   225

XIV.   Suburbia in Excelsis   235

XV.   The Art World   256

XVI.   Taste—Tax Deductible   287

XVII.   Highbrow, Lowbrow, Middlebrow   310

XVIII.   Exit the Lawyer's Wife   334

Afterword   343

Sources and Acknowledgments   353

Index   358

ILLUSTRATIONS

With their sources

Following page 50

"Youth" from the series "The Voyage of Life" by Thomas Cole, "published exclusively for the members [of the American Art Union] of 1849" (*photo New York Public Library*)

"The Greek Slave" by Hiram Powers as it was exhibited at the Düsseldorf Gallery in New York City in 1858. Engraving by R. Thew (*photo New York Public Library*)

"Distribution of the Art Union Prizes" at the Broadway Tabernacle, New York City, 1847. Drawing by T. H. Matteson; lithograph by Davignon (*photo Metropolitan Museum of Art, N.Y.C.*)

"Mr. and Mrs. Ernest Fiedler and Family, 1850." (*coll. Mrs. William Lathrop Rich, photo Museum of the City of New York*)

Greek Revival mansion at Barrytown, N. Y. (*photo by the author*)

Greek Revival dwelling, Sheffield, Mass. (*photo by the author*)

"Highland Gardens," the residence of Andrew Jackson Downing at Newburgh, N.Y. No longer standing (*coll. the author*)

Andrew Jackson Downing, frontispiece of *Landscape Gardening and Rural Architecture* (1859) (*coll. the author*)

Gothic Revival house, Hudson, N.Y. (*photo by the author*)

Drawing room from the Robert J. Milligan house, Saratoga Springs, N.Y. (1854-56), now in the Brooklyn Museum Collection (*photo Brooklyn Museum*)

"Italian Villa" from Currier & Ives series "American Country Life, May Morning," 1855 (*photo New York Public Library*)

"Central Park, Summer," (chromolithograph) by John Bachmann (*photo Metropolitan Museum of Art*)

Federated Church, Croton Falls, New York (*photo by the author*)

"Consummation of Empire," from the series "The Course of Empire" by Thomas Cole (*coll. New-York Historical Society, N.Y.C.*)

Luman Reed, detail of a portrait by Asher B. Durand (*coll. New York-Historical Society, N.Y.C.*)

"Crucifixion" by Lorenzo Monaco in the Jarves Collection, Yale University (*Yale University Art Gallery*)

James Jackson Jarves, photograph (*Yale University Art Gallery*)

"Rest on the Flight into Egypt" by Paris Bordone from the T. J. Bryan Collection (*coll. New-York Historical Society, N.Y.C.*)

Thomas Jefferson Bryan, detail of a portrait by William O. Stone. (*coll. New-York Historical Society, N.Y.C.*)

"Interior View of the Metropolitan Museum when in Fourteenth Street, New York," by Frank Waller, 1881 (*photo Metropolitan Museum of Art, N.Y.C.*)

"Attractions in the Metropolitan Museum of Art," 1880 (*photo Metropolitan Museum of Art, N.Y.C.*)

Paintings from the Jarves Collection in the new galleries at Yale University's School of Fine Arts (*photo Yale University Art Gallery*)

"The Great Fight for the Championship," published by Currier & Ives, 1860 (*New York Public Library Print Coll.*)

"The Great Russian Ball at the Academy of Music, November 5, 1863" by Winslow Homer (detail) (*Harper's Weekly, photo Metropolitan Museum of Art*)

"The Slave Auction" by John Rogers (*coll. New-York Historical Society, N.Y.C.*)

Advertisement for Rogers group, "Neighboring Pews," in *The Century*, 1886 (*photo New York Public Library*)

Following page 122

Tremont House, Boston, 1830 (*photo New-York Historical Society*)

Court of the Palace Hotel, San Francisco, 1878 (*photo New York Public Library*)

The Gem Saloon in New York, 1854, by A. Fay (*coll. Edward W. C. Arnold, photo Museum of the City of New York*)

San Francisco saloon in the Gold Rush days (*Harper's Magazine*)

"Sunday on the Union Pacific" (*Culver Service*)

Main saloon of the Mississippi River steamer *Great Republic* (*Steamboat Photo Co., Sewickley, Pa.*)

"The Champions of the Mississippi," published by Currier & Ives, 1865 (*photo Metropolitan Museum of Art*)

Main Saloon of the Hudson River liner S. S. *Drew,* published by Endicott & Co. (*photo Mariner's Museum, Newport News*)

Grand Foyer of Radio City Music Hall, New York (*photo Cosmo-Sileo, Radio City Music Hall*)

"Armsmere," the residence of Col. Samuel Colt, Hartford, Conn.

"Residence & Laboratory of G. G. Green, Woodbury, N. J.," by Pfeil & Golz (*Bella C. Landauer Coll., New-York Historical Society*)

The Centennial Exposition in Philadelphia, "View on State Avenue, Looking West," sketch by Theo. R. Davis (*Harper's Weekly, 1876*)

The Eastlake organ, exhibited at the Centennial Exposition

"Art Furniture at the Centennial—Display of Howard & Sons, London" (*Harper's Weekly, 1876*)

A Queen Anne house (*coll. the author*)

An Eastlakian interior (*coll. the author*)

A bed in the Eastlake manner (*coll. the author*)

An "old home made new." Built in 1766, remodeled in 1890, Great Barrington, Mass. (*photo by the author*)

The "artistic young lady" of the 1880's (*Harper's Magazine, 1882*)

"The Six Mark Teapot" (*Punch, 1880*)

Following page 210

The grand staircase of "Biltmore," Ashville, N.C. (*Copyright photo Courtesy of Biltmore*)

Residence of William K. Vanderbilt, New York, by Richard Morris Hunt (*photo Metropolitan Museum of Art, N.Y.C.*)

"Biltmore," Asheville, N.C. (*photo by Biltmore*)

Columbian Exposition—"The Grand Court at Night," drawn by Charles Graham (*Harper's Weekly*)

Columbian Exposition—"The Golden Doorway to the Transportation Building," drawn by H. D. Nichols (*Harper's Weekly*)

"Reception at the Art Museum, Cincinnati," 1893, drawn by Frank O. Small and W. A. C. Pape (*Harper's Weekly*)

Wurlitzer Juke Box, 1941 (*photo Rudolphe Wurlitzer Co.*)

Interior of the 1890's by Perkins Hanley (*photo New York Public Library*)

An Oriental Booth (*Ladies' Home Journal, 1896*)

Browne Funeral Home, Thompson, Conn. (*photo by the author*)

A Queen Anne-ish house in Piermont, N.Y. (*photo by the author*)

"A $5000 Colonial House" by Ralph Adams Cram (*Ladies Home Journal, 1896*)

"An Artistic House of Half-Timbered Construction" by Will Bradley (*copyright, 1905, Ladies' Home Journal*)

Glass and textiles by Louis C. Tiffany (*from The Art Work of Louis C. Tiffany*)

Hall of Louis C. Tiffany's flat in East 26th St., New York, in 1883 (*photo Museum of the City of New York*)

Young Elsie de Wolfe in a "cozy corner"

Elsie de Wolfe bedroom

Elsie de Wolfe dining room (*three de Wolfe photos from Byron Coll., Museum of the City of New York*)

A New Jersey bungalow (*photo by the author*)

A Concrete House in Phillipsburg, N.J., 1917 (*photo Portland Cement Association*)

Sears, Roebuck furniture: iron bed (1905), "Arts and Crafts Library Suite" (1905), "Mission Art Glass Lamp" (1915), "Reed Rocker" (1905), "Hall Rack" (1898), "Morris Chair" (1915), (*from Sears, Roebuck & Co. catalogues*)

The Armory Show, New York, 1913 (*photo Museum of Modern Art*)

"Nude Descending a Staircase" by Marcel Duchamp (*photo Philadelphia Museum of Art*)

"The Rude Descending a Staircase" by J. F. Grisworld (*The New York Sun, Inc.*)

Following page   266

The executive dining room of J. Walter Thompson, Inc., New York (*photo J. Walter Thompson, Inc.*)

The "modernistic" men's lounge of Radio City Music Hall (*photo Radio City Music Hall*)

"A modernized early American home," a set from the motion picture "Susan and God," 1940 (*photo by Clarence Bull, Museum of Modern Art*)

French provincial in Highland Park, Ill. (*photo by author*)

Tudor country house in Englewood, N.J. (*photo by author*)

Spanish Colonial suburban in Englewood, N.J. (*photo by author*)

Davenport College's Gothic façade, Yale University, New Haven, Conn. (*Alburtus-Yale News Bureau*)

Davenport College's Georgian façade, Yale University, New Haven, Conn. (*Yale News Bureau*)

Buckminster Fuller's "Dymaxion" house (*photo Fuller Research Foundation*)

Ladies Home Journal's "Tomorrow's Small House" by Philip Johnson (*copyright by Ladies' Home Journal, photo Museum of Modern Art*)

Good Housekeeping's "Western Style" house by Allen G. Siple (*courtesy of Good Housekeeping*)

Air view of Levittown, Pa. (*photo Levitt & Sons, Inc.*)

A Levitt house of 1929 (*photo Ralph Steiner*)

A Levitt house of 1947 (*photo Ralph Steiner*)

Levitt houses, 1954 (*photo Levitt & Sons, Inc.*)

A Cape Cod house and a ranch house in a New York suburb (*photo by author*)

Machine Art catalogue of the Museum of Modern Art (*photo Museum of Modern Art*)

Industrial Art of the Centennial—a chandelier (*author's collection*)

Crane bathroom fixtures pre-Dreyfuss (*photo Henry Dreyfuss*)

Crane bathroom fixtures post-Dreyfuss (*photo Henry Dreyfuss*)

Exhibition in The Glass Center of the Corning Glass Works, (*photo Corning Glass Works, Corning, N.Y.*)

Pierre Roy's painting for a Dole Pineapple advertisement (*photo Dole Pineappple Co.*)

Charles Howard's painting for a Container Corporation of America advertisement (*photo Container Corporation of America*)

"A Woman Weighing Gold" by Jan Vermeer (*Weidener Coll. National Gallery of Art, Washington*)

"Supper at Emmaeus" by Han Van Meegeren (*photo A.C.L., Brussels*)

Following page 322

Tuscan villas by George Platt, 1860's (*coll. George Platt Lynes*)

Concrete houses, 1917 (*photo Portland Cement Association*)

Ranch houses in Levittown, Pa. (*photo Levitt & Sons, Inc.*)

"Old home made new" by William M. Woollett, 1878 (*coll. Sterling A. Callisen*)

"Old home made new," Chicago (*photo by the author*)

"Old bank made new," Great Barrington, Mass. (*photo by the author*)

Cast-in-place concrete house, Port Chester, N.Y. (*photo Portland Cement Co.*)

"Olana," Frederick Church's residence at Hudson, N.Y. (*photo by the author*)

Temple atop a skyscraper—New York Central Building, New York (*photo by the author*)

Grauman's Chinese Theater, Hollywood (*photo J. C. Milligan, Los Angeles, Motion Picture Daily*)

"Crucifixion," attributed to Andrea Mantegna (*coll. New-York Historical Society*)

"Kindred Spirits" by Asher B. Durand (*coll. New York Public Library*)

"Fourth of July," Currier & Ives (*coll. New-York Historical Society*)

"Arrangement in Gray and Black, No. 1" by James McNeill Whistler (*coll. Musée du Louvre, Paris*)

"Pygmalion and Galatea" by Jean Léon Gérôme (*coll. Metropolitan Museum of Art, N.Y.*)

"Custer's Last Fight," by Otto Becker (1895) (*August A. Busch, Jr.*)

"L'Arlésienne" by Vincent Van Gogh (*Coll. Metropolitan Museum of Art. N.Y.*)

"Portrait of the Artist's Mother," by James McNeill Whistler

D. W. Griffith in "The Crossroads of Life," 1908 (*Museum of Modern Art Film Library, N.Y.*)

"The Crossroads of Life," an early D. W. Griffith film

"L'Arlésienne" by Vincent Van Gogh

"Whistler's Mother"

Gothic Revival house, Rhinebeck, N.Y. (*photo by the author*)

Construction of a Queen Anne house (*coll. the author*)

Entrance to Lever House, New York (*photo Lever Brothers Co.*)

The Wilson Patent Adjustable Chair, 1876 (*coll. the author*)

The BarcaLounger, 1954 (*Barcalo Mfg. Co.*)

Locomobile horseless carriage, advertisement 1899 (*Harper's Weekly*)

The main saloon of the S.S. *City of Hickman* (*photo Mariner's Museum, Newport News*)

The Restaurant of the Metropolitan Museum, formerly the Roman Sculpture Court (*photo Metropolitan Museum of Art, N.Y.*)

PART ONE

The Public Taste

CHAPTER I

Enter the Lawyer's Wife

". . . You can't get high aesthetic tastes, like
trousers, ready made. . . ."
W. S. GILBERT, from *Patience*

Several years ago a friend of mine in a moment of husbandly expansiveness deposited $7,000 in his wife's bank account. "There," he said to her. "You've been wanting to do over the living room. There's the money. Now do just as you please with it. And don't get in a decorator. Do it your own way, so that it expresses your personality."

My friend, who is a very successful lawyer and a generous man, was puzzled and dismayed by the effect that his lavish gesture had on his wife.

"You know?" he said to me a few weeks later. "It's a funny thing. I've got to go to the West Coast on business and this time I'm going to take my wife with me. She's just got to get away. She can't make up her mind what to do. She doesn't know whether she wants French Provincial or Early American or Modern or what. She wanders around from shop to shop trying to make up her mind. Now she's taken to crying about it. She's so upset about the whole business, I think she's got to get away from it for a while."

Surely the lawyer's wife, whom I have never met, seems to have been far from sophisticated in matters of taste, but the dilemma that confronted her on a large scale often confronts a great many of us on a small scale. We are constantly called upon to make decisions that, in a sense, give our taste away. The fact is that we take it seriously, not only as an ornament of life but as one of its almost inescapable

3

problems. Taste is our personal delight, our private dilemma, and our public façade.

The mere matter of how we decorate our homes is only a minor part of our concern. There are pressures on our tastes from all sides, pressures that even the most reluctant among us can scarcely ignore. The making of taste in America is, in fact, a major industry. Is there any other place that you can think of where there are so many professionals telling so many nonprofessionals what their taste should be? Is there any country which has as many magazines as we have devoted to telling people how they should decorate their homes, clothe their bodies, and deport themselves in company? And so many newspaper columns full of hints about what is good taste and what is bad taste? In the last century and a quarter the purveying of taste in America has become big business, employing hundreds of thousands of people in editorial and advertising offices, in printing plants, in galleries and museums, in shops and consultants' offices. If the taste industry were to go out of business we would have a major depression, and there would be breadlines of tastemakers as far as the eye could see.

This is not, however, a catastrophe we are likely to encounter, because the taste industry has gradually become essential to the operation of our American brand of capitalism. It is in the nature of our economic system not merely to meet demand but to create it. One of the ways that demand is created is by changing people's tastes, or at least inviting them to change, and by making the pressures to give up what seemed good yesterday for what should seem inviting today so strong that they are almost impossible to resist.

But the story of American taste is far more entertaining and capricious and human than just an economic one. It is a history of dedicated and lively men and women, their ideals and ambitions, their jealousies and their quarrels, their frustrations and foibles and successes.

It is their story that I will try to tell in this book—not the whole story of American taste, by any means, and not the story of every aspect of our taste. If you are a connoisseur of art or architecture or decoration (and it is with visual taste that we will be almost exclusively concerned) you will find that some of your favorite people or styles have been given very short shrift or no shrift at all. I have selected only those men and women, whatever we may now think of their accomplishments, who seem to me to reflect most clearly the ebb and flow of taste.

But this is personal history not art history. It is what has happened to the taste of several generations of lawyers' wives and businessmen's wives and professional men's wives and farmers' wives and to their busy and preoccupied husbands as well. We shall have to look into saloons and Pullman cars, into hotels and river steamers, into art galleries and housing developments, into suburban homes and palaces of the rich and parlors of the frontier, into the offices of corporation executives, and into the lives and minds of architects and artists and connoisseurs and merchants and manufacturers.

Periods of taste are never quite as manageable as historians would sometimes like to make them. They slide gradually from one into another, though occasionally there are upheavals that seem to set apart a vanishing era of taste from a new one. Since our story is one of democratic taste in America, I should like to start in the last years of the 1820's when, it seems from this perspective, the long period of control over taste by a landed and intellectual aristocracy came to an end. For a long time the gentlemanly classes had set the standards of society and from their comfortable mansions they handed down the precepts of taste in art and architecture and fashion. But when Andrew Jackson was elected to the presidency in 1828 on a wave of cocksure Americanism there came with him not only a new "age of the common man" but the beginning of what I would like to call the Age of Public Taste. Taste became everybody's business and not just the business of the cultured few.

Life for those who swept "Old Hickory" into office was high and wide if not particularly handsome, as Mrs. Frances Trollope, who arrived from England in December, 1827, was at some pains to record in her famous (and at the time notorious) *Domestic Manners of the Americans*. Mrs. Trollope, a bustling and bonneted little lawyer's wife with sharp, observant eyes and a sharp tongue, spent three years in this country. She came here with a scheme to recover her fortunes by establishing a bazaar in the frontier city of Cincinnati, and the calamitous failure of that enterprise did nothing to soften her attitude toward the "total and universal want of manners in both males and females" which she found here. Mrs. Trollope was quite aware that something very strange was afoot in the social structure of the New World, but she regarded it as the collapse of the standards of European society rather than as the growing pains of what was to be not only a new political era but a new era in the history of taste. She despaired of America's ever amounting to anything like a civilized nation until it repudiated Thomas Jefferson's "mischievous sophistry," as she called it, that all men were born free and equal. "If refinement once creeps in among them," she wrote in the final sentence of her book, "if they once learn to cling to the graces, the honors, the chivalry of life, then we shall say farewell to American equality, and welcome to European fellowship one of the finest countries on the earth."

But the brash younger generation in America was in no mood to kowtow to the second-hand European manners of the old established aristocracy; they were cocky and men everywhere in the country were filled with optimism and self-confidence. The future of America seemed assured; its power as a nation was no longer a dream of revolutionaries—it was not just a hope but a fact. There was plenty of work to do; there was the whole West to open, and there were all sorts of new industries to be got under way. There were inland waterways to be built and railroads to be laid. There was a great deal of money to be made by the industrious, the sharp, and the unscrupulous. Almost at once new kinds of tastemakers appeared on the scene to tell people how to spend their new-found wealth.

It was not until almost everybody could afford to be concerned with taste that the tastemakers, as we know them today, had any real function. The play in which they have acted divides itself, rather arbitrarily, into three acts. In the first act, which I call the Age of Public Taste, they tried to discipline everyone to a higher appreciation of the arts and to a nicer sensibility to their surroundings. They managed to arouse the public interest to a very considerable extent, but they found to their dismay that the Public Taste was not to be controlled. And so they turned their attention to the Private Taste. They aimed their fire at individuals—at the rich who were presumably looked up to as models of behavior and at housewives in whose hands local standards of refinement and culture were maintained. The curtain came down on the Age of Private Taste when in our own century the tastemakers became exercised about what is now familiarly (but I think mistakenly) called "mass culture." It was then that the curtain went up on the Age of Corporate Taste, and the tastemakers took to working through mass communications media and vast corporations to reach millions upon millions of people.

At the beginning of the Age of Public Taste the novelist James Fenimore Cooper, who was fretted by the turn taste seemed to be taking, wrote in alarm to his friend Horatio Greenough, a prominent sculptor and in some respects one of the wisest men of his day: "You are in a country," he said, "in which every man swaggers and talks, knowledge or no knowledge; brains or no brains; taste or no taste. They are all *ex nato* connoisseurs, politicians, religionists, and every man's equal and all men's betters."

Even three-quarters of a century later there were those who blamed the free-wheeling spirit of the Age of Jackson for all the evils that had befallen American taste. Just after the turn of the twentieth century an architect named Joy Wheeler Dow wrote bitterly: "It was Old Hickory who issued the emancipation proclamation to young America, absolving him from the time-honored and universal fealty to Art. But young America was deceived; it was a campaign lie. Young America was not emancipated at all. Another master was set over him, and that master was unrelenting expediency, who forthwith usurped the throne of Art."

From our vantage point in the middle of the twentieth century the prospect does not seem nearly so bleak, but since the days when public taste was "emancipated" it has traveled a path of windings and turnings, of peaks of frivolity and abysses of dinginess. It has crossed through fairylands filled with imitation castles, decorated with silks and velvets, and through dismal towns all painted brown. It has produced buildings of stark beauty and crude bombast. It has followed the enticements of faddists and has been led by the serious preachments of missionaries for art. But it has never been without honest striving, or without vitality or individuality, and it has never been allowed to escape for long from the checkrein of humor. Through the story of our taste has run a constant theme— if America is to be great, America must have culture.

The number of variations that has been played on the theme has been remarkable indeed, but as the curtain went up on the Age of Public Taste the theme rose from only a few scattered voices, and even in those there was a note of desperation.

CHAPTER II

Every Man a Connoisseur

"I have always suspected public taste to be a
mongrel product, out of affectation by dogma-
tism."
                    ROBERT LOUIS STEVENSON,
                    Virginibus Puerisque, 1881

Thomas Cole, who had a great deal less to complain about than
most American artists of his day, wrote in his diary in 1838:
"I am out of place . . . ; there are few persons of real taste; and no
opportunity for the true artist to develop his powers. The tide of
utility sets against the fine arts."

Cole was one of the most popular painters of the time; his romantic landscapes, filled with lofty sentiment and intricate detail,
were dear to the hearts of what was for those days a very large
public. But if there were few people of "real taste," as he said, it
was not because there were not a great many people who were
trying to have taste. If the "tide of utility" was set against the fine
arts, it was at least a new and exciting kind of utility that was
making a great many people conscious of the niceties of taste who
had never before had occasion to give the matter much thought.

In the 1830's a totally unfamiliar element had emerged in the
problem of taste. It was mass production. Suddenly almost everybody, instead of just a wealthy and cultured few, could buy "tasteful" carpets and chairs, wallpapers and curtain materials. They were
not only cheap but they were to be had in great variety. Inventions
for manufacturing objects with which to decorate the home came
in rapid succession, each more miraculous than the other. In 1837

8

William Compton patented a "fancy weaving loom" and just seven years later the first wallpaper printing machine was imported from England to America. In that same year Erastus B. Bigelow invented a power loom for making ingrain carpets, and not content with this, in 1848 he produced an even more remarkable contraption—a loom to make Brussels and tapestry carpets, which were eventually to cover the floors of America with flora and fauna in colors that sang at the tops of their lungs.

The home-decorating industries boomed. In the twenty years following 1840 the value of factory-made furniture and upholstery leaped from seven million dollars worth a year to twenty-eight million. Styles ran riot. The new mechanical methods of making furniture gave designers a free hand to indulge their delight in ornamentation, and they tried to outdo themselves and each other in fanciness and frippery. Heirlooms began to find their way to the attic as the new chairs and sofas, bedecked with fruit, flowers, and beasties and standing on twisted spindles, crowded into living rooms and parlors. There were thousands of different kinds of chairs selling for as little as a dollar apiece, and as a historian of American manufacture has commented, "If the seriousness of design suffered and individuality was lost in the flood of machine-made products . . . this was compensated by the benefit of even vulgar art to a multitude of consumers, for whom the incipient and factitious elegance of early factory goods represented the first step in household refinement."

Most men (in those days as now) were inclined to consider themselves exempt from any concern with household taste; that was a woman's business and the ladies were far more interested in fashions and fancywork than they were in culture. The man of action looked forward, however, to the day when he could build himself a fine house suitable to his station in life and in keeping with the republican spirit of the day. A suitable house to most men in the thirties was a Greek temple (modified to domestic use) with fine white columns and often a splendid pediment. To achieve such a mansion he needed only the money (which was plentiful), the land (which was cheap), and a carpenter. Architects were a luxury which only a very few people bothered to afford, for there were plenty of books, such as *Benjamin's House Carpenter* and *Shaw's Civil Architecture* in which any clever builder could find all he needed to know to produce an imposing or a modest Greek Revival house with all the proper ornaments and details.

Into these houses, for the most part, went a miscellany of heavy horsehair sofas, elaborate mirrors with gilt frames, portraits of bonneted ladies peering out of backgrounds as thick and black as tar, and carpets covered with tremendous flowers in bright colors. In the 1830's, the walls were delicately tinted, for it was too expensive to import wallpapers from Europe and the wallpaper industry had not yet got its start in this country. At the parlor windows there might be lambrequins, and about the room, if the house was a formal one, as Mrs. Trollope noted in *Domestic Manners of Americans*, a clutter of "little tables, looking and smelling like flower beds, portfolios, nicknacks, bronzes, busts, cameos, and alabaster vases, illustrated copies of lady-like rhymes bound in silk, and, in short, all the pretty coxcomalities of the drawing room scattered about with . . . profuse and studied negligence." Mrs. Trollope found such a plethora of bibelots all too rarely to suit her European notions of elegance. In modest homes the Windsor chair and the simple rocker were still the standard pieces of living-room furniture and the floors, scrubbed white, had only rag rugs on them. In such houses there were likely to be no pictures on the walls.

When factories first began to pour tasteful objects into American homes the householder got little guidance down the path of decorative refinement from the magazines and newspapers. The tastemakers were slow to recognize what it meant for the machine to introduce the muses to the masses. Magazines such as Peterson's *The Lady's World of Fashion* and *Godey's Lady's Book* were filled in the thirties and forties with the latest word from Paris and London on styles in dress, along with inspirational poems, and sentimental and moral tales to beguile the weary hours of the females in their restricted lives, but decorating columns were still a decade away. Magazines had little interest (beyond instructions in various kinds of fancywork) in what ladies hung on their walls and put on their floors. Newspapers carried a very considerable number of advertisements for household goods—for Italian window shades with landscapes painted on them, for French shades that were said to be "very beautiful Gothics, entirely new . . . also Roman and Grecian architecture," for Brussels carpet and for chairs— but they offered their readers no advice on decorating. It was not until the 1850's that housewives were deluged with hints about what they should do to be tasteful and genteel in the appurtenances of their homes.

Compared with the emotional pipe organ that advertisers today play so skillfully, with stops for envy, greed, fear, and lust, the advertising of the 1840's was primitive indeed. There were no surveys and no account executives. There were no professional copywriters— a literary breed that did not come into being until the very end of the century. Each merchant wrote his own advertisements, which were, except for the scandalous claims of hundreds of patent medicines and contraceptive powders and pills, merely lists of items for sale with their prices. Now and then one of them would indulge in slight fancifulness such as "War! War! War! The Wig Makers have declared war against our neighbor Dr. Jayne, because of his hair tonic . . ." but advertising men had barely begun to influence taste. They had yet to learn how to strike terror into the hapless housewife because her draperies were dowdy. The first advertising agencies, however, (they were merely buyers and sellers of space) started in the 1840's and they coincided—just as one would have expected—with the beginnings of mass production of goods and chattels to glorify the American home.

While the decorating industries were bringing the first sweet sips of "refinement" into thousands upon thousands of homes, the fine arts were on the verge of a boom. What had been a few stalwart flowers growing in the wilderness suddenly became a tangle of weeds.

Not even in the great commercial and cultural centers of Boston, New York, and Philadelphia had the arts been in anything like robust health. Prudery, Ignorance, and Self-consciousness, the three Philistine fates, whose motto is "I don't know anything about art but I know what I like," were the enemies that those who were interested in educating and refining the public taste saw all around them. Skirmishes against public indifference were being fought, but they were not serious battles, as they later became, in a large campaign. In New

York as early as 1802 artists had banded together to organize an academy in hopes that they might dignify their position in the community, improve the level of public taste and—not in the least incidentally—expand the market for their wares. But the gallery that they offered to the public was more noble than interesting. It was largely a musty collection of plaster casts of antique statues ordered by mail from Paris. No one but a few art students paid much attention to it. In Philadelphia Charles Willson Peale, who was a distinguished naturalist as well as a prominent portrait painter, managed to organize the local artists into an academy. To accomplish this he had to fight a running battle with local prudery for nearly fifteen years, and when he proposed that the academy should have life classes in which students could draw from the nude, a large contingent of dilettantish young men walked out. They dispatched a protest "highly disapproving of the inconsistent and indecent" suggestion. When Peale borrowed a copy of the "Venus de Medici" from an English painter who had brought it to this country, he was not permitted to show it publicly and had to keep it in a locked case only to be shown clandestinely to a few friends.

Art museums as we think of them today—collections of paintings and sculpture and decorative and religious arts—were scarcely thought of anywhere in the 1830's. That is not to say there were no museums in which art was shown, but most museums then were private commercial enterprises in which a few paintings were shown along with pigs with eight feet, Indian relics, mastodon bones, and other curiosities of nature, archaeology, and science. Though some of the museums had a basically serious purpose, almost any trick that would induce the public to part with a quarter for admission was worth trying.

But art was not entirely without honor. The paintings that Americans liked best in the 1830's were tremendous battle scenes and other historic moments frozen in paint. They were impressive for the number of figures, both military and allegorical, who romped and swooned, posed and died in them. The public was happy to pay admission, as they now do at the movies, to examine their wealth of meticulous detail and their noble sentiments. Equally exciting to the *"ex nato* connoisseurs," as Cooper called them, were the vast romantic landscape paintings of the Hudson River valley and the Catskills and the rugged hills of Vermont, in which every leaf and twig, every crag and falling drop of water was depicted with loving care. In the horse-hair privacy of their parlors women gazed with sentimental delight on the engravings that appeared in such magazines as *Godey's Lady's Book*—scenes of children being scolded or cuddled, of lovers in the least compromising sort of intercourse, and of dewy-eyed maidens with names like Cymbeline and Clarissa taken from the slick paintings of the British Royal Academicians.

Sculptors purified the classical nude and made it decent, hiding the horrid fact of nakedness behind such impeccable names as "Purity" and "The Triumph of Chastity." They talked not about breasts but about bosoms, and there were no such things as legs; there were only limbs. The current fashion for the classical in sculpture was at logger-heads with current sentiments of decorum, and when Horatio Greenough, a man who talked and wrote far more sense about art than nearly all of his contemporaries, produced a Zeus-like statue of George Washington, half-draped in something like a bed sheet, the public was horrified.

By and large, however, the attitude toward art and artists was one of colossal public indifference. Mrs. Trollope had seen in Cincinnati, where she had stayed two years, a calamitous attempt to start an Academy of Fine Arts. Even in her travels in the Eastern part of the country when she came on a desire "among persons of the *first standing in society*" to patronize the fine arts, she found it "joined to a pro-fundity of ignorance . . . almost inconceivable." To this was added the patriotic notion that the artists of America were as good as any in the world.

However proud of their artists Americans pretended to be, they were singularly unwilling to produce cash from their pockets to provide the kind of patronage that makes the arts prosper. Attempts to es-tablish art galleries had encountered bored indifference from the public. There were a few dealers in New York and Boston and Phila-delphia who sold paintings and prints to a few collectors, but the public imagination had by no means been captured. It took a young portrait painter named James Herring to launch a scheme that was in the speculative, commercial spirit of the day, and with it he set off the first art boom of any real consequence that America had ever seen.

Herring started in the art business in a perfectly conventional way. In the autumn of 1838 he opened a gallery at 410 Broadway in New York "for the promotion of the fine arts in the United States." He called it the Apollo Gallery and, according to the catalogue of his first exhibition, he meant it to be a "suitable depot" in which artists might exhibit their works on a temporary basis, and as a "place of resort" for lovers of art "where they may expect to find a rich variety of subjects for study or for sale." Herring charged 25 cents admission and sold his catalogues for 12½ cents.

But he was neither an ordinary painter nor an ordinary art dealer. He was a man with a scheme and a vision, and he knew that if he wanted to make art popular with Americans he would have to do more than just hang paintings on his gallery walls for "lovers of art." He would have to give the public something to talk about and, more important, something to gamble on. He had heard of a scheme that had been tried in Scotland and had worked there extremely well. Artists, dealers, and the public all had gained from it, and he promptly set about to introduce a similar scheme here. To the lofty purpose of art patronage it added the lowly appeal of the lottery ticket. The scheme was this: People were invited to pay $5 for an annual subscription to the Apollo Association. Each subscriber would then receive "a large and costly Original Engraving from an American painting." He would also receive a ticket with a number on it which would entitle him to a long shot at one of a number of genuine, hand-painted pictures by American artists in an annual lottery to be held at the Association.

This was no fly-by-night scheme. It was founded on the highest motives with impressively solid citizens on its board of directors (or legislature, as it was called), and it was patronized by the most respectable people.

In 1844 the Apollo Association changed its name to the American Art Union. William Cullen Bryant, who was happy to lend his name and august presence to any organization that seemed to promote culture, was installed as the Union's new president in that same year, and the Union prospered. The money taken in from subscribers not only covered the cost of the engravings, but also enabled the Union to "purchase paintings and sculpture, statuettes in bronze, and medals, by native or resident artists." These were put on exhibition at the gallery for all to see until the gala evening in December when they were distributed by lot to the lucky ticket holders, "each member having one share for every $5 paid by him."

It was a gala evening indeed. At first the lottery, which was the climax of the Annual Meeting of the Union members, was held in the lecture room of the New York Society Library at the corner of Broadway and Leonard Street, but as the membership and excitement grew, neither the Library nor the Union's new gallery, where it customarily displayed its paintings, was big enough, and the great hall of the Broadway Tabernacle was engaged. There, under a dome supported by elegant Corinthian columns, ladies in their most luxurious crinolines and gentlemen in their top hats waited while two little girls, with hair hanging down their backs and frilly pantaloons protruding below their petticoats, drew the lucky numbers from urns.

In its first year the Union had only eight hundred subscribers, but it set about the problem of building its membership in an energetic and thoroughly American manner. "The Art Union, in the management of its business," the *Art Bulletin* reported retrospectively in 1853, "purchased its stock, advertised and exhibited its goods, employed its agents and clerks just like a merchant." The methods paid off. By 1844 the membership had risen to something over two thousand, and this was just a start, though extracting $5 from each of these new patrons of the arts had not been an easy matter. "Among our subscribers, but a very small part have been volunteers," one of the managers reported at the Annual Meeting in 1844; "the remainder have been procured by the faithful services of our agent, who has visited nearly every town of any importance in the Union." As the manager was at some pains to point out, ". . . our soil does not yield these rich fruits without thorough culture."

With cultivation, however, the fruits became richer and juicier, and the Union was soon in almost complete control of the American market for works of art. It grew not only in membership but in the number and variety of paintings that went to the lucky members. In the year that it changed its name, it distributed ninety-two paintings at the lottery; four years later it distributed more than four hundred and fifty, for which it had paid artists $40,907. There was scarcely a town of any size from Bangor, Maine, to St. Louis, Missouri, that didn't boast one winner. By that time there were "Honorary Secretaries" whose job it was to handle the local business of the Union, to receive subscriptions, and to deliver the engravings to the members in their vicinity. There were secretaries in nearly four hundred cities outside New York; including, in fact, one in Rio de Janiero, four in Canada, one in Santa Cruz, and one all the way across the Atlantic in Munich.

And still it grew. In 1849 Thomas Cole's exceedingly romantic painting called "Youth" from a series with the encompassing title "The Voyage of Life" was one of those that the Union engraved for its members and also put in the lottery. Art lovers of the day found the series so tempting that not only did the attendance at the Union's gallery exceed half a million people in that year, but the number of subscribers jumped to more than sixteen thousand. The lottery itself became such a popular occasion that the Union had to set a deadline for the receipt of subscriptions; Johnny-come-latelies were sending in their $5 right up to the last minute just for the gamble and the party, and this did not seem to the management of the Union quite respectable or quite fair to the members who subscribed early and thereby gave the Union some idea of how much art it could afford to buy during the year. "The acorn which almost by stealth we planted ten years since," the President of the Union gloated, "has become an oak. Under its spreading branches, Art reposes itself in grateful security, sheltered from many of the storms which often frown upon genius and talent. What a change has been wrought in the space of a few short years, in the prospects and hopes of American artists!" It was almost too good to be true; it was, of course, too good to last.

By no means everyone was pleased with the way the Union did business, least of all those artists whose work was overlooked and who did not share the delights that were to be found aboard the gravy train. The grumbling started early; indeed in the very year that the Union changed its name the managers were defending themselves against attack from "some professed friends of the cause," who thought that the Union's system had a tendency to encourage mediocrity. The Union considered this no argument. What, it wanted to know, was the matter with mediocrity? "This fear of mediocrity in Art comes with an ill grace from a community like ours," the Union retorted; "no one affects to fear mediocrity in religion or learning, why should we fear it in art? . . . Someone may rise by and by, and for *his* sake we are content to encourage a host of lesser lights." It found the business of cultivating the public taste a long slow process; art was not something to be indulged in "only by the rich and effeminate"; it was for everyone. How could America have great art until it had a great many mediocre painters? How could the citizenry learn to love great art before it had learned to love any art at all? "Good taste is of all things the most gradual in its development, and of all pleasures it can with most propriety be said to grow on what it feeds on." This was the stand of the Union on aesthetic appreciation; and furthermore mediocrity, if that is what it was, seemed to be paying off.

The argument wasn't good enough to satisfy the artists who were not asked to participate or to placate those who resented seeing what they considered rubbish being handed to the public as art. Rumblings of discontent began to be heard in the studios. Accusations of low pecuniary motives were hurled at the Union. Some of the older artists thought that young flashes-in-the-pan were being allowed to cast obscuring shadows over the ruins of their hard-earned reputations. The New York *Herald*, a lively newspaper that loved nothing so much as a good cause and a good fight, took up the cudgels against the Union, declaring that it was not a legitimate business but an immoral and illegal lottery. In 1851 the New York Supreme Court handed down a decision that the operations of the Art Union violated the law and that its lottery must be abandoned.

And so it was. In December, 1853, the Union held its first and last annual sale of paintings, with the announcement: "A competent legal tribunal having decided that the plan hitherto pursued of distributing works of art by lot was in conflict with the provisions of the constitution, the committee have deemed it necessary to adopt a new medium of communication between the artist and the public." The sale was not a success. Thousands of Americans who were happy to own works of art that they could get on a gamble were not willing to hand over any substantial amount of money for the same privilege. What had looked to many like a true flowering of the aesthetic spirit seemed to vanish with the disappearance of the little tickets with numbers on

them. It was a disappointing spectacle. Only a few years before it
had looked to one president of the Art Union as though America was
"nobly pursuing her destiny" in recognizing the arts. "Perhaps there
is no nation in the world," he said, "which displays a more decided
taste for music and painting than our own. . . . What a hope is this
to animate the heart of genius!"

But genius didn't like the market place, and had brought the giant
Union to the ground. If we look now at some of the paintings that the
Union thought best suited to the living rooms of America, we are
tempted to think that the grumblings in the studios were not without
justification. Many of them look to us inept, sentimental, formless,
and more likely to fetch sighs from romantic maidens than praise
from posterity. But there is no denying that the Union in its way had
done yeoman's service. Not only had it provided a source of income
to American artists that was unlike anything they had seen before,
but it actually had been instrumental in encouraging many young
men to make careers for themselves in the arts. Whether this was a
blessing or not is questionable, but John Durand in his biography of
his father, Asher B. Durand (many of whose landscapes were distributed through the Union) notes that in 1836 the number of artists
in America could be counted on one's fingers but that "in 1851 when
the Art Union fell under the ban of law, American artists formed a
large band." In the eleven years of its existence the Union distributed
some twenty-four hundred works in addition to the subscription engravings, and as Durand wrote: "The Institution, if not a creator for
a taste for art in the community, disseminated a knowledge for it and
largely stimulated its growth. Through it the people awoke to the fact
that art was one of the forces of society."

The American Art Union died suddenly, but the idea died slowly.
Within a few years after its unsuccessful attempt to operate as a normal picture gallery, several new organizations using the Union's ideas
appeared. One was the Cosmopolitan Art Union, with headquarters
well outside the jurisdiction of the New York courts in Sandusky,
Ohio. Another, the International Art Union, was started by some
dealers, Messrs. Goupil, Vibert & Co., for the purpose of introducing
into America the "chefs d'oeuvre of the European School of Art."
Both of these organizations prospered and in their various ways,

through publications and exhibitions, did much to spread the aesthetic word abroad.

From all this varied activity in the infant art world of America one might get the impression that the public was being seduced away from the kinds of raucous pleasures that they long had enjoyed. Nothing could be further from the truth. The most popular museum of the day was the wholesome but bogus emporium of outlandish entertainment operated by P. T. Barnum. Barnum hailed the public to come and see a facsimile of "the great picture of CHRIST HEALING THE SICK IN THE TEMPLE, by Benjamin West, Esq., THE ALBINO LADY; and 500,000 curiosities." This combination of art, freaks, and oddities became Barnum's formula, and if it was not a new one, he developed techniques for exploiting it which almost made it seem so. Other promoters used art as an excuse for more salacious entertainment. Consider for example what happened when a sculpture called "The Greek Slave" by Hiram Powers was first shown in New York in 1847. It was a tremendously decorous success. The slave was a tidy nude maiden with classical features and hair bound in a fillet. Her hands were loosely fastened with a delicately carved chain, and her expression was so demure, and her pose so circumspect, that even the prudery of Philadelphians could not have been offended. She looked, indeed, as though she were fully clothed in her own skin. When she was put on display thousands of men and women paid admission to see her, and such was her reputation as a piece of high art that even children were permitted to view her blameless nakedness. It didn't take the sharpers long to realize that here was a good thing. A man who called himself Dr. Collyer introduced at Palmo's Opera House in New York what he described as "a new movement in the fine arts." Here he attracted the public in droves, from the most fashionable to the least refined, with a *tableau vivant* which he advertised as "living men and women in almost the same state in which Gabriel saw them in the Garden of Eden on the first morning of creation." In no time at all there were "taverns, hotels, saloons, and other drinking houses, where young men and women were exhibited as *tableaux vivants*, in every form and shape, and for every price from six pence up to fifty cents."

It was men like Barnum and Dr. Collyer and Herring of the Art Union who understood the temper of the new democratic approach to taste. The aroma of art was sweet in the nostrils of the public; they liked the idea that the arts had been liberated from aristocratic peonage and now belonged to everyone; they liked to be able to talk about art and to pose as its patron; they enjoyed the publications of the several Art Unions and the sensation of cultural fellowship that came from learning the lingo of criticism and the names and biographies of painters here and abroad. But aesthetics served straight is a liquor that only a practiced and dedicated few can down without choking. The public needed a chaser. The Art Union gave it to them in the form of gambling; Barnum gave them freaks and oddities along with "masterpieces" of art; Dr. Collyer sweetened the drink with sex. It was on such a basis that culture and commerce met at the beginning of the Age of Public Taste, and it is on much the same basis that they have maintained their close relationship ever since.

But commerce has never been allowed to go unchallenged. Thomas Cole had bitterly complained that "the tide of utility sets against the fine arts," and other men have ever since his day tried to stem that tide. They have tried to discipline the public taste for art and architecture. They have struggled manfully against the incursions of machine-made vulgarisms, as they would call them, in order to raise the public's sights to more noble vistas in which the arts might bring beauty and serenity into their lives. They have fought to establish America as a land where the arts might flower as they have flowered nowhere since the great days of the Renaissance.

It has been a good fight, and for the most part a clean one. But the banners under which it has been waged have sometimes borne strange devices indeed, and sometimes it has seemed as though the terrain over which the battles have been fought was an imaginary one. The tastemakers have often skirmished in a dream landscape that bore little resemblance to the tough cultural contours of America's growing industrialism.

CHAPTER III

Smiling Lawns and Tasteful Cottages

"Beautiful birds build tasty nests."

On the evening of December 20, 1844, when the American Art Union met for the first time in the lecture room of the New York Society Library to distribute its coveted prizes, one of the two tellers who had been selected to supervise the lottery was a tall, slightly built young man of rather Spanish appearance. His hair was thick and black and he wore it very long, even for those days, so that it hung down in the manner of a bob below the edge of his high white collar. His eyes were dark and large and looked at everything with the optical hunger of an artist, and, though his manner was extremely reserved, even a little haughty, there was readiness in his smile. This young gentleman, and there was not the slightest doubt that he was a gentleman, was twenty-nine years old and already famous, not only in America but in England and France as well. His name was Andrew Jackson Downing, and he was a landscape architect from the town of Newburgh, New York, on the west bank of the Hudson. No one had a greater influence on the taste of Americans a century ago than he, and no one had a more profound impact on the looks of the countryside.

It was not odd that he was a landscape architect, though the profession was almost unknown in America in the 1840's, but it was very odd that a landscape architect should have rallied so many of his contemporaries to a standard of taste as gentle and romantic as his. In 1844 he had less than eight years of life left to him, and yet twenty years after his dramatic death, the author of "The Easy Chair" in *Harper's Magazine* commented that "no American has built for himself a more permanent monument than Downing the landscape gardener."

There is scarcely a monument left, scarcely a garden or a house or a terraced hillside, to which we can now point and say Downing did that. But there is scarcely a building still standing from the 1840's and 50's or a city park in which Downing's ideas, sometimes distorted almost beyond recognition, cannot be detected. "So long as men are forced to dwell in log huts and follow the hunter's life," he wrote, "we must not be surprised at lynch law and the use of the bowie knife. But, when smiling lawns and tasteful cottages begin to embellish a country, we know that order and culture are established." He believed this with every bone in his rather fragile body and with every cell in his alert and studious mind, and it was to this principle that he devoted himself.

Downing, in a manner of speaking, was born in a garden. His father, who had been a wheelwright, bought a piece of land on the outskirts of Newburgh, and there, in view of the Hudson, built a small red cottage in which he raised a family of five children. To support them he became a nurseryman, and Andrew, who was born many years after his brothers and sisters, played alone in the garden and among the trees in which his father and one of his older brothers worked. He was a precocious child but not a robust one, and being shy and rather dreamy he kept to himself and had few friends. His father died when Andrew was only seven. While young Andrew went to the Montgomery Academy nearby and hoped eventually to go to college, his brother took over the management of the nursery. But college was financially out of the question, and when he left school at sixteen his mother, a practical woman, suggested that he go to work as a clerk in a dry-goods store. No prospect could have pleased him less, and he persuaded his brother to take him as a partner in the nursery. He went at his job with a scientist's curiosity and a poet's romanticism.

His acquaintance with the great world beyond Newburgh, a world of gentlefolk with aristocratic manners and tastes, was first made on the hillsides overlooking the Hudson. The elderly Baron de Liederer, who was the Austrian Consul General, had a summer place in New-burgh, and as he was an amateur naturalist, he grew interested in the young fellow at the nursery who seemed so knowledgeable and had so much curiosity about plants and minerals. Through the Baron young Downing met the Armstrongs who lived in a splendid villa nearby and who entertained friends from as far away as England. Downing was indelibly impressed by their civilized manners and he set about to pattern his behavior on theirs. He was not, however, a dilettante, and he worked hard at his books and at his job until by the time he was twenty-one he was a recognized horticultural authority in the Hudson Valley and was welcomed into all of the great houses as "a gentleman, a scholar, and . . . most practical man."

As the young man grew a little older, he became more and more fascinated with the problems of rural architecture, and less with the science of plants and trees, though the two were always inextricably interwoven in his concept of the good life. His own house was a perfect, almost too perfect, example of the new taste for English Gothic that he was trying to convince his countrymen to accept. In 1838, when he was twenty-five, he married a young lady who lived in an estate directly across the Hudson from the little red house in which he had been brought up. Her name was Caroline DeWindt and she was the great-granddaughter of John Adams, the second President of the United States. The DeWindt home was a gay, relaxed, and comfortable old Dutch mansion, overflowing with eleven DeWindt children and their friends, and "indolently lying in luxuriant decay" with a spacious piazza and lawns sloping down toward the river. It contrasted sharply with the jewel-like house that Downing was to build for himself and his bride.

Downing's house was considered by his friends to be extremely pleasant. He tried to build into its walls and the shapes and dispositions of its rooms, as into its facades and furnishings, the taste that he so passionately hoped all rural Americans would take to their hearts in the cause of civilization and refinement. By the standards of its own day it was "a simple house" in what was then called the Elizabethan style, but which we now think of as Gothic Revival. It was built of stone—neatly symmetrical, with slender, octagonal towers at either side of the peaked entrance and matching verandas whose roofs, decorated with ornamental woodwork, were supported by slender columns and shallow arches.

The Gothic living room looked out upon a meticulously manicured lawn, set about with rustic chairs and urns dripping with blossoms. The trees and flowering shrubs were so planted and trimmed that the village below the house was obscured from view, but they provided little vistas that seemed to incorporate the Hudson into Mr. Downing's small estate of five acres. He called it "Highland Gardens." In executing his perfect house in its perfect landscape he had set out to prove "that a beautiful, and durable, and convenient mansion could be built as cheaply as a poor and tasteless temple."

Downing was not the first to attack the "tasteless temples" that the Greek Revival had scattered about the hillsides and lowlands of America, but no one attacked them with more vigor or with more success. He was an eloquent fighter for his ideas, and the public, which was no more averse to listening to a new prophet of taste then than it is now, greeted his words with enthusiasm, and set about in its own way to apply his doctrine. In 1841 and 1842 he produced two books, one *A Treatise on the Theory and Practice of Landscape Gardening*, and the other called *Cottage Residences*. They were immediately successful and, as one of his contemporaries said, "invaluable to the thousands in every part of the country who were waiting for the master-word which should tell them what to do to make their homes as beautiful as they wished."

"Certainly the national taste is not a matter of little moment," Downing wrote, ". . . whether a young country and progressive people shall develop ideas of beauty, harmony, and moral significance in their daily lives, whether the arts shall be so understood and cultivated as to elevate and dignify the character, whether the country homes of a whole people shall embody such ideas of beauty and truth as shall elevate and purify its feelings; these are questions of no mean or trifling importance."

The tone of Mr. Downing's attack on the problem of taste was loftily moral. "A dwelling house should look like a dwelling house," he said. For a home to look like a little Greek temple was dishonest, an aesthetic and moral lie. "Vices may be expressed in architecture as well as virtues: the worst parts of our nature as well as the best," he wrote. He had one eye on the extravagances that he saw about him and the other on the works of John Ruskin, the most famous aesthetic moralist of his time. "A house built only with a view to animal wants, eating and drinking, will express sensuality instead of hospitality . . . gaudy and garish apartments . . . will express pride and vanity instead of a real love of what is beautiful for its own sake." He went even further than that. He believed that a house that was beautiful ceased to be so if lived in by a dishonest man. "Much of the character of everyman may be read in his house." Take heed!

But Downing's morality was by no means ascetic; he liked and approved of comfort, and he could apply morality to it as well as to the structure of a house. "Verandas, piazzas, bay-windows, balconies, etc.," he said of those comfortable appurtenances, "are the most valuable general truths in Domestic Architecture." How pleasant truth could be! What a pleasant man Mr. Downing's contemporaries found him!

Most of them, that is, but not all. There were dissenting voices, both sophisticated ones and humble ones—highbrow critics and low-brow practical men.

The *Broadway Journal*, a lively weekly magazine that was published in New York for a few years in the forties and of which Edgar Allan Poe was an editor, found a great deal to laugh at in Mr. Downing's books and in the people who professed to follow him so slavishly. It had special scorn for those who went so far as to hire an architect. "A man who is not capable of deciding whether a Greek temple or a Swiss cottage be best adapted to his wants," the journal's reviewer said, "is not worthy of a house at all, and instead of applying for a plan of a mansion, he should apply to the county officers for admission to the almshouse." He didn't even let Mr. Downing get away with his own Highland Gardens and threw back in his face his remark that "the expression of purpose in architecture is conveyed by features in a building." "This is very good," the reviewer retorted, "but in the example of his own house at Newburgh, we observe two octagonal blind towers which have puzzled us exceedingly to guess at their uses. Perhaps they may be cases for depositing fishing rods— we can conceive of no other use for such appendages."

The reviewer was being either very advanced for his time or very old-fashioned in his attitude toward the taste that Downing was attempting to promote. He found the Italian villa and the Gothic cottage, illustrations of which filled Downing's books, "as foreign to our language as the dialects of Boccaccio and Chaucer" and as unsuited to our countryside and climate, and he couldn't resist teasing him for being such a stickler for taste. Downing had said that he had "witnessed with pain" a solecism in taste that was not uncommon —green blinds or Venetian shutters on houses in the "pointed or English cottage style." To this the reviewer replied in the truly American pragmatic spirit that is often indistinguishable from Philistinism, "It is better to commit a solecism in taste than sit in the dark, and if nothing short of green Venetian blinds can render an English cottage endurable in our scorching summers, it would be better to pain an architect . . . than to be roasted or parboiled by leaving them off for the sake of avoiding a solecism."

If this is highbrow criticism which anticipates the functional point of view, let us look at the opinion of a hearty fellow who was a professional farmer, or at least a professional writer for farmers. His name was Lewis F. Allen, and in a book called *Rural Architecture* published in 1852 he made a plea that farmers behave like the good simple people they are supposed to be and "leave all this vanity to town-folk, who have nothing better—or who, at least, think they have —to amuse themselves." There is some question which he disliked more, "refined taste" or fashion, but there was no doubt that a "parlor" sent him into a paroxysm of disgust. "No room, in any house," he said, "should be too good for occupation by the family themselves— not every day and commonplace—but occupation at any and all times, when convenience or pleasure demand it." Downing would have agreed with that in principle, but Downing, for all his humble beginnings and protestations about smiling lawns and graceful cottages, had assumed the aristocratic point of view. He wanted everyone to live surrounded by tasteful objects, with leisure to use their parlors and to cultivate their gardens. He wanted them to paint their houses in muted colors or, as he called them, "soft and quiet shades"; he considered white paint to be vulgar because it did not harmonize with the tones of nature. This was too much for the author of *Rural*

Architecture to accept. "We are not among those," he said, "who cast off, and on a sudden condemn, as out of all good taste, the time-honored white house with its green blinds. . . . Hundreds of our otherwise pretty and imposing country houses have been daubed over with the dirtiest, gloomiest pigments imaginable, making every habitation which it touched look more like a funeral appendage than a cheerful, life-enjoying home. . . . The fashion which dictates them is a barbarous, false, and arbitrary fashion; void of all taste in its inception."

Void of all taste, indeed! Who in America had better taste than Mr. Downing? There were a great many refined and cultivated people who believed that no one did. Mr. Allen, however, was evidently not one of them. Why, he had even been into country houses where he expected to find good simple folk and "on being introduced to the 'parlor' actually found everything in the furniture line so dainty and 'prinked up'" that he was "afraid to sit down on the frail things stuck around by way of seats, for fear of breaking them." He would not have been at home in Mr. Downing's library with its delicately carved "Gothic" chairs. But even so, Mr. Allen had absorbed some of the moral architectural doctrine that Mr. Downing had been preaching. Downing insisted that the material of which a building was constructed "should *appear* to be what it is." "To build a house of wood so exactly in imitation of stone as to lead the spectator to suppose it is stone," he wrote, "is a paltry artifice, at variance with all truthfulness." And Mr. Allen echoed him several years later with ". . . all imitation or device which may lead to a belief that it may be other than what it really is, is nothing less than fraud . . . upon taste and architectural truth."

It was easy to disagree with Mr. Downing on matters of taste and detail; it was even easier to take the superficial aspects of the designs that he published in his books and turn them into something as pretentious and fancy as he meant them to be honest and restrained; but it was impossible to ignore him, or to deny the sincerity of his beliefs in the power of taste as a civilizing agent.

Downing had few intimate friends but many warm acquaintances, and nothing pleased him more than to entertain them at Highland Gardens. He was a most thoughtful host, and yet there was always between him and his friends a solid barrier of reticence. "In social intercourse," one of them wrote, "he was like two persons: the one conversed with you pleasantly on any topic, the other watched you from behind that pleasant talk, like a sentinel." It was as though he were afraid of being caught off guard, as though if he were to drop for a moment the reins with which he held himself in rigid control he would give way to hysteria. In the presence of no one but his wife were the reins ever permitted to slacken, and, so, many people found him haughty and cold in his manner and thought him hard and mysterious.

Among the friends who came to Highland Gardens was one of the most distinguished architects of the day, Alexander J. Davis, whose offices were in New York. Before he had become an architect, Davis had made a reputation for his drawings of views of New York and Boston, and his renderings of buildings were considered superior to any that had been produced by an American before. When Downing wanted drawings to use as illustrations for his books, he turned quite naturally to a perfectionist like himself. The architectural ideas of the two men were in perfect sympathy. Davis had designed a Gothic residence as early as 1832, and, as he was a sensitive barometer in the intellectual climate of his time, he anticipated the popular taste in many instances. It was he, for instance, who claims to have introduced the bay window of which Downing made so much in his day and Boston has made so much ever since. As Downing had no architectural training, he relied heavily on Davis to make his rather rude sketches into elegant plans and elevations.

When Davis embarked on his architectural career in the 1820's as the partner of an older and well-established practitioner, Ithiel Town, professional architects were, as we have already seen, rarely consulted by private citizens. It was, of course, necessary to employ an architect to design a state capitol or a college hall (Davis did a number of both), but private building was another matter. As an architect who came from England to set himself up in practice in New York in 1832 discovered, "the majority of people could with difficulty be made to understand what was meant by a professional architect; the builders, that is the carpenters and bricklayers, all called themselves architects, and were at that time the persons to whom the owners of property applied when they required plans for building." A man who wanted to build a house would look around at what was already standing and decide which model suited him best, and then he would get a builder to make him one something like it. It was Davis who, to a very great extent, was responsible for convincing the public that architects had their domestic uses, and *Brother Jonathan* magazine was pleased to note in 1843 that "within the last few years . . . the banks of the Hudson have been studded with gems of villas and cottages, and we can see by these as well as by the public buildings and private mansions of this city, that the march of *taste* is accelerating." And then the magazine added with doubtful clairvoyance: "The time is not far distant when an American gentleman's villa will be held up to the world as a model of the perfection of beauty. . . ."

Brother Jonathan gave most of the credit for this state of affairs to Messrs. Davis and Town and their "unceasing exertions" to educate the public. Downing, for all his admiration for Davis, thought that *Brother Jonathan* took too rosy a view of the state of taste and, as he suspected that Davis had something to do with the articles that were appearing in the magazine, wrote to him to keep his skirts clean of such vulgar publications. "I beg," he said in a letter written in the winter of 1844, "you will not . . . allow the editors of that or any other paper to write slang articles on taste in your name. I think it does you harm, and I do not hesitate to say this as I am sure you are aware how entirely I have always endeavored, as far as [possible] in my humble way, to advance your professional interests." Evidently the sorts of things that chilled Downing's blood were such outrageous clichés—or so at least he would have thought them—as *Brother Jonathan's* recommendation that castellated architecture was most suitable for the highlands of the Hudson, pointed Gothic for the romantic intervals below the highlands, and the Italian villa style for "clear and sunny glades."

Architects in Downing's day, as in ours, had their troubles with clients who had notions of their own. Strong-minded women were quite ready to tell them how to build, on the one hand, or to take their most tastefully designed rooms and fill them with an unholy clutter, on the other. One of Davis's clients, Ruth Fay, knew her own mind and wrote in no uncertain terms about these modern notions and frivolous practices:

I have a decided objection to the present ambitious or pretentious style of house architecture. It does not comport with our means. Nor is it adapted to houses of the dimensions we usually build. We take our plans from castles and palaces and apply them to cottages and pigsties. Whereas the old manor houses of England and France are much more appropriate. What I want is a house with no waste spaces, the rooms all living-rooms, substantially well finished and comfortably furnished, *with an exterior of perfect simplicity of design.* . . . We can then put on finials, towers, etc., which are more frequently used to hide defects than for any other purpose.

There is no record of whether Mrs. Fay liked what Davis produced for her, but the chances are that he was allowed to get away with no nonsense and few, if any, finials. Most women of the day, however, had a taste for fanciness, and those who could afford to indulged it with a lavish hand.

The parlors of prosperous city houses fairly dripped with what was popularly known as "the French taste." Carpets were soft and flowered. "I raly thought my boot was sinking inter the floor," wrote the fictional country bumpkin Jonathan Slick to his father after his first visit to a wealthy New York mansion. "It seemed jest like walking over the onion patches, when they've jest been raked and planted in the springtime." At the windows were silk draperies, or lace curtains with elaborately tailored lambrequins, fringed and tasseled. Footstools covered with pictures in needlepoint of "lambs and rabbits sleeping among lots of flowers," cherrywood chairs carved in curlicues, sofas upholstered in shiny black or sometimes in bright red velvet, with fancywork cushions on them, endless little tables with bowed and ornamented legs left scarcely any space to move about in the room. On the walls were flowered French wallpapers, gilded mirrors, and probably a romantic landscape by Church or Durand or some lesser light who sold to the Art Union. In the corner was a whatnot in which were displayed porcelain figurines, shells, china dogs, small pictures in lace and velvet frames, and on the mantelpiece was a gilded nymph draped over a clock or a branch laden with stuffed birds under a bell glass.

Many country parlors in the East, as we have seen, affected the city manner, while in the West even the mansions of the wealthiest citizens were somewhat less "advanced." The Gothic cottage and the Italian villa were slow to invade the hinterland, and in his *Life on the Mississippi* Mark Twain describes in great, but by no means loving, detail the "frame house porticoed like a Grecian temple" that was the only proper residence for a prominent citizen and his family. The decoration was just as indiscriminate, just as cluttered, and just as fancy as that of a city house—if less expensive. The wallpaper and the flowered carpet came from American not French mills, and the bric-a-brac in the whatnot was of a homelier sort—shells with the Lord's Prayer or a portrait of George Washington carved on them, a "specimen" of quartz from California, Indian arrow heads, butterflies pinned to a card, and a locket containing a "circlet of ancestral hair." The variety was infinite. The pictures on the walls were likely to be stiff portraits of grandpa and grandma run up in a hurry by an itinerant painter, and a large engraving of *"Washington Crossing the Delaware"* from the famous painting by Emanuel Leutze, or, as Mark Twain said, "a copy of it done in thunder-and-lightning crewels by one of the young ladies—[a] work of art which would have made Washington hesitate about crossing, if he could have foreseen what advantage was going to be taken of it."

Downing and his friend Davis would have considered such clutter not only uncomfortable and disturbing to the spirit but an offense against "correct taste." Downing, especially, had no patience with fads (though of course he was inadvertently responsible for starting some himself) and he cautioned his readers against "the blunder of confounding *fashion* with *taste.*"

By 1850 Downing, who was then thirty-five, was nearly as well known in England as he was in America. His treatise on landscape gardening and his book on cottage residences had sold well there, and he had established himself as a horticultural authority of the first rank with his exhaustive work on *The Fruits and Fruit Trees of America*, which was published in 1845. His monthly articles in the *Horticulturalist*, a new magazine of which he was made editor in 1846, and his election as a corresponding member of the Royal Botanic Society of London, along with membership in the horticultural societies of Berlin, the Low Countries, and a handful of other august bodies had spread his reputation far beyond America. He had even received "a magnificent ring" from Queen Anne of Denmark in acknowledgment of the pleasure she had taken in his books. Recognition in England especially, the land of ancient country houses and elegant gentlemen, meant a great deal to Downing, and in the summer of 1850 he took advantage of the invitations that had been pressed on him by eminent English horticulturalists and set sail.

His interest had shifted largely away from gardens to architecture, as the publication of his book *The Architecture of Country Houses* in this same year testifies, and one of his principal reasons for going abroad was to find a promising young architect for a partner. After a summer of basking in the delicious atmosphere of spacious country houses, delightful parks and highly cultivated English landscapes, he went briefly to Paris where he found the sort of architect for whom he was searching. He was a young Englishman named Calvert Vaux, just twenty-five years old, who had been trained by a well-known London architect as an articled apprentice. Vaux returned with Downing to America and set up with him in the business of designing houses in offices at Newburgh.

As an architect Calvert Vaux turned out to be a sound practitioner, a tasteful and ingenious but undistinguished designer, and a very successful professional. He was a friendly man, and popular, and an unremittingly good citizen of his adopted country. Like Downing, he was devoted to the task of improving the public taste, and he never flagged in his enthusiasm for the spadework that Downing had performed in his books. "The popular taste must be imposed indirectly," Vaux wrote in a letter to a friend in 1860, eight years after Downing's death, "and I see no hope for an advance till the newspapers and magazines help to improve the standard. Men like Ruskin have pushed matters along with great effect in England—none of them professional men but all cultivated students with a liking for their subject." Downing was, certainly, the principal spokesman for Ruskin's architectural ideas in the United States, and Vaux added: "The value of Downing's books here has been great, not because of their technical excellence, for they are very poor in that quality, but because they are full of life and interest. It is the man and not the architect that wins the popular ear, and he compels his readers to allow that the subject is entertaining and enjoyable."

Vaux, however, did his share of publicizing what he considered to be good taste. He wrote for *Harper's Magazine*; and he published a book called *Villas and Cottages* in which the buildings look finicky and fancy compared with those in Downing's *Country Houses*; he talked architecture far better than he made it. His principal contribution to American life resulted from what he had learned from Downing about landscaping; it was he who persuaded Frederick Law Olmsted to undertake with him the design for Central Park in New York in 1856.

The story of Central Park is a long and complicated one, filled with political shenanigans, personal jealousies, and business intrigues. The fact that the park ever came into being at all is a testament to the intelligence, vision, and perseverance of Vaux, and much more especially to that of Olmsted, who threw up the job five times before he managed to get the politicians in line. One city park, more or less, would not seem to be important, but it must be remembered that Central Park was the first head-on attempt to stem the tide that was engulfing every piece of urban land for real-estate speculation and to stave off the increasing misery of city dwellers entirely imprisoned by brick and stone and mortar and pavement. But further than that Olmsted not only fenced off a piece of land; he converted a swampy, barren, and rocky area into a countryside with lakes and green meadows and grottoes, with hills and groves of trees and gardens. And he did it so skillfully that his plans for underpasses and carriage roads, bridle paths and walks have remained almost unchanged for a century from the time he and Vaux laid them out, and they still work in the age of the automobile.

But Downing never saw Central Park, studded as it was with many of his ideas. When Downing was alive it was still a dream in the mind of that rural poet who lived in New York, William Cullen Bryant. Mr. Bryant complained that his walks were being impeded by the growth of the city, and when Mr. Bryant spoke he was listened to. Downing had his own troubles with parks and politicians, though, when he was commissioned in 1851 at a salary of $2,500 a year to design public gardens near the Capitol in Washington and to landscape the White House and the new Smithsonian Institution there. A congressman, as congressmen are wont to do, decided that the

$12,000 that had been appropriated for the White House grounds was an outrageous waste of public funds and charged that, moreover, Downing was being overpaid for his services.

Politics worked somewhat differently in those days from the way they do now, and Downing requested President Fillmore to summon the Cabinet and discuss the matter, saying that unless the bickering could be done away with he was going to go back to Newburgh and stay there. The Cabinet met with the President, and Mr. Downing rolled out his drawings and explained them. They decided that his plans were the best that had been offered and that his salary was reasonable, and from then on Mr. Downing had no trouble from congressmen.

But he did not live long enough to see the trees and shrubs that he had ordered to be planted grow in the public gardens of Washington. In the spring and early summer of 1852 Mr. Downing and his partner were at work on the designs for an elegant summer home for a client in Newport, Rhode Island, and on the 28th of July he set out from Highland Gardens to inspect the work that was in progress and to talk with his client. Mrs. Downing decided to go with him; and her mother, Mrs. DeWindt, with her youngest son and daughter, and Miss Armstrong, an old friend, planned to take the river steamer as far as New York. Two boats were running that morning, the *Armenia* and the *Henry Clay*, and Mr. Downing and his party took the first one that came along. It was the *Henry Clay*, a trim new ship of which her owners were very proud. Her builder and part owner, Thomas Collyer, was aboard that morning and, as the captain had taken to his bed with severe indigestion, Mr. Collyer was in command.

It is most unlikely that the Downings would have got on board at all if they had known what the *Henry Clay* was up to, but they could not have been more than a few feet from the Newburgh pier before they were told by frightened passengers that the *Henry Clay* and the *Armenia* were engaged in a desperate race to determine which was the better and faster ship. It had been nip and tuck all the way from Albany, but the *Henry Clay* had pulled ahead, her stokers piling on the coal until her boilers were so hot that it was impossible to walk from the bow to the stern of the ship without being almost fried by their heat. Sparks flew from the tall twin smokestacks and ladies pled with men on board to insist that the race be abandoned. All attempts to persuade Mr. Collyer or the crew to give in to sweet reasonableness were turned aside with the comment that there was no danger.

The Downings had just finished dinner in the elegant saloon of the ship—which was, by that time, only twenty miles from New York—when Mrs. Downing saw smoke blowing toward them from amidships. In a few moments the *Henry Clay* was ablaze across her beam. In the panic that ensued the Downings were separated by the crowd and lost sight of each other. In desperation Mrs. Downing and her mother and the children leaped over the side into the water. Mrs. Downing was able to grab two deck chairs that floated near her and was swept upstream and out of harm's way by the incoming tide. It may have been her husband who had thrown those very chairs from the upper deck. One account of the tragedy records that he was last seen high on the boat throwing chairs into the river to help the passengers floundering in the water; another account says that he was drowned in a struggle to save his mother-in-law.

On the following afternoon his body was brought to Highland Gardens and laid in his library, as a thunderstorm, according to his friend Mr. Curtis, "burst over the river and crashed among the hills, and the wild sympathy of nature surrounded that blasted home."

Two days later in the New York *Daily Tribune* the author of his obituary called him "a man of genius and high culture" and spoke accurately when he said: "His chief aim was to refine the taste, and elevate the social life and habits of his countrymen to something like the ideal proper to freemen."

Taste in America had changed a great deal between the time when Mrs. Trollope returned to England in 1831 and the death of Mr. Downing, but if we are to believe the architectural and social historians it was for the worse rather than for the better. The days of Downing are now known as the age of "Carpenter Gothic"—"a perfectly awful farrago of libelous details—pointed arches, clustered columns, buttresses, parapets, pinnacles. . . . And with these awful monuments, cheek by jowl, Italian villas, very white and much balconied, Swiss chalets, and every other imaginable thing that . . . the admirable Mr.

Downing could invent, with, for evidence of sterling American ingenuity, the 'jigsaw and batten' refinement of crime." The author of
this diatribe was Ralph Adams Cram, writing in the *Architectural
Record* in 1913. You may recall that Mr. Cram also worked in the
Gothic style, and was the architect of the Princeton Chapel, nick-
named "the God Box," and of the Cathedral of St. John the Divine,
which is considered by critics of today to be one of the most curiously
clumsy anachronisms of our time.

But if Mr. Downing was responsible for inspiring a great many
carpenter-builders and inferior architects to construct parodies of his
cottages and villas, he was also an inspiration to many who tried to
bring order out of architectural chaos. One of the strangest of those
who seem to have been influenced by Downing's words, if not by his
taste for the Gothic and the Italian villa, was a man named O. S.
Fowler who had achieved both fame and fortune by writing books
about the occult science of phrenology. Mr. Fowler had come to the
conclusion while Downing was still alive that the most sensible and
economical dwelling was an octagonal house built of what he called
"gravel walls." Such was the influence of the famous reader of cranial
bumps that hundreds of such houses cropped up all over the country
—some of gravel wall construction, some of wood, and some of stone.
In the introduction to his book on the octagonal house, which he
called *A Home for All*, and which was published two years after
Downing's death, we can hear the faint, but distorted, echo of the
landscape architect's impassioned plea for an architecture suitable
to the character of its owners.

"Beautiful birds build tasty nests," wrote Fowler. ". . . as a general
rule, a fancy man will build a fancy cottage; a practical man, a convenient home; a substantial man, a solid edifice; a weak man, an illy
arranged house; an aspiring man, a high house; and a superior man
a superb villa."

This was the kind of cliché that Downing would have found distasteful, but as he sailed down the Hudson on his occasional trips to
New York and looked at the miscellany of castles, and villas, and
chalets along its banks, he would have been forced to admit that the
phrenologist's reading of the bumps on the landscape was all too
accurate.

CHAPTER IV

The Art Missionaries

"In matters of taste the public is a child. . . ."

While Downing and his circle of friends and followers were busy tidying up the landscape and exhorting their fellow men to lead more cultured lives in more tasteful surroundings, another group of missionaries was hard at work on a different facet of the public sensibilities.

The taste for the "fine arts" in America, quite unlike the apathy that Mrs. Trollope had encountered, was becoming a head-over-heels fad for picture collecting. Like a colt feeling its first oats, taste was getting out of hand entirely, or so at least some of the more thoughtful artists and critics and collectors of the day believed, and it was high time to break the frisky young beast to harness. The men who took upon themselves the responsibility for this heroic act were a varied lot who often disagreed with one another—not only about how the public should be trained but about what was good taste in pictures and what was bad. They were in this respect quite like the artists, critics, and collectors of our own day, and then as now they sometimes fell to squabbling among themselves. On the whole, however, they saw eye to eye on the ultimate goal. They all believed that if a national gallery of art could be established, it would provide a touchstone for taste, and that such an educational and cultural institution would be a stabilizing influence in the state of pandemonium which reigned in the world of the fine arts.

"It has become the mode to have taste," wrote James Jackson Jarves, the most articulate of the critics and collectors of the fifties and sixties.

"Private galleries in New York are becoming almost as common as private stables."

In the early sixties when Jarves made this observation, he was scarcely exaggerating, but to him and to others like him the private galleries smelled no sweeter than the private stables. "The anti-respectable notion of art," he wrote, "the joint offspring of the utilitarian habits of a country new to civilization and the religious tenets of Puritan settlers, has given place in the common mind to a notion almost as one-sided and ignorant in the opposite direction. It inclines to take a sentimental view of the functions of the artist, as of an exceptional being not amenable to the usual rules of criticism, and, covering them with poetical haze, allows the imagination to accept the promise for the fulfilment." This was a radical change indeed. How had the public taste, which had been so prudish and so aloof to the fine arts, come to clasp them so enthusiastically and indiscriminately to its bosom? The activities, and especially the aggressive salesmanship, of the Art Unions had, of course, played an important role in making art respectable and in putting it in the parlor. But what had turned indifference to collecting into a rage for it—in New York, in Washington, in Baltimore, and in Boston?

The answer, as you might expect, was the enthusiasm of a few single-minded men like Jarves himself. Let me introduce you to some of the most important ones—a wholesale grocer who gave up business to become a connoisseur and collector, a bearded dilettante who unsuccessfully tried to give away his important collection of "old masters," and a painter from Vermont whose charm and wit persuaded Boston to be more up-to-date than Paris in its taste for French painting.

When Jarves wrote in the sixties that "the spirit that sustains trade, debases art" he was not thinking of a spirited tradesman named Luman Reed who had devoted the latter part of his life to elevating art and the men who made it. And neither was the painter Thomas Cole thinking of his friend and patron, Reed, when, as you will remember, he bemoaned the fact that "the tide of utility sets against the fine arts." Quite the contrary. Reed was the ideal and unique art patron of his day, and he was, in some respects, more responsible for what became the fad for collecting than any man of his time.

Luman Reed, a square-jawed man with black hair and friendly eyes, was an up-state New Yorker from Green River, and precisely the sort of man who would make the deepest impression on the taste of the business community. He had started work in a general store with his father when he was a boy, had shipped as a sailor in his teens on a merchant sloop on the Hudson, and when he was in his twenties became his uncle's partner in a wholesale and retail grocery business in New York. By the time he was thirty, in 1815, he had taken over the firm, and seventeen years later he was ready to retire with a very comfortable fortune. He had made a reputation for being a completely honest but very astute trader, an exacting employer who was trusted and loved by those who worked for him, and a modest and intelligent man. In 1832 he gave up his grocery business and built himself "a fine house but not a palace" on Greenwich Street. It was considered by his contemporaries to be one of the noblest mansions in the city, built by the most accomplished workmen of materials of the highest quality. While it was under construction, Reed became absorbed by a new interest; he decided to collect pictures. At first he bought a few "old masters," but he was quick to realize that what was being sold to him by Michael Paff, Esq., a posh dealer of the day whose name became a legendary joke, was largely fraudulent, and he turned his attention to the works of men of his own generation.

One of these was Thomas Cole, who had just established himself in new quarters at the corner of Wall Street and Broadway and who was at work when, according to Cole's biographer, "There came in, one day, a person in the decline of life,—took rather a hasty turn around the room, serving for a gallery, and went out without a word. There was that, however, in the appearance of this silent visitor, as he looked quietly but intelligently from picture to picture, which could not be readily forgotten." The visitor, of course, was Reed, though a man in his forties is not usually considered by any but very young biographers to be "in the decline of life." Probably the biographer counted backward from the date of Reed's death because, it is true, he did not have long to live.

Reed became so absorbed in collecting that before his new house was completed he decided to make the top story of it into a gallery. It was the first room built by an American for the sole purpose of hanging pictures. He kept the gallery open one day a week so that the public might see his collection, and he met there in the evening with painters and such agreeable conversationalists as Washington Irving, James Fenimore Cooper, and William Cullen Bryant. He believed that artists were a special breed who should be encouraged and supported by practical men like himself, and when one of his business friends commented to him, "These pictures, Mr. Reed, must have cost considerable money," he replied, "They did; the outlay is my pleasure. I like it, besides the artists are my friends, and it is the means of encouragement and support to better men than myself."

It is no wonder that the artists were not only very fond of Reed but had great respect for his judgment and taste. He was, as Asher Durand's son wrote, "the first wealthy and intelligent connoisseur who detected and encouraged native ability in other directions than portraiture." Not only did he commission pictures from such men as Cole, and Durand, and William Sidney Mount, but he paid the expenses of several artists to go to Europe to study, and when he ordered paintings he always, except in the case of portraits (he commissioned Durand to do a series of the Presidents), left the subject and treatment entirely to the artist. He enjoyed their company and they enjoyed his; they were greatly impressed by the soundness of his perception and the acuteness of his criticism, and they sought his advice. They even elected him the only non-artist member of the exclusive Sketch Club. He never quibbled about prices, and when Cole, to whom he had given a commission, brought the picture to him, Reed asked him how much he wanted for it. "I shall be satisfied if I receive $300," Cole said, "but I should be gratified if the price is fixed at $500." "You shall be gratified," Reed replied, and he ordered five more paintings from him at the gratifying price.

When Reed died in the early 1840's, Mount wrote to Durand: "How pleasing was his address! How well he understood the feelings of the artist! He was one we shall always love to remember." But it was not only the artists who revered him; his friends in business did too, and they took measures to prove it. Thirty of them banded together and raised $13,000 with which to buy his collection and with it to found what they optimistically hoped would be a permanent memorial to him. They established the New York Gallery of Fine Arts.

Founding an institution is never easy, but founding an art gallery in New York in the forties was almost a feat of legerdemain. First of all there was the matter of a suitable building to house the pictures. For a couple of years the Academy of Design was glad to hang the collection, but this was merely a stopgap. The committee of businessmen wanted to persuade the city fathers to let them have the Rotunda, an elegant small building that had been built on city property near the City Hall in the early part of the century for the purpose of displaying a panorama painting that depicted, of all things, the Gardens of Versailles; it was now in disuse. They appealed to James Harper, the mayor (and one of the original Harper & Brothers), who gave the scheme his blessing subject to the approval of the Common Council. The members of the Council were no better than they should be, and Durand reported that "some bribery was used and a good deal of 'lobbying.' " The whole scheme, however, almost washed up on the shoals of ridicule when a celebrated hotel manager and member of the Board of Aldermen was called upon to make a speech in defense of the project. He didn't know anything about art, but his son, who collected pictures, did and he tried to coach his father on what to say. Oratory was florid in those days, and when the moment came for the alderman to dwell upon the beauties of art and civic betterment he "became so entangled and confused in his argumentative use of Greek and Renaissance terms and facts" that it was a miracle that the Common Council didn't laugh the scheme out of existence.

But it didn't. The gallery died of public indifference. When the editor of the New York *Herald* was asked to put a notice in his paper announcing that it was to be opened and that public subscriptions at a dollar a year would be solicited, he was appalled to note that the men behind the scheme "know more about pork and molasses than they do about art!" But he printed a notice all the same. The gallery was opened to the public, which stayed away, and the trustees were able to sell and persuade friends to accept only a thousand subscriptions. In two years, since not even the trustees themselves could be persuaded to come to meetings to elect officers, the pictures were taken down and presented to the New York Historical Society, where they may still be seen. As a demonstration of the "refined taste" of the forties they are incomparable.

Luman Reed's influence on the public taste, however, was more considerable than this indifference would seem to show. "To our princely merchants," an early historian of American art wrote shortly after Reed's death, "Luman Reed, Esq. has set an example of a mode of expending the gifts of fortune very different from the ostentatious display of the dining or drawing room." Private collections of American paintings became a standard accouterment of prominent businessmen. A fashion had been set that was to last for many decades, though very few of the new collectors could boast of Reed's honest enthusiasm, discriminating eye, or genuine respect for artists.

While Reed was assembling his gallery of American pictures a somewhat younger man from Philadelphia, an eccentric dilettante with inherited wealth, was pursuing the muse of painting through the pleasant cities of Europe. His name was Thomas Jefferson Bryan; temperamentally he could not have been more different from the practical merchant Reed. He was a romantic sort, and he bought "old masters" with a lavish hand if not always with what we would now consider discriminating taste. He thoroughly enjoyed himself, but his aim was not merely one of self-indulgence. He believed that America should have a national museum, and he collected his pictures with this end in view. He wanted to provide the nucleus of a great gallery to which Americans could bring their untutored sensibilities and be ennobled by acquaintance with the great works of the past. He offered his entire collection, upward of three hundred pictures, to the city of Philadelphia but, as Jarves wrote ten years later, "these rare old pictures were looked upon by the city fathers as unworthy of houseroom." So in 1853 he rented the second story of a building on Broadway in New York, and opened a gallery to which the public was invited.

Bryan by this time was a strange patriarchal figure with flowing white hair and a splendid Whitmanesque beard, and he presided over his gallery seated in a great armchair and dressed in a red velvet cape. The paintings on the walls, which were "covered with mellow tints," sported many of the most famous names in the history of art—Albrecht Dürer, Jan Van Eyck, Mantegna, Velásquez, and others as impressive. Most of the pictures were from the Low Countries and from France and England; there were only a few from Italy and a few from Spain. The collection was called "The Bryan Gallery of Christian Art"—Christian as opposed to heathen, for by no means all of the paintings were of religious subjects. "A call on him," wrote Henry T. Tuckerman, a critic and poet who was one of the most voluble promoters of the need for a national gallery, "was like visiting a venerable burgomaster of Holland, or a merchant prince of Florence, in her palmy days. . . . He seemed to belong to another sphere, and we to have wandered from Babel to Elysium in thus entering his gallery from bustling and garish Broadway." Bryan had chosen his pictures with the greatest care and, considering the state of art history in his day, with considerable knowledge and imagination. He cleaned the pictures himself, a thing no modern collector would dare to do, and he watched over them. He would not employ any attendants for his gallery, but was always there himself when it was open. He was not a boastful collector, and was quick to point out defects in his pictures, which, as a contemporary noted, was "as delightful as it is rare." If the attributions of many of them now seem to us to have been outlandishly lofty and naïve, we must remember that he was playing very close to par for the course in those days and that the scientific methods of attribution now in vogue were unknown then.

Visitors to the gallery were charged 25 cents admission and 12½ cents for a descriptive catalogue with a preface by Richard Grant White, the father of the architect Stanford White. In his introduction to the catalogue White disclaims any responsibility for "the authenticity of any attributions" as he did not pose as an expert, but he said that Mr. Bryan was "eminently qualified for the labor he assumed." White and Bryan, like Jarves, believed that the public taste in pictures had reached appalling depths, and that "to correct the defects of taste" there could be "no better kind of discipline than the thoughtful contemplation of old pictures of merit." White blamed the Art Unions, "our fashionable picture marts," and "our legion of illustrated works" for the depredation of taste, and he let fly with a barrage of polite invective which is rarely equaled by modern critics, even when they are talking about the popular art of our day: "Floras and Doras, with big eyes and little mouths, big arms and little hands, big busts and little waists, big bustles and little feet; manikin men, all forehead and favoris; portraits of homely old women flattered, in Books of Beauty, into a conventional prettiness and unnatural youth, far more repulsive than their own actual comeliness: such are the works of art which 'sell.' "

No insurance company would issue a policy to Mr. Bryan to cover his pictures, exposed as they were in his Broadway gallery, except at exorbitant rates. He wanted to have them in a safe place, and after six of them had been stolen, he loaned them temporarily to Cooper Union. The thefts, however, rather pleased him; if the public thought they were worth stealing, he reasoned, then the public taste must be improving. James Jackson Jarves, who was also a collector, agreed with him. "At first such property could be exposed with impunity," he wrote. "There was no one to do it the poor honor of thieving, still less of depreciation. Since the discovery that it has a marketable value, some of Mr. Bryan's pictures have been stolen. One of mine has also disappeared, and another was cut into after they were made free to the public. Both Mr. Bryan and myself regard these larcenies as symptoms of progress." Jarves, as we shall see a little later, was an incorrigible optimist.

And so apparently was Bryan. He went right on buying "old masters" until he died on a ship returning from a collecting expedition to Europe in 1870. Shortly before his death he gave his Gallery of Christian Art, which by that time had swelled to 381 pictures, to the New York Historical Society, where they now hang on the same floor with Luman Reed's quite different collection.

Reed and Bryan, both amiable and generous men, both of them pioneers in collecting, and both seriously interested in improving the public taste and the condition of the arts in America, had reason to act with missionary zeal. There were plenty of benighted and ignorant heathen ready for conversion, but it wasn't the aesthetic creed that appealed to the converts; it was the ritual. Instead of setting a *style* for collecting, Bryan and Reed had merely set a *fashion*. It became a fad to buy pictures—good pictures, bad pictures, new pictures or old ones (so long as they weren't "primitives"), American pictures or European ones. For all of their good intentions Bryan and Reed, like so many serious lovers and promoters of the arts, had been instrumental in starting one of the silliest art booms that has ever struck America.

The art market soared after the Civil War in much the same way that it soared after World War II. The art dealers, to use a phrase of the era of the recent boom, never had it so good. Or to use a reporter's phrase from the 1860's, "art has been volcanic!"

Let us take a look through several pairs of eyes at the equivalent of our modern Fifty-seventh Street as it was a little more than a century ago. The eyes are those of a writer for a weekly magazine, *The Round Table,* those of a "reformed" but anonymous art auctioneer who described his activities in *Harper's New Monthly Magazine,* and those of several disgruntled artists who wrote for a short-lived art magazine called *The Crayon.*

Artists and dealers, like writers and publishers, are always engaged in a kind of guerrilla warfare which now and again flares into open combat. It flared in the 1860's. "Crass commercialism" is the common epithet flung by artists at those who handle their products, and commercialism is inevitably connected in the artist's mind with ignorance, lack of taste, and a fast line of talk. An artist writing to *The Crayon* in 1860 summed up what was in the minds of many of his colleagues when he said of the art dealer: "He studies the nature of the public impressibility; he knows how to work the mine of crude sentiment and to turn it to account. With a small outlay of capital and muscular energy he is able, through the press and business agents, to create an excitement in behalf of very ordinary material; he can create public attention upon any one work or man so as to make the public see them in magnified proportions and really believe both to be marvelous productions."

He was quite right then; he would be quite right now. The art auctioneer, who wrote in *Harper's* and called himself "Smith," confessed as much. He and his partner, "Stipples," who "possessed all the requirements for selling pictures . . . good looking, of good address and gentle manners, with great flow of language and impudence unbounded," opened a gallery in a third-floor-back on Broadway for which they had collected "a lot of very poor paintings." The rooms were always full of people who were willing to climb the stairs to look at them, so they decided to charge a 25-cent admission fee, but they had to drop it because "it extinguished the crowd." At first they sold pictures from the wall, like any modern gallery, and school marms trailing a line of children would come and walk solemnly around the gallery while Stipples spouted high-sounding phrases that he had learned by "having crammed for art-talk from a manual on the subject."

After a couple of years of selling old portraits to "Western gentlemen" who had moved to New York and wanted some ancestors to hang on their walls and other "cast iron paintings," the partners decided to turn the gallery into an auction room for art. Business picked up considerably and Smith and Stipples learned a good deal about the public taste. "It is the picture that tells a story that I like most and can sell best," the author says. "Good cradle pictures are usually salable at from forty to sixty dollars at auction." He had his troubles with pictures of animals, though some sold better than others. "Cattle and sheep," he noted, "have often given me a great deal of trouble. Pigs are generally more in demand. One cow looking over another cow's back is very well liked." He had a harder time selling a picture of a horse's head than one of a dog. "A terrier looking out of a hole," he noted, "is good for a certain sum."

It was the "old masters" that really gave them trouble. Stipples took care of that aspect of the business, and the worse the picture the more eloquent he became. The same "old masters" would turn up again and again on the block, some because they had been "sold" to a bogus buyer, of whom they always had a few at each sale, and others because their owners would keep them for a few years, lose their money, and put them back on the market. It was said in those days that "the average holding of a Fifth Avenue mansion" was about three years. Stipples and Smith had one perennial called "Sibyl's Head" that they found in a cellar on East Broadway and bought for $6.50 and were asking $3,000 for, though they thought they had spent too much for it in the first place. Evidently they had their share of "good pictures" too, paintings by well-known artists of the day, and they did well with them.

There was one painting that the auctioneer passionately disliked. It was called "Landing of the Pilgrims," and he describes it as "the worst picture that I ever saw in our auction rooms, and utterly worthless." In trying to get rid of it Stipples in his smoothest and most unctuous manner gave it this build-up:

Ladies and gentlemen—It is not more than once in a century that such a painting as this is exhibited. The owner, a gentleman of enormous wealth [Sensation and awe in the audience!] would have taken it with him to Europe, where he resides ten months of the year, had he not hesitated to deprive the country of so valuable a work of art. I hope that his patriotic motives will be appreciated by you. [Applause.] The subject, as you see, is one of the noblest in the world, and the treatment is—but it would be presumptuous of me to praise the work of the man who painted it. When I mention the name of Squilgee you will understand my diffidence. I may point out to you, however, one or two points in the picture in which the artist has excelled himself. That blasted tree in the foreground is an exquisite bit of painting. The short herbage beneath it is crisp and juicy. . . . You will also observe the prismatic effect of the light on the background. . . . But I need not direct your attention to what must be so obvious to the crowd of art-judges before me.

And he concluded his peroration with, "An opportunity is now offered for some one here to become the owner of one of the greatest paintings of modern times." It was knocked down to a bogus buyer for $400.

"Of course it is not for me to direct the public taste," Smith wrote, and then he added, "Yet it seems a pity that the best works of our best painters should be constantly knocking about auction rooms in company with the worst, and that no National Gallery exists where they would be the property of the people, and where those who wished to paint might have good models to paint from."

This was the constantly recurring theme of the fifties and sixties—the need for a national gallery. The art market was, as you can see, a shambles, for the emporium of "Messrs. Smith and Stipples" was the rule and not the exception, and some sort of anchor to windward was needed.

The reporter who wrote about the art market for *The Round Table* approached it from the point of view of the consumer and not the auctioneer, but what he saw was much the same. "The city is literally flooded with pictures," he wrote. "Day after day new announcements are made of sales of private collections." People flocked to the galleries to inspect the "dross" that was going on the block. "For days before a sale, the galleries . . . are crowded from morning until night, heterogeneous throngs of people that constantly come and go." Old ladies, especially, came to the galleries, and though they didn't pay much attention to the paintings, they would sit around the stove and look at the catalogue or at each other. Young women came to show off their new clothes, and men who seemed "to have no idea upon art beyond the commercial one" would stand very close to the pictures and occasionally touch them "as if to test the soundness of the drygoods" on which they were painted.

The art auctioneers were a breed not quite like any other. They always called the purchasers "collectors," and they combined the attributes of the bully, the snob, the satirist, the wit, and the cooing dove. They were "cajoling in one sentence and withering in the next"; they were masters of obfuscation, and the names of the great painters fell like drops of honey from their tongues. None of the wealthy collectors of the day exposed themselves to the auctions; they visited the displays beforehand by appointment and sent their agents to buy for them. Those who had no agents and little knowledge not infrequently discovered that they had bid in "paintings" which were nothing more than "cheap, colored lithographs, varnished over to look like oil paintings."

Is it any wonder that *The Crayon* said, "In matters of taste, the public is a child . . ."? Or that Jarves commented that ". . . we are only a step in advance of savages who fail to discriminate in a painting between a man, house, horse, tree, or ship?"

James Jackson Jarves, however, was at heart an optimist and he believed that possibly, just barely possibly, the moment was at hand when the arts would burst into blossom on the fertile soil of his native land. The nineteenth century had not seen the likes of Jarves before; he was a new kind of tastemaker, new, that is, to the Age of Public Taste, and a man at whom it will pay us to take more than a cursory glance.

His predecessors in the forties, men like Downing and Reed and Bryan, had for the most part one single aim in view—to interest the public in tasteful objects, in architecture and pictures and the embellishments of the home, and to engage their attention and focus their view on the place of the arts, both decorative and "fine," in a society of free men. The Art Unions had done a tremendously effective job of making pictures known to thousands of people—of making America art conscious. They had done little—or worse than little—to refine taste. You will remember that the president of the American

Art Union in 1844 wanted to know "what is the matter with mediocrity?" Downing in his quite different way was more interested in
persuading his compatriots to put their minds on the benefits of
architecture and on how to lead decorous lives in suitable surroundings, built with honesty, than in educating them to sophisticated
appreciation of architecture as an art. Jarves, on the other hand, was
not a popularizer, in the sense of trying to create a market for art in a
large way; he was concerned far less with the quantity of taste than
with its quality. He was pleased when an English magazine called
him an "art missionary," for he hoped in his quiet but articulate way
to lead converts out of the swamp of popular taste to the upland
meadows on the side of Parnassus where the air was more rarefied and
the view more ennobling.

The story of Jarves has recently been told in great detail by Francis
Steegmuller in his book *The Two Lives of James Jackson Jarves*,
and there is no need for us to dwell at length on the peregrinations of
this Bostonian whose father was the founder and for many years the
president of the famous Sandwich Glass Company. But let us look at
that part of Jarves's life that is intimately involved with the eccentricities of taste in America just after the middle of the last century.

Jarves was forty-three when he and his wife, after living for thirteen
years in the Hawaiian Islands—where Jarves started a newspaper,
dabbled in politics, and tried his hand unsuccessfully at business—
arrived in Paris in 1851. The Jarveses had planned to settle down in
the French metropolis, but after six months they decided to make their
home in Italy. Those six months, however, changed the course of
Jarves's life completely. He discovered the Louvre, and he discovered
at the same time a new vocation. At first he was overwhelmed and
confused by the sheer mass of what he saw. "The long gallery," he
wrote in an article for *Harper's New Monthly Magazine*, for which
he was an intermittent correspondent, "in which are the paintings of
the older Italian, Flemish, Spanish, and French schools is nearly a
quarter of a mile in length." This was a tremendous dose for a conscientious observer who had never given art much thought, and he
complained that there was no systematic guidebook to help him sort
out which paintings were important and which were not. "Repeated

visits, however," he went on, "taught me that taste expanded and improved in the contemplation of its masterpieces."

In the spring of 1852 the Jarveses moved to Florence where the company was brilliant and the atmosphere was perfumed with the delightfully musty aroma of antiquity. There, among other distinguished expatriates from England and America, were Robert and Elizabeth Barrett Browning; Mrs. Jameson, the author of *Sacred and Legendary Art*, which had been published in 1848 and was well-known to subscribers to the American Art Union through the *Bulletin*; and, of all people, Mrs. Frances Trollope, now a successful and prolific novelist, up to her eyes in spiritualism. It was only a matter of months before Jarves was exploring the mysteries of early Italian painting, and was steeped in the books of John Ruskin, Mrs. Jameson, Alexis François Rio, the French author of *The Poetry of Christian Art*, and Lord Lindsay, whose three-volume *Sketches of the History of Christian Art* was a compendium of information about early painters that Jarves found invaluable. He was soon on the road to becoming the most distinguished and one of the most readable American writers on art in the nineteenth century, a collector who anticipated the fashion in America by several generations, and a tastemaker whose influence, which was mostly indirect, has until recently been largely overlooked.

Jarves, a willowy man who was plagued with poor eyesight and frail health, was at his writing desk a good deal of the time, and he frequently visited America in connection with the publication of his works. Neither *Art Hints*, which was roundly lambasted by the loyal and touchy art press for "directing the finger of scorn and contempt upon the best works of our best men," nor another book, *Art Studies*, which an advanced "little" magazine of the day said was "*soaked* in conventional doctrines," had made him popular with either the contemporary painters or the bright young visionaries of the day. But Jarves knew and understood the art world of America, and, if he was critical of it, he was not unsympathetic to any efforts that it was making to spread the arts or to raise the public taste. He believed that "a harvest is to be reaped . . . sooner than many think" in the American fields where art was cultivated.

His own attempts to plow the fields were not happy ones. He had spent ten years in Florence collecting a formidable group of about

The Lotteries That Started An Art Boom
Thomas Cole's "Youth," above, was one
of the most popular engravings ever distributed by the American Art Union,
whose annual lottery at the Broadway
Tabernacle in 1847 is shown below.
Hiram Powers' "The Greek Slave," on
view at New York's Düsseldorf Gallery
in 1858, was the darling of her day.

DISTRIBUTION OF THE AMERICAN ART-UNION PRIZES.

When a Suitable House Was a Greek Temple

The Greek Revival drawing room above was in the New York house of Mr. Ernest Fiedler in 1850, but it might easily have been in the cinnamon and white mansion, below, left, on the banks of the Hudson at Barrytown. The little octagonal extension on its north side is a library, said to be the work of A. J. Davis. The more modest "temple" next to it is on the Main Street of the town of Sheffield, Massachusetts.

The Man Who Domesticated Gothic

To Andrew Jackson Downing the houses on the opposite page were "tasteless temples." His own house at Newburgh, New York, was in what he considered the more "honest" Gothic style. He was responsible for the vogue for little "carpenter Gothic" houses like the one below in Hudson, New York, on which the scroll saw was used so lovingly. Its original coat of paint was surely not white but a "tasteful" somber hue.

Mid-Century Elegance, Inside and Out

This 1854 drawing room in the "French taste," a fashion of which Downing said, "Its lightness, elegance, and grace renders it especially the favorite of ladies," would have been considered quite suitable for the "Italian" (or "Tuscan") villa depicted by Currier & Ives below. The drawing room, once in Robert J. Milligan's home in Saratoga Springs, is now in the Brooklyn Museum.

What Downing Left Behind

Downing's dream of "smiling lawns and tasteful cottages" left its imprint most spectacularly in such public parks as New York's Central Park (shown above from the north in an 1865 view by John Bachmann) and in "carpenter Gothic" edifices such as the Croton Falls, New York, church below. Downing designed neither, but his inspiration was responsible for both.

Collectors Without Honor:

Luman Reed (above), James Jackson Jarves (left), and Thomas Jefferson Bryan (below) were indefatigable collectors and promoters of the arts in the days before America had any real art museums. Here they are shown next to typical pictures from their collections: Reed with Thomas Cole's "Consummation of Empire," Jarves with a "Crucifixion" by Lorenzo Monaco, and Bryan with "Rest on the Flight into Egypt," once attributed to Giorgione and now called a Paris Bordone.

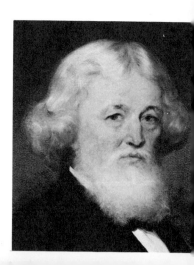

Touchstones of Taste in the '70's

Before the Metropolitan Museum moved to its present site in 1880 it occupied two downtown buildings. Above, left, is the way it looked to the painter Frank Waller in its second home on Fourteenth Street. *Frank Leslie's Illustrated Newspaper* recorded its establishment in the nucleus of its present building in Central Park with the drawing above, right. Below are a few of Jarves's "pre-Giottesque ligneous daubs" now exhibited in Yale's new fine arts building.

Everybody Could Afford Taste

Patterns, prints, and sculpture were turned out for the mass market by the 1860's. Prints like "The Great Fight for the Championship" by Currier & Ives sold by the thousands. The crinoline at the left (drawn by Winslow Homer) might well have been cut from one of Mme. Demorest's millions of patterns. John Rogers sold more than 100,000 "groups" such as "The Slave Auction" and the one advertised in *The Century* in 1886.

NEIGHBORING PEWS. Price, $15.00.

These groups are packed, without extra charge, to go with safety to any part of the world. If intended for Wedding Presents, they will be forwarded promptly as directed. An Illustrated Catalogue of all the groups, varying in price from $10 to $25, and pedestals (in mahogany and ebony finish), can be had on application, or will be mailed by inclosing 10 cents to

JOHN ROGERS,
860 Broadway, corner of 17th St. New-York.
Take the Elevator.

one hundred and thirty early Italian paintings, "characteristic specimens" he called them; he did not claim that they were masterpieces. It was his dream that they would someday form the nucleus of a national gallery of art in America, where, he strongly believed, there was need of such an institution as a litmus of taste for the people and an example to artists. Collecting became an obsession with him. As his finances dwindled and he was obliged to borrow money against the pictures, and as the villa where he lived with his family became more and more cluttered with "specimens," his relations with his wife, which had long been anything but agreeable, became next to impossible. He was determined to get the collection to America and to persuade the city of Boston to purchase it, for as a Bostonian he had longed since childhood to make a magnificent gesture that would establish him as a distinguished citizen of the city and its leading patron of art. The paintings had cost him, so he said, $60,000, but he was ready to make a generous gesture, and he offered them for $20,000 "to any association or individuals pledged to make it finally the nucleus of a permanent gallery for Boston, the final arrangement for exhibition (hanging, lights, and temperature—the last an important consideration for pictures on wood) to be entrusted to me, and the collection to be kept together as a whole under some distinctive name." Such, possibly, as his own.

The trustees of the Boston Athenaeum were quick to see a cultural bargain, and they offered to put up $5,000 if the remainder could be raised by public subscription. Jarves, himself, went so far as to subscribe $1,000 anonymously. But the citizens of Boston were unimpressed and unresponsive. They had not the slightest interest in what *The Crayon*, which had no love for Jarves or his attacks on contemporary American painters, called "pre-Giottesque ligneous daubs." And if this quasi-official publication of the artists was not up to accepting Italian primitives, how could the public be expected to care? They emphatically did not, and the Athenaeum's effort failed. Mr. Jarves had his treasures shipped to New York where they were put on exhibition for the first time in the new fireproof quarters of the New York Historical Society in the winter of 1860-1861.

Jarves had no intention of giving up his attempts to sell the collection at a bargain to found a national gallery, but the financial shoe was pinching him badly, and he was forced to part with a few pictures one by one. None of those he let go, however, were part of the "historical sequence," so important, he believed, for educational purposes. He could find no institution in New York that would take them even at his low price, and he finally arranged with the trustees of Yale College to accept them as collateral for a loan of $20,000. Yale had just built a new art gallery, and was glad to have the collection to cover what might otherwise have been bare walls, and Jarves, who already had a pressing mortgage on the pictures and hoped that Yale might someday be willing to pay $50,000 for them, was glad to have them housed and to have some cash in hand.

He was unable to meet the interest payments on the Yale loan, and the pictures were offered for sale by auction in 1871. Until the last minute Jarves thought that the paintings were to be knocked down individually and that he might realize a considerable sum from their sale. But Yale insisted that the collection be auctioned as a single lot. The sale was a dismal occasion. Only a few stragglers and a few newspapermen came to New Haven to witness Jarves's bitter disappointment. In a single bid Yale bought the pictures at a remarkable bargain—the amount of the loan and the accrued interest, $22,000.

Jarves's estimate of the value of the collection was extremely conservative in terms of the value we attach to his pictures today. The Jarves Collection at Yale, which has recently been cleaned and rehung, is now considered one of the great collections of primitives outside Italy, and single pictures in it, such as the Pollaiuolo or the Sassettas, if they were to reach today's art market, which is hungry for quality, would bring more than Jarves's asking price for the whole lot of them.

In retrospect it is easy to say that the public taste was not yet ready for primitives, but in justice to Jarves's contemporaries it must be added that the public taste is *never* ready for primitives. They become acceptable and palatable only when they have been enshrined in the fastnesses of museums or have become a part of daily life, as they do when they remain in the churches and monasteries for which they were originally painted. Since there were no American museums, in the sense that we know them now, at the time Jarves was trying to convince the public to rally and build one, there is little wonder that no one could be found to support a public subscription for a boatload of flat saints and martyrs on gilt backgrounds, Madonnas with Byzantine black eyes, and little landscapes with what looked like paper dolls set in them. Nothing could have been further from the American taste of the sixties, which had been educated by the Art Unions to accept lush and sentimental maidens, dreamlike landscapes, and smooth-as-satin marble nudes as the highest manifestations of art. Is it any wonder that they found Jarves's primitives "extremely repulsive," or that a Yale undergraduate remarked that the martyrdoms of the saints looked like something you might expect to find, not in an art gallery, but in a dissecting room?

As not infrequently happens in the paradoxical art world, Jarves, by digging around in the distant past and unearthing for his contemporaries a way of looking at the world that was half a millennium old, became a man ahead of his time. Taste, in some respects, was not to catch up with him for several generations, and neither was the historical approach to the study of art, which he believed so important, to become recognized by American universities as a legitimate subject of inquiry for nearly half a century. He introduced to this country the idea that art could and should be studied as a historical progression of styles, and his insistence that his collection was important as an educational instrument because of its "historical sequence" was a brand-new and revolutionary idea for which he had to do battle. But his function as a thorn in the mid-century flesh was one that is most important to us for the moment. He got under the skin of those who were complacent about the progress of art in America, and he made them extremely irritable. "Let us carefully sift the seed as it is sown," he wrote in *The Art Idea*, "and not wait until the tares are big and strong before trying to uproot them. A bright vision of national growth in art does indeed come before our mental sight, but that must not tempt us to overlook the fallow Now. . . . It is a duty to vindicate art, not to foster national conceit, stimulate personal vanity, or pander to individual interests."

This is not the kind of talk that makes a man popular with complacent artists, collectors, or dealers, and Jarves had special words for the critics: "Sagacious on-the-fence critic!" he flung at the reviewer for a daily paper who tried hard not to offend anyone. He berated artists and critics alike for the "present pernicious system of befogging and befooling" the public, and pleaded for "that sort of criticism which justifies its faith by reason and honest likings." Jarves was not afraid to make enemies, and he made many. He believed that the arts were more important than the feelings of individual artists or the interests of dealers, and that, of course, is a sure road to unpopularity in the art world.

But Jarves was not alone, though his methods were often more acrimonious than those of others, in his crusade to raise the quality of the public taste. Steps were being taken by a good many men besides Jarves to try to make the field which was so lush with weeds and tares produce some lovely blossoms. In Boston, New York, Baltimore and Washington men had their hands to the plow. William Morris Hunt, a very gifted young painter who had studied in Paris and returned to marry a lady in "the charmed circles of what was considered the best society" in Boston, came among the Brahmins like a missionary among the heathen. He found their ignorance about art and their indifference to the aesthetic values he thought important an aggravation and a challenge. To him there were no painters as great as Jean François Millet, Corot, and Daubigny and he lectured and wrote with wit, charm, and eloquence about these members of the Barbizon school with such effectiveness that, as one of his biographers has said, "Boston attained the glory of providing the first market in America for those masters' works at a time when they were not yet fully recognized in France."

In Washington William C. Corcoran, a financier, gave $300,000 to build a museum "to be devoted to Art-purposes, and particularly the encouragement of American Genius." The building was finished just before the Civil War broke out, and it was temporarily taken over by the government for the headquarters of the ordnance department. It opened as a gallery in 1870. Mr. Corcoran had given it a magnificent endowment of $1,000,000 and seventy-nine paintings from his own collection. In Baltimore William T. Walters was collecting the pictures that were to become the nucleus of the Walters Gallery, while in New York men like August Belmont, who collected 110 paintings while he was the American Minister to The Hague and A. T. Stewart, the department-store magnate who bought a picture from Meissonier by cable for $70,000 sight unseen, were bringing foreign works, few of which are still in fashion, to our shores.

All of this activity was surely not without its encouraging aspects. Not only did Jarves see cause for hope, but so also did the critic Tuckerman. "Within the last few years," he wrote in 1867, "the advance of public taste and the increased recognition of art in this country, have been among the most interesting phenomena of the times." Not only were American painters studying in Rome, Paris, Florence, and Düsseldorf, but there were now "native ateliers" in Chicago, Albany, Buffalo, Philadelphia, Boston, and New York. Not only were the principal cities holding exhibitions of art, but so were such smaller communities as Providence, Troy, Utica, Portland, Maine, and Charleston, South Carolina. Art was everywhere. Jarves even noted that the looks of store fronts were improving. "Compare the stores of 1850," he wrote, "homely wall surfaces broken up by graceless apertures, as destitute of ornamentation as a mud scow, with those of 1860, with their plethora of carving, classical orders, rococo fancies, striking bits of originality, and here and there ingenious adaptation, in fine, the universal struggle for beauty in some shape or other."

Like so many movements to improve the taste of Americans, the cries for a national museum from critics, from collectors, from artists, and even from art auctioneers brought an echoing voice from Americans in Europe. It was at a celebration of America's ninetieth year of independence held at the Pré-Catelan in the Bois de Boulogne in Paris that the indefatigably public-spirited Mr. John Jay made, as he recalled some years later in a letter, "the simple suggestion that 'it was time for the American people to lay the foundation of a National Institute and Gallery of Art and that the American gentlemen then in Europe were the men to inaugurate the plan.'" From the lips of such a distinguished personage the suggestion, he recalled, "commended itself to a number of the gentlemen present, who formed themselves into a committee for inaugurating the movement." What the critics, collectors, and artists, for all their pleading and cajoling had never been able to do, a statesman, who must have heard their pleas, did with a single utterance. The result of Jay's suggestion was the Metropolitan Museum of Art in New York, which now calls itself with justification "the greatest treasure house in the Western Hemisphere." After a five-year period of anguishing gestation, over which William Cullen Bryant presided as cultural physician, it was born in a private house on Fifth Avenue that had been made over into a dancing academy. A "fine turnout of ladies and gentlemen" in bustles and Prince Alberts came to the opening reception, and within three months more than six thousand visitors had inspected, evidently with almost unanimous approval and surprise (even Bostonians were impressed), the collection that had been assembled. Before it finally occupied a building on its present site in Central Park, it moved to a mansion on Fourteenth Street, where it stayed for six years. The present Metropolitan conceals behind its marble Beaux Arts façade a somewhat Gothic structure that was designed by Calvert Vaux as its permanent, and in the taste of its own day, magnificent home.

The dream of the art missionaries—of Reed and Bryan, of Jarves and Tuckerman and the art auctioneer—had at last come true. What was in effect a "national gallery" that would henceforth be the touchstone of taste had become an actuality. But the public taste was by this time off on a new and different, and, we are inclined to think today, dismal joy ride. Touchstone or no touchstone, there seemed to be no way to keep the public taste in order.

Possibly the publishers of Tuckerman's *American Artist Life* came very close to the truth when they printed in the "advertisement" that appears in the front of the book the following statement by a "foreign writer of acknowledged authority": "There are standing controversies in Art, which are perpetually breaking out afresh: they take new forms with every new age, but they are always essentially the same. These violent dogmatic decisions crush and wither the timid likings of plain people, which might have developed into cultivated taste."

CHAPTER V

Art and Fashion—Cheap and Popular

"Taste is like conscience; all have it. . . ."

After the Civil War and before the depression which came in the early seventies, the North was full of song and gaiety. George Makepeace Towle, an American who had been living in England and had come home, pricked up his ears and noted that he had heard boys in the street singing and whistling Mozart and Rossini, and hand organs grinding out the arias from *Faust* and *Lucrezia Borgia*. He also heard "Negro melodies" and ballads and was astonished at the way "a new song spreads through the states like wildfire." Minstrel shows packed in nightly crowds in the "opera houses" of nearly every sizable community, and farces, stump speeches, banjo solos, clog dances and Mr. Bones delighted the multitudes. A contest for the national anthem was a heated topic of dispute; should it be "Hail, Columbia," or "The Red, White and Blue," or "America, 'tis of Thee" (as he called it) or "The Star-Spangled Banner"? And even then "Hail to the Chief" was played for dignitaries. "There is singing everywhere," the visitor noted. In high society "the universal custom of piano-playing and singing . . . is the *sine qua non* of evening parties and sociables." Singing was even taught in the schools.

But that was not all that impressed him. The theater, after years of being thought indecent, had come alive. There were more performances of Shakespeare in America, he noted, than there were in England. There was "tragedy, fine old comedy and the 'free and

65

easy' burlesque . . . the empire of short dresses, gaudy scenery, and slangy nonsense." It was a gay time, a time of relief after war, a time of easy money, easier morals, building booms and land speculation. But what about art for the people? That was well taken care of, too.

Genuine, hand-painted oil pictures, or even chromos that had been touched up with thick varnish by unscrupulous auctioneers to make them look like the genuine article, were obviously out of the reach of most Americans and, indeed, outside their interest. Pictures, however, were not beyond anybody's reach—nice colorful pictures, suitable for framing, in a tremendous variety of sizes, subjects, sentiments, and moralities. And, what is more, everybody seemed to concur in the belief that no room was adequately decorated, whether it was a parlor or a dining room, a saloon or a poolroom, unless it had pictures on its walls. "Pictures," said Messrs. Currier & Ives, "have become a necessity." The extent of their business amply bears this out.

When Catherine Beecher and her more famous sister, Harriet Beecher Stowe, wrote their household guide, *American Woman's Home*, in the sixties, they suggested that any woman who was decorating her living room set aside about twenty per cent of her budget just for pictures. Out of a total sum of $80 for tasteful and useful objects, approximately $60 was to be spent as follows:

Wallpaper and border	$ 5.50
Thirty yards matting	15.00
Center table and cloth	15.00
Muslin for three windows	6.75
Thirty yards green English Chintz	7.50
Six chairs at $2.00 each	12.00

This left just under twenty dollars for pictures, and the Beecher sisters recommended the following chromos which "when well selected and of the best class, give the charm of color which belongs to expensive paintings":

Miss Oakley's charming little cabinet picture of "The Little Scrap-Book Maker" for	$ 7.50
Eastman Johnson's "Barefoot Boy"	5.00
Newman's "Blue Fringed Gentians"	6.00
Bierstadt's "Sunset in the Yosemite Valley"	12.00

If you couldn't afford to buy frames for them, the Beechers suggested that you make a rustic frame of twigs with the bark still on them and glue "a cluster of acorns" or some small pine cones in the corners. There were, of course, a good many women who could not afford such expensive chromos, and to them the Beechers recommended "engravings which finely reproduce much of the real spirit and beauty of the celebrated pictures of the world."

But for thousands and thousands of other families who could afford neither chromos nor engravings, there were still plenty of pictures to be had. If the test of time is to be regarded as a factor in judging taste, then it would seem that those who could afford the least for their pictures either had, or had forced on them, better taste than those who bought the engravings or the chromos, which have largely disappeared. The cheap, hand-colored lithographs published by Messrs. Currier & Ives are now considered to be not only interesting as documents of the last century, but, according to many people today, worth collecting as "art."

Currier & Ives was not the only firm that produced lithographs by the thousands, but it is certainly the most famous and in its own way did by far the biggest business. The partners were almost entirely without artistic pretensions, but they were rigorous guardians of the quality of the craftsmanship that went into their product. They called themselves, quite frankly, "Publishers of Cheap and Popular Pictures," and no firm ever had a slogan better borne out by its product. The pictures were cheap, all right; the small prints (the smallest were about three by five inches) sold for from 15 cents to 25 cents apiece at retail, and the large folio prints (the biggest were eighteen by twenty-seven) went for a top price of $3. There is no question that they were popular. Currier & Ives had agents all across America, and they maintained a London office that was the center of distribution for Europe.

The core of the operation was a factory on Spruce Street in New York. There most of the drawings were made, the stones prepared, the printing done. Currier & Ives did not use a color lithography process in which the various tints were printed from several stones. They printed only the black drawing and the colors were added by hand. On the fourth floor in the rear was a space reserved for "artists, lithographers, and letterers." A relatively small proportion of the

hundreds of different prints that Currier & Ives published were designed by artists other than those in the regular employ of the firm.
And the tricky and delicate operation of transferring the sketches to
the smooth surface of the lithographer's stones was performed almost
entirely in the Spruce Street factory. Occasionally the work of
nationally known artists, such as Eastman Johnson and John Trumbull, was copied, and now and then stones were sent out to especially
expert lithographers to prepare, but for the most part the entire operation from design to coloring was done on the premises. On the fifth
floor a group of about a dozen carefully trained young women, mostly
of German descent, sat around a table on which was propped a fully
colored print. Each of them had before her a copy of this same picture
and a single color which she applied and then passed the print along
to her neighbor. When the prints had finally gone the rounds the
woman in charge, called the "finisher," did the final touching up, and
the pictures were ready for sale. Only the finest Austrian colors were
used and they were guaranteed not to fade from exposure to light.

The main outlet for the sale of the pictures was the firm's store on
Nassau Street, a commodious establishment with a long table down
the center on which the merchandise was stacked, and bins around
the walls, above which were prints framed and unframed and some
of the original paintings from which they were taken. Each bin had
an inventory of its contents tacked to its lid, and when the lids were
opened they became easels for displaying the prints. Outside on the
street were tables where overstock was sold at bargain prices, and each
morning peddlers would come with their carts and purchase a supply
of pictures to hawk through the streets during the day.

Nathaniel Currier, who started the firm in 1834, and James Merritt
Ives, a younger man whom Currier had taken on as a bookkeeper at
first and then invited into partnership, understood the public taste, or,
perhaps, between them they *had* the public taste. It was nothing if
not catholic. There was hardly a subject that didn't find its place in
their catalogue of pictures, though they avoided scenes in which
people were working too hard; they preferred pastorals in which men
and women and children all seemed to enjoy themselves, playing as
they worked or just playing, and even in winter scenes with the

ground covered with snow and the air clear and crisp nobody was permitted to look discomforted by the cold.

In the Currier & Ives prints, country life is inevitably idyllic; so is life in city parks. The Indian is always a noble savage, brave in defeat; he never conquers. The West is always lovely prairies. And as Morton Cronin has remarked in his revealing study of the subject matter of Currier & Ives, "Even prize fighters pose like undressed statesmen." Irishmen and Negroes are the butts of most of the jokes in the comic prints, and industrial workers are treated as though they didn't exist. Evidently the partners did not think that factory life had any appeal as salable subject matter for pictures. A catalogue which they sent to prospective agents in the seventies listed "nearly eleven hundred subjects" in the following remarkable categories: "Domestic, Love Scenes, Kittens and Puppies, Ladies' Heads, Catholic Religious, Patriotic, Landscapes, Vessels, Comic, School Rewards and Drawing Studies, Flowers and Fruits, Motto Cards, Horses, Family Registers, Memory Pieces, and Miscellaneous in great variety." But even this list omits two of their most popular categories—trains and burning buildings. Except for the comic scenes, the political and temperance cartoons, and some of the more topical fire and train pictures, many of the paintings reproduced would have found themselves completely at home on the walls of the Art Unions.

In the last few decades, since they have become collectors' items, Currier & Ives prints have turned up in nearly every part of the country. The firm had regular agents in many cities and sporadic peddlers and traveling agents who bought the small prints for six cents apiece at wholesale and sold them, presumably, for whatever the market would bear. Currier & Ives claimed in their letter to agents that their experience of over thirty years had enabled them to "select for Publication, subjects best adapted to suit the popular taste, and to meet the wants of all sections." They also claimed that their pictures had become "a staple article which are in great demand in every part of the country." They might also have added Europe for, as Harry T. Peters records in *Currier & Ives, Printmakers to the American People*: "In France the comics and the clipper-ship prints were especially popular, while Germany and Great Britain preferred the views and Western scenes."

There were in New York a dozen or more other firms producing prints for the popular market, but none of them rivaled Currier & Ives in quantity or craftsmanship or variety of subject matter. Some of them, however, were equipped, as Currier & Ives were not, to produce "chromos," or more properly "chromolithographs" in which the colors were printed from a number of different stones instead of being applied by hand. Occasionally they made prints for Currier & Ives, and in the long run the competitors' methods were found to be more modern and their prints sold for higher prices to a middle class clientele, of the sort the Beecher sisters were writing for.

This was a portion of the art public in which, one might think, a man of such sophisticated sensibilities as Jarves, the collector and critic, would have no interest beyond general well-wishing. But there was an artist of whom Jarves thought highly who was very much concerned with this public. He was a sculptor named John Rogers, one of the artistic phenomena of the time and an artist so essentially American and so entirely nineteenth century in his point of view that he tells us more about the public attitude toward art than any of his contemporaries. He was, indeed, a sculptor for the people, a man without airs or graces but with a very considerable talent for modeling in clay and for understanding the public mood. In *American Woman's Home* the Beecher sisters had noted that ". . . a few statuettes, costing perhaps four or six dollars, will give a really elegant finish to your rooms." They must have had Rogers in mind, though he had inferior competitors. Everybody knew him; everybody knew what the Beechers meant. By the time they published their book in 1869 Rogers was not only a household name but a household ornament. His little groups of figures, most of them about sixteen inches high (they are now collected as "Rogers Groups"), were the anecdotal delight of everyone, whatever their station, from the President to the modest housewife, from the sophisticated critic to the barkeep. Rogers was to his day what the *Saturday Evening Post* covers, with their cozy views of the life of *Saturday Evening Post* readers, try to be to our day. His subjects were people with the dignity, fallibility, and humor of real people depicted by a man who had in his nature an abnormally normal distribution of sentiment, patriotism, compassion, generosity, skepticism, humor, and practicality. And, of course, a talent that enabled him to say almost precisely what he wanted to say—which was never anything very profound but was always observant. Rogers was, if anybody has ever been, the embodiment of the Public Taste. If he were alive today he would, one feels, be the producer or director of movies that would be both box office and a little too good for the highbrows to slough off. He was a maker of "documentaries" and his talent was, as the highbrows say, "authentic."

In a completely unflamboyant way he was a man in revolt against the sculptors of his own time. He started life as a mechanical draftsman and amused himself by making little figures in clay, but in 1858 he took himself off to Rome to indulge in the serious study of sculpture in the manner of any number of other ambitious young artists of the time. He was quick to realize that the pseudo-classicism that Hiram Powers and Horatio Greenough and the rest had set out to master was not for him. Almost immediately on his arrival in Rome he wrote to his father: "I don't think I shall ever get into the classic style. I do not take to it. I think my best course is to pursue the path that I have begun and make small figures in bronze or very nice plaster . . . and not attempt any *high art*, for I shall certainly step out of my depth if I do." He knew his own mind, and he knew his limitations, and he had his eye on his future prospects. He adds: "I think if I get my name up for that style and represent pure *human nature* I can make a living by it as well as enjoying it exceedingly."

Human nature was the least concern of most sculptors of the day; they were polishing marble to immaculate and largely meaningless smoothness in hopes of achieving the artistry of Canova. But Rogers was more interested in people than in "high art" and he thought that sculpture should tell a story. Evidently his contemporaries and his teachers in Rome were rather rough on him because he liked to incorporate in his little statues what he called "accessories," by which he meant realistic details that helped to tell the story. In explaining this to his father he also explained better than anyone else the immense popularity that "The Greek Slave" had enjoyed for so many years both in England and America. "Look at the Greek Slave," Rogers wrote, "there is nothing in the world that has made it so popular as that *chain*. The chain showed that she was a slave and

the whole story was told at once. There are plenty of figures as graceful as that and it is only the effect of the chain that has made it so
popular."

Rogers gave up Rome after a few months and got himself a job in
Chicago doing piecework drafting for a concern that didn't have a
great deal for him to do. He spent his spare time modeling little figure
groups and in 1859 he gave one of them, "The Checker Players," to
a charity fair called the Cosmopolitan Bazar. People crowded around
it with delight, pointing out the accuracy of the details and laughing
at the humor of the figures. It was the hit of the Bazar and the papers
in Chicago the next morning all had pleasant things to say about it.
The piece was auctioned off and it brought $75, a very substantial
price. "This success set me to thinking," he wrote his family, "how
I could turn it to account." And turn it to account he did.

The question was how to produce such groups in quantity at prices
low enough so that they could be bought by almost anyone. He took
his problem to an Italian craftsman in Chicago who knew how to
make casts and from him he learned all he could and then proceeded
to refine the techniques in his own way. Within a year he was in New
York and ready to set up in business. He launched himself with a
most ingenious but very simple trick which showed how well he
understood the public mood. While still in Chicago he had made a
group called "The Slave Auction," which included a diabolical-
looking auctioneer. Of this figure he said, "I have rather idealized and
[I] make such a wicked face that Old Nick himself might be proud
of it—two little quirks of hair give some impression of horns." In the
group were also four slaves, a woman, a man, a young girl, and a baby
in arms, and, as he said, "I am entirely satisfied to stake my reputation
on it, and imagine that the present excitement on the subject will give
it great popularity." Before leaving Chicago he was determined to get
what publicity he could for the group and he wrote his mother, "I am
going to put all modesty in my pocket and make a perfect balloon
of myself. I think a little brass and gas will carry me through." He
invited the gentlemen of the press to have a look.

When he tackled New York he was dismayed to discover that many
shops were uneasy about handling the casts of "The Slave Auction";
they were afraid they would alienate their Southern customers. So

Rogers tried a trick that was a great deal more successful than he thought it would be. He hired a Negro boy to carry the little sculpture through the streets and to take orders from anyone who might be interested in buying a copy. The boy very shortly ran upon one of the leading abolitionists of the day, Lewis Tappan, who was delighted with the group and immediately went to Rogers with a list of other abolitionists to whom he might sell the piece. Among these was Henry Ward Beecher, the famous thundering preacher, who was so impressed that he not only befriended Rogers but harangued his congregations with the virtues of his work.

Rogers' reputation soared, not only among the people but among the *cognoscenti*. Three years after his arrival in New York he was elected a member of the National Academy of Design, and a writer in the rural magazine, *Farm and Fireside,* wrote: "What Hogarth is in the pencil, Canova and Michelangelo in marble, Reynolds and Landseer on canvas—all the excellencies of these masters in art have their illustration in the plaster of John Rogers." This kind of recognition was all very well, but Rogers was in business and he meant to capitalize on his reputation. Slowly—for he spent a great deal of time perfecting each group before he released it to the public—he built up a collection of very salable pieces which he marketed through stores, mostly jewelers and stationers, and by mail. He advertised in magazines: "Mr. Rogers' studio is at 212 Fifth Avenue. He mails free to any address a handsome catalogue containing illustrations of all his groups, with descriptive notes. . . ." The prices, depending on the size of the group, ranged from $6 to a top of $25. A few pieces which were intended for the garden, and therefore were fairly large and of more durable material than the clay groups, brought as much as $40. But Rogers was determined that he would keep them inexpensive. "I want them," he wrote, "to be within the means of everyone to buy."

He made it as easy as possible for the purchaser. With every group went elaborate instructions for unpacking so that the group might not be damaged, and in case something did break off (plaster is not a strong material) there were instructions for mending it (he recommended shellac for glue) and for repainting the surface with a mixture of zinc white and burnt umber. For an extra 50 cents he would supply a brush and enough paint to redo completely about three groups.

In 1864 he made a present to President Lincoln and received the following letter of acknowledgment: "I cannot pretend to be a judge in such matters, but the Statuette groups Wounded Scout—Friend in the Swamp which you did me the honor to present, is [sic] very pretty and suggestive, and I should think excellent as a piece of art—Thank you for it." Lincoln was more cautious about setting himself up as an expert on art than some later Presidents such as Calvin Coolidge, who turned down six Cézannes which were offered to the White House, and Harry Truman, who commented to the press about a picture by Yasuo Kuniyoshi, "If that's art, I'm a hottentot!"

About 100,000 Rogers groups were sold in the thirty years between 1860 and 1890. There were subjects to appeal to all tastes, sentimental scenes of lovers, touching scenes of soldiers returning from the wars, happy family groups, comic illustrations of Washington Irving's stories, historical groups, portraits of famous men, and so on. For many years evening parties were organized around *tableaux vivants* in which the participants would dress in white, with their hands and faces whitened, and against a black velvet background pose in the exact attitudes in which Rogers had posed the figures in his groups.

There has rarely been an artist in America who was so universally admired as Rogers. "In the interest of culture and refinement," one critic wrote in 1873, "we are always glad to call attention to the works of that noble laborer in art, John Rogers. . . . True this is an era of cheap reading. . . . Beautiful chromos, too, reproducing the inspirations of the great masters, are almost given away. But how is it with sculpture? Here it is that John Rogers stands alone, occupying undisputed the post of honor. . . . Who has not heard of his 'groups'? Who has not at one time or another seen one or more of them—and stopped and gazed lingeringly, with unfeigned delight?" This is what one might expect from a reviewer in those days when it was more fashionable to praise all American art than it is today. But what about Jarves, who thought so ill of most American sculptors as imitators and superficial, if slick, craftsmen? Here, in part, is what he had to say about Rogers: "We know no sculptor like John Rogers, of New York, in the Old World, and he stands alone in his chosen field, heretofore in all ages appropriated by painting, a genuine production of our soil, enlivening the fancy, enkindling patriotism, and warming the affec- tions, by his lively, well-balanced groups in plaster and bronze. Although diminutive, they possess real elements of greatness. In their execution there is no littleness, artifice, or affectation. . . . His is not high art, but it is genuine art of a high naturalistic order, based on true feeling and a right appreciation of humanity."

Rogers must have been pleased by this complimentary appraisal of his work because Jarves saw in it precisely what Rogers had tried to put there. If he felt the need of any vindication for not having pur- sued "high art," which is, considering his temperament, unlikely, here it was from the pen of the loftiest connoisseur of the day. Rogers' career was a long one; he lived until 1904, though the fashion which had made him the best-known and best-loved sculptor of his day turned to other kinds of household ornaments as the century came to a close. Certainly no sculptor in America, before his time or since, so captured the public imagination and taste, and no one sold sculp- ture of quality to such a mass market.

The mass production of art for the home, in the way Currier & Ives and John Rogers turned it out, was a new kind of assault on the public taste, a new way of making every man an art patron and every housewife a collector of however modest pretensions. Like the production of fancy wallpapers and Brussels carpet, like the thousands of factory-made chairs and bolts of flowered chintz, it was part of the impact of industrialism on taste. Only in a market geared to the millions could prints and sculptures have been sold by the hundreds of thousands. But mass production went further than the decoration of the home; it had by the 1870's overtaken the decoration of the person as well. Ready-made clothes for men were beginning to be common; factory-produced uniforms during the Civil War had con- vinced many men that such garments were preferable to homemade ones, and many women were delighted to forgo the chore of making their husbands' clothes. The personal tailor, of course, was still con- sidered *de rigueur* for those who could afford him, especially among city businessmen with a position to maintain. But the war had taken many women out of their homes to work in the factories and the fields and they became accustomed to buying out of their wages all sorts of articles that they had once made for their families at home—canned goods, prepared cereals, underwear, and, of course, the factory-made clothes and shoes for their men which now appeared on store shelves.

Their own dresses were another matter. When *Harper's Bazar* (as it was then spelled) published its first issue in 1867, the editor announced that $300,000,000 was being spent annually in America for dry goods to be made into clothes by the women of the family. Consequently the demand for dress patterns was tremendous and the pattern business was conducted on a scale that dwarfed even the operations of Currier & Ives.

These were the days of the crinoline—not just for the ladies of fashion, but also for their maids, and not just for those who lived in the cities of the Eastern Seaboard but even for the women who lived in the sod houses of the West and for women working in the fields. The fashion, however, was in its last days, probably because women were tiring of it, or Paris felt the need of a change, and not because, as *Harper's Bazar* insisted, it was a menace in a china closet and a very real fire hazard. Women all too often swept their tremendous skirts into the fireplace, or against the stove, with disastrous results. *Harper's Bazar*, proclaiming from a platform which it thought was built of common sense, made a plea for "suitable dress" for Americans. The trouble with dress in America, as *Harper's Bazar* saw it, was that it was overstandardized. "The uniformity of dress," the editor wrote, "is a characteristic of the people of the United States. The man of leisure and the laborer, the mistress and the maid, wear clothes of the same material and cut. The uniformity that results is not favorable to the picturesque. . . ." Their solution to the male aspect of the problem was to get the laboring men of America to wear "The French blouse" which, they insisted, "has vindicated its title to the drapery of a free man in many a bloody encounter on the barricades and on the streets of Paris." As for women, the editors would have been happier if they could have told the difference between the mistress and her maid, the lady of fashion and the working girl—a lost cause in America if ever there was one, and happily lost.

The center of fashion was, of course, still Paris, though the fountainhead of fashion news and of women's tailoring was Berlin.

Harper's Bazar announced with pride that it had established connections with "the leading European fashion journals, especially the celebrated *Bazar* of Berlin, which supplies the fashions to the newspapers of Paris, whereby we secure the same fashions . . . simultaneously with their appearance in Paris and Berlin, the great centers of European modes." It also announced: "We shall endeavor to maintain a spirit of pure and hightoned morality."

No women in the world, America believed, were as well dressed as American women, and a writer in Appleton's *New York Illustrated* wrote proudly: "It is safe to assert that the United States may challenge the world to show, in any country, so many elegantly-dressed women. Not only in the large cities, but in country places and small villages, the same distinguishing characteristics are observed, an air of fashion modified by a general fitness, which is not discernible in other lands, except among the *élite*, and not always there."

Until quite recently there have been recognized regional differences in styles in America, and some parts of the country have been loath to accept what the style-setters and tastemakers of the Eastern Seaboard cities have recommended as fashionable. In the days after the Civil War, when women plied expert needles in order to drape their bustled figures in untold yards of goods, bedecked with fringe and lace and ribbon and pleated taffeta, it was the dress pattern industry of New York that serviced the whims of women everywhere. "The paper pattern business," pronounced a journalist of the day, "in the development of the useful and the beautiful, and in its magnitude as a commercial enterprise, best illustrates the progress of the age and the civilization of the nineteenth century."

Of all the firms that made and scattered patterns abroad none could hold a candle to Mme. Demorest's Emporium of Fashion in New York. It was the soul of elegance, or so, anyway, a reporter from Appleton's *New York Illustrated* believed when he visited the showrooms and factory on Union Square in 1876. But further than that it was big business. Mme. Demorest (the "Mme." for the French touch) was the wife of a publisher, W. Jennings Demorest, who issued a number of family magazines, illustrated papers, and fashion journals and boasted that two of his magazines (he didn't say which ones) had circulations of a million copies—more than likely an exaggeration.

Mme. Demorest's business, however, surely served a great many millions of women. The factory on Union Square not only had a display room, or "main *salon*," to which the ladies could come to select, in an atmosphere of "grace and elegance of design," patterns in a "large variety suited to every style of face and figure—the wonderful adaptation of costume to wants of all ages and classes," but conducted a vast rapid-fire mail-order business. Orders poured in every day from thousands of agents scattered over America and Canada and Cuba and South America, and to keep up with the demand Mme. Demorest bought the pattern paper at the rate of five thousand reams at a time and envelopes in quantities of two million. The six floors of the little factory hummed with the activity of two hundred girls. On one floor artists and designers were running up new ideas for dresses and preparing illustrations for the envelopes; on another experts who could cut as many as one hundred and sixty-eight patterns at a time wielded their shears. There were folding rooms, stuffing rooms, mailing rooms, and stock rooms. It was Mme. Demorest's boast that every order was filled the day it arrived, and of some of the more popular designs she sold as many as fifty thousand patterns.

Mme. Demorest's activities were not limited either to the Western Hemisphere or to patterns. She had an office in Paris that serviced the European trade (descriptions on all pattern envelopes were printed in French, Spanish, and German as well as in English), and on the side she operated a corset factory. The Paris office, it was claimed, did more business in twenty-four hours than all of the other pattern houses in Europe did in as many days. With the female figure constrained to assume the shape demanded by the patterns that Mme. Demorest's distributed, the corset business was a natural and unquestionably profitable side line.

She was a woman of strong principles and very considerable versatility. As a girl she apprenticed herself first to the dressmaking trade and then to the art of millinery, and when she opened her original, modest shop in New York (she came from Saratoga) she began by importing fashions from abroad which she adapted "to the taste of our people, giving the benefit of her skill and establishment, not only to the wealthy and fashionable, but to persons in middle life and to the lowly." But fashion for everyone from the New York swells to the ladies "among the mines of Colorado, on the Pacific coast, in the dense forests, or in the interior of the continent" was not her only contribution to the welfare of women. Her mass production of the tissue-paper pattern "banished the old, tedious, painful method of fitting dresses" and gave employment to more than ten thousand women who were trained to use her method.

Mme. Demorest was no snob and no caterer to the prejudices of the rich. In the days when "respectable and intelligent colored girls" could not get jobs in "fashionable" establishments, Mme. Demorest hired them, "gave them the same wages, and a seat in the same work-room that was assigned to others." The ladies of fashion were shocked, "flaunted out of the rooms, and announced that they would not patronize an establishment that employed negro girls." But Mme. Demorest stuck to her guns, and the ladies, who were unable to find any place that matched the services of Mme. Demorest's Emporium, had no choice but to come back to her shop.

It is not surprising that Mme. Demorest was considered one of the wonders of her age. She was constantly winning medals of honor and diplomas and "other evidences of the appreciation of merit" at expositions, with the result that she was the most decorated lady of her day. She was also considered a prime cultural asset. "This house," wrote the reporter from *Appleton's*, "is the representative establishment of the world. . . . Its enterprising management deserves great credit for the benefit they have bestowed in the cultivation of taste, and the sound and practical principles which have been constantly united with the aesthetic."

The marriage of the practical and the aesthetic was an idea that Americans liked in the nineteenth century just as well as they claim they do now. Currier & Ives and John Rogers both built their reputations on the principle that there needed to be nothing top-lofty about art and that it was a commodity that people could use and enjoy without pretentions or large bank accounts. Mme. Demorest and her husband followed the same line in the dissemination of style and fashion, and in another of their side lines, the sale of "oil chromos" (notably "The Old Oaken Bucket," "Home Sweet Home," "After the Storm," and "The Captive Child") which they also offered as premiums with subscriptions to their magazines.

This was the heyday of cheap and popular art for everyone, for most people agreed with Gervase Wheeler, who wrote books to help every man have a pleasant home, when he said: "Taste is like conscience; all have it, but they may blunt it; drown its voice, and finally so deaden themselves to its power as to prevent its warnings and warp its influence; it becomes strengthened by use, and the more it is listened to, the stronger and more correct it will become, so as finally to be to the heart what sound judgment is to the mind."

CHAPTER VI

Palaces for the People

"Monstrous palaces of gorgeous sloth and immoral ease . . ."

When Charles Dickens arrived in Boston on a winter Sunday morning in 1842 the Hub of the Universe was looking its brilliant best. The air was cold and clear, the houses were bright and their brass was polished, and the signboards in the streets were resplendent with color and glistening with gilt lettering. The famous visitor was in a good mood. His experience with the customs officials when he disembarked from his eighteen-day journey on the packet boat *Britannia* had been surprisingly amiable; he was used to the "servile rapacity" of French officials and expected similar treatment at the hands of Americans. Instead, he found them polite, good-humored, and efficient. What is more he thought the city "a beautiful one" with large and elegant dwelling houses, handsome public buildings, and fine shops, managed, he noted, by men who called themselves merchants and not tradesmen. But more astonishing than the general air of cleanliness and gaiety of the city was the hotel to which he had been escorted on his arrival by an editor. It was called the Tremont House, a building that Bostonians referred to as "one of the proudest achievements of American genius." Dickens was impressed. "It has more galleries, colonnades, piazzas, and passages," he recorded in his *American Notes*, "than I can remember, or the reader would believe."

Surely his English readers would not have believed, for there was nothing in Europe anything like it. The Tremont House, when it opened its doors on October 16, 1829, with a dollar-a-plate banquet attended by such august gentlemen as Daniel Webster and Edward Everett, was a hotel such as the world had never seen before. Here were sumptuousness and elegance that all but blinded the proud Bostonians and the visitors to their city. Here for the first time was a hotel that broke with all of the old traditions of innkeeping, of crowding the guests into trundle beds, or making them sleep on floors, of courtyards filled with chattering peddlers and creaking carriages, of lobbies which were also barrooms, and room clerks who were also bartenders. It was, indeed, a palace for the people, not only in its elegant structure, its mosaic marble floors, and richly carpeted corridors, its drawing rooms, reading rooms, ladies' parlor, and its decorations in the very latest French taste, but in its treatment of guests as well. Here was service such as no one but the very rich, and they only in their own homes, had ever dreamed of before. A husband and wife could actually get a room to themselves with a bowl and pitcher in it. There were singles and doubles and no need to brush one's teeth at the pump in the courtyard. There were curtains at the windows, and there was free soap—not the individually wrapped little bar with which we are familiar, but a cake of yellow soap that served guest after guest until it was used up. Soap was still an expensive luxury, but then the Tremont House was the very essence of luxury in every way, and it set a style which grew in elaborateness and elegance until it reached its peak about fifty years later in San Francisco.

Once the Tremont House was built every city wanted its own palace hotel, partly as a matter of civic pride, partly as a cool matter of good business. These "monstrous palaces" set a pattern of taste for "gorgeous sloth and immoral ease," as *Harper's Weekly* called it, that the traveler in America learned to expect not only where he came to rest in a great city but en route as well. Palaces greeted him in cities when he disembarked from other palaces that floated down the wide rivers, or rolled along over the ever-expanding rails. Such was the ebullient taste of Americans when they were liberated from the restrictions of their own household budgets; such was the dream world in which any man or woman who could muster the price of a hotel room, or a steamboat cabin, or a berth in a Pullman car might relax, among surroundings that few Oriental potentates could excel.

The designer of the Tremont House, and the man who showed America that anyone can have access to a palace, was a Yankee from Marshfield, Massachusetts, named Isaiah Rogers. He was the son of a ship builder and, naturally enough, he apprenticed himself to a carpenter when he was sixteen and of an age to learn a trade. When he was twenty he journeyed to faraway Mobile, Alabama, where there was a competition for a design for a theater; he won the job, but he did not stay to see his building completed. In 1822, when he was twenty-two, he came back to Massachusetts and went to work for Solomon Willard, a prominent Boston architect, master mason, and sculptor. A group of local businessmen were already fired with enthusiasm for the idea of building a hotel in Boston that should far excel any in America, and it took them ten years to raise the $300,000 that was needed to realize their ambition. When the money seemed assured, young Rogers was given the commission to design the Tremont House; it was claimed to be the biggest building in America at the time.

Rogers was an able architect and a man of considerable mechanical ingenuity, and his Tremont House was both well designed and full of gadgets that made great publicity for the hotel. It had, for one thing, more extensive plumbing than any other building in the country and an elaborate system of speaking tubes from the desk in the "office" (as the lobby was then called) to the various suites and rooms. The office which served as a grand entrance hall with a desk for the room clerk was his invention. Up to that time it had been part barroom, part office, with racks for luggage behind the desk. Rogers provided a separate luggage room and introduced formality and dignity as well as optical grandeur into the room where guests first arrived and received their first impression of the hotel. He also introduced the "reading room," a library with newspapers from all parts of the country and books, use of which was free to guests in the hotel and was available to residents of the city for a small annual fee. This, it should be remembered, was in the days before the public library. In 1830, the year after the Tremont House was opened, the publishers Gray and Bowen of Boston issued a book called *A Description of the Tremont House, with Architectural Illustrations*. Anyone concerned with the construction of a hotel for the next fifty years used this book as a basic guide, and the general plan that is still in use in most hotels today can be directly traced to Rogers's basic scheme. The entrance that Rogers designed for the Tremont House, a Doric portal in the Greek Revival manner that was then the undisputed architectural style for all imposing buildings, became a cliché that hotel builders used nearly everywhere until the 1880's. A hotel was scarcely considered a hotel at all unless its guests entered between Doric columns.

Inspired by Rogers' sense of comfort, eye for elegance, and mechanical ingenuity, palace hotels, as they were called, began to rise in ever-increasing magnificence across the land. John Jacob Astor, who was determined to build what he thought would be a permanent monument to himself, commissioned Rogers to design a hotel that would overshadow the Tremont House and would be the pride of New York. He bought a plot facing City Hall Park and, though some New Yorkers thought he was foolish to build in a location that was not convenient to most modes of transportation, he financed a caravansary with a massive granite façade on Broadway that was a touchstone, according to a hotel magazine, for "everything that was gorgeous and impressive in a New York hotel." After it opened in 1836 it was the choicest meeting place in the city, and "on a fine day at noon, and an hour or two after," a journalist of the day reported, "crowds of beauty and fashion, domestic and imported, fill this part of the promenade of Broadway, for Astor's hotel is on the fashionable side of Broadway, and here you are sure to find the elite of the commercial metropolis. Nothing could tempt them to cross over to the Park side of the street." Rogers moved south and then west leaving a trail of elegancies behind him in Mobile, in Charleston, South Carolina, in New Orleans, in Louisville, in Nashville, where he built the famous Maxwell House, and in Cincinnati. He was a staunch Greek Revivalist wherever he went and though he was still building in the 1860's, long after the Gothic Revival had gained ascendancy, he persisted in the manner and style that had made him famous in his youth.

Once Americans had had a taste of richness there was no end to their appetite for it, and the businessmen who financed hotels and the managers who operated them, usually on lease, did their best to satisfy the national palate that hungered for comfort dipped in a sauce of glitter and gold. Even in San Francisco just a few years after a carpenter named Marshall from New Jersey had accidentally struck gold in 1848, an English traveler, Frank Marryatt, reported that "the places of universal resort were the drinking Saloon and the Gambling House. With a keen eye to profit, the proprietors of these establishments had fitted them up with a splendor irresistibly captivating to men who for months had seen no dwelling more attractive than a rude hut or tent. Pillars, apparently of crystal, supported the gilded roofs. The walls were ablaze with huge mirrors, alternating with pictures of the worst French schools, of the most brilliant coloring and the most questionable designs. . . . Miners in ragged woolen or greasy buckskins; Mexicans in gay serapes and slouched hats; Chinamen with long tails and basin-like hats; Negroes, hodmen, merchants, mechanics, thronged around the liquor bars and the *monte* tables." Possibly this bar was in the What Cheer House, which is reported to have been the miners' favorite, where sleeping was "cheap" and the bar was lavish. Cheap, to be sure, meant a bunk, not a bed, for $30 a week with, as the Reverend William Taylor of Baltimore who visited San Francisco in 1849 reported, "the third plague of Egypt, accompanied by a Lilliputian host of the flea tribe" thrown in. The Parker House, which was a frame building two stories high, boasted a barroom and gambling hall that cost $30,000 to construct and is said to have been rented to a concessionaire for $15,000 a month. A bed in a "miserable little room" could, and often did, cost $250 a week. The elegant trappings for the bar and gambling rooms reached San Francisco by ships that had sailed seventeen thousand miles from the East Coast around the Horn. Once Isaiah Rogers had whetted the taste for public elegance, no trouble was too great, no expense too lavish to give the public what it wanted or more than it had ever dreamed of.

The story of the hotels of America has been told in some detail by Jefferson Williamson, and in his book *The American Hotel* he has written: "Mine Host was the first businessman in America to appreciate the advantages of glitter and ostentation. It was he who inaugurated the plate glass age. From 1830 onward landlords did their utmost to outdo one another in impressiveness of architecture, in use of marble, mirrors, and gilt, velvet, satin and plush. They spent money for 'sinfully extravagant' hand carved mahogany, walnut, and rosewood, and for sumptuous furnishings and knick-knacks of all sorts."

There were two nineteenth-century hotels, one in New York and one in San Francisco, that outdid all the rest in lavishness. The earlier was New York's St. Nicholas (on Broadway between Broome and Spring Streets), which was opened in 1853; it was the first hotel in America to cost more than a million dollars. According to the New York *Tribune* of the day it was "the *ne plus ultra* of expense, of richness and luxury." To another reporter it was "a display of barbaric splendor, rather than art or true refinement." It had window curtains that cost $700 apiece, and gold-embroidered draperies that cost $1,000. Its twenty-two-foot ceilings were alive with curlicues and scrolls, and its sofas and chairs were upholstered in Flemish tapestry. There were mirrors everywhere, and Turkish rugs and window hangings of damask and silk. And over nearly everything was gold leaf laid on with such a lavish hand that an English comedian made New Yorkers roar with his quip that he didn't dare to put his shoes out to be polished at night "for fear the management would gild them."

It was nearly twenty-five years later that San Francisco opened its famous Palace Hotel, a monumental structure that cost $5,000,000 and remained the epitome of luxury until it was destroyed in the earthquake and fire of 1906. It had nearly a thousand rooms and five hundred baths, with no room less than sixteen feet square and many that were twenty. There was a six-foot marble mantel in every room; there were French plate mirrors and modern gas lights. Its public rooms—parlors, ballrooms, children's dining room, billiard room with dozens of tables, music room, and "committee rooms" for poker or *monte,* and many others—surpassed in luxurious comfort and massiveness of scale any that had hitherto been conceived. But its principal boasts were its bay windows, of which it had four hundred, and its courtyard, covered with a canopy of glass. *Leslie's Weekly Newspaper* described it in 1878 with awe: ". . . The immense court, with its circular carriage sweep, broad promenade, banana trees, and palms, lending a tropical note, impressed itself on the memory of countless visitors. Monday evenings became the fashionable time to gather for family reunions. Then all the gas chandeliers were ablaze [there were 155 of them, with 503 lights in globes of all colors], and the music of the orchestra pervading the elegant surroundings crystallized the brilliance of the festivities."

The Palace was built with Comstock Lode money and was the private dream of William C. Ralston, president of the Bank of California, who was known as "the Rothschild of America." Unfortunately he never saw his pleasure palace completed, for on the afternoon of August 26, 1875, the same day that his bank, which was considered as sound as the U.S. Treasury, suspended operations, the financier walked to his death in the sea. Californians were understandably thunderstruck, but not for long. Ex-Senator William Sharon of Nevada, Ralston's partner in many financial dealings and a man commonly known as "The King of the Comstocks," stepped in and not only saw that the bank reopened but that the Palace Hotel was completed. Less than six weeks after what had looked like doomsday, Governor Leland Stanford and his wife were the first guests to sign their names on the hotel register.

The hotel business and the public taste for grandeur had come a long way since Isaiah Rogers designed the Tremont House. Not only were city hotels such as the Palmer House in Chicago, with its barbershop floor studded with silver dollars, heavens and havens for travelers, but resort hotels such as the United States and the Grand Union in Saratoga provided them with fairylands for their holidays. The United States, which opened the same year as the San Francisco Palace, was even bigger than the pride of the West Coast, and if the Palace was so colossal that guests were constantly getting lost in it, the United States was a magnificent wedding cake encrusted with ornament that might well have been squeezed out of a pastry cone. The simile is not inexact, for George M. Towle, who visited Saratoga in the seventies, noted that the balls that took place every evening at the United States were "great matrimonial fairs, where the marriageable wares were shown off at their best." For those who took their vacations in the winter and who liked a more exotic atmosphere than the familiar gingerbread of Saratoga, there was the minaretted Tampa Bay Hotel which advertised itself as ". . . perhaps the grandest structure ever designed for such a purpose. A wonderful Moorish palace, constructed fire-proof, and fitted and furnished regardless of cost to place it as a hotel unsurpassed at this time. No sightseer in America can afford to omit a visit to Tampa and the Tampa Bay Hotel." Sightseers today will find that the hotel is now Tampa University.

People who work in palaces are likely to put on even greater airs and graces than those who inhabit them only as visitors, and room clerks were no different in the seventies from what they are now. "I tell you the American hotel clerk is the concentrated embodiment of dignity," a writer in the trade paper, *Hotel World Review*, reported in 1878. "Perhaps you don't know what I am driving at. Just go and ask one of these bedroom potentates of the whereabouts of some friend of yours, who may be an inmate of the house. Words fail to convey the idea of the way in which you will be crushed. Not that the great men are rude, oh no! But there is a majesty, a loftiness, an exaltation, a consciousness of power in their words, looks and gestures, which reduces the inquirer, in his own estimation, to the last verge of inferiority. Christians who are always strong to humble and abase themselves, whose besetting sin is pride—just a dose or two of hotel clerks. Whenever I feel that I need taking down a peg or two, I have a never failing remedy. I merely step into a first class hotel and ask, 'Is Mr. Smith stopping here?' The great man, after four or five minutes, lifts his eyes, and I feel that I am a worm: he speaks, and I am a Chinaman."

Though there are some European cultures that have brought the snobbishness of hotel clerks to an even more refined pitch than we have in this country (England, in this respect, knows no peer), all foreign cultures are indebted to America for the concept of the palace hotel. Some of them have improved on our ideas of service and have as many as four waiters to our two to serve a simple meal. Nowhere, for example, does one find such colossal bathtubs as in Rome or such elegant liveries as in the Ritz in Paris. In our own day we have seen rich simplicity in the modern manner begin to replace baroque and Oriental ornateness in a few recently built hotels such as the Terrace Plaza in Cincinnati and the Statler in Washington. But they are still palaces for all their modern modish look. Hotels for a long while have imitated the popular concept of how the very rich have lived amid their luxuries, and now that "modern" houses are built almost exclusively by the rich who can afford great expanses of glass and great expanses of curtains to cover them, it is not unnatural that hotels should turn to them for inspiration. Nor is it surprising that they should in some respects imitate Hollywood concepts of luxury, with swimming pools still grander than those of the movie stars, and lobbies, some of them, that combine baroque ornament, often painted white, with furniture that derives from the advanced "functionalism" of the 1920's and 30's. The looks of the palaces have changed, but the mood of their designers and the people who luxuriate in them has remained much the same as it was when Isaiah Rogers found that the public had a heart of golden aspirations.

If Americans were not restless, if they were not so used to packing their bags on the slightest provocation and setting out for new places, and if American merchants and entrepreneurs were not so eager to attract transients to their cities, we should probably have had more sensible if far less entertaining architecture. But as a nation of travelers we have come to expect while on the move luxuries, both optical and physical, that few of us enjoy in our own homes. Indeed the hotels of the last century scarcely matched in elegance some of the modes of transportation that brought guests to their Doric portals. Only a handful of men owned homes as ornate as the steamboats that plied the Mississippi and the Hudson or as luxurious as the Pullman Palace Cars that made the run from New York to Chicago in forty-eight hours in the seventies. If we walk up the gangplanks and climb the steps of some of these conveyances, feel our feet sink into their splendid carpets, and let our eyes roam over their carved panels and tinted windows, we will see that the people's palaces that floated and rolled are every bit as revealing of the public taste as those that stood still.

"To a few people living in New Orleans and St. Louis," Mark Twain wrote of the Mississippi boats, "they were not magnificent, perhaps; not palaces, but to the great majority of those populations and to the entire populations spread over both banks between Baton Rouge and St. Louis, they were palaces; they tallied with the citizen's dream of what magnificence was, and satisfied it."

It was stiff competition for passenger traffic that converted the

Mississippi river boat from a simple workaday hauler of cargo into a ship that was a palace above and often a frightful, plague-ridden steerage below. In the early days of the river boats travelers had the choice either of sailing or of being jammed and joggled in stage-coaches, and comfort, especially for those who could afford to pay the cabin rate, favored the boats. It was a ship called the *General Pike* that set the pace as early as 1819. She was an all-passenger craft with a cabin decorated with marble columns, a rich carpet, mirrors and crimson curtains, and once she had established a standard of elegance on the river, boats became fancier and fancier and the competition for ornamentation more and more lively.

A writer for *Harper's New Monthly Magazine* who embarked on a steamer at St. Louis in the late fifties noted there was always a choice of ships and, as he said, "Of course you seek one of the finest boats— one which you 'guess' will be likely to go within two days of her advertised time. You mount the stairway and find the cabin on the second deck. . . . This cabin is a saloon extending over the whole boat, except a small space in the bow, and in some boats is nearly three hundred feet long. This great hall is sure to be finished with white and gold, and to be, as the newspapers say, 'very gorgeous indeed.'"

For the most part the captains of the ships were in business for themselves, and it was they who decided what their boats should look like and what constituted a really splendid floating palace. The interiors were designed and executed by steamboat joiners and dec-orators who found their inspiration, in all probability, in architectural plan books and manuals of ornament, and then attempted to create floating Nirvanas that would bedazzle the customers. And bedazzle they did. "The magnificence of the saloons of the Mississippi river boats is far famed," a visiting British engineer wrote in 1861, "and they form a strange contrast to the rest of the ship. They are . . . unbroken by columns, by tie rods, or by the engines (as in the Eastern river boats), and there is very little color used in their decoration, except in the carpets and furniture, for they give a preference to white paneling, covered with florid carving. From each beam, fretwork and open lattice work hangs down, and the constant repetition of this carving, illuminated by colored lights thrown from the painted glass skylights on each side, in a saloon over two hundred feet long, produces one of the most beautiful effects of light and shade I have ever witnessed."

Not everyone agreed with him, as a lady named Gail Hamilton made quite clear in her memoirs. She found the boats: ". . . an indefinable sham splendor all around, half disgusting and wholly comical. The paint and gilding, the velvet and Brussels, the plate and the attendants show bravely enough by lamplight, but the honest indignant sun puts all the dirty magnificence to shame." Westerners did not see eye to eye with this lady from the Eastern seaboard, even though they might grudgingly have admitted that the carved white paneling was indeed allowed to collect grime and that the quality of the joinery was as often as not hasty and shoddy. The river boats were their palaces in spite of the fact that it was necessary to post notices asking passengers not to sleep with their boots on and to refrain from whittling the furniture, and even though "rough wear reduced the original elegance of the saloon to a sorry shabbiness long before the vessel had served out its brief span."

Each captain, of course, had to decide just what proportion of his investment would go into the basic necessities of his ship, the shallow hull and the engines, and what he would splurge on gingerbread and gewgaws, on stained glass and carpeting, on inlaid panels and ornate chandeliers. The record of one boat, the *Ambassador*, built in 1840, which weighed 352 tons and was regarded as "a large and handsomely finished" vessel, shows a total cost for the ship of $60,000. Of this the hull accounted for $12,000 and the structure, decorations, and furnishings of the cabin absorbed $31,000. Some captains looked upon such extravagance with scorn; others went a good deal further in their attempts to benumb their passengers with the giddy atmosphere of gilt and glitter. Few of them, however, and none of those with big ships that were competing for the passenger trade, failed to indulge in some degree the exuberant taste of the mid-century. The tremendous circular boxes which concealed the side wheels that propelled the boats were often painted with sunbursts and ornamental lettering. Their tall and slender smokestacks not infrequently were crowned with gilded metal leaves that stuck up like the feathers on a badminton bird and the ironwork spreader bars between the stacks

were as elaborately wrought as New Orleans balconies. Their pilot-
houses were Gothic pastries.

The sleeping accommodations were often fancier than they were
spacious. A typical cabin was about seven or eight feet square, though
some of the bigger boats on the Lower Mississippi provided in the
1880's a luxurious combination bedroom and parlor that was twelve
by twelve. Occasionally a ship boasted a nursery, quarters for the
servants of cabin passengers, and even an encrusted and befringed
bridal chamber. In general, however, according to Mark Twain,
"every state-room had its couple of cosey clean bunks, and perhaps a
looking-glass and a snug closet; and sometimes there was even a
wash-bowl and pitcher, and part of a towel which could be told from
mosquito netting by an expert—though generally these things were
absent, and the shirt-sleeved passengers cleansed themselves at a long
row of stationary bowls in the barber shop, where were also public
towels, public combs, and public soap."

These were the public palaces of the West, grander than anything
on shore, grander than anything most of the people who traveled
on them ever saw anywhere else. Their Greek Revival decorations in
the early days were a long way from the formal elegance of the
designs of Thomas Jefferson, just as the gimcrackery of the later boats
was a long way from the restrained and gracious Gothic of Andrew
Jackson Downing. But it was the nature of the public taste to delight
in the sight of richness, for here was a world in which luxury and
comfort far beyond the needs of any man was lavished on every man.
Here the men and women whom Mrs. Trollope found so gauche
and priggish could bask in tinted light among splendors of princely
proportions. Here, many of them believed, the tastes of the crude
and insensitive underwent the tempering of refinement.

The side-wheelers that plied the Hudson and Long Island Sound,
and those that splashed the waters of Lake Erie and the St. Lawrence,
were in some respects even more remarkable than the Mississippi
boats. For one thing they were less like barges with castles built on
them and more like ships with the fittings of palaces, for instead of
being flat-bottomed and snub-nosed, they were long and sleek with
sharp and graceful prows; they were closer relatives of the packets

that crossed the Atlantic than of the barges that moved slowly along
the canals. Charles Dickens was even more impressed by one of the
lake steamers than he had been by the Tremont House. The *Burlington* that took him from St. Johns to Whitehall on Lake Champlain
delighted him on all counts. "This steamboat," he wrote, "is a perfectly exquisite achievement of neatness, elegance, and order. The
decks are drawingrooms; the cabins are boudoirs, choicely furnished
with prints, pictures, and musical instruments; every nook and corner
in the vessel is a perfect curiosity of graceful comfort and beautiful
contrivance." Dickens gave all of the credit for this to the ship's
captain, a gentleman named Sherman "to whose ingenuity and excellent tastes these results are solely attributable."

But the story of the Eastern side-wheelers is usually not that of a
single captain of excellent tastes, for only in the early days of the
century were the boats owned and controlled by the men who sailed
them. There is no need for us to dwell here on the cut-throat competition between Commodore Cornelius Vanderbilt, who in his
younger days was a genuinely seafaring man, and such scoundrels as
Daniel Drew and Jim Fisk who were past masters at stock watering,
customer milking, and monopoly building. ("There goes Jim Fisk,"
said a contemporary wit, "with his hands in his own pockets for a
change.") In his excellent book *Sidewheeler Saga* Ralph Nading Hill
has recently retold the battles of these financial prestidigitators and
the effects of their manipulations on shipping and railroading. But the
heat of the competition which they generated had its effect on the
magnificence of the ships they owned and sponsored, and on those of
other owners as well.

Palace ships transported the high life as well as the low life up the
Hudson on their way to take the waters at Saratoga or to do business
at Poughkeepsie or Albany; others steamed up Long Island Sound
to make the train connection at Fall River to Boston or to
deposit the "four hundred" at fabulous Newport. Whereas the
Mississippi River boats offered their passengers one long unbroken
saloon in which to conduct their social life, the Eastern boats had
some of the qualities of an opera house. From a balcony that made a
promenade past the upper tier of staterooms the traveler could look
down into the saloon with its grand staircase at one end, blossoming

gas chandeliers, columns, an expanse of figured carpet, carved tables
and chairs, and a piano at which any passenger so minded could fill
the saloon with music. The staircase in one ship, the *St. John,* owned
by Drew, was carved from Santo Domingo mahogany and was inlaid
with white holly. It cost $25,000. On one of Fisk's ships, the
Plymouth Rock, there were thirty-two suites, decorated with gilded
furniture upholstered in plush and silk and velvet, and the ship's bar
was done up in white marble. In general the Eastern boats were more
richly colored than the Mississippi boats and did not rely solely on
gleaming white with gold trim for their elegance. Rich woods were
contrasted with painted panels ornamented with griffins and maidens
and bouquets. Bronze rosettes touched with gilt, columns painted
salmon color against Van Dyck brown backgrounds, richly carved
cornices and brackets, and thousands of yards of maroon carpeting
made a voyage to Fall River, except for those who were used to such
lavishness in their own palaces at Newport, an excursion into a dream
world. Even the ferry boats that crossed back and forth from Manhattan to New Jersey were workaday palaces when Jim Fisk controlled them, and their cabins had "panels painted a soft green with
pearl stiles, and arches of lilac, pink and pearl, and mirrors throughout."

In the 1850's railroad cars were dusty and hard-seated. They were
heated by iron stoves that roasted those who sat near them and left
those at the ends of the cars shivering with the cold. It was George
Mortimer Pullman who changed all this, for once he applied his
wits to the design of the cars they became as elegant and comfortable
as the side-wheelers. When Captain Douglas Galton came to America
in 1856 to report on the American railroads to the Lords of the Privy
Council for Trade, he noted that Americans took their ideas of railroad carriage design more from ships than from carriages. He noted,
furthermore, that their purpose was to accommodate large masses of
people with a minimum outlay for first cost and that everyone was
treated "without privilege or exclusiveness, or of superiority of one
traveler over another." In general he found our one-class system
superior to either the second- or third-class carriages of the British
railroads. There were sleeping cars as early as 1838 that ran between

Baltimore and Philadelphia, rough affairs in which there were double-decker bunks that could accommodate twenty-four passengers who slept with their boots on. Twenty years later George B. Gates invested $5,000 in two sleeping cars for the Cleveland to Buffalo run, but they were not popular. It was on such a primitive sleeping car, during a trip between Toledo and Chicago, that young George Pullman, who had been trained as a cabinetmaker, began to plan the sleeping car that was to revolutionize American railroading. In 1858 he got permission to rebuild two coaches owned by the Chicago and Altoona Railroad into sleeping cars, but it was not until about five years later that he produced the "Pioneer." It was a splendid rolling parlor fifty-four feet long and ten feet wide with considerably more headroom than those common coaches of the day that had been converted for sleeping purposes. The Pioneer cost the large sum of $20,000 to build and it was too wide for many station platforms and too high to go under many bridges. The assassination of President Lincoln, however, put Pullman's contraption, which might otherwise have rusted on a siding, into business. A car suitable to the mournful dignity of transporting the body of the martyred President was needed and only the Pioneer was considered sufficiently magnificent. Bridges were raised and platforms rebuilt to accommodate the car and in it the body of the Great Emancipator was carried from Chicago to Springfield.

From then on Pullman and his Pullman Palace Cars were among the wonders of American railroading. The Civil War had given the railroad business a tremendous boost, and the public welcomed Pullman's succession of improvements—the palace sleeping car, the parlor car, and the dining car, all tricked out in the most up-to-the-minute ideas of elegance, of plush and chandeliers and inlaid woods and tinted windows, of fringe and scroll work, and the inevitable figured carpets.

Like many another man who has found his way to the heart and pocketbook of America by providing people with comfort and elegance, George Mortimer Pullman was convinced that he had made a contribution to the dignity of his compatriots as well. "I have always held," said Mr. Pullman, "that people are greatly influenced by their physical surroundings. Take the roughest man, a man whose lines have brought him into the coarsest and poorest surroundings, and bring him into a room elegantly carpeted and finished, and the effect upon his bearing is immediate. The more artistic and refined the external surroundings, the better and more refined the man."

Another moralist, and one in his time almost as well known as Pullman and just as successful in his own line of business, took quite another attitude toward Pullman's contribution to American refinement. This was Edward Bok, the famous editor of the *Ladies' Home Journal* around the turn of the century. He was dismayed at the fanciness and frippery of American architecture and interior decoration; he crusaded against what he considered the monstrosities of the nineties. He blamed the low taste of Americans for ornateness directly on their experience with the Pullman Palace Cars. He might also have added the steamboats and the hotels, for they were all equally palaces for the people and all equally reflected their desires for luxury at the same time that they whetted their appetites for richness.

In a very real sense the hotels and steamboats, the Pullman cars and bars are outside the tradition of American architecture and decoration and outside the province of the tastemakers who consider themselves serious. Like the opera houses, and movie palaces, the recreation piers, and fairground bandstands, they belong with the circus wagons and calliopes and juke boxes as part of the carnival arts. No one takes them seriously for they were never meant to be serious. A house is a place where a man expects to be joyous and bored and contented and faced with tragedy and in which he can shut himself away from the world, and when he creates his home he is willing to listen to sober advice about how best to build and how best to decorate. But when he ventures forth either for business or pleasure he moves into a world where he is wafted on swan boats and bedded down in crystal palaces, where he is entertained by women as beautiful as angels (if not so discreet) to the sounds of erotic music and the tinkling of glasses. For the moment he loses himself in the fairyland of the carnival—a prince whose comfort is the first concern of a retinue of servants, and whose eye is filled with riches by scores of artists. In such surroundings and in such delights what matters it to him whether what he beholds be "tasteful"?

CHAPTER VII

Packaged Taste

"The soothing influence of an Eastlake bookcase on an irritated husband has never been sufficiently calculated. . . ."

Plush and crystal were all very well for palaces of recreation and travel, but in people's homes, so the tastemakers of the seventies thought, such frivolity was not only out of place but downright immoral. It was high time, they felt, for discipline to be applied. During the fifteen years that followed the Civil War three head-on assaults were made upon public taste—in interior decoration, in architecture, and in the appreciation of art. Eastlake, a disciple of William Morris and Ruskin, undertook to implant reasonableness in American living rooms, hallways, dining rooms and bedrooms; the so-called Queen Anne or Elizabethan Cottage Style of building engaged in a winning battle to the death with Gothic; the Centennial Exposition at Philadelphia not only exposed millions of men and women to the greatest (in size) art exhibition ever seen on this or any other continent, but tried to effect the sacred marriage of industry and the household arts. The language of the tastemakers in the seventies, as we shall see, has a familiar ring for us today; their arguments have again become fashionable in our time. If their principles and moral pronouncements were much the same, the results they achieved were, to say the least, quite different.

But before we watch the assault of this new band of aesthetic missionaries on the public taste, let us see what had happened since the quiet and persuasive voice of Andrew Jackson Downing was silenced by the explosion of the *Henry Clay* in 1852.

97

Had Downing lived until the seventies he would have been saddened indeed by the parody of his dream of smiling lawns and tasteful cottages. Many of his ideas, to be sure, had persisted. A large number of towns had Societies of Rural Art and Rural Taste who were seeing to it that "in place of staring bridge guards, painted white, were vine wreathed rustic railings or fanciful iron balustrades." The societies were even taking the tasteless householder in hand. "If a house were to be repainted," said an account of their activities in 1875, "it seemed to put off, with its painful white lead and Paris green, the old life of unchanging labor and to put on, with its modest livery of cool browns and grays, the new life of aesthetic impulse and occasional leisure, of books and croquet." It was true, too, that many lawns smiled with crescent-shaped flower beds and urns dripping with nasturtiums and ivy or bright with geraniums; evergreens like stately dunce caps stood as sentinels before Gothic cottages and Tuscan villas. But the restraint that Downing counseled and the quiet that he believed to be essential to refined taste had for the most part been drowned in the bitterness of civil war and in the building boom that followed it.

Gothic had turned from dignity to inexpensive jigsaw fussiness, and the Italian villa had lost its relatively simple shape, had donned the Mansard roof crowned with elaborate wrought-iron railings and had become what we now think of as "pure Charles Addams." The rich had found neither the Gothic cottage nor the villa elegant enough for their taste nor ostentatious enough to suit their position. In San Francisco Charles Crocker lived in a Mansard palace that might well have been built to house a museum, but for fancifulness it did not compare with the Oriental eccentricities of spectacular dimensions and equally spectacular contours that other men of great wealth affected.

Colonel Colt, the inventor of the revolver, lived in Hartford in a house appropriately called "Armsmere," "a long, grand, impressive, contradicting, beautiful, strange thing," as a writer in the *Art Journal* then called it, that was a distant relative of an Italian villa with "an Oriental, capricious, glass dome in the rear contrasting strangely with the lofty solid tower at the front, as if the owner had begun by being an English lord, and had ended by being a Turkish magnate, looking out on the Bosphorus." Each day thirty men rolled, cut, and trimmed the lawns of Armsmere and tended its ponds and fountains and swans. At garden parties a band composed of German armorers from the Colonel's factory played concerts while the guests nibbled on exotic fruits from the Colonel's 2,634 feet of greenhouses.

P. T. Barnum lived in a minaretted glory called "Iranistan" in Bridgeport, Connecticut, but no one's house excelled in fantasy the home of Frederick E. Church, a painter who made a sizable fortune out of his landscapes, which sold for as high as $10,000 apiece. It was a villa which its owner called "Olana" and it was located just south of Hudson, New York. From its porch its owner looked down over the river and nearly a mile of landscaped meadows and trees that had been disciplined into romantic disorder by his friend Olmsted, the designer of Central Park. The painter himself had designed the villa with the practical assistance of Calvert Vaux, and it was "built in the Persian style, so far as the climate and the requirements of Western civilization permitted." It had walls two and a half feet thick, partly stone and partly brick set in Oriental patterns. Its minarets and cornices and porch were painted in gold and rich colors, its roof was covered with slates of green and red and black. It can still be seen from the Rip Van Winkle bridge at Hudson.

Such were the Mansard houses of the middle classes and the Oriental houses of the new rich. The taste for the exotic had been fed by trade with the Middle and Far East and by such popular books as Washington Irving's *Tales of the Alhambra.* Magazines were filled with descriptions of faraway cities in India and Egypt and Persia. Admiral Perry's celebrated treaty with Japan in 1854 had not only caught the imagination of Americans but had started a flow of a new kind of Oriental wares to this country. The great Crystal Palace exposition in London in 1851 and the Paris Exposition of 1867 had brought together the artistic outpourings and crafts of strange lands and had opened the eyes of Americans who had visited them to all sorts of undreamed-of decorations for the home—Persian carpets and brass samovars and Moorish furniture inlaid with mother of pearl. All these were combined with the elaborately ornamented rosewood chairs and tables and sofas turned out by furniture factories, with mirrors in gilded scroll-saw frames, and whatnots aching with bibelots. "It has become proverbial among European manufacturers," wrote an architect in the seventies who was determined to bring order out of chaos, "that whatever is so wanting in good taste as to ruin it for the home market, will do for the United States. In fact, Europeans have found to their sorrow the folly of sending their choice productions to what they, perhaps with some justice, consider a land of barbaric tastes."

Such a statement could not have surprised anyone; ever since Mrs. Trollope's day Americans had had their barbarity thrown in their faces by compatriots who had traveled to Europe. But it was true that the time was ripe for a new maker of taste to herald a brave new era. No one had added a dash of fresh spice to the aesthetic arguments about how people should live since Downing's death, and he would have been the first to admit that his words had grown dim in the public ears. After a long period of extremely tasty debauchery, there were many Americans ready to hit the sawdust trail to salvation, and Charles L. Eastlake, the new messiah, was on hand to help them.

"Suddenly the voice of the prophet Eastlake was heard crying in the wilderness," *Harper's Bazar* reported. " 'Repent ye, for the Kingdom of the Tasteful is at hand!' "

Actually Eastlake spoke in a rather quiet voice and he was directing his sermon on taste to his compatriots in England and not to Americans at all. The effect of his words, however, was almost equally magical on both sides of the Atlantic. No prophet of taste in our era has ever precipitated such a pell-mell revolution with such a slim volume as did Eastlake with his *Hints on Household Taste*. It was published first in this country in 1872, three years after it was issued in England, and immediately became the manifesto and the testament and the book of revelations, all in one. Households were completely refurbished to follow its teachings; furniture manufacturers and upholsterers were forced to scrap their old designs and patterns to follow its dicta; young brides declined to set up housekeeping with anything that it did not certify as "artistic."

If the furniture and the aesthetic trappings that Eastlake so persuasively recommended seem to us now as cumbersome as anything that the nineteenth century produced, we must remember that to our grandparents not only had they the fascination of a new look, but that the arguments that went with them had the ring of high moral purpose and high aesthetic ideals. Here was a chance not only to redecorate but to be saved at the same time.

Charles Lock Eastlake bore a name that in its day was famous. His uncle, Sir Charles Eastlake, was the president of the Royal Academy and a painter as highly thought of as any in the middle of the century in England. The nephew was a man of modest artistic talents who vacillated between an ambition to be a painter and an inclination toward architecture. He was good enough at the latter to win medals for his architectural drawings and to be appointed Secretary of the Royal Institute of Architects. But he also liked to paint water colors, and he liked to write. His first book, *Hints on Household Taste*, rocketed him into quick fame; he never produced another that had such a popular success. He did not pose as a scholar but his scholarship was adequate to his purposes, and Lord Beaconsfield appointed him keeper and secretary of the National Gallery in 1878. He was responsible for rearranging and classifying the picture collections under the schools to which they belonged (an innovation in museum practice at the time) and for putting them under glass to protect them from the atmosphere of London. Eastlake was bitterly disappointed when he failed to succeed to the directorship of the Gallery; he retired in 1898 and spent the next eight years, until he died, writing social essays and comments on art.

Like Downing, Eastlake was concerned not only with aesthetics but with morals, though he faced them aggressively rather than with Downing's gentleness. He was disgusted with the low state to which taste had fallen, and with the way in which the public invariably seemed to scamper off in pursuit of the latest fad, no matter how silly or extravagant or capricious. He was especially hostile to everything he considered to be sham and showy rather than, to use his favorite word, "sincere," and he blamed the intolerable situation about equally on women and on shopkeepers. It was not that he failed to understand the fickleness of taste, but he could not condone it. "This absurd love of change—simply for the sake of change," he wrote, "is carried to such an extent that if one desires to replace a jug or a table cloth with another of the same pattern, even a few months after it was first bought, however good the style may have been, it is extremely difficult, sometimes impossible to do so. The answer is always the same. 'Last year's goods, sir. We couldn't match them now.' " He blamed the purchasers and not the manufacturers. "So long as a thirst for mere novelty exists independently of all artistic considerations, the aim at Manchester and Sheffield will be to produce objects which, by their singular form or striking combination of colors, shall always appear new."

This kind of impatience with novelty-seeking and the tone of Eastlake's attack sound almost monotonously familiar to us today. We have been continually exposed to the entreaties and attacks of critics, designers, and promoters of modern houses and furniture who have tried to make us lead more reasonable lives in more "functional" surroundings. But to Eastlake's contemporaries this was a new note, a clarion call. The very notion that simplicity of design and "sincerity" of construction should be identified with good taste was an astonishing reversal of Victorian notions of luxury and comfort. And that good taste could also be inexpensively come by was nearly revolutionary. "Excellence of design," Eastlake pronounced, "may be, and, indeed, frequently is, quite independent of cost. . . . Some of the worst specimens of decorative art that I see exposed for sale are expensive articles of luxury. Some of the most appropriately formed, and therefore most artistic, objects of household use are to be bought for a trifling sum."

We have often heard such sensible sentiments expressed in our time by the Museum of Modern Art, whose design department has for some years held exhibitions of inexpensive "useful objects" on which it places the aesthetic equivalent of the Good Housekeeping Institute's seal of approval. But such words in the era of fringe and whatnots, of pots of ferns hanging by chains in bay windows, and ottomans upholstered with needlework baskets of kittens, had all the impact of a revelation. Immediately the new messiah of taste was surrounded with apostles who spread and interpreted and amplified his words and who gathered converts to his fold.

Eastlake's ideas of "functionalism," though that word was not to come into the language of design until about half a century later, took something from Ruskin, who believed that "the essential and necessary structure of an object should never be lost sight of nor concealed by secondary forms or ornament" and something from William Morris and his handicraft movement. Eastlake had no patience with unnecessary curves, so essential a part of the furniture designed in the "French taste," because they seemed to deny the essential function of a piece of furniture, which should be strong of construction, forthright in its purpose, and, above all, comfortable. A chair or table or even a mantelpiece to be sincere should be put together with wooden pegs and dowels and not with nails and screws. A wooden peg had "sincerity," a nail did not. "I do not exactly see," he wrote, "how veneering is to be rejected on 'moral' grounds," but he disliked it because it was used to cover shoddy cabinetwork and because it was inclined to blister.

It is not difficult to see why such sensible ideas, which combined moral uplift, high aesthetic ideals, practicality, and physical comfort, should have delighted so many. Nor is it difficult to understand why so many writers and other promoters of the public taste should have rallied to make Eastlake a household word and something of a household deity. This was the tidiest parcel of taste anyone had seen in a long while—a veritable C-ration for the sensibilities. Eastlake had not only offered a new look, but he had given a complete set of practical instructions for putting it into effect. More important than this he had also provided a neat and easily mastered set of arguments that any housewife could learn and recite with conviction. This was packaged aesthetics for everyday use. The catch phrases—"sincerity," "picturesqueness," "the quaint," and "the artistic"—became part of every woman's vocabulary and (think how Eastlake would have disliked it) of every upholsterer's stock in trade. As *Harper's Bazar* said nearly ten years after the Eastlake fad had struck America, "with . . . eagerness we turned to hear of this new thing. . . . We began to talk about 'harmonies' and 'gradations,' about tiles, plaques, embroideries, bric-à-brac, and the 'sincere' in joinery and decoration, as if we knew what we meant. . . ."

If people did not know what they meant, it was no fault of Eastlake's three principal disciples in America, the aesthetician and art promoter Charles Callahan Perkins of Boston, Mrs. M. E. W. Sherwood, the grandmother of the playwright Robert Sherwood, and Charles Wyllis Elliott, a writer who was also a shopkeeper.

Charles Perkins, who edited the American edition of *Hints on Household Taste* and wrote an elaborate preface for it, was a cultural pillar of Boston. He was president of the Handel and Haydn Society for which he occasionally conducted concerts and wrote music. He was also the president of the Boston Art Club. Before his interest was temporarily diverted by Eastlake to interior decoration, he wrote two successful books on Italian sculpture, which brought him favorable notice at home and in Europe. Furthermore he was one of the very first men to lecture on the history of fine arts in an American college. In 1857 he had given a series of lectures on "The Rise and Progress of Painting" at Trinity College in Hartford. His taste, however, was conservative, and he was one of the Bostonians who had put the cold hand of rebuke on James Jackson Jarves's attempts to found a museum with his collection of Italian primitives as its nucleus. Perkins, who was an able writer, was also something of an aesthetic snob, and if Americans had any hopes that Eastlake's remarks about the sorry state of public sensibilities did not apply to them and were only for the British, he abruptly disabused them in his preface. "Nowhere . . . is modern sterility in the invention of form so marked as in America," he wrote. "We borrow at second hand and do not pretend to have a national taste. We take our architectural forms from England, our fashions from Paris, the patterns of our manufactures from all parts of the world, and make nothing really original but trotting wagons and wooden clocks."

He had a remedy to offer, however. Part of the remedy was to read Eastlake and go forth and sin no more; the other part cannot but remind us of T. S. Eliot's plea for the establishment of a firm intellectual aristocracy. Perkins wanted all questions of taste left in the hands of cultivated men like himself. "We do not see how taste can be elevated," he wrote, "until the world grows wise enough to submit to be governed in it by men of cultivated artistic feelings. . . . We submit questions of law to jurists, and questions of theology to theologians, but we do not defer to men of taste . . . because we believe in the most stupid of all sayings, *de gustibus*, etc."

Perkins would not have thought Mrs. Sherwood, who shared his devotion to Eastlake, his equal in "cultivated artistic feelings," but what she lacked in sensibility she surely made up for in enthusiasm.

As often as not she signed her many magazine articles with just her initials, and she was identified by *Appleton's Journal*, to which she was a regular contributor, as "M.E.W.S., the accomplished lady, a distinguished member of New York Society . . . who will continue her sparkling papers on Social topics and her eminently picturesque stories." No one in her time wrote so picturesquely about architecture and decoration as Mrs. Sherwood and no one could wrench so much meaning out of a chair or a tile or a bookcase as she. Her enthusiasm for Eastlake was unbounded, as her enthusiasms and her distastes were wont to be; though she was as much of a social snob as Perkins was an aesthetic snob, and suffered throughout her life from acute rheumatism, she could always discover some new excitement in anything she took it upon herself to examine. Only Mrs. Sherwood could have written of the blight that lay upon taste before Eastlake appeared and the wonders that it had wrought in such a way as this: "Who knows how much of incompatibility of temper, sorrow, passionate discontent, mutual disgust, may not have grown out of these unhappy surroundings? Nay, Indiana divorce laws may be perhaps directly traced to some frightful inharmoniousness in wallpaper. The soothing influence of an Eastlake bookcase on an irritated husband has never been sufficiently calculated. . . ."

"We must have beauty around us to make us good," she said, glancing at "immoral ugly furniture, tasteless carpets, badly conceived chairs, and vulgar bookcases," and then her eyes lit upon a tile. Eastlake thought highly of tiles as ornament, but Mrs. Sherwood went still further. "There is much morality in a tile," she wrote. "It is a patient instructor, never deserting its pulpit, never failing in its own steadfast devotion to duty. Build Aesop's fables, with their immortal teachings, into your fireplace. . . ." What an easy way to be saved!

One of the objects of Mrs. Sherwood's enthusiasm was Charles Wyllis Elliott. She saw him as "the Apostle Elliott of American interiors" who "has not only preached and practiced reform, but has written a book, last and greatest of knightly effort." The gospel that Mr. Elliott preached was the testament of Charles L. Eastlake, of course, and the reform that he practiced was in terms that the master must have applauded. His headquarters were Boston, but he did not open his shop there until he had traveled extensively in Europe looking for the kind of medieval wrought-iron candlesticks and hinges that Eastlake pictured in his book as examples of "sincere" craftsmanship. Elliott, according to Mrs. Sherwood, "had a passion for bric-à-brac," for which he had searched especially in Holland where he "unearthed much in that great repertoire which is quaint, sincere, and valuable." But he was not only interested in the quaint; he wanted to make good, honest furniture available at prices that everybody could afford. In those days most of the furniture makers in America were Germans and the pieces that they made were based on French designs. Elliott took it upon himself to adapt the familiar shapes to new uses and to produce chairs "as honest in material and as strong as the old ones, but not so clumsy."

His success in Boston, according to Mrs. Sherwood, whose claims should be generously discounted, was considerable. "It has become a crime now in Boston or its elegant neighborhood to have an unbeautified room. A horsehair sofa, which was once but a misdemeanor, has become one of the capital sins since Mr. Elliott has made it easy and cheap to have a set of furniture beautiful and artistic in the place of the old abominations. No one dares to select a wall-paper which would offend the principles of William Morris, while sideboards and bookcases of medieval design, with lovely keys which Lucretia Borgia might have worn at her girdle, and which Benvenuto Cellini may have originally designed, lock up the tea and sugar from pilfering domestics. Doors swing not on modern hinges but on long brass ornamental bars, which make the old conundrum possible, 'Why is a lady like a hinge?'—'Because she is a *thing to adore*.'"

It is not surprising that the shift to Eastlake and his foursquare furniture should also have caused a good deal of poking around in the attic for "antiques." Many people mistook Eastlake's examples of old brass hinges and wrought-iron fire fenders, his drawings of furniture from the sixteenth and seventeenth centuries, and his talk about how sensible it had once been to use a spear for a curtain rod, for a signal to dress up any room with any old piece that had a look of antiquity. Under pressure from the considerable numbers who demanded "Eastlake furniture," manufacturers (who had no love for Eastlake because of what he had written about the shoddy work they turned out) began to run up tables and chairs and bookcases and cupboards that were a parody of what Eastlake had in mind but which at the same time had an undeniable affinity to his own pieces. They were angular and bulky, and about as close to Eastlake in spirit as the overstuffed modern of today is to the early designs of the Bauhaus. "Hardly any branch of manufacture applied to the furnishing of houses," *Appleton's Journal* reported in 1876, "has been more successfully revived of late years than that of brass articles." Tiffany's was doing especially well with filigree brass clocks, inkstands, candlesticks hammered into faces, griffins, and arabesque patterns. Tiles were everywhere—Japanese designs were especially popular and were readily copied by American manufacturers; any stylish fireplace was set about with tiles, and Japanese fans, china, and occasionally peacock feathers ornamented the mantel.

Mr. Perkins, Mrs. Sherwood, and Mr. Elliott were by no means the only American apostles and interpreters of Eastlake in the seventies. No one distilled Eastlake's ideas more successfully for the general reader than Mrs. Ella Church Rodman in her book *How to Furnish a Home.* She believed, and made others believe, that there was "no reason, either in prose or in rhyme, why a whole house should not be a poem" and that "furnishing may be done artistically without following rigidly all the rules of high art." She did, however, suggest a few fundamentals: ". . . there must be fitness, appropriateness, proportion, simplicity, harmony, and durability." Downing as well as Eastlake would have approved those fundamentals, and so would such decorating authorities as Edith Wharton and Elsie de Wolfe a generation later. When Mrs. Rodman wrote: "A pine table is a proper thing, but a pine table that pretends to be black walnut is an abomination," she was taking the words out of the mouths of the "functionalists" half a century before they were old enough to speak for themselves.

Perkins and the others who so ardently promoted Eastlake had a good deal to account for before they got through. Their efforts to cultivate the public taste with the use of a nice neat formula ended, as such efforts so often do, in producing exactly the kind of faddish novelty-seeking that Eastlake so railed against. "Not a young marrying couple who could read English," a writer in *Harper's Bazar* reported in 1876, "were to be found without *Hints on Household Taste* in their hands, and all its dicta were accepted as gospel truth. They hung their pictures and curtains just as Mr. Eastlake said they should; laid their carpets, colored their walls, hinged their doors, arranged their china, bought their chandlesticks, insisted on their andirons, procured solid wood, abjured veneering, and eschewed curves, all after Mr. Eastlake's own heart."

If they had hewed as close as this to the Eastlake line, America would have had a deadly monotonous look; it got to have a fairly monotonous look as it was, but each interpreter of Eastlake and each purchaser of the quaint and the picturesque added his own fillip, and soon what was intended as a return to simplicity had developed into a whole new fanciness of its own. But Eastlake was only one of the influences at work on the public taste. The architectural protagonists also had their shoulders to the commonweal. They labored to create one of the most plausibly explained and most unlikely-looking architectural excursions that has ever taken place on this soil.

Gothic had been mistress long enough and by 1870 the lovers of architecture found her faithless. Once she had been called honest, once her garlands had been thought piquant and tasteful, but now in her advancing years she had gone in for gimcrackery and was concealing her age under a false face of romanticism that did not fool the young and vigorous. "One of the principles upon which the promoters of the Gothic revival insisted with energy and eloquence," wrote H. Hudson Holly, one of the advocates of change, in 1878, "was 'truth in architecture.' . . . But the new reformers say that truth is not the peculiar possession of Gothic architecture; and, indeed, *modern* Gothic has often found the temptation of an age that loves to be deceived too strong for it." The new architecture that they recommended to take its place was called the "Queen Anne Style" for reasons which are almost opaquely obscure. Actually it seems to have been a tossed salad of Elizabethan, Jacobean, and the style of Francis I with the structural underpinnings of none of them. It was ideally suited to the mood that cherished Eastlake, for it was picturesque at the same time that it was "honest," and "artistic" at the same time that it was "practical." Its sharply peaked roofs, second-

and third-floor balconies, spindled verandas, occasional stained glass windows, and corner towers were considered to be "harmonious" with the "sincere" and the "quaint." What was still more important, it was an architecture equally suitable to the wealthy and to the poor, and it demanded no skills in building of which every American carpenter was not the master.

Architects by the 1870's were beginning to be accepted as useful professionals by more and more members of the public, and in the Queen Anne style the architects saw an opportunity to make a marriage between art and the vernacular methods of building. It was nonsense, they had decided, to continue with the Gothic, which bore no relation to the needs of the people or the skills of builders. They reasoned that if we were ever to develop a national architecture we must take into account the skills and materials at hand. An Englishman, John J. Stevenson, writing in *Harper's Magazine* in 1876, said: "The interest of refined and educated minds for the last thirty years has been directed not to improving the vernacular style, but to the hopeless attempt of supplanting it by another, which appeared at first to flourish, but has not taken root in the soil of the country." Queen Anne offered just the opportunity that the architects wanted —they could apply to the vernacular methods of building the "artistic" qualities of "refined and educated minds."

When the English architects spoke of the vernacular they meant the traditional heavy frame construction built of thick, stout timbers. But the American architects were quick to adapt the Queen Anne house to the "balloon frame" which had been developed by American pioneers in the 1830's. Instead of heavy timbers it was made of light two-by-fours nailed together. It was a simple, inexpensive, and sturdy method of building made possible, in part, by the fact that nails, instead of being hand-wrought, began to be turned out cheaply by machinery. For the most part, frame buildings in America had been simple, foursquare structures with no architectural pretensions whatsoever; Queen Anne was a welcome chance for the architects to correct this lack of "artistic" quality.

"The epoch of Queen Anne," wrote George William Curtis in 1886, "is a delightful insurrection against the monotonous era of rectangular building and of the divorce of beauty and use. The distinction of the present or recent dispensation is that the two are blended, that neither the house nor anything in it need be clumsy or ugly." Curtis, you will remember, had been Downing's friend nearly forty years before he wrote these words in "The Easy Chair" in *Harper's*, and the blending of the useful and beautiful was part of the credo of his old friend. But more Americans (partly because there were more Americans) took to the fad for Queen Anne than had listened to Mr. Downing. "Whether you will pay five thousand or fifty thousand dollars for your house, the good Queen Anne will have it a pretty and convenient house, and if you choose she will furnish it prettily and conveniently."

One needs only to look at the houses in nearly any long-established town to see how extensively the good queen left her imprint. Originally most of her houses were painted in somber, artistic tones, in browns and reds; now many of them have been "vulgarized," as it would have seemed to their builders, by white paint. Many a New England village that today will not put up a "modern" building lest it destroy the character of the town, and will build stores in the "colonial" style because they are thought to be in keeping with the architecture of the rest of the village have, in fact, a predominance of Queen Anne houses and a minimum of genuine "colonial." In the seventies Americans were not timid about being "modern" and bankers were as happy to give mortgage loans on a modern Queen Anne house as on a Gothic one. The country was not yet old enough to have become self-conscious about reviving its youth.

To introduce a new kind of architecture and to endear it to the public is usually a long, slow process of cajoling, preaching, explaining, and proselytizing, but the public took Queen Anne to its bosom with an agility that surprised its protagonists. As one of them said, "I have frequently noticed that whereas formerly the introduction of any novelty excited a certain amount of adverse criticism, that it took some time to remove . . . Queen Anne . . . became popular at once, not only among the educated, but even among the rustic populations." The reaction was very like that which had greeted the preachments of Eastlake, and the reasons for Queen Anne's acceptance were much the same. Here was an architecture that was easily explained, easily built by local carpenters either from architects' plans or from plan books, and which was justified with a tidy set of arguments with a suitably lofty moral and aesthetic tone.

If we were to close our eyes to what a Queen Anne house looked like and just listen to the arguments that were used by architects to justify it, we might very well think we were hearing the voice of a "functionalist" of our own time. Listen, for example, to William M. Woollett, a courtier of Queen Anne and the author of a little book called *Old Homes Made New* that was published in 1878. Woollett explained how you could take a Greek Revival house, complete with columns and a pediment, and with the application of some ingenuity and imagination and sound architectural principles make it over into an up-to-date Queen Anne. Here are the principles that he lays down:

First: That the convenience of the plan, its best distribution and adaptation to the wants of the particular individuals by whom it is to be occupied, and the site on which it is to be placed, should in all cases be the paramount consideration.

Second: That the exterior should grow naturally from the plan, its outline being fixed and determined by that . . . that it should also be a consistent following out of the proper and natural uses of the materials of which it is built; each material being fully acknowledged.

Third: that the architectural effect should be obtained by the natural combinations and workings of the constructive portions of the structure, and not by adding or planting on these features: and again by the natural variety of the outline rather than by the richness and variety of the detail.

Fourth: That the proportionately greatest work of art in architecture is that which produces the most effective result at the least expenditure of labor and detail in design, which, in the practical mind of the American, is also money.

If what was simplicity to Woollett seems like fanciness to us, and if exteriors which grew naturally from the plans have been considered by nearly everyone for fifty years to be monstrosities of bad taste, we should remember that the houses were as natural settings for Eastlake furniture as a flat-roofed, glass-walled house is for the furniture we call modern today. They were as strictly *de rigueur* for the "artistic craze" of the seventies as their modern counterparts are for the "functional craze" of our own day.

Like "modern architecture" and "modern furniture" Queen Anne architecture and Eastlake furniture grew together as part of the same movement, and if there had been any chance that they might have been cults that flourished locally and were unknown except in the sophisticated communities of the East, the Centennial Exposition of 1876 at Philadelphia saw to it that many millions of Americans were exposed to their elevating atmosphere and to a veritable avalanche of other art besides.

The repercussions of the Centennial on American taste were tremendous. Rising above the Schuylkill River was the biggest exposition that had ever been held anywhere in the world, six times more costly than the Crystal Palace in London in 1851, bigger than the Paris Exposition of 1867, bigger even than the Vienna Exhibition of 1874, which boasted fifty acres of buildings and which cost nearly ten million dollars to construct. It was a tribute, according to those who planned it, to "the unparalleled advancement in science and art, and all the various appliances of human ingenuity for the refinement and comfort of man" in the century since the United States were born. On 236 acres of splendidly landscaped grounds, seven enormous buildings, together with many smaller annexes and exhibition halls erected by the States of the Union and by foreign governments, looked down on the river. For the opening ceremonies on May 10 Richard Wagner had written a Grand March "especially for the occasion" and John G. Whittier read a "hymn" that he had composed to celebrate the nation's one hundredth birthday. Nothing on so grand a scale, so exotic, or so euphoric with "culture" had ever been seen in America before. Americans drank deep of the heady wine of art, and the hangover lasted for at least a quarter of a century, or longer than anyone cares to remember.

The artistic center of the Exposition was Memorial Hall, which was also called the Art Gallery. It was a permanent structure of granite and brick and iron that rose one hundred and fifty feet in the air and was topped by a large ball on which stood a heroic figure of Columbia. "At each corner of the base of the dome," the *Art Journal* recorded, "is a colossal figure representing the four quarters of the globe; while over the corners of the four corner-pavilions are colossal cast-iron eagles with wings out-stretched. The frieze around the entire building is highly ornamented." Through Memorial Hall's iron and bronze doors, with the coats of arms of all the States and Territories emblazoned on them, flowed paintings and sculptures and examples of what was then called "industrial art" from all over the world. Even the seventy-five thousand square feet of wall space for pictures and the twenty thousand square feet of floor space for statues was insufficient; a large brick building had to be added on the rear to accommodate the artistic outpourings of the civilized world.

"Never before in the United States," wrote a reporter for *Appleton's Journal* shortly after the Exhibition opened, "have there been gathered together in one place so many works of art representing so great a variety of nations." On the whole, however, he found the exhibition only "a fairly good one." He thought the English pictures, which he divided into three types, "pre-Raphaelite, sentimental, or ideal," somewhat inferior to his expectations. As for the French, he was indignant because the work of the painters who were represented was "puerile" compared with the excellent Corots, Bretons and Millets which had already been seen in this country through the offices of William Hunt, the Bostonian; he also was disappointed that Bouguereau was not represented. He felt better about the American art: "this, we venture to believe," he said, "is the best collection we have ever had. It consists of about six hundred pictures in oils and water colors and covers the names of nearly all the artists of distinction from Stuart, Copley, and Benjamin West to Eastman Johnson and Sanford Gifford." He did not note that neither Ryder nor Eakins, the two American painters of the seventies whose reputuations have become the most lustrous of any in our time, were not included at all. It is true that Eakins' painting of "The Gross Clinic" was shown at the Centennial, but not as a piece of art. It was considered too realistic, too bloody for a period that believed that "a work of art can never afford to be repulsive or disgusting," as the *Appleton's* reporter said; it was hung elsewhere with the medical exhibits.

If the Appleton's reporter was not greatly impressed the public was of quite a different mind. Reminiscing many years later William H. Ellsworth in *A Golden Age of Authors* noted that the Centennial had "implanted an appreciation of art which was new to the American people." The objects that confronted the top-hatted gentlemen and the ladies in the bustles and flowing trains and tight bodices, with parasols in their gloved hands, were rich indeed. The effect of the paintings and sculptures was sufficient to arouse a new public interest in the fine arts and to set a new generation in pursuit of art as a career. But the American home felt the greatest impact from the displays of "industrial art" objects and from the various manifestations of Eastlake and Queen Anne which were everywhere in evidence but which were most particularly to be seen in the British Pavilion.

"What a grand and comprehensive division it is! 'Industrial Art!'" wrote a critic named Walter Smith in his elaborately illustrated book on the exhibition, which in its second edition was called *Household Taste.* "The union of two great elements of civilization—Industry, the mere mechanical, manual labor, and Art, the expression of something not taught by nature, the presentation of that ideal, the mere conception of which raises man above the level of savagery." If refinement and civilization meant the meeting of the machine and ornamentation, here was man's release from savagery with a vengeance. The industrial art show included everything from a silver epergne depicting Neptune and Triton with nymphs and walruses bedecked with flowers and crystal pendants to a brass chandelier ornamented with griffins; it ranged from a "Renaissance" bedstead with a tufted baby-blue silk headboard and dark raw-silk draperies to a tremendous cast-iron fountain set about with urns, the product of the Mott Iron Works. Never before had Americans seen such refined craftsmanship, or design that they thought so exquisite. It was a great stimulus to "art manufacture" in this country. "The specimens from abroad, of furniture, carpets, hangings, and embroideries," wrote H. Hudson Holly, "formed an opportunity for the art student such as may not occur again in many years. Most of our cities (except New York, which, in its greed for wealth, appears to have no time to give to the development of art) took advantage of the chance offered, and stocked their museums with works of this kind." Possibly New York was right, and the other cities too hasty in their enthusiasm, but the mood for fancywork was everywhere. "Two years after the Centennial," John A. Kouwenhoven records in his *Made in America,* "the sale of jigsaw blades had leaped from a few thousand a year to about five hundred thousand a month."

Critics today look back upon the Centennial Exhibition as an architectural and artistic calamity that produced not a single new idea but was, rather, the epitome of the accumulated bad taste of the era that was called the Gilded Age, the Tragic Era, the Dreadful Decade, or the Pragmatic Acquiescence, depending on which epithet you thought most searing. It is difficult for anyone now to turn the pages of the many guides to the exhibition and its arts and examine the careful engravings of the furniture and bric-a-brac, the chandeliers and sculptures without a mixture of tolerant amusement and a sad sense that here was a tremendous straining toward artistic achievement that was doomed from the start. It was all show—show of technique, show of rich materials, show of virtuosity—with no driving conviction behind it, no intellectual substance, and no fight. At most it was a rear-guard action, an attempt to defend what it considered the niceties of handicraft against the incursion of the machine. The "union of the two great elements of civilization, Industry . . . and Art" was an illusion; it had not yet been discovered that the machine could produce a new kind of art, and the tradition that art and an encrustation of ornament were inseparable was as old as the business of silversmithing and architecture. But if the progeny of this misalliance of art and the machine seems to us to have been ludicrous, the public and many of the critics of the day felt otherwise. The exhibition "like a Fairy's wand," according to Mrs. Sherwood, had banished bad taste from all right-thinking Americans.

The result was a wave of tastefulness that was known at the time as the "Artistic Craze." Gone were the elaborately floriated Brussels carpets in favor of muted, conventionalized patterns or Oriental rugs; gone, too, the "heavy frescoes, inartistic 'reps,' the crimson curtains against white walls, the staring papers, and the furnace holes in the floor." It was to the Pre-Raphaelite painters, Burne-Jones and Dante Gabriel Rossetti, and to the handicrafter William Morris, so Mrs. Sherwood wrote, that "the lovers of artistic interiors owe an immortal debt, for they started in England an art crusade against the bad features of household furnishings, which was born in the reign of George the Fourth." She had forgotten, for the moment, her old idol Eastlake. "If the man of the next century," wrote George William Curtis, meaning us, "should ever see the amusing little opera of

Patience, which has so pleased us who are his great-grandfathers and queer old ancestors, he will understand not only that this age was the renaissance of taste, and not only that it had its contemporaneous caricatures of its characteristic tendency, but that it was conscious of them and greatly enjoyed them. The droll 'aestheticism' which produced a figure like Oscar Wilde and a kind of social cult evident enough to give point to the pictorial laugh of *Punch* was only a ravelling out of the solid and golden fabric of refined and elegant taste. The worship of the teapot is only an extravagance of the impulse which designs the beautiful house and fills it with beautiful things."

What was considered a beautiful house after the Centennial was very likely to be as somber in tone inside as it was outside. It was the era of the brownstone front and of stamped leather walls. But let Mrs. Sherwood tell you what was considered good taste: "Nothing can be more beautiful," she wrote, "more orderly, more harmonious, than a modern New York house which has blossomed out in this fine summer of perfected art." One of the houses that she most admired was the home of Dr. W. A. Hammond on West Fifty-fourth Street. "The walls [of the dining room] hung with deep crimson and maroon leather stamped in gold, with figures of chimerical animals of medieval design; the ceiling Renaissance of the fifteenth century" pleased her, but what delighted her most was the doctor's office which she found excellently suited to the function of diagnosis. It was decorated as "an Egyptian retreat, with the lotus, the scarabaeus, and the procession of slaves, huntsmen, and animals," and what is more, "the hawk-headed goddess, the dog-faced deities of Egypt, the inscrutable eye of the high priest as he presides over the fireplace" were part of the functionalism. "This room," Mrs. Sherwood observed, "is devoted to consultations on the mysterious diseases of the brain, and is fitly dedicated to that subtle Egyptian intellect which saw so clearly behind the veil, and read, as no other people have read, the enigma of life."

Doctor, lawyer, beggarman, thief—everyone was expected to have taste, and those who did not were exposed to the most ruthless ridicule by the tasteful. "There never was a time," Clarence Cook, the author of a volume called *The House Beautiful*, wrote in the Centennial year, "when so many books written for the purpose of bringing the subject of architecture—its history, its theory, its practice

—down to the level of popular understanding, were produced as in this time of ours. And from the house itself, we are now set to thinking and theorizing about the dress and decoration of our rooms: how best to make them comfortable and handsome; and books are written, and magazine and newspaper articles, to the end that on a matter which concerns everybody, everybody may know what is the latest word."

For half a century, from the time Mrs. Trollope came to America and found its citizens boorish, priggish, ill-educated and smug until the afterglow of the Centennial with its aura of aesthetic sophistication, the tastemakers had concentrated their efforts on improving the Public Taste. Downing had dreamed of tasteful cottages for everyone; Jarves saw in the ornamented store fronts of Boston the seeds of a Renaissance in America; the Art Unions had tried to bring an appreciation of the fine arts to every section of the country. The founders of the museums in New York, and Boston, and Washington, and Baltimore had labored to provide touchstones of taste to guide the public. It had been a long slow battle with public indifference, with faddishness, with misplaced exuberance, and with Philistinism. But by the 1880's something new had happened to the social structure of the country. For half a century America had been, as much as it has ever been, a one-class society. Not everyone was equally rich, but everyone had an equal opportunity to exploit the wealth that was to be reaped by the persevering, the adventurous, and the unscrupulous, and the gulf between the rich and the poor was, compared to what was to come at the end of the century, a narrow one. When the tastemakers applied themselves to "the Public Taste" they meant everybody's taste, and to a very considerable extent the taste of the rich was only the taste of the poor on a more lavish scale.

But this was changing. The rich were becoming fabulously rich, so rich that their taste was divided by a towering wall of wealth from the taste of the rest of the people. They might, almost, have lived in different worlds. While the Public Taste was not forgotten by the tastemakers, their real quarry became the rich. If the taste of the rich could be made as sublime as their wealth could afford to make it, they reasoned, tastefulness would filter down to the middle classes and to the poor. It was not surprising that their interest should shift, as it did, from the Public Taste to the Private Taste.

PART TWO

The Private Taste

CHAPTER VIII

Stately Homes

". . . it was as if some angel had descended
in the night while he slept, and had whispered one magic word with which he was
ever after to immortalize himself, namely—
'Adaptation!' "

George Washington Vanderbilt II inherited scarcely more than
a fraction of his father's estate. When the railroad magnate,
William H. Vanderbilt, dropped dead of an apoplectic fit in his
library at 640 Fifth Avenue late in the afternoon of November 28,
1885, he left a fortune the size of which astonished even those who
knew him well. It was double the value of the $90,000,000 that he
had inherited from his father, the old Commodore, and as a broker
of the day noted, the estate "if converted into gold . . . would have
weighed five hundred tons, and it would have taken five hundred
strong horses to draw it from the Grand Central Depot to the Sub-
Treasury in Wall Street." Of this massive sum young George, who
was twenty-three when his father died, received only $10,000,000
and the house at 640 Fifth Avenue. It was little enough compared
with what fell to his brothers: $67,000,000 to Cornelius II and
$65,000,000 to William K., but George, very soon after his father had
died, put his fortune to what he thought was good use. He built the
most palatial mansion that America has ever seen, and he built it at a
time when palaces of surpassing splendor were the order of the
day for such families as the Astors, the Goelets, and the Belmonts.

George Vanderbilt's house, if a massive limestone château can be
called by such a homely name, was "Biltmore." From its leaded-glass

windows its young owner surveyed his princely domain of 130,000 acres of North Carolina woodlands. In its library he sat beneath a magnificent ceiling, painted by the ebullient Venetian master, Tiepolo, a work of art that he had acquired in Europe on the condition that he keep secret where he had got it and what it had cost him. Around him (he was a studious young man) were twenty thousand richly bound volumes on his favorite subjects—forestry, art, and ancient and modern languages. In his banqueting hall, whose ceiling was seventy-five feet above its highly polished floor, he dined with friends surrounded by Gobelin tapestries and warmed by a triple fireplace. In his print room he examined his collection of Dürer engravings or a chess set that had once belonged to Napoleon I. There were forty masters' bedrooms in the house and the steep roof that covered it was the largest, whether for a public or private building, anywhere in the country.

To plan his gardens young Vanderbilt had secured the services of Frederick Law Olmsted, the designer of Central Park; to manage his forests he employed Gifford Pinchot, who was then, like Vanderbilt, still in his twenties. It was the first experimental forest in America, and J. Sterling Morton, the Secretary of Agriculture of the day, noted somewhat wistfully, "He employs more men than I have in my charge. He is also spending more money than Congress appropriates for this department." The hundreds of employees who worked the farms and forests lived in a village, complete with church and hospital, that Vanderbilt had constructed for them; they provided him with a choir for his private chapel.

When George Vanderbilt conceived his plan to live in a palace and devote his fortune to experimental forestry, it is not surprising that he should have chosen as his architect a man well known to the family. Richard Morris Hunt had not only built William K.'s house at Fifty-second Street and Fifth Avenue, the very model of a French château that had made its designer famous, as one of his contemporaries noted, "almost before it was completed," but who had also built the family mausoleum on Staten Island. There in a $300,000 version of the Romanesque chapel of Saint Gilles at Arles, his father was entombed, and for fear of body snatchers was guarded by watchmen who were required to punch a time clock every fifteen minutes.

Palaces for the People

The rather austere structure above is Tremont House, opened in Boston in 1829, the first "palace" hotel anywhere in the world. Before long every city of any size in America and Europe had a palace hotel of its own, such as the San Francisco Palace (below), whose luxury and elegance made it one of the wonders of America in the 1870's.

Ornamentation Spans the Continent

The rococo saloons above and below, left, were a continent apart in the 1850's. Above is the Gem Saloon of New York, featuring stuffed birds and a tremendous mirror, and below is a saloon in San Francisco during the gold rush when the rest of the city was shacks. It wasn't long before one could span the continent in a rolling palace such as Frank Leslie's train on the Union Pacific, below, right.

Gothic Takes to the Water

Outside as well as inside scroll saws turned ships into floating wedding cakes.
Above is the main cabin of the *Great Republic,* a Mississippi River steamer
built as a "boat to end all boats." Her flower-carpeted cabin was three hundred
feet long. Below, Currier & Ives "The Champions of the Mississippi" com-
memorates the kind of race that often led to exploding boilers and disaster.

Glitter and Gold—The Foolproof Formula

Splendid staircases, enormous chandeliers, rich carpets, and above all gilt have been the *sine qua non* of America's public palaces. Above is the main saloon of the *S. S. Drew*, a Hudson River steamer. Below is a modern palace, the grand foyer of Radio City Music Hall. Half a century changes the design but the spirit stays the same.

The Carriage Trade at Home

Industrialists in the 1860's had their private palaces. Above is "Armsmere," the Hartford, Connecticut, home of Colonel Samuel Colt, the inventor of the revolver. Its Oriental domes and minarets ornament a basically Italian villa. Below a patent medicine king uses his mansard villa and factory to advertise his "ague conqueror" and himself. His portrait is on the vase of roses.

The Fair That Made America Art-Conscious

Millions of Americans discovered "taste" at the Centennial Exposition in Philadelphia in 1876. Besides the vast exhibition halls, they saw such architecture, domestic in scale, as the state buildings above. They delighted in the Eastlake organ, below, left, and were wonder-struck by such "art furniture" and mantels as those on display in the British exhibit, below, right.

They Called It "Queen Anne"

The typical "Queen Anne" house above and the room to the right were recommended by the same architect, H. Hudson Holly, two years after the Centennial. The room is in the Eastlake manner, as is the "sincere" bed in which the lady reclines below. Next to her is an "old home made new" in Great Barrington, Massachusetts. Built as a foursquare brick house in 1766, it was remodeled in the Queen Anne manner in 1890.

The Artistic Craze

The trappings of the ubiquitous "artistic young lady" of the decade following the Centennial were very much the same in America and England, from which the craze came. Ornamental tiles, precious teapots, Japanese fans, peacock feathers, and Pre-Raphaelite hair-do and flowing dress constituted her setting and her costume. The ladies on this page are from *Harper's Magazine* and from *Punch*.

THE SIX-MARK TEA-POT.

Æsthetic Bridegroom. "IT IS QUITE CONSUMMATE, IS IT NOT?"
Intense Bride. "IT IS, INDEED! OH, ALGERNON, LET US LIVE UP TO IT!"

It had been the magnificence of Hunt's house for William K. that (according to legend) had made Mrs. Astor, the mentor of New York society in the seventies, accept the Vanderbilts into her fold; it had been the quality of its design that had caused Charles F. McKim, of the famous architectural firm of McKim, Mead, and White, to say that he often walked up Fifth Avenue late at night to look at the house because he slept better after feasting his eyes on it. But there were other reasons as well. Mr. Hunt was the most amiable of men and an architect rare in his capacity to get along with his clients. "The first thing you've got to remember," he once said to his son, "is that it's your client's money you're spending. Your business is to get the best results you can following their wishes. If they want you to build a house upside down standing on its chimney, it's up to you to do it, and still get the best possible results." With such an attitude toward his profession, there is no wonder that he found so many friends or that George Vanderbilt should have been happy to turn to him for the realization of his dream.

Biltmore was, and still is (it is now open to the public), a massive structure of Indiana limestone based on the Château de Blois, with pinnacles and steep roofs, and a forest of chimneys and gables. When George Vanderbilt saw Hunt's plans for the house he was so pleased that he had a spur of railroad built to the site from Asheville to expedite the construction, and he imported hundreds of artisans from France to lay the walls and apply the ornament. Accounts of its cost vary by several millions of dollars; some say $3,000,000, some say $5,000,000; whatever the figure, it evidently mattered little to George Vanderbilt or, indeed, to Richard Morris Hunt.

To most critics of architecture today Hunt is anathema. Though he may have been a more expert designer and a man of more refined tastes and greater knowledge than most of his contemporaries, his influence on American building is looked upon darkly. It is not that his own buildings are considered to be any more ridiculous than those of his fellow architects, but the style that he played so large a part in setting has, in many expert opinions, been a disastrous backwater in the progress of our architecture.

Actually Hunt was in no sense an innovator; he was a sail that caught the ambitious breeze that blew off the great fortunes of the seventies and eighties and drove the ship of taste into luxurious and splendid harbors. He was the artistic conscience of men and women of great wealth to whom display and ostentation were a highly competitive game. For the most part his clients were the scions of the men who established the great fortunes; it was the second, third, and even fourth generations of wealth who represented a new leisure class such as America had never known before. The founders of the fortunes were too interested in amassing wealth, too occupied with playing the great industrial game, to devote the same ingenuity and inventiveness that their sons and daughters did to spending their fortunes. There is no easier or more pretentious way to spend money than on building palaces. "They are inveterate builders, are these American millionaires," wrote a historian of the "stately homes." "What with the six or seven great New York houses of the Vanderbilt family, and their still larger number of country estates; it could be plausibly argued that among them they have invested as much money in the erection of dwellings as any of the royal families of Europe, the Bourbons excepted."

More than any architect of his time, more than McKim, or Mead, or White, and more than H. H. Richardson, the designer of Trinity Church in Boston and one of America's most inspired architects, Hunt epitomizes the rich and official taste of the decades following the Centennial. It will pay us to consider the career of this handsome, humorous, hard-working, and friendly man upon whom wealth was heaped by the wealthy and to whom honors were accorded by the world.

Hunt was born in Brattleboro, Vermont, in 1827, the same year that Mrs. Trollope came to America. His father, who was a prominent jurist and a congressman, died in Washington when Richard was only five, and he was brought up by his maternal grandmother and by his mother. Mrs. Hunt was a woman of somewhat uncommon talents as a painter and, according to Henry Van Brunt, one of Hunt's first pupils, was "fortunately for the future of Art in America . . . a woman of high spirit, great force of character, and of accomplishments far in advance of her time." In her two sons (Richard's brother was William Morris Hunt, who became one of America's most distin-

guished painters and was, as you will recall, the man who introduced
a taste for French painting to Boston) Mrs. Hunt realized the artistic
ambitions that it was almost impossible for a woman in her day to
attain for herself. She took her sons to Europe in 1843, and while
William pursued the art of painting in the studios in Munich and
Paris, Richard, who had thought that he wanted to be a soldier, went
to work in the atelier of a prominent Parisian architect named Hector
Martin Lefuel. In 1846, when he was nineteen, Richard enrolled at
the École des Beaux-Arts. He was the first American architect ever
to get his training there, and he was the first of hundreds; it was
largely through his influence that later in the century it was the ambition of every young American architect to study at the Beaux Arts,
and a great many of them realized their ambition. Eight years later,
he went to work for his first architectural instructor, Lefuel, who had
quite recently been appointed to the august position of supervising
the design and construction of the additions to the Louvre by which
Napoleon III intended to memorialize his reign. Young Hunt, who
was by this time, to all outward appearances—in speech, mannerisms,
and dress—a complete Frenchman, was put in charge of the construction of the Pavillon de la Bibliothèque. "There is a certain picturesque surprise," one of his contemporaries recalled many years
later, "in the spectacle of a Yankee lad giving form and character to
one of the imperial monuments of France."

The Frenchified Yankee lad decided, however, that though Lefuel
assured him that a great career lay before him in France his responsibility and his future were in America. "It has been represented to me,"
he wrote to his mother at Christmastime in 1855, "that America was
not ready for the Fine Arts, but I think they are mistaken. There is
no place in the world where they are more needed, or where they
should be more encouraged. Why, there are more luxurious houses
put up in New York than in Paris! At any rate the desire is evinced
and the money spent and if the object is not attained, it is the fault
of the architects. . . . There are no greater fools in America than in
any other part of the world; the only thing is that the professional
man has got to make his own standing."

When Hunt arrived in New York, a tall young man of twenty-
seven, with deep-set eyes and a splendid mustache (he had been called

"the handsomest American in Paris"), the profession of architecture, as we have already noted, was scarcely considered a profession at all. But Hunt brought with him the most extensive training that any American architect had ever received, an intensely industrious temperament, a devotion to academic detail, and—almost as important as any of these —a considerable architectural library. He had collected it at some sacrifice of the expensive pleasures of Parisian gaiety, and it was an investment that paid him rich returns, for as the architect Henry Ives Cobb, Jr., has observed, "Those were the days when to be original meant having an architectural book that none of the other fellows had." Shortly after he reached New York he was offered a job by Thomas U. Walter, who was in charge of the dome that was being added to the Capitol in Washington. He was gratified to receive a salary of $50 a week, which, next to that received by Mr. Walter himself, was the largest paid to anyone on the project.

In general, however, the practice of architecture in America was not all that Hunt had hoped it would be, and when he returned to New York to set up a studio of his own, things were slow. They were not, however, dull, for he soon found himself involved in a lawsuit that, as it turned out, was more important to the profession of architecture in America than it was to Hunt himself. At the request of an eccentric and wealthy dentist named Dr. Parmly, Hunt, while still in Paris in 1855, had made some sketches for a house that the dentist planned to build for his daughter and son-in-law. When he got back to America, Hunt went to work on developing the sketches into detailed plans and Dr. Parmly was evidently pleased with them. When Hunt went off to Washington he turned the work over to another architect, but not until after he had received his client's approval. On returning from Washington several months later he again took over supervision of the building and when it was almost completed he presented his bill. The house cost in the neighborhood of fifty or sixty thousand dollars, and Dr. Parmly was, so the account goes, "outraged at the charge of five per cent which also covered the designs for interior decoration." The dentist had paid $450 on account, and that, so far as he was concerned, was all he was going to pay. Hunt sued. To architects this was a *cause célèbre*. A jury of the New York Supreme Court found in Hunt's favor, and though it awarded him only two and a half per cent, the minimum architectural commission in those days, the point had been established: architects were professionals and their services not only commanded respect but proper remuneration. The case also had the effect, we are told, of generally raising the standards of architectural practice and of improving professional methods.

They could have done with improvement, and Hunt found other ways besides suing his clients to do what he could. He was one of the founders of 'the American Institute of Architects, and its first secretary. "Before this establishment [in 1857]," Henry Van Brunt wrote, "community of thought, mutual friendship hardly existed among architects. The hand of each was turned with jealousy and suspicion against his brother. His processes of design and his business methods were personal secrets. Each concealed his drawings from the rest, as if they were pages of a personal diary. Even books and prints were carefully secluded from inspection by a rival. Pupils were apprentices and as in my own case, often looked with eager and unsatisfied eyes through the glass of their master's locked bookcases. There were no ethics of practice, no common ground of mutual protection, no uniformity of action or thought, no national literature of architecture. The current professional periodicals of England and Germany furnished the sole inspiration of nearly every architectural office in the land."

The Institute may have brought the architects together, but it also set them at each other's throats. In its early days the Battle of the Styles, as it was called, was raging tempestuously. The advocates of the Gothic revival, full of the rich arguments and even richer vocabulary of Pugin and Ruskin, defended the "natural forms" of the pointed style, while the advocates of the "classic" were led by Hunt with his wealth of knowledge of the architecture of the Renaissance and his Beaux Arts training. The arguments became so heated and the members of the Institute found them so engrossing that it was finally necessary to pass a resolution to exclude "this dangerous subject" from the Institute's discussions.

Hunt was a natural teacher—demanding, enthusiastic, generous, and concerned. Shortly after he had set himself up in practice in New York he was approached by three young men who aspired to be architects. They pleaded with him to take one of the studios in the Tenth Street Studio Building, which he had just completed, and to instruct them in the manner of the Beaux Arts; there was no university in America at that time that thought architecture worth teaching. Henry Van Brunt, George B. Post, and Charles D. Gambrill were his first pupils, and they were joined later by Frank Furness and William R. Ware, who became one of the founders of the school of architecture at Columbia University, the first in this country. Hunt was a taskmaster, insistent on "plans on rigidly scholastic lines" and "strict classic forms" and a proper study of all styles of all ages. His criticisms were, Van Brunt says, "pungent and severe . . . genial and picturesque" and given with "inexhaustible humor." The pupils worked at a long table in a large room whose walls were covered with plaster casts, and Hunt encouraged them to "draw, draw, draw, sketch, sketch, sketch!" "If you can't draw anything else," Furness recalls his exhorting them, "draw your boots, it doesn't matter, it will ultimately give you control of your pencil so that you can more readily express on paper your thoughts in designing."

Hunt was living at this time on Washington Square in what sounds to us now like a jungle of travel souvenirs. His walls were "rich with hangings, old panels, sculptured or painted, and modern studies from the studios of Paris." In carved cabinets were bronzes and medallions and Venetian glass and "curiosities of fine handiwork in all the arts." Scattered about the room were medieval missals, embroideries, musical instruments, "masterpieces" of forged and wrought metalwork, and examples of faïence, and a collection of "strange and costly toys of every era of civilization." Hunt's tastes were nothing if not catholic and to the eyes of his contemporaries the place had "a mellow look."

In the early sixties Hunt went back to Europe, where he stayed for several years. If he had done no important work, built no splendid buildings before he left, he had accomplished something more important. He had implanted in a group of young architects an enthusiasm for what were considered in those days sound classic architectural principles. He had, indeed, laid the foundations of what was later in the century to be hailed with almost euphoric self-adulation by the architects as the American Renaissance.

Without patrons, which means without a great deal of wealth seeking to be used for personal gratification, there could be no Renaissance. No one, not even the Astors or the Belmonts, was as rich as the Vanderbilts with their vast railroad holdings, but all across the land were millionaires. In Chicago the Potter Palmers had made a fortune in real estate and hotelkeeping, in San Francisco the Crockers and the Huntingtons and the Floods and the Leland Stanfords had amassed fortunes in railroads and real estate and other bonanzas of the Gold Rush. Social competition was acute among the rich, and standing was determined, to some extent, not only by the lavishness with which one entertained but by the size and magnificence of one's house and by the richness of its collections of paintings and tapestries and tiger rugs and chandeliers and by the number of such houses one owned and where they were situated. The most spectacular cluster of palaces (they were called "cottages" by their owners) was, of course, at fashionable Newport, a resort that Bostonians had looked upon as their own until New Yorkers such as the Astors and the Belmonts and the Vanderbilts had spotted it with their ostentatious summer homes. "There comes back to me a phrase uttered by Charles Eliot Norton . . ." wrote Van Wyck Brooks in speaking of the man who introduced the History of Art to Harvard. "It was to the effect that the picture of heaven in the Book of Revelation—with its excess of precious stones—was such as might have been conceived 'by a New York woman.' What a phrase was that for expressing how Boston and Cambridge felt about the gaudy New York splendor that had vulgarized their beloved Newport."

Where the arts were concerned, the vulgarizers of Newport were a timid, unadventurous lot. They were willing, indeed eager, to spend vast sums from their fortunes on palaces and on all manner of arts, fine and applied, to furnish them; but where taste was concerned they wanted to be absolutely safe. Paul Bourget, the French novelist and critic, spoke of "the sincerity, almost the pathos, of this love of Americans for surrounding themselves with things around which there is an idea of time and stability." And he added, "It is almost a physical satisfaction of the eyes to meet here the faded colors of an ancient painting, the blurred stamp of an antique coin, the softened shades of a medieval tapestry. In this country, where everything is of yesterday, they hunger and thirst for the long ago." But Bourget, though he may have satisfied himself with this explanation of the houses he visited, only half glimpsed the truth, and the half he saw was sentimental. The fact was that the rich were rich enough and lived enough apart from the world to be conservative; they could look to the only models of wealth and station that they could find that were comparable with their own—the great houses of Europe and the palaces of Renaissance princes, who had also made their money as traders and financiers. Americans have always been avid consumers of books of etiquette because American society is fluid and men and women are constantly moving from one social level to another and are eager not to offend or to appear boorish. There were no books of etiquette to which the rich could apply for instructions on how princes should live in this country, and so they turned to the only models available to them—to the standards of European elegance, and with the aid of architects they adapted those external trappings to their own extremely rigid, refined, and on the whole boring mode of life.

Indulgence in extravagant architecture was certainly better than suicide from boredom. James Jackson Jarves was deeply concerned in the late sixties with "the increasing number of young men born to great incomes" who wound up with delirium tremens or death by their own hands. One young man of his acquaintance had poisoned himself and "another buried his lassitude of life in the turbid Thames." If these young men, he reasoned, especially the more intellectual among them (the stupid ones could content themselves with sports), could be got interested in intelligent patronage of the arts, how much better off they, and the world, would be. To oversimplify in still another direction the explanation of the great houses and their vast collections, it seems at least partly true that the scions of wealth built and furnished so feverishly as a kind of occupational therapy to help them keep their senses.

When Hunt came back from Europe in 1868 he reopened his New York office (he had been away all during the Civil War and returned to find the country in a state of boom prosperity), and he was kept busy with commissions. He seemed, in the early days of his career, to have a talent for getting into disputes and one of the first jobs he worked on after his return caused many eyebrows to rise. He designed an apartment house, the first, it has been said, in New York. According to Alan Burnham, the principal authority on Hunt, "This building was the center of much of the 'French flats' controversy, in which it was conceived as wicked and immoral to house several families under one roof, as theretofore only the lowly tenement had attempted this type of domestic arrangement." Several years later he built the Tribune Building in New York, one of the first elevator office buildings in the country. But his great opportunity and his great reputation did not come until the end of the seventies when he was commissioned by William K. Vanderbilt and his socially ambitious wife Alva to build them a house on the corner of Fifty-second Street and Fifth Avenue.

"Formalized barbarism" it has been called by James Marsden Fitch, a critic of our own day, but to most of Hunt's contemporaries it was a revelation of beauty, purity of design, delicacy of detail, and above all of elegance. It was a château in the manner of Blois, and not the least of its astonishing characteristics was the material of which it was made. New York millionaires had been quite content to live in almost identical brownstone mansions, and here suddenly was Mr. Vanderbilt blossoming forth in pinnacles and turrets built of a gray limestone and topped with a slate roof. Even Ward McAllister, the social arbiter of Newport and Mrs. William Astor's confidant and attendant, was constrained to admit that Hunt's building was sufficient justification to invite the Vanderbilts to the Patriarch Balls at Delmonico's.

There was one dissenting voice amidst the general clamor of praise from the architects of Hunt's day, a voice from the Middle West, from an architect far more intellectual and far more inventive than Hunt, and one of the pioneers of the architecture we now think of as modern. "Must I show you this *French château*, this little Château de Blois, on this street corner, here in New York, and still you do not laugh?" It was Louis Sullivan who asked the derisive question. "Must you wait until you see a *gentleman* in a silk hat come out of it before you laugh? Have you no sense of humor, no sense of pathos? Must I tell you that while the man may live in the house physically (for a man may live in any kind of house, physically), that he cannot possibly live in it morally, mentally, or spiritually, that he and his home are a paradox, a contradiction, an absurdity, a characteristically New York absurdity; that he is no part of the house, and his house is no part of him?" It was almost as though Andrew Jackson Downing had restated his warning that "much of the character of everyman may be read in his house."

But to most men no such pertinent and impertinent questions occurred. "It was as if some angel had descended in the night while he slept," wrote the architect Joy Wheeler Dow in *American Renaissance* in 1904, "and had whispered one magic word with which he was ever after to immortalize himself, namely—'Adaptation!' " To Dow, who regarded Hunt as "probably the most remarkable architect this country has produced," his hero had saved American architecture from the dreadful reign of Queen Anne and Eastlake.

By the eighties the American Renaissance was well launched and a new Battle of the Styles was being waged. In Boston H. H. Richardson, who had followed Hunt at the École des Beaux-Arts by several years, and who like his elder was abroad during the Civil War, was busy adapting the ponderous Romanesque architecture of Southern France to New England churches and libraries, to railroad stations and private homes, with astonishing ingenuity and effectiveness. In New York plans came rapidly off the drafting tables of McKim, Mead, and White and of Carrère and Hastings for country and city houses, for public buildings and offices in all sorts of styles. The wealthy could live in adaptations of Georgian, or French Renaissance, or Colonial, or, as the Henry Villards did, in a palace on Madison Avenue and Fiftieth Street in which the Medici would have been very much at home. Architectural offices were humming with activity all over the country. The nation was now almost completely tied together with railroads and waterways, and in spite of financial panics and conflicts between labor and capital, between agriculture and industry, and between the partisans of high tariffs and free trade, there was building everywhere. Real estate operators were experimenting with housing developments for workers; the wealthy were inspired to indulge in lavish philanthropies that needed to be housed. These were days when there were no income taxes and a man might make as much as several million dollars a year while the men who worked for him might with luck make as much as four or five hundred. For architects good, bad, and indifferent these were halcyon days.

Hunt's fortunes continued to increase. He built town houses for the Elbridge T. Gerrys and the John Jacob Astors on Fifth Avenue and "cottages" for the Ogden Goelets, several for the O. H. P. Belmonts and for the Vanderbilts at Newport. If they inspired awe and envy by the massiveness of their façades, they bedazzled by the glitter and sumptuousness of their interiors. Entrance halls were two or three stories high, layer upon rich layer of balconies and balustrades, of carving and wrought iron, of chandeliers and sculptured nymphs and graces, of tremendous allegorical ceiling paintings and friezes. With a lavish hand he used white marble and pink marble and green marble and gold and still more gold. Hunt gave his clients Moorish rooms and Byzantine rooms and Palm Courts and Jacobean suites; bowls of orchids ornamented the marble-topped tables he helped his clients to select, exotic birds sang in Oriental cages he had suggested for their solariums, and the grand staircases would have been fit setting for a princess in train and coronet to descend to meet her courtiers. No wonder Hunt was the trusted darling of the New York rich. He was their taste and their sense of fitness.

But he was not spoiled by them. First of all he was an architect who exacted of himself the most rigid standards of scholarship, for he believed that his art reached its highest achievements, not by originality and inventiveness, but by an intelligent adaptation of the great styles of the past to the needs of the present. To him architecture was an accretion of the best that man had produced, and it little became the artist to throw away that heritage in favor of his own whims. Furthermore, he loved craftsmanship and he admired the men who worked for him, the artisans who built the walls and carved the details, who fitted the pipes, and laid the tiles. And they admired him in return and liked him for the respect he showed them and for his humor and his sympathy. One day when he was inspecting the work on the William K. Vanderbilt house on Fifth Avenue just before it was completed he noticed a small tentlike affair in the ballroom and he asked one of the stonecutters what it concealed. Inside was a life-size portrait figure of himself dressed as a workman with a mallet and chisel in his hands. The stonecutters had made it as a tribute to him, and

Vanderbilt was so pleased with his new palace that he permitted it to be installed high on the house.

By 1890 there was no question that Hunt, now sixty-three, was to most of his contemporaries the grand old master of American architecture. He had designed the base for the Statue of Liberty on Bedloes Island; he had put a new façade on the Metropolitan Museum and had built the Astor Library. He was at work on the plans for Biltmore and was soon to remodel Cornelius Vanderbilt's cottage at Newport, "The Breakers," a matter of alteration that cost its owner $3,000,000. There were those, to be sure, who preferred the kind of elegance that McKim, Mead, and White produced; their eclecticism was somehow less archaeological than Hunt's and seemed fresher and less ponderous. There were those who thought that Richardson was the greatest architectural genius that America had produced, but by the nineties he was dead at a tragically early age, his great promise only half-fulfilled. In the Middle West Louis Sullivan was immersed in the new aesthetic suggested to him by the use of steel construction and plate glass and there was a promising young draftsman named Frank Lloyd Wright working in his Chicago office. But when the Columbian Exposition was planned it was Hunt who was given the Administration Hall, the most prominent of all the buildings, to design.

"It was the World's Columbian Exposition of 1893," wrote Henry Steele Commager in *The American Mind* just a few years ago, "that condemned American architecture to the imitative and the derivative for another generation." But to the architects who planned it and the sculptors and painters who ornamented it, nothing so glorious had ever been offered to the American people. It was "The White City," gleaming with plaster of Paris. Every one of its tremendous structures was bedecked with heroic sculpture and fluttering flags and was reflected in Lake Michigan or in the lagoons or in the artificial pools. "As a scenic display," wrote Henry Adams, "Paris has never approached it," and no wonder. Frederic Law Olmsted and his young assistant Henry Codman had chosen the site and brought order out of a chaos of wasteland along the lake shore. The Chicago architects John Wellborn Root and Daniel H. Burnham, the most famous practitioners in the city, were given supervision over the architectural plans, but they felt that the exposition should represent the architects not merely of the Middle West but of the whole nation. Hunt's old pupil Henry Van Brunt and his partner, Frank M. Howe, were summoned from Kansas City; McKim, Mead and White from New York, Peabody and Stearns from Boston. "When . . . in 1893," wrote Van Brunt in his eulogy of Hunt, "several of us were summoned to act together again with him on the great national arena at Chicago, the natural dominance of the master again asserted itself without pretension, and we once more became his willing and happy pupils."

The result of his tutelage was an array of Beaux Arts classicism as white and richly ornamented as a congregation of royal brides. The hundreds of thousands of mustachioed men in bowlers and women in leg-of-mutton sleeves who wandered on foot, or were pushed in wicker "rolling chairs," or were wafted in the gondolas on the lagoons and reflecting pools gazed up at domes and lofty columns capped with acanthus leaves, at ranked arches and sculptures symbolizing every virtue known to man. Taller than all the rest was Daniel Chester French's colossal statue of The Republic, sixty-five feet from the hem of her dress to the laurel wreath that crowned her tresses. "See here, old boy," exclaimed Augustus Saint-Gaudens, under whose direction the sculpture was planned and erected, "do you realize that this is the greatest meeting of artists since the fifteenth century?" His question was directed to Burnham, and it was not, in his terms, without justification. Here were all the great architects of the day; here were Frederick MacMonnies and Daniel Chester French and Saint-Gaudens himself, all sculptors; here were painters—John La Farge, Mary Cassatt, Alden Weir, Kenyon Cox, Edwin Blashfield, Gari Melchers, an imposing congregation indeed. And the public was both bewildered and impressed.

"In the choice of the classic style," wrote Talbot Hamlin, a devoted admirer of the American Renaissance, "the consulting architects only symbolized popular taste; in the actual creation of the tremendously impressive group of buildings . . . they did more; they astonished, delighted, and fixed popular taste." To him the Exposition was "the symbol of the arrival at full birth of that which may be called modern American architecture."

Another observer was less sure of what the White City meant to

America. "One sat down to ponder on the steps beneath Richard Hunt's dome," wrote Henry Adams in his autobiography, "almost as deeply as on the steps of Ara Coeli and much to the same purpose. Here was a breach of continuity—a rupture in historical sequence! Was it real, or only apparent? One's personal universe hung on the answer for, if the rupture was real and the new American world could take this sharp and conscious twist towards ideals, one's personal friends would come in, at last, as winners in the great American chariot-race for fame. If the people of the Northwest actually knew what was good when they saw it, they would someday talk about Hunt and Richardson, LaFarge and Saint-Gaudens, Burnham and McKim, and Stanford White when their politicians and millionaires were otherwise forgotten. The artists and achitects who had done the work offered little encouragement to hope it; they talked freely enough, but not in terms that one cared to quote; and to them the Northwest refused to look artistic. They talked as though they worked only for themselves; as though art, to the Western people, was a stage decoration; a diamond shirt-stud; a paper collar; but possibly the architects of Paestum and Girgenti had talked in the same way, and the Greek had said the same thing of Semitic Carthage two thousand years ago."

In Hunt's mind there could have been little of the kind of concern that we now associate with the idea of an architecture for the people. Architecture to him meant grandeur in the classic tradition, something to look upon with awe and, if possible, with reverence, as one looked upon the possessors of vast fortunes with awe, even if reverence for most Americans was impossible to summon. Hunt's career, his artistic ambitions, and his aesthetic creed were inextricably interwoven with the emergence of a new aristocracy in this country, an aristocracy of wealth which, like Hunt's architecture, was ephemeral. A few of the houses he built for the rich still stand but the spirit that inspired them like the fortunes that built them has dwindled. Some, like Biltmore and The Breakers, are now open to tourists; some, like the William K. Vanderbilt house on Fifth Avenue, have disappeared; others stand empty with their lawns gone to hay and their gardens to brambles. The American Renaissance, the age of elegant eclecticism, passed from Private Taste to Public Taste and then to limbo.

Hunt was readying The Breakers for the arrival of the Vanderbilts at Newport when he died. In the last few years of his life honors had been heaped on him. He was the first architect to receive a doctor's degree from Harvard, and both Yale and Princeton had followed suit. He had been elected to the French Académie des Beaux Arts, an honor that, according to his obituary in the New York *Herald,* was "an implied compliment to American architecture as well." He had been made an honorary member of the Royal Academy of British Architects and was the only American to win its Gold Medal; he was an associate of the Society of Engineers and Architects of Vienna, and an academician of the Society of St. Luke in Rome, "the oldest institution devoted to arts in the world." For the last few years of his life he suffered "from cruel bodily distress" but he carried on with his profession until his sixty-eighth year, a "vigorous, virile, energetic, tempestuous character."

He died in his "cottage" at the head of Church Street in Newport where he had lived for more than twenty-five years and where his brother William had lived before him. "Every season the cottage and its extensive grounds resembled more a hotel than a private residence," a local reporter noted, "so many guests and visitors were constantly on hand." Newport was shocked, not just wealthy summer Newport but its permanent residents as well, for the Hunt family had become so closely identified with the affairs of the resort that they were looked upon by the natives more as permanent residents than as summer people.

One would expect the eulogies for such a man to be filled with rich and laudatory adjectives. From the members of his profession and from the press, they were, indeed, plentiful, flowery, and evidently sincere, for he was a man who made friends easily and kept them, and he had brought honor and position to his profession. One is less likely, however, to expect the following "resolutions" sent to his widow from the workmen of Baltimore and signed by representatives of the carpenters, bricklayers, stone cutters, plumbers, electricians, stonecarvers, tile layers, marble cutters, woodcarvers, coppersmiths and painters on account of "his generosity, sympathy, and services in behalf of the worthy laboring men of all classes . . . :

therefore we who have worked under him, deeming it fitting that we record our love and appreciation of him have

Resolved that in his death our country has lost its greatest architect, and our skilled workmen, artists and sculptors have lost a kind, considerate and constant friend, for neither his great fame nor his wealth ever caused him to be forgetful, indifferent, or careless of the rights and feelings of his fellow men and laborers who were aiding in an humbler way in erecting these beautiful buildings, which only marvelous genius could have imagined and planned. . . .

Resolved that to him more than any other man of our time all the representative workmen of this country are indebted for the elevation of their trades and arts to the position which they hold in the rank of the great army of skilled workmen.

Though he was not able to be on the job at The Breakers for the last two weeks of his life, and was forced to stay at home with what seemed to be "nervous prostration," he conducted his business from his bed. It was not until the night before he died that the doctors told his family that he seemed to be in danger.

"Upon his deathbed," his first pupil, Henry Van Brunt, told a gathering of the members of the American Institute of Architects in a final tribute to the most distinguished of its founders, "he was seen to raise his hand and, with the fine gesture of the artist, to trace as with a pencil in the air a line of beauty, delicately but firmly fitting the act of grace to the unconscious study of his imagination."

CHAPTER IX

Societies for Truth and Beauty

"Some of our social ideals are against art.
There are those of us who want to be artists
and give themselves, and yet want to be
gentlemen and hold themselves back."

Economic depressions treat artists no better than any other men who have to make their livings, but they do not do badly by the inspiring muses.

Just before the Centennial Exposition blossomed so confidently above the Schuylkill, financial panic had swept across the country. In the three years that preceded the fair and in the two that followed it some fifty thousand commercial enterprises in America had failed, and yet, as you will recall, there had never been so much interest in the arts. The "artistic craze," the Eastlake fad, and the rule of Queen Anne in architecture flowered in a swamp of economic despond.

Nearly twenty years later, when the White City made millions of Americans gasp with astonishment at the water-reflected splendor of the Beaux Arts in Chicago, the country was again in the grip of a depression—a far worse one than its predecessor. Three times as many businesses went under in 1893 as had disappeared in 1873; more than 550 banks failed, and railroads, large and small, went into receivership. Men in bands wandered the streets looking for work, and it was the next year that the few remaining members of Coxey's "army" to reach Washington were arrested for not "keeping off the grass" that Andrew Jackson Downing had planted for the Capitol grounds.

No longer ago than the 1930's the greatest depression of all brought into being the greatest experiment in government patronage of the arts that this country has ever seen. If the artists who worked "on relief" for the WPA Art Project produced more than the usual amount of mediocre and bad art, they also produced some good, and there is no denying that the depression was an era of uncommon fecundity in the arts in general. The muses were certainly busy. It was out of this Depression also that the New York World's Fair of 1939 grew on the bad lands of Long Island and established "modern" architecture once and for all as the *sine qua non* for commercial and industrial building.

But whether depressions have a salutary effect upon the arts or not (and there are scholars who argue that the High Renaissance was a period of comparable economic slump), it does seem that in times when business is bad and men are out of work, a great many people, and especially a great many women, not only take comfort but find busywork in promoting "the finer things of life." And so it was just after the Columbian Exposition. Suddenly there burgeoned in various parts of the country, and in the Middle West most of all, "study groups" and "art clubs" and "literary circles" and "cultural societies" enough to gladden the hearts of the most ardent artistic missionaries and the most devoted handmaidens of the muses.

But the flowering could not have come about if the soil had not been well prepared and the seeds broadly scattered.

In the decade that preceded the Columbian Exposition of 1893 museums and art schools had grown like mushrooms almost overnight in cities large and small all over the country. Cincinnati, the seat of the famous Rookwood Pottery Works, led all the rest. It was, as a writer in the *Century* said in 1886, "the first of the Western cities to be known as a home of picture collectors and it holds the first place at the present time in the amount of its recent gifts to art." It was mainly the German element of the city's population that had got behind a drive that raised something over a million dollars in six years to establish a veritable fortress of a museum and an art school on a hill overlooking the city. Joseph Longworth, grandson of the Nicholas Longworth who made himself famous as a horticulturalist and was a friend of Andrew Jackson Downing, made the first substantial contribution to the art school on the condition that it be separated from the University of Cincinnati and attached to the museum. The function of the school, in which there were more than four hundred young men and women enrolled by the mid-eighties, was not merely to train painters and sculptors; the marriage of the arts and industry that had been consummated at the Centennial Exposition was producing offspring at a prodigious rate, and most of the students were enrolled in classes in "woodcarving, decorative designing, metal-work, and industrial art." A high percentage of them, of course, took art training merely for the entertainment and cultural uplift that association with the arts afforded, and in most art schools of the day the young ladies outnumbered the young men by five or six to one.

Cincinnati was not alone. Chicago had its Art Institute housed in a Romanesque building designed by Burnham and Root, the architects who were later to have charge of the plans for the Columbian Exposition. Its moving spirits were Charles L. Hutchinson and Martin A. Ryerson, men whose temperaments and talents complemented each other and differed greatly. Hutchinson was an energetic money raiser and promoter, a banker who had inherited a fortune from a father who was known as a rowdy trader on the wheat exchange. Under the pressure of his enthusiasm the Art Institute soon outgrew its first permanent home and moved into its present far larger and more elaborate building. In his book *Battle for Chicago*, Wayne Andrews records that Hutchinson "when told that the trustees were considering the appointment of a conservative director, growled and said, 'I am afraid that they may get someone who will make a mausoleum out of the Institute instead of a three-ring circus.'" Ryerson was a quite different sort of man—studious, quiet, of Quaker-like manner and also, evidently, of Quaker-like business acumen. He was educated at Harvard and in Europe and was a lawyer by profession and a man of wealth by inheritance. It was he who was the eyes of the museum. He traveled in Europe, buying paintings for his own collection and for the Art Institute, and his taste, which was ahead of its time, was matched by his skill at purchasing. He bought pictures by the Impressionists, and especially by Renoir, at a time when, to say the very least, they were considered poor investments; they were, indeed, considered by most collectors and many critics of the day to be outrageous daubs and an insult to refined taste. As the result of Ryerson's perception the Art Institute has one of the richest collections of Impressionist pictures anywhere in the world.

St. Louis was ahead of Chicago in establishing a museum and so was San Francisco. Pittsburgh and Milwaukee did not get under way until the mid-eighties, and by that time there were art societies and museums even in such cities as Denver, Colorado, and Jacksonville, Illinois, not generally known in those days as seats of culture. Kansas City had a museum; the University of Michigan had "a growing collection"; Nashville, Tennessee, had a thriving "Art Association" for exhibitions. The fine arts, which were a stepchild of American culture in the days when the grocer Luman Reed had given up his business to collect art, were now the focus of a great deal of attention, the cause of the expenditure of a great deal of private as well as public funds, and the producers of a few artists whose work we still consider worth looking at.

Not everyone, to be sure, was equally enthusiastic about the ways in which art was being brought to the public, and the priggishness that had so disgusted Mrs. Trollope in the 1830's was still a matter to be reckoned with sixty years later. A medal that Augustus Saint-Gaudens was commissioned by the Government to design as the "prize medal" for the Columbian Exposition depicted on one side a scene of Columbus landing on the soil of America, and on the other side was the figure of a nude boy holding a shield on which the prize-winner's name would be engraved. "Then came the catastrophe," wrote Saint-Gaudens's son. "Previous to the striking of this medal, the Page Belting Company of Concord, New Hampshire, improperly obtained a copy and printed a caricature of it so villainous that the boy, who on the original stood as a bit of artistic idealism, appeared in all the vulgar indecency that can be conveyed by the worst connotation of the word nakedness. At once the morality for which our nation is notorious took fire." The hue and cry was considerable and the Government, as it always does in matters of art, took the path of caution and had a decorous substitute for the offending boy run up by one of the medalists at the mint.

In Massachusetts, just about a decade before the disgrace of Saint-Gaudens' naked youth, Governor Butler recommended that the legislature abolish the State Normal Art School because, he claimed, it had demonstrated its "uselessness" by the fact that the students modeled "nude human figures in clay." "Line drawing for industrial purposes," he insisted, was as far as any school supported by public funds should go.

The art that took the public fancy and also the fancy of that special group known as the "art public" was eminently decorous and uplifting, proclaiming the full calendar of virtues, domestic and heroic, in little pictures for the drawing room and massive murals for public buildings. It was art that baffled no one by its subtleties and shocked no one by revealing unpleasant truth. It was as though Keats had been rewritten to read, "What we think is beautiful is truth, and anything we do not think is beautiful is an outrageous lie." Blindfolded Justice looked down from public walls, nymphs wandered in idyllic groves, cows lowed in peaceful pastures, and children in lace collars hugged each other. It was on such painting as this that the art societies feasted in the name of culture.

"The development of 'the true artistic spirit,'" wrote an anonymous author in Scribner's in 1896, "which should 'beautify life and ennoble every industry,' has been, of course, the aim of all these creditable movements, but minor and more personal motives have not been wanting. It has even been asserted that social ambitions, the desire of prominent citizens to appear as art patrons, have been responsible for the birth of more than one promising art association."

Whatever the motives, however pure or however venal, in the economically despondent days following the Columbian Exposition the true believers and the merely ambitious banded together "for the promotion of art among the people."

Chicago, with all the liveliness of a young city that was determined to establish itself as the Athens of the West, was the most active of all, and of all the art societies that it boasted there was none so ambitious as the Central Art Association. Unlike the Art Union with its overtones of commercialism and its spicy element of gambling, the Central Art Association was as pure as the artistic sentiments it purveyed. But like the Art Union its influence spread far beyond the limits of the city in which its headquarters were located. It was

founded by Mrs. T. Vernette Morse of Chicago in March, 1894, and
in less than three months it held a general meeting in the Art Institute. Four years later it was incorporated and had three thousand
paying members, who if they lived in Chicago paid $5 a year and if
they lived elsewhere paid $3. It had ten departments: architecture,
ceramics, historical study, house decoration and industrial art, illustrating and engraving, municipal and public improvement, painting,
public school improvement, sculpture, and traveling exhibitions.
There was no aspect of the public's art sensibilities it was not prepared to tackle. Its general meetings, which were held annually,
became known as "art congresses," and one of the speakers who addressed the membership at the 1898 congress on the subject of "Art
in the Home" was a young architect named Frank Lloyd Wright.
In the following year two more departments were added, one for miniature painting and the other "the Truth and Beauty League for boys
and girls under eighteen." Within the year three thousand youngsters
had by hook or crook, but most likely by a mass concentration of the
committee on the department of "public school improvement," been
enrolled. By 1901 the Central Art Association and its publication, an
illustrated monthly called *Arts for America,* had, for reasons which
are obscure, disappeared from the public eye.

The short life of the Central Art Association was a merry one, full
of youthful zeal and backed by eager young men and women who
found the newness of Chicago an incentive not only to creative activity
but to spreading the artistic word. This young group met in the studio
of Lorado Taft, a bearded, clear-eyed, and even-featured young
sculptor in his early thirties who had recently returned from Paris,
and who had worked on statues for the Agricultural Building of the
Exposition. There Taft and Hamlin Garland and Charles Francis
Brown spent long evenings packing crates of paintings to send out to
cities and towns in the Middle West—an early experiment in the
traveling exhibitions which are now a regular part of the stock in
trade of such purveyors of taste as the Museum of Modern Art and the
American Federation of Arts. Garland was a novelist who though still
young had made a reputation, as the *Critic* magazine put it in 1898,
"because he has so exhaustively set forth his discontent with all kinds
of human conditions as to make himself a very satisfactory mouthpiece

for the dissatisfied." Brown was a painter, and the three of them called themselves "the Triumvirate." Their dissatisfaction was not with any apathy toward art but with the means of feeding those who hungered for it. "Taste has been considerably raised by reading," Garland wrote in a disquisition on the Central Art Association of which he was briefly the president. "The thing needed is contact with the actual work of the artist. Yet with all this crudeness and bad taste, there is a pathetic desire to do better. People, especially women, long to share in all that is brightest and best in art."

The Central Art Association gave its all to provide the "brightest and best." Their inspiration came from one of the most curious phenomena in the history of American culture—the movement known as Chautauqua. Anyone who was brought up in rural America and is over forty must remember the big circuslike Chautauqua tents with pennants flying from their poles and culture and entertainment and moral uplift filling their audiences with a vast sense of civic pride and wonder at the nobility of man and his works. But the Chautauqua that inspired the Central Art Association was a quite different matter from what it came to be after 1910, and it will pay us to digress for a moment to look at a movement that can only be explained by a nationwide hunger for some firsthand contact with the cultural aspects of life.

The founder of Chautauqua, a young minister from Camptown, New Jersey, named John H. Vincent, had not the slightest idea when he laid out an outdoor map of the Holy Land in a grove of trees near his little church that he was starting a unique movement in mass education. His purpose was, quite simply, to brighten up the teaching of Sunday school and to show young men and women how to conduct Sunday school classes. He was gratified at the numbers that turned out to follow him about his map as he talked, and he decided that he might expand his work by providing courses by mail to those who lived too far away to come to Camptown. In this simple way Vincent introduced "correspondence courses" for the first time to American education. His audience grew rapidly. Several years later he suggested to a friend in Akron, Ohio, that he would like to have a two-week summer session at some appropriate place, and his friend, Lewis Miller, suggested a defunct camp at Lake Chautauqua, New

York, of which he was a trustee. The first "summer school" (another new concept in American education) was opened at the lake in 1874 with forty young men and women, all very carefully chaperoned. By day they studied the Bible under the trees and during the evenings they sang songs by the shores of the lake to the light of campfires. The cost for the two weeks was $6 for each student. The food was good, the teaching excellent, the atmosphere eminently respectable, and the young people went away happy and filled with missionary zeal, not only for teaching the Bible, but for Camp Chautauqua.

It grew like wildfire. The two-week session was extended to two months, and the teaching of the Bible was expanded to the teaching of all sorts of "cultural" subjects. The camp grew into a tent city with thousands of tents and many more thousands of visitors who came from all over America. In the open air pavilions they sat enthralled by the wisdom and wit of statesmen and novelists, poets and humorists, critics and, of course, divines. There was scarcely a famous man or woman of the day who did not come sooner or later to speak to the audiences at Chautauqua. Six presidents of the United States lectured by the shores of the lake—Grant and Garfield, Theodore Roosevelt and Hayes, the martyred McKinley and the jovial Taft. Courses were given in science and philosophy and religion and music. The great singers and the great instrumentalists of the day and even a full symphony orchestra under the direction of Walter Damrosch gave concerts outdoors in "God's temple." Chautauqua became known as a university and by 1893 it was chartered by the State of New York to grant academic degrees.

Nothing so successful as this could exist for long without being imitated, and on the shores of lakes all over the country other Chautauquas, equally respectable and equally devoted to culture and uplift, were started to provide a haven for those who could not travel as far as upper New York State. By 1900 there were two hundred such centers of culture and propriety and, according to the Harvard philosopher William James who spoke at them, smugness. Hundreds of thousands of men and women flocked to the tent cities for their vacations and during the winter they pored over books selected from the seven hundred instructional or inspirational volumes that were issued under the Chautauqua imprint or read the *Chautauquan,* a monthly magazine.

Chautauqua was never greatly interested in the fine arts, except music, and it is not surprising that when the Central Art Association was established with its motto, "For the promotion of good art and its dispersion among the people" it should attempt to be, as Garland described it, "a sort of Chautauqua-system for the study of art." There were, as we have seen, a rapidly growing number of art societies in small cities and towns and it was this tangible evidence of interest that Taft and Garland and Brown and Mrs. Morse wanted to organize "into one central association for mutual aid." They offered those who joined the association not only traveling exhibitions (in which they daringly showed a few "impressionists") but also a lecturer with each show and an opportunity to purchase the pictures. They were so fearful that they might be suspected of commercialism, however, that at first they required checks for the payment of pictures to be made out in the artists' names; subsequently they let the local associations keep ten per cent of the purchase price to cover their expenses and to enable them to raise a little money for further exhibitions. Like Chautauqua, the association issued study courses (Taft was the director of the course in "modern art"), issued pamphlets on such subjects as "the principles of individualism and originality in art," and provided a "bureau of criticism" to which "young artists in isolated towns" might send their work "for helpful criticism."

Within the first couple of years the study courses had been adopted by "hundreds of clubs" and the ladies of the Middle West were following the pages of the Association's magazine with avidity. Janesville, Wisconsin, had held an exhibition of 150 pictures (at an expense of less than 50 cents a painting), the first ever to come to that city. Lincoln, Nebraska, had shown 100 pictures and many other towns and cities had hung the pictures sent them by the Association in hotels and empty stores and in the local libraries. A few towns had decided after this initial contact with art that they wanted "permanent galleries," and Peoria, which was then in the throes of planning a new public library, decided to tack a gallery onto the building. Everyone seemed pleased with the experiment—not only the ladies who were getting culture but, of course, the artists who were having work seen outside large cities for the first time.

For some artists the study groups and culture clubs offered a new kind of opportunity for supplementing their livelihood. One of the most popular of all the items on the varied Chautauqua menu had been the "chalk talks" in which the lecturer illustrated his spiel with pictures that he drew on a blackboard. Taking their hint from this, a number of artists, among them Lorado Taft, became lecturers who were much in demand and who unquestionably were responsible for bringing to many audiences their first opportunity to see how a genuine artist works. Taft, for example, started giving "clay talks," as he called them, as early as 1891 with an "entertainment to a small Evanston club, modeling a clay head into various shapes with running comment." He was astonished when he was paid the rich sum of $35 plus $10 for expenses. The talk was a tremendous success and from then on, according to his wife, "Lorado became a favorite and could have filled every evening with lecture engagements. His beautiful speaking voice and clear enunciation were a great asset." (His good looks must also have been an asset with the ladies of his audiences.) In all, he gave fifteen hundred "clay talks" and his fee went up to $300 plus the expense of shipping nine barrels of clay and models.

The pattern set by the Central Art Association, short-lived though the organization was, was a great deal closer to our present methods of promoting the arts than it was to anything that had happened before. It combined showmanship with earnestness of purpose, entertainment with cultural uplift, and enthusiasm with an infinite belief in the American public's ability to absorb the "finer things of life." The traveling exhibitions, lectures, study courses, and art congresses presented the most completely unified attack on taste that had ever been launched by a small, eager group of artists and art lovers in America. The ways in which our larger museums today attempt to spread their influence beyond their walls into the community, and beyond the immediate community into the hinterland owe a great deal to the ideas that originated in the effluvium of enthusiasm that came in the wake of the Columbian Exposition.

The culture and art clubs of the nineties were, like the women's clubs of today, the social and intellectual outlets of middle-class matrons. But in the excitement about the arts the lower classes were by no means forgotten; they, too, were exposed to Truth and Beauty, and if they were less reverent in their attitude toward the art to which they were introduced than the ladies of the study groups, they seemed to have a gayer and livelier time of it.

The lower classes were not nestling birds with their beaks open waiting for someone to drop in the morsel of art. Quite the contrary. When Mr. A. C. Bernheim of New York returned from London in the spring of 1892, he was filled with enthusiasm and a sense of dedicated purpose. He had seen at Toynbee Hall, an institution of free learning in a slum district of England's capital, an art exhibition which had been arranged to give the poor a chance to refresh their spirits with contemporary paintings. Bernheim saw no reason why the lower classes of his own city should not be given a similar opportunity to become acquainted with art, and he approached the University Settlement Society with his suggestion. The Society took kindly to the idea, but the labor leaders did not. It must be remembered that these were days when "the class struggle" was no mere matter of negotiation, mediation, and sweet reasonableness; these were days when strikes were pitched and bloody battles, when militiamen shot down workers in railroad yards, and scabs and pickets battled quite literally to the death. "The robbed and the robbers cannot sincerely fraternize," said one of the Socialist labor leaders with classic Marxian fervor, "especially when the robber comes asking the robbed to accept as a favor a few crumbs from the feast which is the creation of the latter. . . . The Labor Movement is a class movement, and nothing should be done to weaken the class spirit." Another "radical" taunted those who wanted to set up the exhibition by calling them "seekers after notoriety." But art prevailed over politics and the exhibition opened on June 20 in rented rooms at the corner of Grand and Allen Streets.

There were sixty-six oil paintings and watercolors in the show, and twenty sketches in black and white, and at the risk of weakening the class spirit people flocked to the little galleries to see them. The show was open for forty-one days and in that brief time more than thirty-six thousand East Siders came to look. "The result was," wrote Mr. Bernheim, "that the most bitter and radical of the Socialists became our firmest friends and worked incessantly as 'runners' guiding droves of people to the exhibit. . . . Night after night their leaders might be heard explaining, in glowing terms, the special merit of this masterpiece and that particular school of painting, to groups of earnest listeners."

The lectures of the labor leaders, who evidently decided that if they couldn't lick the forces of uplift they had better join them, have unfortunately not been preserved, but some of the reactions of the common folk have been. Among the pictures exhibited were landscapes by the American Bierstadt and the French Barbizon painters, Daubigny and Corot; there were canvases by the dapper and eccentric William Merritt Chase, by Winslow Homer and the popular French master of Roman circuses, Gérôme. Those who came to the exhibition were asked to vote for their favorites. On the whole they seemed to prefer story pictures to landscapes, and they heartily disliked the Impressionists. "Why, that isn't painting," one visitor said of an impressionist landscape. "That's paint."

Inspired, or perhaps nettled, by New York's success, Bostonians decided to do as much for their poorer citizens and in the winter and spring of 1892-93 they held shows in the North End and South End of the city. The latter was opened in a large wardroom of the old Franklin schoolhouse on March 13 with the Lieutenant Governor presiding. "This show," said one of the visitors, "lays it all over the Art Museum; it's *fresher goods*."

Andover House, a settlement for men, and the Women's College Settlement arranged the exhibition, abetted by a committee of "artists, business and professional men, and women given to good works." About fifteen hundred people a day came to look at the hundred pictures, "the best in Boston," and they were shown about by art students, Wellesley College girls, artists, and "young women of society," who tried to explain the virtues of art. The most popular painting in the show, in the opinion of the men, was "The Village Smithy" by Henry Sandham. The women gave their hearts to "Sleeping Innocence," a nude child by Léon Perrault, and A. H. Munsell's "portrait of the little deaf-mute Helen Keller." The children's vote went strongly for a picture of a spaniel called "Correy" by Elizabeth Strong, who caused a sensation by bringing the "flesh and blood" dog to the exhibition one afternoon. "The children's glee was unbounded."

"Though many have been led to visit the Art Museum through

this exhibition," a reporter wrote in *Harper's Weekly*, "it would be idle to say that any strong artistic impulse has been given to the majority of these people; but into the minds and souls of hundreds of them a light has surely come from another world—a world in which sordidness and toil are not the only things of moment, and where it may be seen that there is other work to be done besides that of brawn."

The famous Jane Addams of Chicago's Hull House also believed strongly in the spiritual value of art and wrote in 1895 of "the attempt of Hull House to make the aesthetic and artistic a vital influence in the lives of its neighbors." With her friend and colleague Ellen G. Starr providing the requisite taste and knowledge of the arts, Hull House gave courses in History of Art to "large and enthusiastic classes" and made available to the neighborhood a "small circulating loan collection" of reproductions of paintings. They were "choice things" ancient and modern, and so popular were several color prints of Fra Angelico angels that the neighbors had to sign up weeks in advance for them. To one woman, the wife of a drunkard who had once been a member of the state legislature, the art at Hull House was her only tie with the finer things she had once known. Another woman, who had lost a second child, borrowed a Fra Angelico angel to hang over the dead child's crib, an improvement, Miss Addams noted, over the wreath of wax flowers that marked the first child's crib.

Miss Addams and Miss Starr believed in quality and they also believed that art was most effectively administered in small doses. Practicing what she professed, Miss Starr started the "Art in Schools" movement by finding a few good examples with which to decorate classrooms in schools in the Hull House neighborhood. The Chicago Woman's Club was quick to see her example as a project to which they might well devote themselves and set up a separate society for "the decorating of all the public schools in the city."

This was in 1895. The taste of all ages and classes of Americans was under attack from many different directions and the surge of aesthetic gospeleering that swept the country in the nineties inspired chauvinistic smugness. Julian Ralph, who made a journey through the West in this same year, was dismayed to discover artistic provin-

cialism in such cities as Cleveland and Minneapolis, and was shocked
by the "hearty contempt" with which an art student spoke to him
of "the un-Americanism of those who go to Paris from this country
to study art." "I have no patience with such folk," the student, a young
lady, had said to him; "they think it a sign of strength to prefer
foreign teaching, whereas it is only a fashion set by weak and silly
people who ape everything that is foreign." It was not a new argument; Emerson had said much the same sort of thing many years
before, but it was surprising from the young and adventurous who,
up to now, had dreamed first of Rome, then of Düsseldorf and
Munich, and then of Paris as the Meccas to which every aspiring
artist should go for training and inspiration.

America's satisfaction with its own art was demonstrated several
years later as the century came to a close, in a new and conclusive
manner that businessmen and housewives understood very well.
When Thomas B. Clarke's collection of American paintings was sold
at auction it brought the unprecedented sum of nearly $250,000.
The auctioneer, who was an old hand at disposing of art goods, both
foreign and domestic, said at the end of the four-day sale that it was
"the greatest which he had ever conducted and that it would be
more far-reaching in its results than any other sale ever held in this
country." A landscape by George Inness called "Gray Lowering Day"
was knocked down for $10,150 and "the American public realized
for the first time that America had produced a great artist." Clarke
had bought the picture originally for $300. Inness's "Delaware Valley"
brought $8,100 from the Metropolitan Museum in New York and
paintings such as Winslow Homer's "Eight Bells" and "The Life
Line" sold for prices "in the thousands."

Just a few years before only Gérômes and Meissoniers, Corots and
Daubignys and Rousseaus would have brought such prices, and only
works by such men were considered worth imitating by the picture
forgers who are always on hand to run up masterpieces to meet the
demands of avid, if not expert, collectors. No better proof of the
arrival of American art, no more specific measure of the value that
was placed on it by collectors, need be found than the fact that in
the late nineties, after the Clarke sale, the fraudulent picture factories started to turn out "Innesses." On a somewhat higher plane

the interest in American art also took a tangible form. The Art Institute of Chicago prepared a special gallery for American paintings. The trustees of the Metropolitan in New York in 1899 were discussing the possibility of following Chicago's lead. "There is every indication," wrote Gustav Kobbe in the *Forum*, "that a wave of development in American art is now sweeping over the country. . . ."

There were others who were not so sure that the millennium had arrived. No one seemed to be able to make the Government in Washington take any interest in the fine arts at all. "The official tendencies," wrote a commentator who was heartily trying to see only the bright side, "are most hopelessly adverse." And even if Andrew Carnegie had founded an institute in Pittsburgh and had given $40,000 "to be expended in the purchase of paintings . . . to be placed in a chronological collection intended to represent the progress of American Art beginning with the year 1896," there were those who wondered just what the arts really meant to most Americans.

"The spread of common school education is against us," wrote the novelist Henry B. Fuller in the *Bookman* in the last year of the century; "everybody can read and write. This is the age of waste paper—of 'widely diffused intelligence.' Art has had its great days when scarcely anybody could read and write." He was anticipating an argument that was to be heard again after the Second World War when intellectuals, appalled by the havoc that they believed the mass media had wreaked upon the public taste, again began to worry about the destruction of real discrimination by indiscriminate education. "We have neither respect nor reverence," Fuller went on. "As has been well said, we are the best half-educated people in the world. We have lost untutored man's capacity for reverence, yet have not reached the capacity for respect that follows upon well-grounded instruction. . . . Furthermore there exists among us an incorrigible propensity to live life rather than to represent it, or discuss it, or to speculate on it. We have a wonderfully fine opportunity to live, and we are taking full advantage of it—like the good and normal Occidentals that we are."

From the perspective of a little more than half a century, Fuller's observations seem to us justified. It is difficult for us to see much value in the art that his contemporaries were most ardently supporting. We look in vain, as we did at the time of the Centennial, among the accounts of the art associations of these days for public acclaim of Eakins or of Ryder, the two artists who have most prominently survived from those days, two men who kept largely to themselves, one a realist, one a romantic. And in spite of all the busy people in the Central Art Association, all the exhibitions for the working classes, and the art schools of the Middle West; in spite of all the high prices paid at the Clarke sale, and the new galleries of American art in the museums, we cannot but wonder if perhaps Fuller may not have said what was in the backs of the minds of a great many ardent missionaries of truth and beauty when he pronounced: "Art today is a poor creature who finds herself in a position sadly false; the circumstances of the case make it inevitable that she should cause trouble for herself and for everybody else. She is a trial, a burden, a bother. . . . Let us not deplore our ineptitude for art, but let us put a stop to mistaken endeavor and call a halt on misapplied energy. . . ."

CHAPTER X

The Peacock on the Newel Post

"It has even been said that the future house
will be of glass."

By the nineties the wilderness in which the prophets of taste were
crying was largely man-made. Half a century had passed and
more since the days when Andrew Jackson Downing warned that so
long as men continued to live in log huts there would be lynch law
and justice would be administered by the bowie knife. The fad for
Gothic cottages and Tuscan villas had come and was gone, leaving
its litter as well as its few jewels on the landscape, and most people
thought it was good riddance. The star of Eastlake had risen like a
rocket, exploded in a great burst, and, to all intents and purposes, had
disappeared, its high-minded idealism buried under a glut of badly
made furniture. The White City in Chicago had convinced most
people that there was nothing vulgar about white paint after all and
that the morality of aesthetics did not require a man to paint his
house in somber hues that melted into the landscape. The development
of a practical elevator following Elisha Graves Otis's invention in the
1850's had made the skyscraper a possibility, and the persistence and
imagination of steel salesmen had finally ignited a few architects, first
in Chicago and then in New York, with a sense of the possibilities
of a new kind of structure.

The man-made wilderness was certainly not a desert, and it was
fast becoming a jungle. Cities were growing both vertically and
horizontally and for the most part without plan or caution. Skyscrapers
of twenty stories astonished urbanites in the nineties and confirmed

them in their conviction that the wonders which industry and invention and "progress" could achieve were endless. To the rich who financed them they were a new kind of castle—this time in the air —filled with the promise of treasure. To the architects who designed them they were temples—no matter to what deity; it was enough to be able to dream on such a scale. If very few of their dreams turned into masterpieces, their buildings were at least the foothills of our present urban landscape, which many men consider, when seen from a distance, to be of impressive beauty.

Beautiful as our skyscraper cities may be, no one has ever had the temerity to call them tasteful. For all the efforts to control taste, to lead it, to entice it and flatter it into refinement, men and women in the nineties, as they do now, seemed to go their own irresponsible way, making silly fads of the most serious aesthetic doctrine and turning the reasonable into the ridiculous. But they did not do it without the help of those who were, by their own account, supposed to be the mentors of taste. The American "passion to sell," as Louis Sullivan called it, brought wave after wave of contradictory advice about the nature of good taste and panacea after panacea by which everyone might be saved from a fate worse, if possible, than unstylish draperies.

We are likely to consider the nineties as the nadir of American taste—the last gasp of the Victorian era with all it implies of clutter, of bric-a-brac, of tassels and fringe and flowered carpets. But while this is true in part, it is true only in the sense that there is no sharp demarcation between one era of taste and the next. By no means all of the art manufactures of the Centennial were broken or stowed away in the attic nor was the spirit of the Centennial with its emphasis on craftsmanship by any means dead. Many people still lived in substantial Tuscan or Mansard villas, the plan books of the day still encouraged the laboring man and the white collar worker to build houses in something very close to the Queen Anne manner, with all of its excrescences of spindles and balconies and towers, if few of its basic virtues.

But if the old hung on in some of its dreariest aspects it was for no lack of new ideas of how man's taste should express itself. Some of these ideas were, as we have seen, efforts to imbue the populace with the sense of "truth and beauty" as it was conceived by the art associations and culture clubs. Others were attempts, like Downing's, half a century earlier to make men lead more reasonable lives in more tasteful surroundings. In the last decade of the century the "quaint" was no longer fashionable but the "artistic" was. Traces of the romantic stayed on and the exotic was popular; the peacock that had once embellished the lawns of stately homes now moved indoors and stood, stuffed, on the newel post. Some of the clutter was gone: the fancy bric-a-brac and china dogs were replaced with ornamental plates from Holland, and tiles from Japan which were no longer displayed in whatnots but on "plate rails" high enough on the wall to avoid the casual shoulder that might knock them off. Handicrafts, especially those that William Morris, the English reformer, would have approved were held in high esteem. Stained glass for the home was coming into its own and ceilings, so lofty in the sixties and seventies, were coming down. In general the air seemed less musty, the rooms less somber, and the out-of-doors more friendly. Americans of the middle class were entering the "era of good taste"—of safe and sound taste, of refinement that could be acquired by the use of simple formulas found especially in the *Ladies' Home Journal*, in encyclopedias of the household, and in books on homemaking. Never before in America had it been so easy to have "good taste" as it was in the mid-nineties. Only those who could not read need have had a shadow of a doubt.

". . . if it be granted for the sake of argument," wrote Edith Wharton and Ogden Codman, Jr., in their book *The Decoration of Houses* in 1897, "that a reform in house-decoration, if not necessary, is at least desirable, it must be admitted that such reform can originate only with those whose means permit any experiments which their taste may suggest." And then the authors put the responsibility squarely on the kind of client that Hunt had so successfully wooed. "When the rich man demands good architecture his neighbors will get it too."

The double optimism of this statement—that the rich might demand good rather than just showy architecture and that if they did it would raise the level of the taste of those who could afford far less —is the very essence of the philosophy of the era of good taste. Both Downing and Eastlake deplored the extravagances of the rich, especially the new rich, and relied on the good common sense of plain people to raise the level of taste by looking at architecture and decoration for their essential usefulness. But the rich were a great deal richer by the end of the century than they had been twenty-five or fifty years before, and they were both more isolated socially and more powerful politically. Relatively few men and women understood the ways in which the great fortunes were amassed—the buying and selling and trading and pyramiding of railroads and steel corporations, the cornering of markets and the breath-taking bravado and cunning with which competitors were left penniless. The mystery that surrounded their financial operations sharpened the popular appetite for information about their lives. They lived, as a consequence, in the glare of a publicity that they contended was distasteful and beneath them but which at the same time the ostentatiousness of their houses and parties openly invited. Their social life, like their business life, was intensely competitive, and characteristically the men left to their wives not only the strategy of social competition but also most matters of taste.

It is not surprising that in the nineties taste and private wealth should have been more closely identified in most people's minds than they are today. The corporation as a patron of the arts and not infrequently as an experimenter with advanced ideas in architecture, with a mixed chorus of public relations voices to proclaim both corporate and artistic virtues, was a phenomenon as yet unknown. The rich man went his own way and neither his business nor his corporate behavior was anybody's affair but his own, and in his private life and private taste he was, presumably, beholden to no one. When it was the mood of the extremely rich man and his wife to spend millions of dollars on all sorts of objects of art with which to decorate and embellish a house that had already cost a fortune, it is no wonder that to most people the exercise of real taste was something reserved to those who could pay handsomely for it.

The idea that good taste can only filter down from the rich to the poor, as though by reverse osmosis, is an aristocratic tradition, and when there is a single closely knit aristocracy of wealth, prestige, power, and education as there was in the eighteenth century, it has some validity. But in a time like our own, when there are many aristocracies—the leaders of business, the intellectuals, the peers and peeresses of the entertainment world—competing to set the standards of taste, the idea that what is good for the rich will be good for everyone seems ludicrous. It raises the same kind of half-amused and half-shocked reaction as Secretary of Defense Wilson's remark that "what is good for General Motors is good for the country."

But what Edith Wharton saw around her in the days when Lenox and Bar Harbor and Stockbridge and Newport harbored the very cream of expensive taste was a long way from the confused social pattern of today. Ward McAllister's "four hundred" socially acceptable families meant something very specific in the American social structure. Those who were in it took it with deep seriousness; many who were not in it desperately wanted to be, and those who could not possibly aspire to it, or thought it ludicrous, at least did not deny that it existed. Here was a phalanx, in tight formation, that could be made into shock troops to attack bad taste. The strategy omitted one vital consideration: when most people imitate the rich they take the show and leave the subtleties, and in the process they bury their natural sensibilities under an icing of socially acceptable clichés.

What happened when the followers of the Hunts and the Stanford Whites who built so lavishly for the very rich began to repeat the pattern on a more modest scale for the merely well-to-do, and finally for the families of moderate means?

The emerging businessman aspired to be an aristocrat—not merely the Carnegies and the Morgans and others of great wealth, but lesser successful men—and there was a reaction against those kinds of architecture that were considered bourgeois. The American Renaissance that Hunt had been so prominent in starting set a pattern that humbler men than Vanderbilts aspired to, and so the architecture that had satisfied their fathers was not for them. "The art prophet which this bourgeois epoch produced," said the architect Joy Wheeler Dow of the Gothic and the Queen Anne periods, "corresponded exactly to it —just such a one as might be naturally expected—John Ruskin, old fogy with ideas of no practical value to communicate to the world." Dow was by no means a first-rate architect, but he was a successful one who built a good number of substantial houses for substantial families, and in his book *American Renaissance, a Review of Domestic Architecture,* published just after the turn of the century, the full fire of the disciple burns brightly and throws its light on the attitudes of architect and client alike.

It was he who said that an angel had whispered "Adaptation" in Hunt's ear and changed the course of American architecture, and since adaptation in a great variety of very odd, sometimes entertaining, and often ridiculous forms was to flower with the profusion of dandelions on the landscape for another three decades, it is worth letting Dow have his say. Here in its purest essence is the adapter at work:

"The right way to adapt a French château for an American house," he explained, "is really to make believe to restore one, pretending for the nonce that one is M. Pierre Lescot, M. Claude Perrault, or M. Gabriel, and that the king or some grand seigneur of the realm has commanded one's services for the purpose." He then demonstrates from his own practice, and there can be no doubt that his client was flattered to be likened to a king or a grand seigneur.

As in the elevation of the house for Mrs. H. at Morristown I made believe to myself that the medieval *tour* was genuine, already there, but requiring immediate restoration. It was easy to set imaginary masons to work pointing the machicolations and curtain. I made believe that long disuse had vanquished the portcullis, leaving its yawning pockets to be disposed of. Commercialism said, "Wall them up." Not I. It would be a pity to lose a particle of the 13th century atmosphere that consents to linger. So I decided upon a bold innovation as the privilege of adaptation. I could anchor the chains for holding up the glass canopy over the carriage entry, in those pockets that once housed the arms of the portcullis, and thus the spooky old *tour* could be saved intact. The main part of the American château is in this case supposedly modern, developed from motives supplied by the minor châteaux of France—the *manoirs,* the *fermes,* with a little American household planning within, necessary for convenience.

Dow does not record how Mrs. H. of Morristown liked her ghostly tower or the slight touch of American household planning that he allowed her for convenience. It almost seems as though neither he nor his client in their mutual thirteenth-century dream world much cared. The point was the dream, not the reality, in just the same way that the ranch house set on a suburban quarter of an acre embodies the dream today.

The dream took many forms, by no means all of them medieval and French. The Swiss chalet was considered especially suitable to the domestic needs of Americans, as were houses inspired by the architecture of Norway and Sweden and Japan. But more important than these was a new interest in America's own past. A Colonial revival, which McKim, Mead, and White introduced, was beginning to spot the countryside as early as the eighties with columned houses with Palladian details in the windows and cornices. Dow recommended them for their "symmetry, restfulness, and good proportion" and noted that "the closer the adaptation, up to a certain point, the greater the success." The skyscraper was a puzzle to most architects; it was no easy trick to adapt a French château to a building that went up twenty or so stories—a precipice punctured with windows. But the architects were undaunted. To look at their skyscrapers one would never guess that the walls were hung on a steel frame and had nothing to do with holding the building up, and Greekish temples and dormered Mansard roofs and Renaissance palazzi sat atop cliffs of brick.

The interiors of the houses were likely to carry out the general spirit of the exterior in their architectural details, and houses that were châteaux outside were likely, for example, to have carved banisters within. But in general the architect's job stopped with the shell and the decoration was left to the client. Edith Wharton and Codman thought this a shocking situation and they claimed that theirs was the first book on *"house decoration as a branch of architecture"* to be published in America or England in fifty years. Not everyone, of course, could afford a new house and the luxury of matching interiors with external styles. Most people were stuck with what they had, and their problem was to touch up the shell as best they could (a coat of white paint, for example, to cover the old browns and dark reds) and to make the interiors as modish as possible.

Modishness in the nineties had a decided air of gentility as opposed to stylishness, the well-bred scent of lavender as opposed to the racy scent of musk. The wives of men in the professions—the law or banking or just coupon clipping—looked down their noses at the wives of men who were in trade. Being "well bred" was more important than being rich, and being both was the key to acceptance in many circles. The mood was very different from the egalitarianism of

Andrew Jackson's day; very different from our own. There was an
aristocracy that took itself seriously; between the rich and the poor
there was a deep and wide canyon, and the bridges across it were few.

The houses in which the gentlemen and the ladies of the nineties
lived emphasized this. If the very rich were princes, the well-to-do
were squires, their walls hung with trophies of the chase or the battle-
field—actual or simulated—or of travel to the Orient or Europe or at
least to the local bazaars where such trophies might be purchased for
decorative purposes. But the key to gentility was "harmony." "Better a
short shrift and the coldest of conventions," said *The Woman's Book*
in 1894, "than the personal impress on walls and in decorations that
violates the laws of harmony, and offends good taste." The key to
harmony was to keep everything in a low but not a somber key—no
loud colors, no gaudy rugs or curtains or wallpapers. Woodwork was
stained "golden oak" and not painted, dadoes were high and above
them the walls were papered in simple floral patterns, preferably
tulips and lilies, or stenciled with basket-weave patterns or fleurs-de-lis
designed by such tasteful craftsmen as Louis C. Tiffany. Suitable
pictures for the living room were etchings or engravings or best of
all, "autotypes of famous works of art"—the sepia photographs from
Alinari in Florence of Leonardo's "Last Supper," Guido Reni's "The
Chariot of Phaeton," or the two fat-faced little cherubs from the bottom of the "Sistine Madonna." Bric-a-brac of the frilly sort was replaced by vases of "Favrile" glass of astonishing iridescence; and in
place of baskets of ferns hung by chains in the bay windows, fan leaf
palms stood in gleaming brass pots in the corners. The fad for the
Oriental was at its peak, thanks to such painters as Whistler and
Mary Cassatt, who had discovered the simple beauties of Japanese
prints in Paris and made much of them in their paintings. Whistler
especially, with his extraordinary capacity for using his eccentricities
to publicize his works, had appealed to the "artistic" housewives.
It was he who introduced the palely tinted or white walls on which
hung Japanese prints of doubtful quality. Vases filled with flowers gave
way to single pine boughs or stalks of iris carefully arranged in the
Japanese manner. Even lanterns and parasols came indoors.

It was the day of the cozy corner, the inglenook, and the Oriental
booth. In the corners of living rooms, not only of houses but of city

apartments, housewives arranged curtains and sofas and cushions to make what were almost rooms within rooms. A few yards of striped material, a few curtain rods spiked with spearheads, a cot, and a batch of pillows were enough to make something an Arab could have called home—a tent. "Starting with the idea that what we do shall be an aesthetic solace, indicative of one's personality," wrote the author of the decorating column in the *Ladies' Home Journal* in 1896, "let us consider the practical construction of the Oriental booth." The Turkish corner was popular, with its hookah, mother-of-pearl furniture, ottomans, and imitation oil lamps issuing a dim mysterious light. For a Japanese corner a parasol suspended from the ceiling with bamboo curtains hanging from its edges, and a round settee beneath made a cozy place for decorous conversation. The simple inglenook could be made by putting high-backed benches on either side of the fireplace or in a bay window. Its distant descendant in our own time is the breakfast nook.

But these were the details of decoration. At the heart of the matter there were changes that presaged a new attitude toward the home, a new feeling for space and airiness. Furniture was getting lighter and bamboo and wicker were increasingly popular, not only for the porch but for the living room as well and for the study and bedroom. Life on the veranda became more important, indeed the piazza, as it was more often called, became an outdoor room with swings hanging by chains from the ceiling, wicker tables stacked with magazines, bamboo chaises longues, elaborate Moorish rush chairs and rugs of grass or even Persian carpets on the floor. Porches began to be glassed in and registers for hot-air heating were arranged so that the outdoor rooms could be used all year round. "It is significant that we are no longer afraid to live in glass houses," wrote Mary Gay Humphreys in *The Woman's Book* in 1894. "It has even been predicted that the future house will be of glass."

Glass served most of the same functional purposes in those days that it does now, but it also served decorative ones that today we think of as ludicrous. The panes on porches were likely to be small, but there was a device then as now known as a picture window—a far cry from its namesake in the modern house. The revival of stained glass was hailed as a minor renaissance in the 1890's and America was especially proud of two artists who were thought to rival the great stained-glass artisans of the Middle Ages. The painter John La Farge was one of them; he designed many windows for churches and for secular buildings, both domestic and public, and was an ardent champion of the medium. The other was an eccentric and talented man named Louis Comfort Tiffany.

Two prominent figures of the nineties, one of them Tiffany and the other the editor of the *Ladies' Home Journal*, Edward Bok, practiced what Edith Wharton preached. They both believed that the taste of the rich was the avenue to the taste of the middle and lower classes, and in their quite different ways they took upon themselves the problem of the public sensibilities. Tiffany's method was by artistic manufacture and by personal example; Bok's was by practical editorial interpretation.

Tiffany was both an innovator and a distorting mirror; he not only reflected the advanced tastes of his time but he made them somewhat grotesque. He was a tastemaker and an artist, businessman and craftsman, dilettante and patron.

In five-and-ten-cent stores today you will find a kind of orange iridescent glassware—plates and bowls and tumblers and vases—for which Tiffany, though he would be shocked, is directly responsible. You will look almost in vain in antique stores and secondhand shops for the glass that Tiffany himself designed. Very little of it comes on the market, for those who have it, though it has long since gone out of fashion and is only just coming back in, are unwilling to part with it. Whatever may be its qualities of design, sometimes simple and sometimes elaborately ornamented, there can be no question about the quality of the material of which it is made. It is heavy, it is extremely lustrous, and its colors at their best are astonishingly subtle. The five-and-ten-cent version of Tiffany glass is a mockery of the taste with which Tiffany sought to imbue his customers in the nineties. His following was a prosperous one, for his wares were not cheap, and the fad for Tiffany glass lasted well into this century. His lampshades of tinted and stained glass in an era when colored glass was an almost inevitable part of the decoration of every house were widely copied, usually in fancied-up versions; a real Tiffany glass lamp was a prized

possession of those who could afford a piece from the master craftsman's own "studio."

Tiffany was a man of extravagant fancies and exotic tastes; he was
inventive, eccentric, and versatile. There was hardly any form of art
at which he did not try his hand. He was a painter, decorator, glass
maker, jeweler (he was the son of the Tiffany of the Fifth Avenue
jewelry store), rug designer, and landscape architect. In each of
these activities he was something of a sport, never working quite in
the mode of his day, though never far from it. He was more of an
exaggerator than a revolutionary, and whatever he turned his hand to
had an outlandish quality. When, for example, he was asked by the
National Theater in Mexico City to design a "glass curtain" he produced a tremendous landscape that included views of the two vol-
canoes that tower above the city. It was a mosaic that weighed twenty-
seven tons, was composed of two hundred panels each three feet
square, and in all included nearly a million pieces of Favrile glass,
"inlaid into a concrete composition." It was obviously a permanent
installation and not a curtain in the ordinary theatrical sense.

When he decorated his own apartments in New York and his
house at Oyster Bay, Long Island, he was scarcely less elaborate, and
when he permitted a book, *The Art Work of Louis C. Tiffany*, to be
published about himself, the same spirit of exotic richness pervaded
not only the prose but the very paper (10 copies on parchment and
502 on hand-made Japan paper—none for sale) and the binding of
red leather, tooled and covered with gilt. This book, which appeared
without the name of an author on its title page, was dedicated "To My
Children" and explains in the foreword that it was written at the
children's insistence because it was against Tiffany's principles to
talk shop at home. "It is this condition . . . which caused their father,"
the foreword says, "to listen to their reproaches and overcome his
natural dislike of anything that savors of selfseeking. . . ." According to
a penciled notation in the copy in the Century Club library (Tiffany
was a "Centurion") the book was written by Charles de Kay; it was
filled with color plates of Tiffany glass, of jewelry which he designed,
and of his paintings. There were also views of his several places of
residence decorated by himself.

One of his homes was on the top floors of an apartment house in

New York called The Bella. Here, as a sample, is how de Kay describes it in part: "As you entered from the lift you found yourself in a lobby, lighted with stained glass, which reached high into the peak of the gable where the beams themselves showed in a rich dull color scheme lighted here and there with plates and studs of bronze, the broad surfaces of the beams showing the knots and grain of the wood. The roof slopes were set with glass tiles to aid the light from the windows, and the windows themselves were made up of rounds of glass of uneven thickness." The walls were India red and the stained-glass window sash was so heavy that an arrangement of pulleys and chains was needed to lift them. Of another apartment atop a building designed for Tiffany by McKim, Mead, and White at Madison Avenue and Seventy-second Street de Kay wrote, "As one enters the studio the vestibule is like a bit from the palace of an Indian Rajah. Beams and trim are carved wood from Hindustan and the wall supports a trophy of curious Indian weapons. The organ loft is full of growing flowers and big oriental vases. Colored tiles . . . iridescent glass, and shelves full of Keramics in subdued tones meet the eye in every direction."

Tiffany's house in Oyster Bay was even more fantastic, with a tremendous dragon spitting water into a pool in the garden, with peacock feathers in brass pots on the mantels, and grottoes made of glass. But all of this was not far in spirit from what *The Woman's Book* of the day recommended. It was much the same as the *Ladies' Home Journal*'s Turkish Corner and Oriental Booth. But it was more so. It was all part of the craft movement inspired by William Morris in England; but it was the craft movement gone slightly berserk. It owed much to the Oriental fad that affected Whistler and Degas and Manet, but it was the Oriental influence with sound and scent effects, with organs and incense. When Tiffany got hold of an idea (and he got hold of the Orient by traveling in the Near East as a young man) no elaboration of it seemed too great—whether in glass or tile or inlaid mother-of-pearl. Tiffany, with a splendid red beard, pointed in the Edwardian manner, had a flamboyant personality that the public found it difficult to resist. He was proud of what he had done to interest the public in the decorative and useful arts, and in the foreword of the gilt and parchment book the author says: "Among the artists who have led the way in this change there is none who has affected the taste of the public more profoundly than Louis Comfort Tiffany."

What survives of Tiffany's profound effect seems slight enough. The enthusiasm for the art of the craftsman so dear to avant-garde hearts in the nineties was, before Tiffany died, supplanted by an equal enthusiasm for the art of the machine. Tiffany's principal legacy is Favrile glass—the iridescent glass whose formula he stumbled on by mistake and which remained a secret of the Tiffany Studios, but to his contemporaries he was noted for his "sincerity" and his very considerable business acumen, and he was called "the William Morris of this century in America."

Tiffany's influence on the public taste (whatever it may have been on the private taste of those who could afford his wares) was a minor diversion compared with the assault of a man fifteen years his junior whose knowledge of art, architecture, and decoration was almost non-existent. That is not to say that the young man was not opinionated in these matters; indeed he knew very well what the public should like and what aesthetic attitudes they should adopt. He knew, for example, that a straight line was better than a curved one, that fanciness was immoral and plainness was goodness. He believed that it was his mission to "make the world a better or more beautiful place to live in," and one of his first attacks on the world was an attempt to rid it of what he called the "repellently ornate." The young man's name was Edward Bok, and he was twenty-six years old when, in 1889, he succeeded Mrs. Cyrus H. K. Curtis as the editor of a six-year-old magazine called the *Ladies' Home Journal*. He was brimming with ambition, energy, and an aptitude for sniffing the winds of fashion. When he took over the *Journal* it had a circulation of 440,000 copies a month; in a few years he had built it to an unprecedented million.

Bok, you will remember, was the man who blamed the bad taste of the public on the lavish example of the Pullman Palace Cars. To him they represented everything that was distasteful in decoration, and besides, he said, they were unsanitary. In his autobiography, *The Americanization of Edward Bok*, he claims that his series of editorials attacking the Pullman Company for its notions of decoration was responsible for the ultimate disappearance of the plush and the lambrequins so dear to Mr. Pullman's and the public's heart. He was flushed with editorial, aesthetic, and moral triumph when a new dining car appeared on the Chicago, Burlington, and Quincy Railroad. He describes it as follows: "It was an artistically treated Flemish-oak-paneled car with longitudinal beams and cross-beams, giving the impression of a ceiling-beamed room. Between the 'beams' was a quiet tone of deep yellow. The sides of the car were wainscoting of plain surface done in a Flemish stain rubbed down to a dull finish. The grain of the wood was allowed to serve as decoration; there was no carving. The whole tone of the car was that of the rich color of the sunflower." The traveling public, he said, greeted it with enthusiasm.

Bok's battle with Pullman was, however, a secondary campaign in his grand strategy; his main forces were massed against the small houses of America. Bok, who had a zealot's capacity for being shocked, found the architecture in which most Americans lived "wretched," and he deplored the money that was wasted on "useless turrets, filigree work, or machine-made ornamentation." The plain fact was that very few Americans could afford to employ architects; most people relied on builders and contractors not only for the erection of their houses but for their design as well. The results were, of course, either fairly simple wooden boxes or wooden boxes tricked up with the clichés of the Queen Anne style—octagonal towers with candle-snuffer peaked roofs, scalloped shingles, spindled porches, and little balconies stuck on wherever ingenuity could find space for them. If you will travel through New England today, looking at each house as you drive down village streets and especially in the outskirts of cities, both small and large, you will find that Queen Anne houses far outnumber any other. Most of them are now painted white instead of the somber colors that were *de rigueur* when they were built, but there is no question that most of the charming towns of New England are far less Colonial than Queen Anne. It was against this influence that Bok leveled his editorial guns.

His method, as he described it himself, sounds like a new one; it was in fact an old one refurbished. In the sixties and seventies *Godey's Lady's Book* had published engravings of houses taken from Downing's book on *Country Residences* and showed their plans. Plan books, giving approximate costs and fairly complete building specifications, had had a lively market for half a century before Bok launched his campaign in the *Journal*. Yet when, in 1895, Bok tried to employ the services of "leading domestic architects" to draw plans and elevations of small houses that he could publish in his magazine, he was greeted with the coldest of receptions; the architects looked upon the suggestion as "cheapening their profession." Eventually he found an architect, whom he does not name, who was willing to go along with him, and he "began the publication of a series of houses which could be built, approximately, for from one thousand five hundred dollars to five thousand dollars."

The response of his readers was immediate and enthusiastic, and "*Ladies' Home Journal* houses" grew like innocuous mushrooms in communities all over the country. Architects and builders were furious; Bok, they claimed, was "taking the bread out of their mouths." But Bok knew better. He was dealing with a clientele that wouldn't employ architects anyway, and the plans that he supplied to the readers who applied for them were good enough for any builder to work with. His two major contributions to small house design were the elimination of the parlor, which he thought was a useless extravagance, and a provision that every servant's room have two windows for cross ventilation and be at least twice the size of such rooms in ordinary houses. One woman in Brookline, who erected twenty-five "*Journal* houses" as a real estate venture, didn't notice until ten of them were built that they had no parlors.

Whole communities of Bok's dream houses sprang up; speculators built them, individuals built them, and as Bok had got estimates on their cost from contractors in various parts of the country no one found himself in the position, so common when one employs an architect, of having the final cost far outrun the original estimate. Finally even the architects were impressed. "I firmly believe," wrote Stanford White shortly before his death, "that Edward Bok has more completely influenced American domestic architecture for the better than any man in this generation. When he began, I was short-sighted enough to discourage him, and refused to cooperate with him. If Bok came to me now, I would not only make plans for him, but I would waive any fee for them in retribution for my early mistake."

Bok also ventured deep into the territory of interior decoration with perfect confidence in his own taste. He knew that interior decoration, as he put it, offered "a field almost limitless in possible improvement" but he wasn't sure of the best way to launch his attack. One day, he recounts, he met a woman at the funeral of a friend whom he was surprised to see there as he had not thought her to be close to the bereaved family. "To be perfectly frank," the woman said to him, "I am going to the funeral just to see how Mrs. S——'s house is furnished. She was always thought to have great taste, you know, and whether you know it or not, a woman is always keen to look into another woman's house." So Bok made it possible in the pages of the *Journal* for women, millions of them, to look into other women's houses. He ran a series of a hundred photographs of rooms and called the department "Inside a Hundred Homes." Bok credits this piece of discreet keyhole-peeping with bringing the circulation of the magazine up to a million readers. He followed it with another picture feature which he called "Good Taste and Bad Taste"; he reproduced what he considered a bad piece of furniture, and said why he thought it was bad, and a good one and explained its virtues, both practical and aesthetic.

As a maker of taste Bok had a greater influence than any other man of his generation. His ideas were uncomplicated by any knowledge of the arts; they were sensible, down-to-earth, and just new enough not to shock anyone by being revolutionary; at the same time they were fresh enough to appeal to the general feeling of relief at throwing off the weight of Victorian fanciness. The changes that he wrought upon the landscapes and in the decoration of living rooms and bedrooms were considerable, but the methods that he used to change taste were more far-reaching in their influence than the changes themselves. He set a pattern in the *Ladies' Home Journal*, where he found that mass appeal to the house-proud aesthetic sense, so long as it was not pushed too hard or too far, was a first-class money maker. Today, thanks to Bok, you cannot pick up any mass circulation magazine that does not, either as a regular department or as an occasional feature, advise its readers on how to decorate their homes, how to look at art and architecture, or how to be up to date on the latest word in aesthetics.

By and large as the century came to a close most people were rather pleased both with the accomplishment and the promise of America. A continent had been tied together, even though the package was not a very neat one and it contained a good many unfortunate slums. The march of culture, however, had been glorious. Look at the universities, at the land-grant colleges. Look at the libraries and museums and art schools. Look, too, at the cultural societies and study groups, at the numbers of artists and architects, at the skyscrapers, and the domed state capitols, and the palaces of the rich. Look in another direction at the housing developments for workers and the uplifting influence of art upon the common people. There was culture for all who would sit at its table and partake; there was even forced feeding for those who hung back: free education was universal. Every facility had been provided to sharpen the aesthetic sensibilities, to train them, to provide touchstones for them, and to turn them to use and, of course, to profit. What remarkable, what measurable, what delightfully statistical progress!

"If the century which is nearly at its close," wrote Candace Wheeler in *The Outlook* in 1897, "has given so largely to the ease and comfort of the laboring mass, it has also introduced into the homes of the rich an element which was in truth somewhat lacking in those days of bare and slender elegance."

To the Edith Whartons and the Candace Wheelers, to the Boks and the Tiffanys it seemed only a matter of time before the taste of the rich, which they felt was improving, would engulf the lower classes. As the 1800's turned with a tumultuous celebration into the twentieth century the stage, they thought, was set for a flowering of taste such as America had never seen before. But in the wings there were mutterings; backstage there were squabbles. When the curtain went up, the same old tug of war was being waged. The truth was what it had always been—that disagreement about taste was far more interesting than harmony. After a century of progress nobody could agree, so far as taste was concerned, what progress really meant.

CHAPTER XI

Suitability!

> "The essence of taste is suitability. Divest
> the word of its prim and priggish implica-
> tions, and see how it expresses the mysterious
> demand of the eye and mind for symmetry,
> harmony and order."
>
> EDITH WHARTON, *French Ways and Their*
> *Meanings*

Elsie, that is just your *métier*," said Elizabeth Marbury to Elsie
de Wolfe shortly after the turn of the century. "Why not go
ahead and be America's first woman decorator?"

Elsie had been an actress, but the stage had been only moderately
kind to her ambitions. Charles Frohman, a consistently successful
producer in the eighties and nineties, had launched her in the first
New York production of *Thermidor*, a romantic drama by Victorien
Sardou, which opened at Keith's Theatre in 1891. For the next decade
she had trouped, first for Frohmann and then with her own company,
but as an actress she was always, so she felt, the little girl who had
made a success in amateur theatricals at Tuxedo Park. She was visiting friends there when the rigidly exclusive resort opened its first
season, and she had attracted attention to herself in a one-act play
called *A Cup of Tea*. In one scene she was called upon to faint on a
sofa, and being something of an acrobat, she did "a double back roll
onto the floor." "This," she says, "was considered very fine acting."
Whatever it was, it was the beginning of her career. It was also the
occasion of her meeting Elizabeth Marbury, already a well-known
theatrical and literary agent, who was to be her life-long and most
intimate friend.

Elsie de Wolfe was a woman of gusto, quick temper, good figure and striking but not pretty appearance. She made a fetish of being unable to understand accounts and of always extracting from her business a whopping profit. She was sure of her tastes, all of which were expensive, and she was celebrated for standing on her head. She was an ardent devotee of calisthenics, raw vegetables, and famous people, and if she was not the first woman decorator in America (and she may have been), she was certainly the first to turn her skill for the niceties of taste into a considerable personal fortune. Her career as an actress ended with a theatrical casualty called *The Wife Without a Smile* in which she played the leading role. Her exit line, and the last she was paid to speak on the stage was: "It can go to the pigs."

Interior decoration, when Elsie set herself up in business in the house she shared with Elizabeth Marbury (it had been Washington Irving's home near Gramercy Park in New York), was scarcely a profession at all; it was an adjunct of the upholsterer's trade. In Downing's day George Platt, an Englishman who came to New York in the forties, had been the most famous decorator in America. He had a shop on Broadway in which he sold furniture that he designed and had made for him by German craftsmen in his own factory in Hoboken, across the river from Manhattan. He had prospered and so had other upholsterers. But it was not until the nineties that there was even a hint that interior decoration might be a suitable profession for women. Ladies might with decorum teach or edit or do social work, but there the respectable professions, if not the jobs, seemed to stop. Actresses, except for a rare few, were still looked upon as women of questionable virtue. Miss de Wolfe makes it quite clear in her autobiography that she would never have gone on the stage had she not desperately needed to support her widowed mother.

If Miss de Wolfe was the first to essay the decorating profession, she was surely not the first to pronounce publicly on its suitability for her sex. Candace Wheeler, about a decade before Miss de Wolfe embarked on her new career, published an article in the *Outlook* on "Interior Decoration as a Profession for Women." There was a great deal of "artistic manufacture," she reasoned, and there were a great many women with "natural good taste." The trouble was that those who could afford the artistic manufactures were not always those with the good taste. Furthermore, she believed that the profession was especially well suited to women because of their "instinctive knowledge of textiles and intimate knowledge of the conveniences of domestic life." Miss Wheeler, however, was under no illusions that natural good taste was a sufficient basis for a professional career, and she bemoaned the fact that there was no school where a girl might learn to draw decorative details and study the historic styles. "One may venture to predict," she wrote, with accuracy, "that for so important and well recognized an art as decoration is becoming, there will be schools and college courses where students can be well and authoritatively trained for this dignified profession."

Elsie de Wolfe had none of the training that Miss Wheeler thought ultimately desirable, but she filled at least one of Miss Wheeler's conditions. She was a woman with what passed for "cultivation and taste and an instinct for arrangement," and she was able to capitalize on the fact that, as Miss Wheeler put it, "there are a large number of homes belonging to the well-to-do members of society who have none of this general cultivation, and are well aware of their own lack of it." Furthermore she was well acquainted with the "well-to-do" of New York and Chicago and San Francisco. She had traveled extensively in Europe and had always had more than a passing interest in furniture and decorative styles. All she had to do was let it be known that she was in business. She sent engraved announcements to her friends; her name and address was on them and "a little wolf with a flower in his paw." Within a week, she says, "orders poured in."

The career of Elsie de Wolfe was a flamboyant one, and since she worked only for wealthy clients she demonstrated to some extent what Edith Wharton (whom she found sharp and cold) had preached —that the taste of the lower classes could be improved by educating the rich. Whether Miss de Wolfe improved anybody's taste is debatable, but change it she did, and her influence went far beyond the delicately tinted walls of the houses she decorated.

Her first big job was the Colony Club in New York, a building on Madison Avenue between Thirty-first and Thirty-second Streets. Stanford White had been engaged as the architect, and Miss de Wolfe's name had been proposed by her friends Miss Marbury and Miss Anne Morgan (J. P.'s sister) to the committee. "Are you out of your heads," said one of the wealthy and petulant founders of the new club, "giving an important job like this to a woman who has no experience?" Stanford White was summoned. "Give it to Elsie, and let the girl alone," he pronounced. "She knows more than any of us." It is difficult now to believe that the Colony Club, the very model of respectability and propriety, could ever have been considered "a menace to the American Home," but the very fact that a group of women should have considered establishing a club in which they were not only the exclusive members but where they could "smoke and have their drinks" was very shocking indeed in 1907.

Elsie's reputation was made by her job on the Colony Club and by the publicity given this shocking institution in which ladies might "imitate the bad habits of their fathers and husbands and brothers." There she introduced one decorative fad of fairly short duration and one that is with us still. The first was the use of lattice indoors to give a gardenlike appearance to the members' dining room; it was copied in country houses and even in city houses all over America for nearly two decades. The second was the use of colorful flowered chintz in what were then called "drawing rooms." In no time chintz hung at windows and covered chairs and sofas and cushions from New York to San Francisco; it was relatively inexpensive, it was gay, and it was easy to work with. Elsie de Wolfe became known as 'The Chintz Lady." Other notions with which she decorated the Colony Club took on less quickly but no less thoroughly. She invented the "vanity table" which opened out in front, so that the ladies might "sit comfortably close to the mirror" while making up their faces, and the "tray table" which she thought of as a convenience for women who wanted "to move from room to room, taking along whatever they happened to be busy with—their needlework, manicure materials, letters, etc."

There could have been no better client than the Colony Club for a woman launching a new profession. Its members were wealthy, prominent, and fashionable, and what was good enough for them was good enough for wealthy, prominent and fashionable women elsewhere—except in Boston. Miss de Wolfe's first big private client was Mrs. William H. Crocker of San Francisco with whom she worked on the decorations of her home, "New Place," at Burlingame. From the Crockers she went to the Ogden Armours of Chicago, and then to the Weyerhausers of Minneapolis. But it was Henry C. Frick, the crusty steel magnate, to whom she owed the founding of her personal wealth.

Frick, who had amassed a huge fortune and in the manner of his day was bent on setting himself up in lordly surroundings, had purchased half a block of Fifth Avenue frontage at Seventieth Street for his palace. Elsie was summoned to decorate and furnish the second floor and was bidden to stand as a fence between him and the gaggle of dealers who were scheming for his patronage. For this he offered her a ten per cent commission on everything she bought for him on the condition that she would take no commissions of any sort from dealers. "If I spend five thousand dollars," he said to her, "you will get five hundred dollars for your knowledge; if it is ten thousand dollars, your fee will be one thousand dollars, and so on." It happened that a portion of the famous collection of Sir Richard Wallace (of the Wallace Collection, a museum in Manchester Square in London) was for sale in Paris and the dealer Jacques Seligman, known as "the Fox," had the sole disposal of it. Frick and Miss de Wolfe were in France looking for furnishings for the Fifth Avenue house when Seligman came to her and offered her the first opportunity to see the treasures which had for some time because of a lawsuit been stored away. She looked, and she persuaded Mr. Frick that he too should look. In half an hour, impatient to keep a golf date which he had postponed briefly in order to see the collection, he spent 350,000 francs for a table, 400,000 for a console, and so on until millions of francs worth of furniture had been purchased. "I followed at his heels, aghast . . ." wrote Miss de Wolfe, "and I realized that in one short half-hour I had become what was tantamount to a rich woman."

She was quite willing, however, to impart her secrets of decoration to anyone who could pay the price of a book, and in 1913 she published *The House in Good Taste*, a volume whose exterior bespeaks its author's taste in interiors. It was bound in a soft gray blue and stamped with gilt and mauve and white. Like many writers on taste in America before her, like James Jackson Jarves and Henry Tuckerman, like Mrs. Sherwood and Candace Wheeler, she was excited by the evidence that she saw of the improvement in American sensibilities. "I know of nothing more significant," she wrote in the first paragraph of her book, "than the awakening of men and women throughout our country to the desire to improve their houses. Call it what you will —awakening, development, American Renaissance—it is a most startling and promising condition of affairs." The key word in Miss de Wolfe's vocabulary was "suitability." "My business," she said, "is to preach to you the beauty of suitability. Suitability! *Suitability!* SUITABILITY!!"

What was suitable to Miss de Wolfe was too expensive for almost everyone else—Louis XVI chairs, Nattier portraits, Houdon busts, Savonnerie carpets—but she gave her readers some hints about putting the pieces of furniture they already owned in convenient (i.e., "suitable") places and about getting rid of unnecessary clutter. In addition to "suitability" she also urged "sincerity," just as had Eastlake, whose furniture she abhorred, and she exhorted her readers to express their personalities: "If you are both sincere, if you both purpose to have the best thing you can afford, the house will express the genius and character of your architect and the personality and character of yourself. . . ." There was a good deal of snobbishness in her attitude toward taste, and she employed familiar techniques of intimidation: "A woman's environment will speak for her life, whether she likes it or not. How can we believe that a woman of sincerity of purpose will hang fake 'works of art' on her walls, or satisfy herself with imitation velvets or silks. . . . A house is a dead-give-away. . . ."

The rules, however, were not complicated, and to have taste need not be beyond any woman's reach. The formula for achieving suitability was to pursue a consistent style, whatever it might be, for "to conform within rational limits to a given style is no more servile than to pay one's taxes or to write according to the rules of grammar." Consistency was the safe and sure road to good taste, and out of the preachments on its behalf came the "period" room.

Compared with the constant struggles of the nineteenth century to achieve a style of its own, this was resignation and admission of defeat. Miss de Wolfe was convinced, as many others were, that the concept of the house had been settled once and for all, and that so far as furniture was concerned "we cannot do better than to accept the standards of other times, and adapt them to our uses." It was sad, she thought, but true. "We have not succeeded in creating a style adapted to our modern life. It is just as well! Our life, with its haste, its nervousness, and its preoccupations does not inspire the furniture makers."

The results of such defeatism as this in high places was bound to show in middle-class houses before very long. The progression was a logical one: from the period room, decorated with authentic period furniture, to the room decorated with factory-made copies of period pieces. Grand Rapids was there to meet the new demand, and it was soon possible to buy for reasonable prices excellent copies of furniture from almost any period. Heirlooms that had been retired to the attic in the fifties and sixties in favor of the new machine-made furniture began to reappear, and out of this same safe formula came the antiques craze which in the twenties was to produce so many "early American" rooms with exposed beams, a kettle in the fireplace, and a spinning wheel beside the hearth. The period room was something any woman could envisage with the help of the decorating magazines, which told her what curtains and what wall colors were suitable to what period. And if she could not afford to decorate her house all in one style, there was always advice at hand on what periods could be combined with the maximum effect to produce a house in good, uncluttered, and suitable taste.

The "correct taste" which Downing had been convinced in the fifties could be achieved only by education was finally being realized, and it was a bloodless thing. The Age of Good Taste was now well under way, and it was factory-produced, decorator-inspired, and inexpensive. It was so easy to be right; only the most careless or most eccentric housewife need deviate from the norm.

The Elsie de Wolfes and the Edith Whartons, their imitators and apostles and followers, as numerous and articulate as they were, by no means had the field to themselves. The first decade of the century, as we have already noted, was full of ferment, and the wine of taste that we are now consuming in such tremendous gulps is the produce of grapes wrathfully trodden then.

"When luxury enters in," wrote Gustav Stickley, the editor of *The Craftsman*, of the American home in 1909, "and a thousand artificial requirements come to be regarded as real needs, the nation is on the brink of degeneration."

Stickley, the son of a Wisconsin stone mason, was in the direct line of aesthetic moralists who tried to make Americans both sincere and sensible about the houses they lived in and about the objects with which they surrounded themselves. He was an apostle of William Morris and in 1884, when he was twenty-six, he moved to Binghamton, New York, where he established a furniture factory in which he set out to practice the traditions of handicraft that Morris preached. His name and his writings are now almost forgotten, but his impact on the landscape and living rooms of the beginning of the century was considerable. It was he who was largely responsible for the bungalow, the forerunner of today's "ranch house" and for the sturdy, foursquare furniture known as "Mission," which was the progenitor of today's "functional" chairs and tables and sofas. As a designer, as a philosopher of the function of the home, as a writer, and as a purveyor of taste he was the furthest possible cry from Elsie de Wolfe. There were details on which they would have agreed—lack of clutter, for example—but on the nature of "taste" they would have been at loggerheads.

The simple virtues, the outdoor life, the "sacredness of the home" and wholesomeness—these were not only Stickley's basic requirements of the good life but of good design as well. He was deeply concerned with what he had seen happen to America: it had grown too rich too fast. "We need to straighten out our standards," he wrote, "and to get rid of a lot of rubbish that we have accumulated along with our wealth and commercial supremacy. It is not that we are too energetic, but that in many ways we have misused our energy precisely as we have wasted and misused so many of our wonderful natural resources." He feared for the children of parents who brought them up in fancy surroundings lest they have it ingrained in them that they could not marry until they could afford equally luxurious houses. He deplored "the kind of life that marks a man's face with the haggard lines of anxiety and makes him sharp and often unscrupulous in business," and he regretted "the extravagance and uselessness of many of our women" and the all too prevalent "touch-and-go attitude toward marriage" which kept the divorce mills of America humming.

His answer to this, or at least part of his answer, was houses "based on the big fundamental principles of honesty, simplicity, and usefulness—the kind of houses that children will rejoice all their lives to remember as 'home,' and that give a sense of peace and comfort to the tired men who go back to them when the day's work is done." The houses that he recommended were bungalows, or, as he called them "Craftsman homes."

The bungalow as we are familiar with it (and who is not?) and Mission furniture were, as Lewis Mumford has said, "the first designs that put California esthetically on the modern map," and like the California ranch houses of today bungalows cropped up in great numbers in the country and suburbs, in small towns and large, all over America. One of its most successful promoters and popularizers was not a Californian but a Chicagoan named Henry L. Wilson, who called himself "The Bungalow Man." What he did to the design of the bungalow must have made the serious Stickley shudder. In 1910 he produced a book called *The Bungalow Book, a Short Sketch of the Evolution of the Bungalow from its Primitive Crudeness to its Present State of Artistic Beauty and Cozy Convenience, Illustrated with Drawings of Exteriors, Floor Plans, Interiors, and Cozy Corners of Bungalows Which Have Been Built from Original Designs*. It cost a dollar and in two and a half years it had gone into five editions. The bungalow had everything that the ranch house has, and a combination, as Wilson points out in his preface, of a background which was both Oriental (the word bungalow comes from the name given to low thatched houses of the Bengalese in India) and Spanish colonial. Wilson did not explain how these two strains met, but in 1910 explanations of this sort were not thought necessary. It was the age of "adaptation."

The bungalow, however, shows few traces of anything that might be called an architectural influence except the Swiss chalet. Its two constant features are wide overhanging eaves and a porch usually supported by piers made of boulders. The bungalow was originally a one-story building, square, with no entrance hall and with exposed beams in the ceiling of the living room. But in most of those illustrated in The Bungalow Man's book there are dormers in the shallow roofs, and the rooms they served were cramped. A two-story bungalow twenty-eight feet by forty-five cost about $2,000.

In describing the evolution of the bungalow and its culmination in what he called the "Spanish Mission Style" Wilson wrote: "The result was quaint and attractive . . . a 'house beautiful' inside and out, the very embodiment of homelike coziness and convenience, inexpensive, but of refined elegance easily adaptable to almost any location, whether mountain, plain, or valley, or on a city's narrow streets, or the broad, shaded village avenues." Wilson knew the public taste, as the number of bungalows that were built from the plans in his book amply testifies, and if he were still in business he would still be building bungalows. He would, however, call them ranch houses, for the ranch house is the bungalow with very minor changes. The roofs of both slope at the same shallow angle; the windows are of almost the same proportions, and many bungalows (like all ranch houses) had large picture-windows. Often the eaves of the ranch house hang far over in the same way as those of the bungalow but instead of boulders to support the porch roof, you find the rugged touch of the ranch house in indoor and outdoor fireplaces. The ranch house is the bungalow pulled out like a piece of taffy and bent.

The relation of Wilson's bungalows to Stickley's Craftsman Homes was very like the relation today of the ranch house to "modern." They were quite different in spirit but they embodied many of the same features, and their details stemmed from the same ideas. Whereas Stickley emphasized "wholesomeness" Wilson played up the "cozy"; whereas the modern architect dwells on beauty of "function," the designer of the ranch house talks about "freedom" and "informality." A "Spanish Mission Style bungalow" built in the suburbs of Chicago in 1910 was the exact counterpart of the ranch houses recently advertised in the *New York Times* as "The New Southwest . . . a dramatically authentic ranch home . . . only a few minutes from Great Neck station—26 minutes from Penn Station." Oh, the deserts of Chicago—Oh, the prairies of New York!

Elsie de Wolfe would have given the bungalow short shrift. Where, she would have wondered, was there any grace or elegance in its squat lines? How could anyone put up with the bulky, relentlessly practical Mission tables that were strong enough to support an elephant, or the squared-off metal and glass lampshades and Navajo rugs with which their owners were encouraged to furnish them? Mission was briefly the rage just after the turn of the century. Stickley made it in his factory at Binghamton in the name of craftsmanship, and the Grand Rapids factories turned it out for a cheaper market. Sears, Roebuck featured it in their catalogues, and it was possible for the housewife to buy a three-piece "Arts and Crafts Library Suite" made of solid oak for $11.95. A square "Mission Art Glass Lamp" that burned kerosene and hung from the ceiling was $7.85. Young couples, eager to break away from the fringe and furbelows that had decorated their families' houses, eyed it with much the same enthusiasm that their parents' generation had coveted the "sincere" Eastlake furniture that was the *sine qua non* of the "artistic craze" of the seventies.

Compared with most of the furniture offered the housewife at the turn of the century it was a very model of sensible taste. It was the era of the cast-iron bed, ornamented with griffons, and painted in combinations of colors—in maroon and white and gilt. The brass bed decorated with medallions, the wicker rocker as baroque as a Neopolitan church, hall racks of golden oak which were a combination hat rack, seat, and mirror, cuckoo clocks with pine cone weights and set about with carved oak leaves, bamboo screens, and objects that were part glass-fronted bookcases, part desks, part vanity mirror, and part bureau all in one—this was the general run of furniture offered by the mail-order houses. For the most part America missed the craze that swept Europe just after 1900—the *Art Nouveau*, which is now coming back into fashion in some quarters and which Elsie de Wolfe called "that avalanche of bad taste which burst upon us in 1900 and had its way until the beginning of the war." "I cannot forget," she says in her autobiography, "those awful chairs and tables supported by flowers contrived to look as if they were growing from the ground. And the mantelpiece of fleurs-de-lis and rushes, carved and painted in their natural colors of purple and yellow and green." *Art nouveau* came to America less in decorative schemes than in artifacts. Louis Tiffany made vases in the manner of growing flowers (iris and water lilies and tulips were the most popular motifs), and pen trays and jewel boxes, pendants and earrings and picture frames, often with maidens in shifts and with flowing hair stamped on them, sold in quantity in inexpensive shops.

But in general it was Mission furniture and the crafts movement that represented the advanced taste of the day, and William Morris was a name to be reckoned with right up to the outbreak of the First World War. He had a few influential disciples who were sincere, such as Gustav Stickley, a few who were talented and flamboyant, like Louis Tiffany, and he had many who merely clung to his coat tails. Of this last group there was none so well-known as Elbert Hubbard in his flat black hat and cape and flowing tie—the Sage of Aurora, New York. There in a sanctimonious atmosphere of social uplift, of handicrafts, and paternalism he conducted the astonishingly successful Roycroft Press that brought the message of the crafts movement in limp leather bindings to millions of Americans.

Hubbard, who came from Illinois, first made his mark as a soap salesman; he invented the scheme of boxing several cakes in a package and later of putting premiums with them, an idea in premium selling which he later was to introduce to the magazine subscription business. By the time he had reached his late thirties he had had enough of soap (he was by then a partner in a firm in Buffalo, New York), and decided that he wanted to wash his soul in culture. He tried Harvard but was restless in the atmosphere of undergraduates. He wrote a few novels, none of which was a success, and then he went to travel in Europe. It was in the early nineties that his path crossed that of Morris and in 1895 he took the $60,000 he had got from his share in the soap firm and established his press.

He was an indefatigable writer, an accomplished phrase maker, and a publicist of no mean talents. Aphorisms tripped from his pen at such an astonishing rate that in Stevenson's *Home Book of Quotations* his name is one of the few preceded by a star which "indicates that quotations from his work are so numerous that no useful purpose would be served by giving the pages on which they occur." Aristotle, Matthew Arnold, Shakespeare and Plato are others in this class, but there any similarity between Hubbard and literary eminence ceases. He produced more than a hundred essays called *Little Journeys to the Homes of Great Men* (ranging from Leonardo da Vinci to J. P. Morgan) and he edited a magazine called the *Philistine* which, after a few years of accepting contributions from others, Hubbard wrote entirely himself. Its first issue appeared in 1895, shortly after he established his press, and soon it was addressed to the "American Academy of Immortals, otherwise the Society of the Philistines. The Association of Book-lovers and Folks who Write, Paint and Dream. Organized to further Good-Fellowship among men and women who believe in allowing the widest liberty to Individuality in Thought and Expression." At its peak, around 1910, the *Philistine* claimed a circulation of 225,000 copies, and Hubbard's name was a household word. His most success-ful venture was a little essay called "A Message to Garcia," which, it has been estimated, sold over eighty million copies. It was bought by the United States Marines and presented to every member of the Corps. The German army and the Japanese army were saturated with it; thousands of American businessmen made sure that each of their employees read the little homily on the virtues of obedience, service, and devotion that told the story, inaccurately, of an incident in the Spanish-American War.

Pilgrims traveled from far and wide to spend an evening in Hub-bard's company at the Roycrofters Inn in Aurora. His wit and his conversational gifts, his massive countenance (which somewhat re-sembled William Jennings Bryan's), and his prophetic voice were revered by hundreds of thousands of people who had read his homilies, heard him lecture, or had seen him on the vaudeville stage. In some respects he was a one-man Chautauqua—a dispenser of opinions on every aspect of taste and culture, always with overtones of spiritual uplift and earthy morality. His reputation in Aurora was anything but savory because of a blatant marital scandal in which he was the central figure, but elsewhere he was looked up to. His influence on taste was far less stolid than the Mission furniture that he promoted and that typified the crafts movement to most people. Out of his press poured little volumes bound in limp leather, printed in heavy black type. They were ornamented with medieval-like designs inside and formalized gilt flowers outside; the paper had a rough, hand-hewn look to it and the quality of the presswork was excellent. To many of Hubbard's con-temporaries he was the embodiment of the artistic spirit, and when a torpedo sank the *Lusitania* in May, 1915, the last influential disciple of William Morris in America went to the bottom of the Atlantic, leaving behind him a great many mourners, a sizable fortune, and a star in Stevenson's book of quotations.

The bridge between Stickley and Hubbard of the craft movement and Elsie de Wolfe of the school of suitability was built of Portland cement. Rarely did they meet on this bridge, but occasionally they could not avoid it. Cement, or concrete, as it was more often called, was an honest material that appealed both to the simple foursquare builder and to the imaginations of the frivolous. It was not as cheap as frame construction, but if it was not fireproof it was extremely fire resistant. Furthermore it was plentiful. In 1908, thanks to the boom given the concrete business by the construction of the Panama Canal, America was manufacturing fifty-five million barrels of cement a year. It is not surprising that the industry should have explored every possible use of its material, or have tried to sell the public on its virtues.

"The Age of Concrete," *House Beautiful* called it in 1908. "Never before was so much concrete used," wrote one of the editors. "You may build a factory or a chicken house out of it, a railroad or a piece of statuary, a canal, except for the water, and a boat to sail upon it; a church to the decorative frieze and the images of the saints. In fact, there is no end to the purposes, both useful and ornamental, to which cement and its big brother, concrete, may be put."

It was almost like making mud pies, and Americans, always fascinated by new materials and new things to do with them, took to concrete with glee. The arguments for using it instead of wood for houses were convincing. In an illustrated book published by the Association of American Portland Cement Manufacturers in 1912 called *The Concrete House and Its Construction* the virtues of the material were expounded. It was not only "fire resisting" but "vermin proof." It had "sound proof qualities" and its "non-conductivity" would save twenty per cent on the family fuel bill. It also assured "low cost upkeep." For those who were not convinced by this array of arguments, there were loftier ones. Concrete house construction would solve the deforestation problem, and its artistic possibilities were unlimited.

Houses in the newly exploited material went up in suburban and rural areas all over the country, from the simplest square boxes and bungalows (Wilson included plans for concrete houses in *The Bungalow Book*) to elaborate country estates for such wealthy families as the F. S. Harknesses in New London, for the H. M. Flaglers at Palm Beach, and the Guggenheims at West End, New Jersey. Architects as renowned as Carrère and Hastings, who designed the Public Library in New York, used it for homes for wealthy clients. Some of the construction was "monolithic," some of it was of concrete block. The cement manufacturers, in the manner of good philosophers of building, counseled: "The fundamental rule of all good architectural design is that the appearance of the building shall express the structural capabilities of the materials of which it is composed."

The decorative possibilities of concrete, however, allowed for all manner of whimsies and extravagances. "A cement garden table recently made is a thing of beauty," said *House Beautiful*. "The raised work looks like the product of a sculptor's tools. It has three legs with lion's heads at the top and lion claws at the foot." That was just a start. There were also "Egyptian sphinxes which look as real as any sphinx you ever saw." And there were cupids and "weeping Magdalens" and an "American eagle all ready to scream."

Scream as the eagle might about "the house in good taste," about "awakening, development, American Renaissance," or about the "goodfellowship among men and women who believe in allowing the widest liberty to individuality in thought and expression," America was on the verge of being engulfed by a typhoon of taste that blew from foreign shores.

By the time the war broke out in Europe in 1914 there were very few practicing American domestic architects whose work forecast the style we now call "Modern." The only one whose name is now familiar was Frank Lloyd Wright. The ideas that had been so cogently expressed by the sculptor Horatio Greenough in a letter to his friend Emerson had been largely forgotten here, but they were remembered in Europe. He had written: "Here is my theory of structure: a scientific arrangement of spaces and forms [adapted] to functions and to site; an emphasis of features proportioned to the gradated importance in function; colour and ornament to be decided and arranged and varied by strictly organic laws, having a distinct reason for each decision; the entire and immediate banishment of all make-believe." The words of Louis Sullivan were also remembered. His attempts to evolve a style that was based on building with steel and that expressed the essential qualities of the new material had impressed architects in Europe more than they had impressed his contemporaries at home. The ideas were here, many of the engineering principles had been developed here, the knowledge to put them into practice was here. But the spark that ignited the public taste was to come from elsewhere.

And when the spark lit upon the dry tinder of respectability, suitability, refined taste, and complacency, what a spectacular conflagration took place! What a glorious explosion! Elsie could scarcely catch her breath.

CHAPTER XII

Whirlwind on Twenty-Sixth Street

"This is not a movement and a principle.
It is unadulterated cheek."

In the late afternoons in 1911, when they had nothing better to do, a small group of young painters used to sit in a little art gallery at 305 Madison Avenue in New York and complain about how badly the world treated them. They called themselves "progressive," and they bemoaned the fact that they had no place except this one gallery in which they might regularly show their wares. If it hadn't been for the enthusiasm, generosity, and ample funds of Gertrude Vanderbilt Whitney, who was a sculptor, they wouldn't even have had this little point of contact with the apathetic public. It was a situation that they found unbearable, and what they decided to do about it caused an eruption in American taste from which we have not yet recovered. It was not at all the kind of eruption that they expected, and it was certainly not what they wanted. It brought the house down around their heads.

The timbers of the house were scarcely robust. The art world in America just after the turn of the century was in a period of acute doldrums. The Academy had a corner on respectability and it was impossible for the younger painters who were tired of the genteel tradition of such painters as Chase and Dewing and sculptors like MacMonnies and Lorado Taft to get their works shown in the Academy's annual exhibition. The respectable public grumbled angrily, as did the equally respectable critics, at the group of young painters who called themselves "The Eight" and especially at those members of the group who had been dubbed the "Ash Can School."

It was not considered nice, and it was certainly not considered artistic, to paint the meaner aspects of city life as these men insisted on doing. What was beautiful, many people wanted to know, about the back alleys of Greenwich Village and the seamy characters who inhabited them? Why should anyone paint pictures of saloons, and rundown markets, and pushcart peddlers, and slatternly women? What was the point of painting subjects that were not beautiful? Was *that* art?

The public thought it most assuredly was not. The painters insisted that there was beauty to be seen everywhere if only you had the eyes to see it, and in defiance of the Academy and of a public that would pay $20,000 for a Bouguereau and only $260 for a Ryder when they both appeared in the same auction in 1910 they organized a Show of Independents. Five hundred pictures were hung without benefit of a jury, but the public was not much interested, and the art dealers had their eyes turned in another gaudier direction.

Wealthy American collectors had discovered Europe with a hungry appetite—not contemporary Europe but the Europe of the safe and glittering past—and the dealers who traded in masterpieces were enjoying a boom such as the art market had never seen before and may never see again. They, too, were contributing to the future of American taste as they embellished the houses of American millionaires with great pictures and sculptures of the past and lined their own pockets with gold. The public taste was the least of their worries, and the plight of the American artist was none of their business. When J. Pierpont Morgan was bent on making his own collection the greatest personal collection of pictures in the world and the Metropolitan Museum of Art, of which he was president of the Board of Trustees, the greatest museum, how could dealers be expected to fret about the pennies involved in selling contemporary pictures? It was the era in which Joseph Duveen bought Gainsborough's "The Blue Boy" from the Duke of Westminster and sold it to Henry E. Huntington of San Marino, California, for $620,000 (Huntington spent more than $30,000,000 in all on his collection) and when Mrs. "Jack" Gardner of Boston was busily making "Fenway Court" into a museum filled with Titian and Rembrandt and Rubens, and many other masters, with tapestries and porcelains and Renaissance furniture. Mrs. O. H. Havermeyer with the help and perceptive guidance of her friend Mary Cassatt was assembling a collection of Goyas and El Grecos and of Impressionists—Renoir and Manet and Monet; and Henry Clay Frick, Elsie de Wolfe's client, was converting his house into a private museum with a room completely decorated by Fragonard (he bought it from Morgan's collection), and galleries hung with such pictures as Rembrandt's "The Polish Rider," a portrait by Gentile Bellini, a St. Francis by his brother Giovanni, a Velasquez, a Duccio and Bouchers and Turners galore. There he sat among his treasures, wrote Ann Burr, his biographer, "on a Renaissance throne under a baldachino, holding in his little hand a copy of the *Saturday Evening Post*" while an organist played his favorite tunes, "Silver Threads among the Gold" and "The Rosary."

From the dealers' point of view the situation was not without its troubles, and many who tried to reap the harvest of American dollars found themselves having to use any means, honorable or otherwise, to recoup their investments. When Roger Fry, the British art critic and painter, came to America at Morgan's bidding to be the director of the Metropolitan Museum and also to assist Morgan in assembling his personal collection, one of his most disagreeable problems was turning aside the constant efforts of dealers to bribe him to buy their masterpieces. Even the august firm of Duveen had to settle out of court with the United States Government for challengeable customs practices. The *Burlington Magazine,* a connoisseur's art journal in London, was greatly concerned in 1904 about what it called "The Consequences of the American Invasion" and the way in which prices had become so inflated that European collectors were not only unable to compete on the market but were selling their greatest works of art to Americans who were happy to pay almost any price for them. The *Burlington Magazine* had no notion that in just a few years there was going to be a European invasion of America, or what sort of an invasion it would be, or what it would do to the art market.

Neither did the progressive young painters who hung around the gallery at 305 Madison Avenue. If they had had any such premonition, it is unlikely that they would ever have formed the Association of American Painters and Sculptors or that the then notorious and now famous International Exhibition of Modern Art would ever have taken place at the Sixty-ninth Regiment Armory at Lexington Avenue and Twenty-sixth Street in 1913.

The Armory Show, as the exhibition is now always called, was a scandal and a triumph, but its origins were casual. Walt Kuhn, an enthusiastic young painter and caricaturist in his early thirties who had natural gifts for showmanship and for making both fast friends and fast enemies, suggested to Jerome Myers and Elmer MacRae that the three of them should get together and organize a large exhibition of progressive American art. MacRae and Myers, like Kuhn, then had pictures on show at the Madison Gallery, and they decided to meet on December 14, 1911, at Myers' studio on Forty-second Street with Henry Fitch Taylor, another painter and the director of the gallery, to talk it over. They started by drawing up a list of artists whom they wanted to have join them and the response was such that soon they had an organization with J. Alden Weir as its president, Gutzon Borglum (who was later to become famous as the sculptor who carved the faces of four Presidents on the side of Mount Rushmore) as vice president, and Kuhn as secretary. Soon there were about twenty-five members in all, among them such men as George Bellows, Jo Davidson, William Glackens, Robert Henri, Mahonri Young, and John Sloan.

It was one thing to form a society; it was another to organize an important exhibition. Where to have it? Where to get the money? For about a year they discussed these questions and tried to find an exhibition hall. Weir resigned as president and, according to Myers, "even the stout-hearted Kuhn" became discouraged. "Finally there came a meeting," Myers recalls, "when hope was nearly abandoned . . . ; it seemed as though our work was all to be wasted for lack of a location. As we were leaving, I told Kuhn that I would go to see Arthur B. Davies."

Myers had no idea what he was letting himself and the painters of America in for when he and MacRae persuaded Davies to become president of the association. At first Davies was reluctant to join; he was anything but a joiner. Finally he agreed, and things began to happen which had the artists breathless. "Thus it was that I," wrote Myers nearly thirty years after the Armory Show, "an American art patriot, who painted ashcans and the little people around them, took part in inducing to become the head of our association the one American artist who had little to do with his contemporaries, who had vast influence with the wealthiest women, who painted unicorns and maidens under moonlight."

Davies was known to his contemporaries as a man who kept himself very much apart from the rest of the art world. At those meetings at which he did appear he sat and said nothing. When he would go to look at paintings in a gallery he was impatient of the presence of other visitors, and if there were more than two or three he would go away. He liked to keep the address of his studio a secret, and one of his contemporaries tells us that on one occasion "an invitation to see his new work in progress was qualified with the condition that the address of his studio must afterwards be forgotten." Another of his contemporaries, and one who worked very closely with him on the Armory Show, recently said of him, "He was morbidly shy, nervous and self-conscious. He was crabbed, and he wanted to be the idol of a little clique."

With his election to the presidency of the Society of American Painters and Sculptors the shy man turned into a dictator. According to Guy Pène du Bois, a fellow member of the association, Davies became "severe, arrogant, implacable" and "governed with something equivalent to the Terrible Ivan's iron rod." Even Gutzon Borglum, who was known for his toughness and his ability to stand up to anyone, couldn't take the imperiousness and venom of the new president. One day when he and Davies were on a trip Borglum said as a joke that if Davies were a sculptor he too could afford a car. Davies snapped back at him, "I could if I were that kind of man." Borglum resigned as vice president and sent his letter of resignation to the *New York Times* where it was printed before the members of the society saw it.

But despite the resentment of the members of the society toward Davies, suddenly the dream of a show began to take shape as a reality. In the process it emerged as something quite different from what it was originally conceived to be.

Most of the accounts of the origins of the Armory Show, and there are many, were written by men who participated in it, but they did not get around to committing their reminiscences to paper until twenty-five or thirty years after the event. As a result there are a variety of versions, quite different stories of who was of prime importance and who played minor roles, of who selected the pictures, and even of who was responsible for changing the basic plan for an exhibition of American works of art into a show that was, in a manner of speaking, "stolen" by the European painters. There seems little doubt that Davies was the fountainhead of ideas, that Walt Kuhn was the energetic lieutenant who carried them out, and that Walter Pach, a painter and a writer but not a member of the society, did yeoman service as guide, salesman, publicist, and handyman extraordinary. There is also little question that old friends became new enemies, that rifts opened which were never closed again, and also that even those who were most intimately involved in the planning of the show had no inkling of what they were letting loose upon America. They expected to surprise and shock the public. They did not expect to start riots, alert vice squads, and be burned in effigy by students.

The original plan of the Armory Show was simply to stage a large and comprehensive exhibition of paintings and sculptures by what the group believed to be the more advanced American artists. With these they wanted to show, as Walt Kuhn said, "a few of the radical things from abroad to create additional interest." Just what the radical young artists of Europe were up to was known to only a few habitués of Alfred Stieglitz's "291" gallery in New York. There the famous photographer who was the earliest active promoter in America of the Post-Impressionist artists of France showed works by Cézanne and Toulouse-Lautrec, by Gauguin, and even by Matisse and the indefatigably shocking Picasso. But "291" was a unique and tiny outpost of the European artistic radicals, a gallery in which scarcely a dozen people could crowd at a time: it made no impact of any account on the public and very little on the American artists. Davies, however, was very much aware of it, and, according to Walter Pach, had bought a water color by Cézanne there and even a Picasso.

It was Davies' interest in the Europeans that changed the complexion of the exhibition, but the change did not happen all at once.

Before there could be any show of any sort, a place had to be found
to hold it and money had to be found to pay the rent, insure the
pictures, and defray the costs of a catalogue. Kuhn undertook to find
the place; Davies went after the money. One of the members of the
Association of Painters and Sculptors mentioned that there were
several armories in New York that let the public play tennis for a fee,
and maybe one might be rented for a show. Kuhn went from one to
another until he found that Colonel Conley who was in command of
the 69th Regiment of the New York National Guard (it was known
as "the Irish Regiment") would let him have his Armory for a month
for $4,000 with a down payment of $1,500. Kuhn appealed to a
friend of his, John Quinn, who was an art collector and also a lawyer,
to take over the legal aspects of the arrangements, and though Quinn,
according to Kuhn, "thought the whole scheme a crazy one" he agreed
to help. Just where Davies got the money for the down payment is
still a well-kept secret, but he got it. He was, you will remember, a
man "who had vast influence with the wealthiest women."

From this moment on the members of the Association of Painters
and Sculptors "retired to their various studios and hoped for the
best," leaving the selection to Davies and Kuhn and the legal details
to Quinn. Davies went off to think things over; Kuhn went to Nova
Scotia on a painting trip and Quinn went about his practice. While
Kuhn was in Nova Scotia, Davies sent him a catalogue of a large
exhibition that was then being held in Cologne in Germany. The
show was called the "Sonderbund" and Davies said in his accompanying note: "I wish we could have a show like this one." Kuhn wired
him saying that if he could get him passage on a ship he would go at
once to Cologne to see the show and get as much of it as he could
for the Armory. In a few days Kuhn was on his way. Davies saw him
off at the ship in New York. "Go ahead," he said to the young painter.
"You can do it." This was in the summer of 1912.

Kuhn arrived in Cologne the day that the exhibition closed, and
saw most of it after it had been taken down from the walls and was
stacked waiting for shipment. Here were Cézannes and Van Goghs
and here too were "the leading living modernists of France." At first
the show had not been much of a success and those people who had
taken the trouble to see it had nothing good to say for the strange

pictures which seemed to them an insult to their sensibilities, out-landish distortions of every rule of good draftsmanship and artistic tradition. But Kuhn was delighted, especially with the paintings by Van Gogh and the sculpture of Lehmbruck, whom he met and per-suaded to lend work to the New York show. From Cologne he went to The Hague, where he saw pictures by the aging Redon, and was so impressed that he took it upon himself to guarantee a whole room in the show to his pictures. He then made a quick trip to Munich and finally to Paris where, suddenly, the prospects became overwhelming. "One night in my hotel," he wrote, "the magnitude and importance of the whole thing came over me." He cabled to Davies, begging him to come to Paris. Davies came by the first boat.

For several weeks Davies and Kuhn "practically lived in taxicabs," racing around Paris talking to painters, borrowing their works, staying up all night. They enlisted the interest of "the formidable M. Vol-lard," the great dealer who had collected Van Gogh and whose anticipation of the public taste for the Impressionists and Post-Im-pressionists was one of the most extraordinary pieces of imaginative art merchandising of the time. It was the American painter Alfred Maurer who had introduced them. Walter Pach was also living in Paris; his acquaintance was broad and his friendships led Davies and Kuhn into many studios they might otherwise have missed. It was Pach who introduced them to the brothers Duchamp-Villon, and thus to the "Nude Descending a Staircase" by Marcel Duchamp, which became the scandal of the Armory Show. No picture in America has ever elicited so many wisecracks, evoked so many cartoons, infuriated so many critics, or dumbfounded and angered so many peaceable citizens.

From Paris, Davies and Kuhn went to London to see Roger Fry, who was then holding a show of "moderns" at the Grafton Gallery. The two Americans were convinced that what they had collected was a far superior group of paintings and sculptures, though they arranged with Fry for the loan of some of the pieces he was exhibiting. By late in November the arrangements had been made. Walter Pach had agreed to see to the endless details of collecting, packing, and shipping in Paris and Davies and Kuhn went back to New York to herald their new prophets.

There was a good deal of the showman in Kuhn. He loved theatrical performers of all sorts, spent a good deal of his life consorting with circus folk, and he was well aware of the importance and magic of ballyhoo. He persuaded Frederick James Gregg, an editorial writer for the New York *Sun*, to take charge of the publicity for the forthcoming exhibition and the painter and critic Guy Pène du Bois was corralled to spread the word wherever he could—especially in *Arts and Decorations,* of which he was editor. Press releases and posters poured out from a little office and Kuhn hustled about, making arrangements with contractors to build booths in the Armory, organizing students to act as ticket takers and guards, trying to get a full list of the works of art so that there might be an accurate catalogue, helping to deal with the American painters whose work was to be shown and countering the complaints of those whose work was not. So many painters wanted to be included that William Glackens was appointed the chairman of a selection committee to cope with them. The catalogue never was completed as pictures and sculpture poured in until the last minute, and an incomplete one was issued in desperation. There were days of frightful anxiety, when the ship on which the paintings and sculptures were coming from Europe encountered storms on the Atlantic and turned up in New York harbor two weeks after it was due. Once the pictures arrived, not the least of the problems was how to make the military drill hall look like an art gallery, but at the suggestion of George Bellows, the painter and lithographer, Mrs. Whitney gave a thousand dollars at the last moment for greenery and other decorations. Swags of evergreen were hung from the Armory balcony and trees were arranged behind them; the hall looked not only handsome but festive.

In all about sixteen hundred pieces of sculpture, paintings, drawings, and prints were assembled at the Armory. There were separate rooms for the Cézannes and Van Goghs, the Redons and the Gauguins. In order to give a proper perspective on the new and revolutionary works there was also a collection of old and revolutionary works—pictures by Ingres and Delacroix and Daumier and Corot, by Puvis de Chavannes, and Renoir and Monet.

There was even a sixteenth-century drawing of geometrical human figures to show the respectable origins of cubism. And of course there were dancing Matisse nudes, and Picasso cubist figures. There were bright abstractions by Picabia and Kandinsky and Léger and somber ones by Braque; there were sprightly landscapes by Dufy and pale maidens with no noses by Laurencin; there were sculptures by Bourdelle and Maillol and moody pictures by Rouault. Indeed, it is difficult to think of a painter or sculptor who is not now considered a "modern old master" who was not represented at the Armory. Side by side with them were the tamer works of the Americans—John Sloan and Stuart Davis, Albert Ryder and William Glackens, Marsden Hartley, Mahonri Young, George Bellows, Edward Hopper, Karfiol, Luks, and dozens of others. It was a mammoth undertaking and an expensive one, but not a single member of the association that fostered it was asked to put up a cent. "It was Davies's party," Kuhn said. No one ever seemed to know exactly where the money came from to meet the expenses of bringing the pictures together, of the carpentry, the hangings, the pedestals for the sculpture, or the benches. Whenever money was needed Davies managed to find it.

The Armory Show opened its doors on the evening of February 17, 1913, and to the strains of band music from the balcony, four thousand people wandered among the bewildering pictures. "All society was there," Kuhn said, "all the art world." At the entrances art students sold catalogues and gave away free badges with the emblem of the show on them—the pine-tree flag of the American Revolution with the words "The New Spirit" printed below it. Davies and MacRae and Kuhn and John Quinn and a dozen or so artist members of the Association were in the receiving line, while Walter Pach, who had hurried to New York from Paris, was busily trying to explain the new art to the puzzled visitors. Quinn formally opened the exhibition with a speech. "It is the most complete art exhibition," he said, "that has been held anywhere in the world during the last quarter of a century." Quinn was an impressive figure, well known as a member of the National Democratic Committee, and as a sponsor of arts of Ireland, especially of the Abbey Players. "He was tall and aristocratic with a profile like a Roman coin's," a painter said of him, "only finer."

But for all the dignity that his presence lent to the occasion, it could not stay the "amazement and amusement" that, according to a reporter, "was written on the faces of the bystanders." They flocked to the rooms where the Post-Impressionists' and the "futurists'" pictures were hung and "so deeply packed was the crowd in front of the freakiest pictures, that it was almost impossible to see them."

Whether fury or bewilderment was the predominant emotion of those who attended the opening, there was a sense of excitement that was undeniable. There was no question that something was happening to the arts and that the safe and sensible tradition so dear to the academicians had locked horns with an outlandish, disrespectful, and, above all, vigorous enemy. "The opening night seemed to me one of the most exciting adventures I have experienced," wrote Joel Spingarn, an aesthetician of Columbia University. "What moved me strangely was this: I felt for the first time that art was recapturing its own essential madness at last, and that the modern painter-sculptor had won for himself a title of courage that was lacking in all the other fields of the arts."

Other critics could see only the madness, and the storm broke in the papers at once. "The Armory show is *pathological!* It is hideous!" said the *New York Times*. "Some of the most stupidly ugly pictures in the world and not a few pieces of sculpture to match them," wrote Royal Cortissoz, respected critic of the New York *Herald,* and he later added: "This is not a movement and a principle. It is unadulterated cheek." Cartoonists had a field day, especially with Duchamp's "Nude Descending a Staircase," which Julian Street referred to as an "explosion in a shingle factory." But in spite of hundreds of columns of type and the almost daily cartoons the public was at first apathetic. On the opening night it looked as though the success of the show were assured, but for the next two weeks almost nobody came and the deficit grew. It was on the second Saturday of the show that indifference suddenly turned into pandemonium.

The slow fuse of publicity finally detonated the explosion, the dam of indifference broke, and the public flooded through the doors of the Armory. "Actors, musicians, butlers, and shop girls . . . the exquisite, the vulgar from all walks of life," according to Kuhn, crowded around the astonishing exhibits. School children by the hundreds were shepherded by indignant teachers through the maze

of "vulgar, lawless, and profane" works of art. Art students came to
jeer and so did celebrities. Caruso, then at the peak of his operatic
career, entertained the spectators by drawing caricatures of the paintings and tossing them to the laughing crowd. The numbers became
so great that the price of admission in the mornings was raised from
twenty-five cents to a dollar so that those who wanted to study the
pictures seriously could get near them. In the four weeks in which
the show was open in New York more than a hundred thousand people
came to admire, to wonder, to puzzle, and to scoff. What had looked
to the members of the committee as though it might be a financial
calamity had turned into a very profitable venture. Not all of them,
however, were pleased with the turn that the affairs of the show
had taken.

"I hope," said the painter Robert Henri to Walter Pach, who was
in charge of selling the pictures and sculpture, "that for every
European picture you have sold you have sold one by an American."
Unfortunately for those who had promoted the exhibition as a means
of bringing American painters to the attention of the public this was
by no means what was happening. The Europeans were outselling
the Americans by a very discouraging ratio. Quinn bought between
five and six thousand dollars' worth of the new foreign art. The
Metropolitan Museum purchased a painting from the show by
Cézanne. It was "one score after another for foreign art," wrote Jerome
Myers, who was wounded and distressed by what he saw happening.
"People became freak-conscious, the normal taste was bewildered.
Faith lost its balance." But worse than that, the art market was suddenly turned upside down. "Art values shivered," he said; "some went
down to zero, others leaped skyward. . . . While foreign names became
familiar, un-American propaganda was ladled out wholesale."

Myers was by no means alone in his distaste for the foreign invasion. Royal Cortissoz called it a subversive movement on the part
of aliens to disrupt American art. "The United States," he said, "is
invaded by aliens, thousands of whom constitute so many acute perils
to the health of the body politic. Modernism is of precisely the same
heterogeneous alien origin and is imperiling the republic of art in the
same way." Cortissoz was never known as a liberal in art matters,
though he was one of the most influential and popular art critics of

his day. But a different, and far more booming voice took quite another attitude toward the foreign invasion. "Messrs. Davies, Kuhn, and Gregg," wrote ex-president Theodore Roosevelt in an article in the *Outlook*, "and their fellow members of the Association of American Painters and Sculptors have done a work of very real value in securing such an exhibition of both foreign and native painters and sculptures." Kuhn had showed Roosevelt around the show on March 4, the day that Woodrow Wilson was being inaugurated. He had been "gracious but non-committal" at the time, but in his article, which he called "A Layman's Views on an Art Exhibition," he pulled no punches.

There was no question that he disliked intensely the Cubists and Futurists and his remarks about them have often been quoted since to demonstrate the true Philistine attitude. But he recognized, as did few of the professional art critics of the day, that here was freedom for the artist and that freedom per se, was good. "There was one note entirely missing from the exhibition, and that was the note of the commonplace. There was not a touch of simpering, self-satisfied conventionality. . . . There was no stunting or dwarfing, no requirement that a man whose gifts lay in new directions should measure up or down to stereotyped and fossilized standards." And then he stated his views on the art itself. "But this does not in the least mean that the extremists . . . are entitled to any praise, save, perhaps, that they have helped to break fetters. Probably in any reform movement, any progressive movement, in any field of life, the penalty for avoiding the commonplace is a liability to extravagance. It is vitally necessary to move forward and to shake off the dead hand of the reactionaries; and yet we have to face the fact that there is apt to be a lunatic fringe among the votaries of any forward movement. In this recent exhibition the lunatic fringe was fully in evidence, especially in the rooms devoted to the Cubists and the Futurists, or Near-Impressionists."

It took a new kind of critical vocabulary to try to explain the strange new art. "Significant form," a phrase devised by an English critic, Clive Bell, fell from many lips. "Tremendously sincere" was the retort to those who claimed that the abstractionists were pulling the public's leg. "I am not competent to say whether these words represent sincerity or merely a conventional jargon," said Roosevelt, and added a very neat aphorism about the language of taste: "It is just as easy to be conventional about the fantastic as about the commonplace."

The repercussions of the Armory Show spread far beyond New York. Never before had art provided so much lively copy to American newspapers and magazines, so many funny stories, so much vituperation, or so much aesthetic heat which shed, so far as the public was concerned, so little aesthetic light. The newspapers, especially, had a field day. "Listen My Children and You Shall Hear/of the Which and the Why of the Daub and the Smear" was the heading of an article in one paper. In another a headline proclaimed:

CUBIST ART EXPLAINED!!!

Did the Armory Show Puzzle You? Just
Read This, Which Tells All About It.

Prize for a translation

There followed an explanation of the new art by François Picabia, one of the exhibitors, in which he said: "This new expression in painting is the 'objectivity of the subjectivity,'" and then added, "Art deals with deep, brooding, fundamental soul states." Most of the public found this laughable; some of them turned laughter to profit in one way or another. On March 23, the *New York Times* reported on an exhibition held at the Lighthouse for the Blind called "The Academy of Misapplied Art"—an exhibition of two hundred paintings "following cubistic, past-impressionistic, futuristic, neurotic, psychopathic, and paretic schools." The hits of the show were a "Matisse" by an eleven-year-old-girl named Nanette Turcas, and a painting by Henry Watrous, a professional artist, that was called "Emotions of a Lady of Sixty-three on Roller Skates." On March 13 a large New York department store ran an advertisement in the New York *Sun*:

The John Wanamaker store presents, tomorrow and Saturday, for the first time in America, Color Combinations of the Futurist Cubist Influence in Fashions in the new Paris Models for Spring. . . . The straight lines of the Cubist, and the color combinations of the Futurists and the Impressionists are presented for the first time in America by the Wanamaker stores.

At the bottom of the advertisement, which filled nearly an entire page, was a reproduction of the Armory Show's insignia, the pine tree and "The New Spirit."

On St. Patrick's Day night the show closed with a noisy, rowdy celebration. "It was the wildest, maddest, most intensely excited crowd that ever broke decorum," wrote an artist who was there. "The huge Armory was packed with the elite of New York—and many not so elite." Artists and millionaires, society matrons and reporters, art collectors and "celebrities too numerous to register" milled about, and at ten o'clock a regimental fife and drum corps saluted the close of the show with a rousing rendition of "Garry Owen." Once the public was cleared out, the artists of the Association and the girls who had taken tickets and sold catalogues started their own celebration. Through each room and section of the show marched the band with the crowd of artists and workers behind them. Champagne was produced, and there were toasts and speeches.

"To the Academy," shouted one artist in derision.

"No, no," retorted John Quinn. "Don't you remember Captain John Philip of the *Texas?* When his guns sank a Spanish ship at Santiago, he said, 'Don't cheer, boys, the poor devils are dying!' "

When Maurice Prendergast, a painter a generation older than the young men who arranged the Armory Show, came to see the exhibition, he looked around for a while, and then in the loud tones that are common to the hard-of-hearing he boomed out, "Too much Oh-my-God! art here."

From New York the show went to Chicago and nearly half of the too-much art was subtracted from it for the exhibition in the Art Institute. All of the shocking pictures, however, were included, and the press build-up that preceded their arrival was a publicist's dream. Serious articles by Harriet Monroe in the Chicago *Tribune* in which she tried to give the rationale of the new art were countered with full-page shockers in the *Record Herald.* ("Hark! Hark! The Critics Bark! The Cubists are coming to town, with Cubist hags and Cubist nags, and Even a Cubist Gown.") But the build-up did not presage the excitement caused by the show itself. Crowds as in New York jammed the Art Institute, but the city fathers of Chicago managed to add a fillip that was missing in New York. His Honor the Mayor publicly pronounced on Picabia's abstraction "The Dance at the Spring." "I see it. Plain as day," he said. "It's Charlie Merriam attacking the trac-

Palaces for the Rich

Richard Morris Hunt implanted the French château on American soil. All three of the pictures on this page are of houses he designed for Vanderbilts. Above, right, is William K.'s house at 52nd Street and Fifth Avenue in New York, and next to it is the main staircase of "Biltmore," below, the stately home he built for George W. Vanderbilt II near Asheville, North Carolina.

High Taste in the Nineties

The Columbian Exposition in Chicago in 1893 followed a decade of eager museum building and proselytizing for the fine arts. Above is Hunt's Administration Building for the Fair and MacMonnies' colossal fountain. Below, right is Sullivan's celebrated Transportation Building, and at its left a reception in the first of the big Middle-Western art edifices, the museum at Cincinnati.

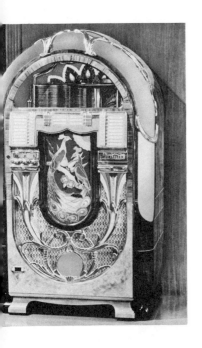

The Persistence of the Peacock

If the room at the upper right were wired for sound it would be almost indistinguishable from the juke box next to it. The peacock moved indoors in the nineties, stuffed on the newel post. Half a century later he turns up on a juke box surrounded with familiar trappings—stained glass, metal curlicues, glittering fabrics. Both the room above and the Oriental Booth (from the *Ladies' Home Journal* of 1896) would have been considered suitable for the Queen Anne-ish house below.

"Good" Taste and "Bad" Taste

Edward Bok, editor of the *Ladies' Home Journal,* conducted a long editorial campaign starting in the nineties against Queen Anne houses in "bad taste." He would have considered the house on the left (in Nyack, New York) an eyesore. He promoted such homes as the "Colonial House" (below) by Ralph Adams Cram (which could be built in 1896 for $5,000) and the little house, below, left, which cost only $1,000 in 1905.

An Artistic House of Half-Timbered Construction

The "Artistic" and the "Suitable"

Louis C. Tiffany lived in what he preached. Above are a selection of his wares and the entrance hall of his flat on East 26th Street in New York in 1883. Below, the young Elsie de Wolfe disports herself in an Oriental Booth in the days before she set out to abolish such clutter and replace it with the "suitable" decoration she designed for the rooms on the next page.

Elsie de Wolfe, "The Chintz Lady," designed the bedroom above and the dining room below for her own house near Gramercy Park in New York, in the first decade of this century.

The people who lived in the houses shown on the facing page had probably never heard of Elsie de Wolfe. The popular furniture for bungalows was "mission," also called "craftsman." With the bungalow and small concrete house are examples of furniture from Sears, Roebuck & Co. in the days when the bungalow was the equivalent of the modern ranch house.

$10.45

$5.95

The Art Exhibition That Overturned the Art World

The placid scene above is the only known photograph of the tumultuous Armory Show of 1913. Of all of the works of art displayed there none caused such anger, dismay, and laughter as Marcel Duchamp's "Nude Descending a Staircase," below, left. It is now in the Philadelphia Museum of Art. Next to it is a cartoon from the New York *Sun* of March 20, 1913.

SEEING NEW YORK WITH A CUBIST

The Rude Descending a Staircase
(Rush Hour at the Subway)

tion merger." And then he added, "A blind man with his hands tied to his back could paint as well with his feet."

And Chicago was loftily moral. Arthur Charles Farwell, president of the local Law and Order League, was reported as saying: "Why, the saloons could not hang these pictures [it was the Matisse nudes that bothered him]. There is a law prohibiting it. . . . The idea that people can gaze at this sort of thing without it hurting them is all bosh. This exhibition ought to be suppressed." An instructor in art at the Waller High School publicly complained that the exhibition was "nasty, lewd, immoral, and indecent." And a clergyman who had brought a group of Sunday school children for their annual visit to the uplifting masterpieces in the Art Institute let out a bellow of indignation when he saw the modern pictures and demanded that the public be protected from these "degeneracies." A few days later a local newspaper carried the headline "Futurist Art Included in State Vice Inquiry."

The inquiry itself amounted to nothing. The chairman of the Vice Commission, whom Walter Pach described as "a nice old state senator," came to look around and especially asked to see a painting called "Prostitution" and the "Nude Descending a Staircase." The former was a moral little picture about the evils of sin and the latter suggested nothing at all to the senator that he could object to. The publicity given to the investigation, however, brought out a kind of clientele that did not usually haunt the Art Institute. Pimps and prostitutes came to look at the "dirty pictures," and went away disgruntled at having wasted their quarters on admission tickets.

It was also in Chicago that the art students, instructors, and employees of the Institute staged a protest meeting at which they dressed in "futurist" costumes, painted their faces in odd colors, and burned a Matisse and Walter Pach in effigy. One of the professors made a "cubist speech" and his wife played "a futurist sonata." The "sonata," which no longer sounds very surprising, was Ravel's "Jeux d'Eau." In general the attitude of the city's mentors of taste was very much like that of the local newspaper reporters. W. M. R. French, the director of the Art Institute, said that Cubism was a "toss-up between madness and humbug."

From Chicago the exhibition went to Boston, but by that time the hilarity which it evoked seemed to have nearly burned out. Boston disapproved and in general stayed away, thinking that it was more seemly to ignore what Cortissoz had called "unadulterated cheek" than to make a fuss about it. The final tally of sales of pictures showed that more than two hundred and fifty had been bought in New York as against fifty in Chicago and Boston together. The total attendance figure is unknown, but Pach estimated that well over a quarter of a million people paid to see the pictures and an equal number had complimentary passes or came on the "free days" at the Art Institute.

The day of accounting to the members of the Association of American Painters and Sculptors came in the autumn following the close of the exhibition, and it was not a happy occasion. The members met at the Manhattan Hotel, and Kuhn, the secretary, placed his report upon the table. Guy Pène du Bois was the first to look at it. He studied it for a moment, shrugged his shoulders, and said, "I resign." Then Robert Henri looked, and then George Bellows, and Mahonri Young, and Jerome Myers, and one after another the members resigned and left the meeting without a further word. The show had been a financial success, but it had also been a financial calamity, so the artists thought, for American art. The evidence of the report was overwhelming: the painters of Europe had captured the imagination of American collectors and with it the market. "Our land of opportunity," said Myers, "was thrown wide open to foreign art, unrestricted and triumphant."

The Armory Show has often been called a turning point in American taste, and there is no denying that it was. But whether taste was turned forward or backward from that point is another question. The immediate influence of the exhibition on the taste of most Americans was scarcely noticeable. Possibly a hundred thousand people out of a population of nearly a hundred million believed that the new art from Europe was a revelation, a sign of new vitality in the visual arts, and a gate to the future. More likely, a few thousand or even a few hundred thought so. The strange paintings and sculptures in the Armory, which most solid citizens took as a direct insult to their sensibilities, produced a small hard corps of disciples and a vast new army of hostiles. Most Americans were confirmed in the conviction that artists are irresponsible members of society, bent on careers of exhibitionism. Even those who had conscientiously followed the paths down which the mentors of taste had led them, determined to refine their taste by reading and travel, by hours spent in museums and still more hours in lecture halls, were unprepared for what was suddenly thrust at them in the name of art. Indeed, they, the very backbone of support of the arts, were the most infuriated of all.

Ever since the middle of the nineteenth century, when Jarves had tried to interest an apathetic public in his Italian primitives, taste-makers had been trying to improve the public taste through all sorts of education. If only, they believed, we could get people to look at pictures, hang them on their walls, know their histories and distinguish their formal, plastic qualities from their superficial sentimental aspects, an improvement in the public taste would be assured. The exhibition at the Philadelphia Centennial in 1876, which almost overnight had made millions of Americans art conscious, had not been an assault on taste; it had been an extravagant but gentle goading. The societies of truth and beauty in the nineties had been inspired by hopes of cultural uplift, by dreams that they might raise the level of good taste among the middle and lower classes by encouragement and entertainment and appeals to civic pride. In the planning and decoration of houses men like Edward Bok believed that if you pointed out the difference between good taste and bad and supplied inexpensive reproductions of paintings by old masters, the level of public taste would be raised. Good taste, indeed, seemed to be an achievable virtue identified in most people's minds with education and refinement.

It was squarely in the center of this target that the slings and arrows of the outrageous Armory Show landed. Is it any wonder that those whose taste was fastidious should have been flabbergasted and furious at the "vulgarities" of color and distortions of drawing that were thrust upon them? How could you apply any of the rules of taste to these "monstrosities?" It was unthinkable!

It was precisely at the safe and sane rules of taste that the Armory Show was aimed—at the Academy, which in its superior wisdom decreed what was good art and what was not, at the critics whose tidy vocabulary of clichés could describe any painting and whose judgments were weighed in the concise language of historical reference, the loose language of lofty sentiment, and the technical language of the studio. A few critics like Clive Bell and Roger Fry were intellectually sympathetic with the new movement and were ready with a new vocabulary to justify it, and not only it, but all art that came before it. Subject matter and philosophical content no longer mattered; all that mattered was "significant form"; it covered everything.

The principal result of the Armory Show was to divide the republic of taste, which had once been like France—a country of many political groups separated by minute shadings of opinion—into two major parties, a nice convenient system that is dear to Americans. The new parties were "Modern" and "Traditional" and until quite recently if you gave your allegiance to either party, you voted the straight ticket. Lately the party lines have begun to blur, as they did earlier in our political system, and the bitterness of the schism that was wrought by the Armory Show has been somewhat, but by no means entirely, sweetened by the passage of time.

"Whatever you think of this show," said one of the laymen who came to the Armory the night the exhibition opened, "our art can never be quite the same again." He was right, and so was another visitor, a banker named James A. Stillman who was being shown around by the sculptor Rudolph Evans. "Something is wrong with the world," he said. "These men know."

PART THREE

The Corporate Taste

CHAPTER XIII

Taste on Wheels

While the eager young American painters were honing their knives to cut the throat of the Academy in 1912, two adventurers were on their way to Flagstaff, Arizona. If the painters had known what was in store for American taste in the visual arts, they would have had their eyes on these two men, one a vaudeville magnate, the other a glove salesman. They were not pioneers in the arts but, unwittingly, they were to discover a sleepy little town and turn it into a bewildering combination of honky-tonk, illusion factory, glorified suburb, and city of despair. The magnate was Jesse L. Lasky and the salesman was his nephew, Samuel Goldfish, who later changed his name to Sam Goldwyn. With them were the script of a moving picture called *The Squaw Man*, a playwright named Cecil B. DeMille, and an actor, Dustin Farnum. On the map Flagstaff looked like the ideal place to make a "Western" but one glance at its characterless landscape from the station platform was enough; the pioneers got straight back on the train and headed for the West Coast. It was by pure chance that a passing acquaintance mentioned to them a quiet suburb of Los Angeles as a likely place to make their film. The suburb was, of course, Hollywood, where no holly grows, and in a rented barn on a peaceful road called Vine Street they made their first feature-length movie.

Messrs. Lasky and Goldwyn, when they headed for Flagstaff, had no more notion what they were letting loose on taste than did Henry Ford when he tinkered the Model T into existence. But the second decade of the century was a time when mechanical gadgets were primary factors in shaping taste into brand-new patterns.

It had, of course, happened before. The power loom and the

power lathe had changed the taste of most Americans eighty years earlier by turning out miles of inexpensive flowered carpet and hundreds of thousands of fancy chairs; the mechanical jigsaw had covered homes with dripping and curlicued ornament; Pullman's gadgets, the sleeping, dining, and lounge cars, had introduced thousands of footloose people to new extravagances of decoration; Roebling's gadget to make steel cable had introduced a new factor of "tension" into American methods of building, and some eager steel salesmen from Pittsburgh had convinced a group of Chicago architects that the material they were making with the new Bessemer process for railroad tracks could also be used to hold up buildings— the skyscraper came into being. Inventors and mechanics and the financiers who promoted them had thrown their gadgets on the market. It was not their business to worry about what the public taste should be; they were concerned with manufacture and merchandising, with keeping production costs down and the desire for new goods up. The public's sensibilities were the concern of the critics and the educators, of the moralists and the artists. Henry Ford, when he put America on rubber wheels, was no more concerned about his effect on taste than the earlier inventors and industrialists or than Lasky and Goldwyn with their script for *The Squaw Man*.

Yet together the automobile industry and the movies shifted the background against which taste in our own time must be portrayed. The consumers of taste were being reshuffled, new kinds of tastemakers began to appear, new patterns and standards of living were emerging, and the characteristics of "Corporate Taste" were just poking their heads above the horizon.

Movies were nothing new in 1912, and though they were looked on darkly as promoters of juvenile delinquency by clergymen, whose congregations and collections they seemed to be stealing, they were not taken seriously by those who concerned themselves with the niceties of taste. The nickelodeon, which had been the inspiration of two Pittsburgh showmen, John P. Harris and Harry Davis, in 1905 had spread across the country, a wildfire of tricked-up elegance and the forerunner of today's movie palace. A nickelodeon was simply a converted store, ornamented with cast-off opera and theater props, sometimes seating as many as ninety customers. It offered a movie show that ran anywhere from twenty minutes to an hour. The usual fare was a one-reel melodrama, a comedy of even shorter length, and a "song slide" which projected popular lyrics on the screen to encourage the customers to sing along with a paid crooner and pianist. There were between eight and ten thousand nickelodeons in America by 1908, with electric signs and fancy names—"Bijou Dream," "Pictorium," "Dreamland," "Theatorium," and "Jewel"—and a major attraction of the day was a thriller called *The Great Train Robbery*. Vaudeville houses, reluctantly aware that this was competition that they could not lick and therefore had better join, took to running movies at the end of their shows, and even the churches opened their parish halls on Saturday nights to discreet selections of movies which they followed by gospel meetings.

But before Goldwyn and Lasky went to the West Coast there were few full-length, eight-reel films made anywhere. New York studios or "factories," as they were then called, were turning out two- and three-reelers on schedules that provided a single day for shooting an entire picture, and the competition was stiff and the tactics of distribution cut-throat. Only in France were the motion pictures thought of as a potential art form rather than just quick, cheap diversion. There in 1908 the "Divine Sarah" Bernhardt was persuaded to play the role of Queen Elizabeth in what turned out to be, like the early television shows nearly forty years later, a theatrical performance photographed in motion. It was not until the war years that in small and large towns all over the country local opera houses (many of which were just meeting halls on the second floor over a block of stores) were equipped for regular movie shows, and piano teachers and church organists found themselves with a new profession. Day after day they rattled off their repertories of sweet and ominous, furious and romantic tunes as they watched the figures on the silent screen hurrying about their business of love-making, cliff-hanging, villain-chasing, and tears-behind-laughter. Everyone knew the musical clichés. The strains of Massenet's "Elegie" or Rubinstein's "Kammenoi-Ostrow" meant melancholy, as distinguished from Rachmaninoff's "Prelude in G Sharp Minor" or "One Fine Day" from *Madame Butterfly*, which denoted tragedy. Joy was summoned by "The Scarf

Dance" or Schubert's "Serenade" or Grieg's "To Spring." The hearts of the public were often wrung, their spines made to tingle, and their sides all but split with laughter, but little thought was given to their aesthetic sensibilities.

The mechanical gadget, hand-cranked and flickering, or, if you prefer, the new medium of visual expression for the artist as well as the financier, emerged only a few years after the Armory Show in a guise that looked as though it might have an influence on the public taste. The early films had been frankly, precipitously, and unself-consciously catch-penny entertainment. No one regarded them as an aesthetic menace, any more than one regards the circus as a threat to taste. Even those who considered the movies immoral did not preach the evils of the effect they might have on the public appreciation of the arts. And if it was immediately obvious that the impact of the Armory Show was far-reaching, no one except perhaps a few visionaries had any notion in 1913 how profoundly the movies were to influence standards of taste. Not that the movies have ever been innovators of new styles and modes. They have only been one (though perhaps the most pervasive one) of a number of implements for spreading "the latest thing," and this thing that they have spread has been for the most part the conservative, safe, and accepted taste that has already had the stamp of suburban and upper middle-class approval. With one important difference— in the movies everything is raised to a slightly higher power. The suburban home in the films, for example, is likely to be larger, more expensively furnished, more tidily landscaped, and more consistent in its character than it ever is in actuality. It is the housewife's dream and not her house, or even the house of her most envied friend.

At first, when the movies were still in their two- and three-reel infancy, the interiors against which the action took place fell into three categories that were known to the trade as "rich, plain, and mean." The director, who in those days was also the art department, had his carpenters build the sets out of painted theatrical flats (moldings, mantels, even the pictures on the wall were painted), and for models he used interiors torn from such magazines as Bok's *Ladies' Home Journal* and from books. It was not until after the burgeoning of the "epic" films—*The Birth of a Nation* in 1915 and a year later

Intolerance—that the young movie industry began to flex its artistic muscles and undertake to build lavish sets, filled with intricate ornamental detail, and furnished with opulent period furniture that made the housewife's mouth water. Art departments became nearly as important as actors, and in the next decade the art director established himself as a purveyor of taste on a scale which even the editors of the mass circulation magazines could not attain. In the days of the silent films, language offered no barrier whatsoever to the distribution of movies to all the civilized and near-civilized nations of the world, and more than half of Hollywood's revenue came from foreign audiences. It was then that the picture of America as a nation of lavish tastes and habits, a portrait that has been a nightmare to our official propagandists for more than a decade, began to spread across the world. It was then, according to Robert E. Sherwood, that a chieftain of a remote African tribe "sent an order to America for a gleaming white barber's chair for use as a throne, explaining that he had seen one like it in an Adolphe Menjou picture." It was only a few years later that Bette Davis appeared in a film called *Dark Victory* and furniture shops and department stores were besieged by women who wanted a sofa "just like the one in Bette Davis's drawing room."

There is no question that the movies influence the taste of many people and that they can make fads even if they do not, except rarely, initiate fashions. But the industry has never posed as a crusader in such matters. It has served to spread, with a speed unknown before, tastes that seemed already sure of public acceptance. A new hairdo on Betty Hutton may become the teen-age standard almost overnight, or the revelation that Clark Gable doesn't wear an undershirt (as he didn't in *It Happened One Night*) may, and indeed did, cause a calamity in the undershirt industry. But the movies' business is not to make taste in any other arts but their own or to foster the notions of decorators or architects; their function is to be dramatic and entertaining and sometimes instructive and this they accomplish by a combination of reportorial (or in movie lingo "documentary") and theatrical techniques that both simulate and exaggerate reality. In the documentary film this is accomplished by focusing rapt attention on the commonplace, on the details of a street scene, for example, on the cracked and blistered store sign, the chalk of children's games on the pavement, the reflection of clouds in a delicatessen window. In achieving theatrical effects the setting is used to heighten the tension or the glamour or the serenity of the scene, and it is not tastefulness that matters but emotional effect. Devotees of simple, clean-surfaced, undressed modern interiors have complained that the movie industry has been lax in not promoting what is "progressive" in architecture and design. The practical fact is that, cinematically speaking, there is nothing interesting in an unbroken surface, and in a room that is skinned down to its bare walls there are no accents of decoration that enable the moviegoers to locate a character when he is shown in a close-up. If the movies have had an effect on that abstract quality known as visual taste, it is probably through the moviegoer's inability to avoid focusing on what the movie director insists that he look at. He is made to consider momentarily details of the visual world over which his eyes have long since grown accustomed to slide without stopping, and in this sense the movies may have trained his perception and possibly his appreciation of the uncommon in the commonplace. But there is no way to measure this, and certainly it is of minute concern to the entertainment world. It is even questionable whether the art films that have been made in such profusion during the past few years and which attempt to interest the public in the works of such artists as Van Gogh, Michelangelo, and Alexander Calder haven't, by being sententious and boring, made more enemies of art than art lovers.

But whether the influence of the movies on taste has been good or evil, the undeniable fact that for years about 55,000,000 Americans a week have paid admissions to see them is a measure of their inevitable impact on what is regarded as acceptable taste. There had never before been a medium that could hold a candle to them either for visual impact or for the vastness of the audience, and yet their tendency has been to perpetuate accepted standards of taste rather than to promote new ones. While developing their own art, they have been, in a sense, the enemy of other arts, as any writer, painter, or decorator who has been to Hollywood will hasten to tell you. It is not merely that they have played taste safe; they have played it in ways that are cinematically and dramatically sound. The quality of movies, *qua* movies, is a separate question from that of the influence of movies on taste in general, and it is well to remember in both connections that, while thousands of second- and third- and tenth-rate movies have poured out of the studios for more than half a century, several hundred first-rate films have also been made. If in half a dozen decades this new art has produced half a dozen masterpieces, it has done at least as well as the arts of writing and painting, and probably better.

So far the young art has gone through three principal stages in its development and is just now entering upon a fourth. The first stage was the simple excitement of putting motion on a flat screen; the second was to add the realm of the heart to that of the nerves, and emotion was added to motion through the telling of stories; the third was to add the dimension of sound to that of vision in 1929 and thus to involve another of the senses; and the fourth and newest one is to add the illusion of personal involvement in the space occupied by the action on the screen. In other words, to use an analogy that is by no means entirely accurate, in a brief span of time the movies have progressed from a primitivism, in which the depiction of action alone was enough to satisfy the artist and the spectator, to simple storytelling against flat backgrounds such as was portrayed in medieval manuscripts. From there they moved to a kind of Renaissance concern with formalized realism with a message. And now Cinerama, 3-D, and CinemaScope try to achieve an overpowering size and depth like the Baroque painting of the seventeenth century in which space encompassed the beholder as well as the figures in the picture. Space becomes limitless and dramatic and in it larger-than-life figures lead an existence of larger-than-life emotions.

And this has been accomplished in a short time by groups of businessmen and artists employing a series of mechanical gadgets. Whether the stockholders and boards of directors of movie companies thought of the movies as an art or not, corporations had got themselves deeply involved in the art business in a way in which they had not been before. They were not just hiring individual designers to make drawings for their merchandise; they were employing many different kinds of men and women with many kinds of artistic skills to work together in making a group-produced art. Sometimes the product had extraordinary harmony; sometimes it was a hodge-podge, but it was always a product of many artists and not of one. There hadn't been anything quite like it since the days of the Gothic cathedral, those monuments (sometimes harmonious and sometimes a hodge-podge) to the skills of many anonymous geniuses—sculptors, woodcarvers, and stained-glass makers. Though their motives were presumably different, the chairman of the board of the movie company and the medieval Cardinal had a good deal in common; neither lacked for congregations of the faithful, or for influence on the artistic tastes of their times, or for the final word on what the artist could get away with.

The influence of the movie industry and that of the automobile industry on taste could not have been more unlike. The assault of the movies was on the eyes of the nation, direct, seductive, and purposeful. The automobile moved in slowly and its effects on taste were the result of changes in the habits and habitats of millions of people and a recutting of many facets of the social structure. Obviously no one played so large a part in this revolution as Henry Ford, and there is certainly no more unlikely personality to have been a prime factor in changing tastes in the arts or one who would have given them less thought. Art, indeed, meant precisely nothing to him.

It was certainly not the design of Mr. Ford's gadget but its price that was to change the face of America. Inexpensive transportation transformed the suburbs from quiet towns in which large, comfortable, verandaed residences sat upon expansive lawns, into bustling "dormitory towns" with small houses of tapestry brick set down on quarter acres of land upholstered with stiff little blue spruces. Before the days of the automobile the Philadelphia "Main Line," New York's Westchester County, and such communities as Englewood and Morristown, New Jersey, were, like towns on the outskirts of other great cities, mostly the summer residences of the wealthy. No one who could not afford to be driven in his carriage to the station each morning, unless he lived in one of the "undesirable" locations near the tracks, could commute to the metropolis and his office. With the arrival of the automobile it became possible even for those who lived five or six miles from the train to gulp down their coffee at seven-forty in the morning and still make the 8:01. For many years the automobile was the rich man's toy, a noisy, undependable, dusty, and liver-shaking contraption that was in much the same class as the private yacht. Closed cars (that is, half-closed cars: the chauffeur sat out in the cold) were only for the very rich, and even as late as 1919 ninety per cent of the nearly nine million automobiles on the roads were touring cars and roadsters with fabric tops and celluloid storm curtains. Just after the First World War those who rode in sedans and town cars or limousines were frankly thought by many people to be the profiteers who were responsible for the high prices of food, bearing out in some degree Woodrow Wilson's prediction made while he was still the president of Princeton that the automobile as "a picture of the arrogance of wealth, with all its independence and carelessness" was sure to "spread socialistic feelings."

Ford, however, took care of that threat with the Model T. He put it into production in 1908 and sold it for just under $1,000. It was his ambition to produce a thousand cars a day and to keep pushing the price down and down. By 1914 Ford was selling a quarter of a million cars a year and of all the cars on the road (there were two and a half million registered in 1915) about half were Model T's. Its price finally dropped to $295. Not only did the city dweller move to the suburbs to lead a semirural life, but the farmer brought his family to town to shop and to the movies whenever he felt like it. What had been an hour trip in a buggy became a ten- or fifteen-minute trip in "tin Lizzie"; what had once been a rare excursion to the country for the city dweller was reversed to become a routine daily trip from home to office and back. But Ford's influence was more far-reaching than just a change in the mobility of the citizenry; he dropped a bombshell into economic thinking.

"Industry must manage to keep wages high and prices low," he declared. "Otherwise it will limit the number of its customers. One's own employees should be one's own best customers." He demonstrated this in a way which rocked not only the automobile industry on its heels but all other industries as well. He declared that henceforth the minimum wage for common labor at Ford plants would be $5 a day and that the working day would be eight and not nine hours. This was in 1914 when the usual minimum wage was less than half what

Ford agreed to pay. To keep production costs low and wages (and therefore purchasing power) high meant that the work on the production line had to be kept at the most intense possible pitch and the worker became more of a robot than ever. But a principle was established that meant, as Frederick Lewis Allen has demonstrated in *The Big Change*, that the gulf between the rich and the poor was to grow narrower and narrower, and that their tastes and their ability to gratify them were to grow closer and closer together. As men and women of the laboring classes became better and better customers (thanks not only to Ford, of course, but to the labor unions that continually pressed for higher wages and more time in which to spend them) industry and the tastemakers became more and more concerned with competing for their favors. Not only did they become customers for what were once considered luxury goods, but they became potential patrons of the arts as well. Their tastes in entertainment, in decoration, in design, and in architecture became primary concerns not only of those who wanted to profit from them but also of those who wanted to alter and improve them for the greater glory of the arts.

Ford's personal revolution had accomplished two interrelated but quite different revolutions in the taste business. On the one hand it had introduced the era of the suburb—the era in which the city dweller not only dreamed of owning his own home in the country but went out and built or bought it by the millions. What were his tastes? Real-estate developers and their architects fell all over themselves trying to find out, and they produced the most conglomerate and ludicrous architecture this country has ever seen in their efforts to be all styles to all men. On the other hand Ford's evolution had raised the social level of a great many people to the place where, if they weren't already worrying about whether their taste was good or not, the decorating and fashion and mass circulation family magazine were going to see to it that they did.

CHAPTER XIV

Suburbia in Excelsis

"Their hearts and their treasure are twenty
miles apart."

Heaven knows what Mrs. Trollope would have thought of the suburbs of the 1920's; they were like nothing under the sky that she knew in America a century before. They were, indeed, quite unlike anything that had ever existed anywhere. As a woman who believed strongly in the virtues of a neatly stratified society, she would have been at a loss to know where to pigeonhole what was to all intents and purposes a brand-new kind of landed gentry. Many of them were only slightly landed and they were gentry in an American sense that Mrs. Trollope had not been able to understand or countenance. They were gentry simply because they were free Americans. The only wealth and position that they had inherited was the tradition of equality, but now they had land instead of landlords.

The weedlike growth of the suburbs was more than just a geographical shift by hundreds of thousands of people from the hot and cluttered pavements of the city to the nearby spaces which, if they were not exactly open, were at least ajar. It was a major upheaval in the social and cultural structure of the nation and in the patterns of the lives of millions of families. America had long been divided into cities and towns and rural areas, and those who lived in the cities and towns did the business and those in the rural areas managed and tilled the soil and tended the cattle. With the arrival of the suburbs came a whole new class of people who lived in the country, where they produced nothing but floral borders and privet hedges and children; they commuted to the cities to do their business. "Their hearts and their treasure," said Agnes Rogers, "are twenty miles apart."

Busy new islands of civilization appeared where there had been dumps and marshes and potato fields. Little sleeping towns that had had many of the aspects of communities hundreds of miles from a metropolis were astonished to wake up and find themselves all but incorporated into the city limits, with populations that doubled and tripled in a decade. What had once been a small cluster of village stores suddenly turned into a flourishing main street with movie theaters and specialty shops, with chain stores that offered overwhelming competition to small merchants, with rows of filling stations, and cars, mostly driven by women, bumper to bumper clogging the thoroughfare. By day the suburbs were nearly deserted by men, who had gone to the city, and the community, its culture and its climate, became a woman's world. In the suburbs a man's home is his wife's castle.

In a manner of speaking it was the third revolution in America in a century and its influence on taste was as profound as the other two. The first was the one that had taken place when the landed gentry of the plantations were being pushed into the background by Old Hickory and his graceless colleagues. It was at that moment that the industrialization of America was about to pour "tasteful" objects into the market for everyone to buy and the scramble for taste was on. But out of the power of the machine was to come a new revolution and a new aristocracy, just as tight in its exclusiveness as the old one. It was made up not only of men who had made fortunes out of manufacture, like Colonel Colt of the revolver, but of those who had made impressive sums of money out of dealing in corporations—the Vanderbilts, and Carnegies, and Morgans, and Fricks—or in municipal real estate like the Astors and Goelets. And a great show of wealth they made, not only in their private palaces and yachts and collections of masterpieces from Europe, but in rigid circles in which they moved aloof and apart from the world that fed them so splendidly.

The exodus to the suburbs was a third, and middle-class, revolution, and never has there been a revolution so bloodless in so many different senses of the word. It was a movement in which the virtues of stability, conformity, and reasonableness were paramount, in which edu-

cation, healthful recreation, and community service were not steps
to the good life but the good life itself. To those concerned with the
level of the public taste it seemed to offer great promise. It seemed to
indicate that Americans were going to settle down and thereby give
the roots of culture a chance to grow and take firm hold. For another
thing the suburbs seemed to offer a place where individual tastes
might have a decent chance to develop, and where children could be
raised without either the onus of rural provincialism or the oppressive-
ness of the crowded city. Perhaps the new member of the landed
gentry had only a five-room house on a quarter acre of land and even
on that there was a heavy mortgage, but at least he was not the ten-
ant of a great holder of metropolitan real estate. A man who owns his
own home is likely to be a great deal more concerned with the taste
that it betrays than a man who pays rent. A home owner's home is
nobody's fault but his own.

From the relatively short perspective of thirty years the houses that
were built in the suburbs in the early and mid-twenties, and in which
a great many people are still living, may seem strangely out of keeping with the new architectural ideas that were bubbling then to the
surface, but they do not seem in the least inexplicable. There is certainly nothing odd in the behavior of the new small landowner who
builds or buys a house that is a smaller version of what the wealthier
landowner has built for himself. The country house from the time
that Hunt introduced the doctrine of "adaptation" had been entirely
that; it was a château or a chalet, it was a Dutch burgher's house or
a steam-heated version of a Spanish hacienda. When the new suburbanite moved out of the city to build his house on a small plot of
land the models that were suggested to him by the *Ladies' Home
Journal* and *House Beautiful* were modest versions of the houses that
sat at the ends of long driveways behind high hedges. The picturesque
again came into fashion, as it had in the sixties and seventies of the
previous century, and what did it matter if a six-room château that
had a slate roof and a turret and was built of granite let almost no
light into its living and bed rooms through the leaded glass of tiny
windows? What did it matter that one's neighbor just across the privet
hedge lived in a doll's version of an English country house, half-

timbered and stuccoed, with the second floor projecting out slightly over the first to make a "charming irregularity?"

Both charm and irregularity were often obtained at the sacrifice of modern methods of construction and of living space, and the ends to which real-estate speculators and home buyers would go to achieve something conventionally out of the ordinary were considerable. In a magazine called *Charm* that was published by L. Bamberger and Company, the Newark, New Jersey, department store, in the late twenties and early thirties there appeared an advertisement that sums up the suburban dream of the period. Under the caption "Enter here . . . and leave the commonplace world outside!" is a description of "a gracious dwelling styled by Architect Frank J. Forster like a Norman French farmhouse." The white oak floors, it says, are "pegged down with hand wrought iron nails . . . the windows of antique glass imported from England." All lighting fixtures and hardware were hand wrought like the nails, and the stone fireplace "was brought from a New England country house more than three hundred years old when dismantled." The crowning touch, however, makes even the New England fireplace in the French farmhouse seem only slightly eccentric. "The hand hewn beams in the livingroom," the copy continues, "and [in] the stone flagged summer porch were cut in the surrounding wood by a Negro axeman brought from South Carolina for the task." How like the days, fifty years before, when Mr. Vanderbilt imported French stone masons to build his château at Biltmore, and yet how unlike!

This particular house was in New Jersey, but its counterpart was in Evanston, Illinois, and Ardmore, Pennsylvania, and wherever there were fashionable suburbs. In less prosperous suburbs there were more modest versions of it—the nails machine made, the beams in the living room cut by power saws and then slightly hacked up to give them a hand-hewn look; the windows had modern "antiqued" glass, and the fireplace was built of any old boulders or tapestry brick. "Quaint" became a popular word again and a desirable quality that housewives went to considerable lengths to achieve in breakfast nooks, in arrangements of living room and bedroom furniture, and in new fashions of bric-a-brac.

It was in the twenties that the "antiques craze" turned every old farmhouse and barn into a potential treasure trove, and aged maple beds and corner cupboards, spinning wheels and cobblers' benches, chests of drawers and blanket chests became the apples of a million eyes. Never has so much old paint been scraped off so much old furniture in order, as collectors said, "to get down to the original wood." Hundreds of houses on back roads and highways in New England were turned into furniture and bibelot shops. Pewter that the family had put away when they could afford china, and luster candlesticks that had been forgotten when they could buy brass or silver came out of the attic or the cold-cupboard to be proudly displayed and sold for gratifying prices to avid collectors. There was hardly a suburban housewife who didn't harbor a secret "little" dealer in a "darling little shop" (or shoppe) to which she would not risk taking even her closest friends. Affluent collectors began to buy entire paneled rooms and build homes to go around them; others built exact replicas of seventeenth-century houses, some even going so far as to scorn electricity and bathrooms. Husbands became experts in antiquing modern copies of old pieces with dirt and linseed oil so that they might not be out of character with the "authentic pieces." John Marquand describes a barn in *Wickford Point* that was done over into a dwelling and in which there was genuine fireproofed hay sticking out of the loft. (Mr. Marquand himself in the thirties bought a seventeenth-century house in West Newbury, Massachusetts, which he intended to move in its entirety to his place on Kent's Island in Newbury; the expense however, was prohibitive.)

Wagon wheels became ceiling fixtures; cobblers' benches became coffee tables; black caldrons and kettles hung on irons in fireplaces; Early American hand-blocked wallpapers were copied for machine production and sold by the mile. There was a boom in hand-hooked rugs, and you could buy them at New England filling stations when you paused for gas. Primitive paintings, especially of farm scenes and dour ancestors in black suits or black bonnets, were patched up where a child's foot had long ago gone through them and were hung over fireplaces in suburban homes. Prints that Currier & Ives had sold for a quarter were handsomely framed in curly or bird's-eye maple and brought a hundred times their original price. Rogers groups again stood on little living-room tables; once they had been considered art, now they were "quaint" and they were "collector's items."

The causes and origins of the popular craze for Early American antiques that reached its peak in the twenties (and is still very much with us though in a more rarefied form)* can be stated in general terms although it is difficult to pin them down to particular decorators and tastemakers. As early as the Centennial Exposition in Philadelphia there were a few collectors of Colonial Americana and some pieces, especially ceramics, were shown then. By the nineties there were a number of wealthy collectors who were working in earnest to gather prize examples of early furniture and handicrafts, but the public was neither aware of nor interested in their activities. In general Americans were too much interested in the remarkable industrial progress and expansion of the nation to care about rummaging around in its own historic past. It was nice to use the past as a point from which to measure how far America had come, but progress was more important than nostalgia. In the Hudson-Fulton celebration in New York in 1909 there was, however, a nostalgic feast. A replica of the *Half Moon* was anchored in the Hudson River, and in a parade for which the city turned out in droves there were floats depicting Washington's farewell to his troops, an Erie Canal barge, Lafayette's visit, and a Colonial house. It was not, however, until the American Wing of the Metropolitan Museum in New York opened its doors in 1924 that the public realized that they should take "Early American" seriously. It was a clarion call: here were the art and handicrafts, the furniture and china and pewter and silver of our ancestors enshrined, catalogued, taken seriously, and displayed as treasure. Robert de Forest, the chairman of the board of the museum, gave the money to build the wing, and the collections came mainly from Mrs. Russell Sage and R. T. H. Halsey, one of the original trustees of the museum.

Henry Ford restored the Wayside Inn at South Sudbury, Massachusetts, filling it with furniture and curios from the seventeenth, eighteenth, and nineteenth centuries, perhaps in repentance for his famous remark, "History is bunk." In Williamsburg, Virginia, the

---

*The *Wall Street Journal* for November 3, 1953, reported: "Post's Grape-Nuts Flakes boxes now contain plans for sawing and hammering out six early American 'antiques,' including the 'courting mirror,' in your home workshop. A panel on the outside of the package bills this as a '15-cent value free.'"

Rockefellers financed a complete replica of the governor's palace and gardens and the refurbishing of adjacent buildings, and the townsfolk, who were employed in the local taverns and shops, wore (and still wear) colonial costumes at their work. Even the A & P was Early American. Williamsburg colors became the standard for decorating the spate of small houses that went up in the twenties and thirties, all paying scrupulous attention to authentic colonial details with almost archaeological zeal. The *Ladies' Home Journal, Good Housekeeping,* and *House Beautiful* were quick to assure their readers that little "plantation homes," Cape Cod "salt boxes," and the Pennsylvania Dutch Colonial homes were all in the best of taste. By the end of the twenties Grand Rapids was turning out copies of all manner of Early American tables and chairs and cobblers' benches and beds for those who wanted the new old look but could not afford to pay the soaring prices that dealers had found they could demand for genuinely worm-eaten pieces with their "original brasses."

"Personality" became a word more and more frequently connected with the house and its decorations. Downing had said in his day: "Much of the character of every man may be read in his house," but the somewhat ominous tone of voice was missing in the thirties of this century. Emily Post, whose reputation rests more on her books of etiquette than on her contribution to architecture and decoration, published a fat volume in 1930 called *The Personality of a House* and in it she said: "Its personality should express your personality, just as every gesture you make—or fail to make—expresses your gay animation or your restraint, your old fashioned conventions, your perplexing mystery, or your emancipated modernism—whichever characteristics are typically yours." Such remarks set a great many women to wondering just what their personalities were—mysterious? emancipated? old-fashioned? It was a challenge and a puzzle, and the soul-searching produced some very odd interiors and probably a good many perplexed husbands. Personality and the early American craze became inescapable. Even Childs restaurants, once famous for their white-tiled walls, businesslike appearance, and chefs in the front windows making griddle cakes, began to redecorate either in the Early American elegant style, or the tavern style, or the Spanish manner. Alice Foote McDougall made a fortune out of suburban ladies who looked upon her restaurants, bristling with ancestral gew-gaws, as the acme of the quaint and the picturesque.

The concern with expressing personality in architecture and decoration was by no means limited to the suburban home. Even our great universities spent millions upon millions of dollars trying to dress up for what they thought was their role. Harvard with money from the Harkness family suddenly began to erect tremendous dormitories (called "houses") in the Georgian manner, each of which looked, as one architect said, "like a lot of New England public libraries with a town hall on top." At Yale the architect James Gamble Rogers turned to the English university tradition and built in a style known as "collegiate Gothic," with the result that undergraduates learned to live in a moat-surrounded building behind tiny leaded window panes and to disport themselves on lawns beneath soaring Gothic towers. There was a city ordinance in New Haven that all buildings facing on the Harkness Quadrangle must be in a sympathetic style of Gothic, and clothing stores and little restaurants were housed in stone gabled buildings, with arched doorways.

Other universities followed the same pseudo-archaeological pattern. Duke spent its tobacco millions on Gothic; Princeton spent its millions the same way, and there is a story, probably apocryphal, that the University of Chicago wrote to the University of Oxford for advice on how to build a Gothic chemistry laboratory. "We cannot help you," wrote back the chemists at Oxford. "We haven't built a Gothic building for four hundred years." The American universities were peopled to a great extent by the sons of suburban families and the academic's state of mind was much like that of the housewife. College presidents and trustees rummaged around in the past, uncertain just what the personalities of their institutions were or how best to express them and give them substance. It was, indeed, a time when America in general was more confused about who and what it was than it had ever been before.

From another quarter a new wind had began to blow, quietly at first and then with increasing velocity until it reached the full cry of a hurricane. It was the wind of "modernism," and for the most part suburban America was content to batten down its doors and windows and ride out the storm. As we look at the suburbs now, about thirty years after the wind first began to blow, we can distinguish some traces of the storm but not as many as one might expect. At first glance the effect seems slight indeed, and considering the intensity of the attack that was leveled at American architecture by those who were promoting the International Style, as it was called, as the *summum bonum*, there are only a few scattered buildings to show where the attack was successful. The real consequences, however, are less spectacular than the few "machines for living" that were built in the late twenties and thirties. The wind blew a good deal of fancy work out of a good many homes and planted in them new and simpler furniture. It provided architects, even those who believed in what they called "traditional styles," with a good many new words in their architectural vocabulary that they were quick to combine into clichés. It simplified and "streamlined" the kitchen, making surfaces smooth and cupboards often flush and hidden; it did not necessarily make the kitchen a more efficient workroom. It increased the size of living-room windows until they became known as "glass areas." But more important than these superficial changes and many others of the same nature, it eventually took the heart out of the "adaptation" movement, out of the archaeological search for styles, and laid the ghost of Richard Morris Hunt, which had stalked the land for more than half a century.

There is no need for us to trace the rise of the "Modern Movement" from its nineteenth-century origins, from H. H. Richardson and Louis Sullivan, from the beginnings of styles based on "tension" instead of on "thrust," but without chauvinism it can be said that much of it started in America, was transplanted to Europe, and was brought back to this country in the 1920's as a European idea. In the American public mind it didn't become a "movement" or a cause at all until after the depression of the thirties was well under way. The influence of the Museum of Modern Art was a prime factor in spreading the gospel of the new architecture. When the museum was founded in 1929 with money given by four or five wealthy patrons including Mrs. John D. Rockefeller, Jr. and Miss Lizzie Bliss, it devoted itself entirely to exhibitions of paintings. By 1931 its young director, Alfred H. Barr, Jr., who had wanted to have a department of architecture from the start, enlisted the help of two friends, both in their twenties,

Philip Johnson, who later became an architect, and Henry-Russell Hitchcock, now one of America's most distinguished architectural historians, and architecture and industrial design became an active concern of the museum. In the spring of 1932 they held their first exhibition of buildings by the men who are now considered the old masters of Modern architecture: Le Corbusier, Mies van der Rohe, Gropius, J. J. P. Oud, Frank Lloyd Wright, and some others. The public reaction was sufficiently violent to cause a considerable amount of argument and a good many columns of publicity in magazines and newspapers. It was Alfred Barr who invented the name of the International Style, and it was in the catalogue of that exhibition that the term "functionalism" (actually used in a derogatory sense) was first publicized.

Modern was a good deal more than just a method of building with reinforced concrete in a manner in which the forms, to use the language of its own arguments, expressed the function and the materials. It was more than just a "flat-chested" style, as Frank Lloyd Wright called it, or as the Museum of Modern Art said, a new system based on building "in terms of *volume* of space enclosed by planes or surfaces —as opposed to mass and solidity." It was a new concept of the way men, if they were sensible, rational beings ought to live, and the concept had not only a structural but also a social morality built into it. Modern was said to be *honest*, whereas "adaptation" was dishonest; the *truth* of architecture was to be found in the new style, not, as the adapters had so fervently believed, in the slow accretion of architectural knowledge over the ages. The Gothic Revival, you will remember, had won the field on the grounds that it was a more *honest* architecture for America than the Greek Revival. Eastlake had preached a doctrine of "sincerity" that meant putting furniture together with dowels instead of nails or screws, an offshoot of the morality of William Morris's crafts movement. The Queen Anne house swept all before it because the vernacular methods of building plus the artistry of the architect were more *honest* than that which was used in Gothic or Italian villas or Mansard houses. Finally came Modern, a new style with an old morality using the same old words—*honesty, sincerity.* Men's ideas of how buildings should look change radically as do their methods of building them; the words they use to justify their revolutionary ideas change not at all. Of all the arts none wraps itself in such a cloak of morality as architecture or assumes so many moral arguments to justify itself; no other art impinges so surely and inevitably on the life of everyone and therefore must justify itself to every man.

"Ironically," wrote Elizabeth Mock in the foreword to a catalogue of an exhibition of Modern architecture in 1944, "here was a style which, more consciously than any other in history, was directed toward the improvement of the comfort and convenience, health and happiness of society, yet there has probably never been an architectural movement more deeply distrusted by the public." In retrospect it seems to have been the very concern with the happiness of society that made people distrust it so. It was not just an architecture of simple style, new construction, and rational function; it was an architecture of do-goodism, and the public was damned if it wanted to be done-good-by. At least not in such "overgrown garages," "shoe boxes on stilts," or "cold white factories," as they called those examples of the International Style of which they saw pictures in magazines and newspapers.

The International Style quickly came to be identified in most people's minds with a phrase coined by Le Corbusier, one of the progenitors and practitioners of the new style. He insisted that a house should be "a machine for living." The idea was enough to send the shivers down the backs of most Americans, as well as most Germans and most Frenchmen. Isolated buildings were built by adventurous souls, but the style caught on nowhere as a fad. It did, however, fire the imaginations of young architects with a zeal as intemperate as that with which Hunt had fired an earlier generation with the glories of the Beaux Arts. A new battle of the styles was on. This time it was not the Classic versus the Gothic, though it might just as well have been; it was Modern versus Traditional.

The reason why this new style (unlike many that had been presented to Americans before) did not catch on tells as much about the people who rejected it as about the style itself. It arrived in all its pristine, chaste, and essentially puritan simplicity at a moment when, as we have noted, a great many Americans were moving to the suburbs to adopt a new way of life. But simplicity was not what they wanted —least of all simplicity with a machine-made look. To nearly everyone "functional" architecture was identified with the factory or with the office—with the skyscrapers that were built in such profusion in the decade before the Depression, and the industrial plants that were all business and very little humanity. "Own your own home!" a slogan so familiar in the twenties as to be almost meaningless, sometimes meant a new house in an established suburb, sometimes a house in a "development" or a "subdivision." But in those days, unlike the mass-produced houses of almost identical shape and style that we have seen rising near all big cities in the last six or seven years, a home-of-one's-own meant a house different from one's neighbor's. Often the difference was merely in the architectural slip cover that went over the plan. It was common for rows of houses with identical insides to be covered with Dutch and Colonial and Spanish outsides. The contractor-builders in the twenties and thirties frequently employed architects not to work on the plans which they ran up themselves but merely to design varieties of exteriors. The houses, many of them, were very shoddily built. ("It is estimated," wrote Walter B. Pitkin in 1931, "that Americans are swindled out of half a billion dollars a year by crooked building contractors.") They gave a semblance of individuality without a trace of eccentricity, and this was what those who became new landowners seemed to want. When they moved into new communities the last thing on their minds was to appear eccentric to their neighbors. Taste was a quality to be carefully strained, and the court of appeal on all such matters was first a peek into your neighbor's window and then a careful study of the women's magazines. In the latter the housewife would find an occasional "Modern" house or interior which the editors presented in order to show they were up to date, and she was likely to find conventional interiors or a style popularly known as "modernistic."

"Modernistic" was the bane of the existence of· those who were seriously trying to promote "Modern." It was, in effect, a sort of jazz-age version of a classic style. The simple rectangles and curves of the Modern were squeezed into oblique angles; mirrors and wall brackets became spiked and askew and were often made of blue glass; modernistic furniture was typified by the bookcase that stepped up like a skyscraper and was capped with a copy of an African mask, or a piece of copper beaten into a bas-relief of a draped female. Fireplaces were surrounded by metal moldings, sometimes combinations of brass and steel in angular abstract patterns or conventionalized flowers. It was, in some respects, a decorator's interpretation of the Duchamps and Picassos of the Armory Show plus the influence of Greenwich Village bohemianism where people sat on poufs and ottomans and burned incense and used long, tapering cigarette holders. As a style, modernistic was far more urban than suburban and it caught on less firmly in people's houses than it did in hotels such as the new Waldorf-Astoria in New York and in the lobbies of such skyscrapers as the Chrysler Building and the Empire State.

The suburbanite, however, gave it short shrift. It was not the sort of atmosphere he, or more likely she, wanted to create, and *atmosphere* was as important as *personality.* The Modern house was unrelenting in its demands for an orderly life. It had no cellar and it had no attic; its style depended on the beauty of simple surfaces free of clutter. It seemed an unlikely place for a man to come home to, throw himself down, put his feet up and shut out the world of work and neighbors. He could scarcely tell, with the walls of glass that were *de rigueur* in modern design, whether he was indoors or outdoors. He insisted it was not for him and never would be. Modern was damn nonsense, and he wanted no part of it, and neither (except in the kitchen) did his wife.

In some ways more important than his own feelings were those of his banker, or loan association manager, who put up the mortgage for him. A Modern house was not considered a good gamble and these men would not finance one. Suppose a man built a Modern house and then moved away, who would take it over? And besides, once that simple concrete exterior began to age, it looked even more terrible than when it was new, and it seemed to age awfully fast. A crack on a clear surface shows like a scar on a woman's cheek; if the walls of a traditional house began to age they could be painted. Some suburbs had zoning laws that prohibited the construction of Modern houses lest they spoil the character and atmosphere of the community.

The arguments for Modern were reasonable and humanistic, but the arguments against it were also reasonable and they were intensely human. "We value," wrote Lewis Mumford in 1932 in a discussion of Modern architecture, "the positive results of science, disciplined thinking, coherent organization, collective enterprise, and that happy impersonality which is one of the highest fruits of personal development." He was right in the abstract, but he was wrong in the many specific cases of men and women who, regimented as they may have been in their suburban communities by standards of taste and custom, wanted to feel that they were free agents in their own homes. All day at work they were the creatures of disciplined thinking and coherent organization and collective enterprise; the last thing they wanted when they came home was happy impersonality. They wanted to feel that they were part of a tradition, part of the gentry who had built homes before, part of a great stream that had risen generations earlier in the headwaters of the American past. Modern architecture seemed to them to have no place in this stream.

The collapse of the stock market in October, 1929 did not change the essential complexion of taste overnight, but taste went ghastly pale and stayed that way for nearly a decade. Private building slowed down to a lethargic shuffle; skyscrapers that were on their way up when the crash came found themselves half-empty towers, ghostly symbols of a recently unbridled optimism. An architecture such as America had never seen in the environs of its great cities grew up in deserted lots and near dumps—shacks of discarded packing boxes and advertising signs, of odd pieces of rusted corrugated iron and broken fence slats. They were called Hoovervilles, and they were the disgrace of the nation. But it was disgrace and hardship that gave the style known as Modern its chance. It was a social architecture, an architecture of reform with dreams of a better society built into its aesthetic doctrine. When the planners who were desperately trying to cope with the famous "third of a nation," ill-housed and ill-fed, began to devise ways of relieving the desperate housing situation, it was natural that they should turn to this simple new architecture for their inspiration. Government projects like Greenbelt, Maryland, were conceived in the new, flat-roofed, and "functional" style, and city planners worked with architects in an attempt to create communities that someday might serve as models to private builders. Towns like Roosevelt, New Jersey, not far from Princeton, were built all at once—single-storied houses, flat-roofed, and with walls of glass; there were housing projects on the outskirts of many cities—most of which looked like clusters of brick or concrete boxes with holes punched in them at regular intervals. They were singularly lacking in the promise of joy, but they were happier than the slums.

The government housing projects did not set a pattern for speculators who were building with private buyers or tenants in mind. Apartment houses in the thirties went right on putting Tudor or French Provincial details on their brick façades. Even after the Second World War had started, the Metropolitan Life Insurance Company financed a tremendous housing development in the vicinity of Washington and it put its money into a glorified traditional American village. Those few adventurous individuals who built Modern houses in the thirties did so in a pioneering spirit. Functionalism was not as functional as it looked or was touted to be; carpenters and roofers were not used to flush windows and flat roofs and joints without moldings, and a little warping could be a calamitous thing. In some ways the adventurers were like the owners of automobiles in 1905; they expected to get out every few miles and look under the hood. Most people did not feel they could afford this luxury, even if they wanted it.

If Modern had failed to make more than a slight and official dent on domestic architecture, it had, by the end of the thirties, caught on and firmly established itself in a good many other nooks and crannies of life. Not only was some department-store furniture beginning to assume the squared-off clichés of functionalism but designers had gone on a spree of streamlining from which they have yet to return. Everything from toasters to refrigerators, from vacuum cleaners to orange-juice squeezers became wind-resistant. The new profession of industrial design was coming into its own, and "machine art" was, like American antiques a decade before, enshrined in a museum in 1934. At the Museum of Modern Art, bearing springs, dentists' X-ray units, electric waffle irons, alarm clocks, cash registers, and any number of other "useful objects" were put on pedestals under spotlights. Modern became almost mandatory for the design of up-to-date shops and gas stations; even roadside diners cast off their old Pullman-car look and emerged gleaming with glass brick and aluminum and furnished with chairs made of bent chromium tubing. The symbol of hope of the decade, a futile but magnificent gesture in the name of peace and prosperity, was the biggest architectural last straw at which a people on the brink of war ever grasped. In 1939 the New York World's Fair rose on a reclaimed Long Island swamp, a city of geometrical shapes, of Trylon and Perisphere, of strip windows and ramps and flat roofs and glass walls. Like the White City of the Columbian Exposition of 1893, which had celebrated the triumph of the Beaux Arts, the New York World's Fair announced in indisputable terms that Modern of a sort was here to stay—at least for a while, and at least so far as industrial building was concerned.

If the Second World War implanted any single architectural idea more firmly than any other in people's minds it was that of impermanence and makeshift. Wartime housing was slapped together with haste and a modicum of attention to style. Temporary buildings—as houses for factory workers, as government offices, as military installations—were the rule rather than the exception, and tens of thousands of families lived in that perfect symbol of American mobility, the trailer. Whether, if there had been no war, Modern would have emerged during the forties as the characteristic architecture of America is scarcely worth speculating about. The fact was that the war left a housing crisis. Another fact was that people were glad to live in anything, even Quonset huts. Conversion from war to peace played some odd tricks on taste, but it did not greatly change it.

"Here is the [Buckminster] Fuller house," wrote a correspondent for *PM* shortly after the war was over, "the first mass-produced house to reach the market. Look at it: it's round, made of aluminum and plastics and stainless steel. Next year there'll be 50,000 of them on the market at about $6,500 each plus the land." Beech Aircraft was going to make them. There was another gadget that someone had dreamed up that would lay a concrete house the way a hen lays an egg. It was a time of dreams; almost anything that anybody could suggest that might actually get a house built was worth considering. Apartments were not to be had except occasionally by bribing an agent or a superintendent or by watching the obituary columns and getting your bid in before the body was buried. People who owned houses wanted twice or three times what they had paid for them a year or so earlier. It looked like a moment when a great many people, having to build from scratch and with GI loans to help them, might almost create an architectural renaissance. Books on how to plan a house, how to get a good architect, how to be Modern or advanced poured onto the market. R. H. Macy and Company held an exhibition of "Homes America Wants"; the designs were originally made for *Good Housekeeping* and the decorations were "created by the magazine's decorating staff under the supervision of Dorothy Draper." At the Museum of Modern Art there was an exhibition called "Tomorrow's Small House"—ten scale models of houses designed at the behest of the *Ladies' Home Journal*. The Museum said, "A million and a quarter new dwellings will be needed each year after the war, a challenge without precedent in American building history."

Good Housekeeping's guess was better than the *Ladies' Home Journal*'s; they claimed that people set great store by "sentiment" and that they would want "the exterior to be a contemporary treatment of some familiar architectural style, the interior to be the ultimate in modern convenience." The *Journal* took a loftier line and the designs it sponsored were strictly in the Modern idiom. One of the houses that *Good Housekeeping* had selected was described in the *New York Times*: "The most inviting, if not the most practical for this locality, is probably the ranch house planned by Allen G. Siple of Beverly Hills, Calif." It is doubtful if even the editors of *Good Housekeeping* had any idea what was going to happen to the ranch house in the next decade.

Something else, however, happened first, something that was to establish a brand-new suburban pattern that even contemporary critics of our culture looked upon with wide-eyed dismay. Hundreds and then thousands of almost identical houses began to spread out over a 1,400-acre tract of land on Long Island. In 1945 William J. Levitt started to build Levittown, and by 1948 he was putting up houses at the rate of 150 a week until he had completed 6,000 of them. Now, as I write this five years later, there are 70,000 people in Levittown. Eric Larrabee said in *Harper's*: "His [Levitt's] house is the model-T equivalent of the rose-covered cottage—or Cape Coddage, as someone has called it. It is meant to look like the Little Home of One's Own that was a subsidiary myth of the America Dream long before Charlie Chaplin put it into 'Modern Times.'" Levittown is not alone; Lakewood, a suburb of Los Angeles is even larger than Levittown, and Park Forest, thirty miles south of Chicago, now is approaching a population of 30,000. Not even the Federal Government, that insures mortgages on the houses in these new mass-produced suburbs, knows how many such developments there are, but as Harry Henderson, who has made a study of the way people live in them, has written, "One can safely assume that their combined population totals several million people."

The quality of these mass-produced communities that distinguishes them from the suburbs of the twenties and thirties is that their populations are highly mobile and that they are almost entirely inhabited by families in the same age and income groups. They are, in effect, single-class communities where there is no living on the wrong side of the tracks, and any spiritual tracks that there may be are not determined by income or background or promise; they are determined by personality.

"The standardized house," wrote Harry Henderson in *Harper's* in November, 1953, "creates an emphasis on interior decorating. Most people try hard to achieve 'something different.' In hundreds of houses I never saw two interiors that matched—and I saw my first tiger-striped wallpaper. (The only item that is endlessly repeated is a brass skillet hung on a red brick wall.) Yet two styles predominate: Early American and Modern. . . . Taste levels are high. My interviews with wives revealed that their models and ideas came primarily from pictures of rooms in national magazines. Nobody copies an entire room, but they take different items from different pictures. At first women said, 'Well, moving into a new house, you want everything new.' Later some altered this explanation, saying, 'Nearly everybody is new. . . . I mean, they are newly married and new to the community. They don't feel too certain about things, especially moving into a place where everyone is a stranger. If you've seen something in a magazine—well, people will nearly always like it.' So many times were remarks of this character repeated that I concluded that what many sought in their furniture was a kind of 'approval insurance.' "

Here was something new in the attitude of the suburbs. True, "approval insurance" had long been basic to the housewife's exercise of her taste or her adaptation of the taste of the magazines, and "something different" is merely a play on the old theme of expressing one's personality. What was new was that there was no ladder in the suburban community that one might climb conscientiously, hoping one day to reach the top rungs. One does not move up in a one-class suburb; one moves out—to another suburb where the houses and the lawns are bigger, the trees older and taller, and the atmosphere is one of permanence not transience. Eventually the families that prosper will presumably arrive in the old, established suburbs—not the ones so close to the metropolis that they have been all but absorbed into it, but those like Winnetka or Pasadena or Montclair. There the top levels of corporate management, the corporation lawyers, the consultants to industry live in spacious houses set back from the same street on which lower but aspiring management lives in smaller replicas of the big houses. There the taste of Elsie de Wolfe and her successors to positions of eminence in the field of decoration, hold sway—chic but styleless elegance, luxuriousness with an air, comfort without daring or distinction.

But less and less do the tastes of the relatively poor and the relatively well-to-do seem to differ in the ways in which they are expressed, and there is no better example of this unity of taste than the ubiquitous ranch house. It has become the standard new suburban dwelling in the suburbs of New York as of Boston, of Chicago as of Cincinnati or Seattle or, of course, Los Angeles. It varies in price from the least expensive (around $7,000) to any amount a man can afford. In a single suburb of Chicago, for example, you can buy ranch houses that cost $10,000 or $65,000 just a few hundred yards apart, and the expensive one will be merely a larger, more carefully built and more completely gadgeted version of the former. Stylistically they are sired by the same California notion of the good life. They are all one-story cottages with gently sloping roofs and out-sized picture windows. Some (the expensive ones) are long and some are U-shaped with patios; some have a slight touch of the Cape Cod cottage, some have Spanish Colonial touches, some have "dropped" living rooms and "split levels," but somehow the romantic appeal of the West is built into all of them. The suburban ranches are often a quarter of an acre or less, and the view from the picture window is of another picture window. The pervasive Western spirit of the open range and the barbecue, of sunshine and leisure is nonetheless nationwide. For the nostalgic pleasures of exhuming the early American past, this generation has substituted the romantic dream of the prairie. The enchantment of Paul Revere, hero and silversmith, has been displaced by Hopalong, and the American architectural tradition of making things seem to be what they are not has found a new expression.

The looks of the suburbs have changed radically since the early years of the century. Not only have they grown tremendously in size but they have become layers upon layers of architectural styles. Many that were entirely composed of individual houses now are crowded with sprawling apartments; many of the new ones have been laid out with a careful eye to avoiding thoroughfares that might endanger the lives of children; many now have shopping centers with ample parking areas instead of the crowded main streets which suburban growth made infuriating. Regional differences in taste have all but disappeared, and if you were to be put down blindfolded in the new suburbs of any large American city it would be difficult to tell whether you were in the East or the West, the North or the South. Sears, Roebuck, and Company, the largest retailers in the world, have given up the custom of printing different catalogues for different parts of the country; the same sofa covered in the same material sells at almost precisely the same rate in each of the six sales districts into which they divide the country. The same is true of lamps, and pictures for the wall, and women's dresses.

This ironing out of regional differences in taste does not mean that America has come to be a place where everyone likes exactly the same things, as the pages upon pages of different styles of furniture in the Sears catalogue bear witness. It means several other things. It means that our highly mobile suburban population take their tastes with them, rub them against new friends and absorb new tastes at the same time that they are depositing their old ones in the new community. It means that styles and fads and tastes travel faster than they used to—through the movies, through magazines with circulations in the several millions, through radio and TV. The time lag between the introduction of a new style and its popularization has been narrowed down as communications media feel impelled to provide their audiences constantly with something new and different.

But what does it mean in progress of taste? Is the national taste any better now than it was in the 1890's? Is it any better than it was when

Edward Bok spread the *Ladies' Home Journal* houses across the country at the same time that Wilson, The Bungalow Man, was marketing the precursor of the ranch house, and the Portland Cement companies were promoting the Age of Concrete? It is a question that each reader will answer first in terms of his own home and the homes of his friends. "On the whole," he will say, "I think taste has improved." But then he will look beyond his own immediate circle at the tastes of millions of people he does not know, and he will say, "On second thought I'm not so sure."

CHAPTER XV

The Art World

"QUESTION: Is there any hope for the baseball player to learn about art?

"ANSWER: Baseball players are not so dumb
as you think. Their attitude is about the same
as that of the art world towards the general
public."

WOODSTOCK ART CONFERENCE, 1947

Not long after the surrender of the Japanese brought an end to
the Second World War, I asked a Wall Street broker, who
was (and still is) an avid and discerning collector of contemporary
American paintings, why he thought art was having such a boom in
this country. "It's just a fad," he said. "It's like those miniature golf
courses that were everywhere during the depression. Art has
caught on."

Art had indeed caught on, but the boom turned out to be more
tenacious than the miniature golf craze that had whiled away the
doldrums of the thirties. There had been art booms in America before. The Art Unions in the 1840's had been largely responsible for
the first one, when the excitement of the lottery had turned indifference on the part of many people into an apparent concern with the
higher reaches of the sensibilities. Again after the Civil War, when
fortunes came and went with such precipitous rapidity, art whisked
in and out of galleries and auction rooms. The speed with which it
changed hands delighted the dealers even if it made the serious promoters of the arts, men like Jarves and Tuckerman, apprehensive
about the frivolity and snobbishness of the public taste. Still another

boom had been set off by the Centennial Exposition in Philadelphia in 1876, when the largest collection of paintings and sculptures that had ever been gathered anywhere exposed millions of Americans to a taste for what passed for art in those days—anecdotes in costume, romantic landscapes, glassy-eyed maidens, and nudes armed against impropriety by skin as pure and impervious as porcelain.

Superficially the start of the latest art boom can be laid to nothing more complex than the acute scarcity of consumer goods for a few years after the war was over. You will remember that refrigerators and automobiles, stoves and washing machines, vacuum cleaners and even bathtubs were nearly impossible to come by in the middle of the last decade and that waiting lists of customers for hard goods were discouragingly long. Money, however, was not scarce and neither was art, especially art made by Americans, and a great many families that might otherwise never have found themselves in possession of any pictures but color reproductions began in modest ways to buy drawings and paintings. New collections were thus started, and the person who once begins to run an art fever is likely to find himself with a galloping disease. Art dealers were quick to see the possibilities of the new market that had opened to them, and the virginal collector on a small scale became a quarry well worth pursuing. But the postwar art boom cannot be explained as simply a mere matter of economic scarcity of supply and eagerness of demand. Its roots lie deeper than that in soil that had been carefully cultivated, fertilized, and watered for a long time by an eager band of tastemakers—museum officials, art critics, dealers, teachers, and aesthetic messiahs.

The present art boom (for it continues even though its character differs somewhat from the first postwar flush) is the result of a conscientious, expensive, and on the whole well-organized campaign against Philistinism. The campaign reaches back to the days when Luman Reed gave up his grocery business to become a collector and Bryan presided over his private Broadway gallery in a velvet cape, but by contrast with those early bearers of the aesthetic standard, the group that now calls itself the Art World can compete as a pressure group with any commercial association or lobby in financial resources and public relations techniques. They are a well-trained, if not well-disciplined, band of zealots who have constituted themselves a sort of

Salvation Army of our sensibilities. The ways in which they work to bring the light of art into the dark caverns of the Philistine mind have been greatly refined since the days when the Metropolitan Museum was founded in 1873, since the heyday of Chautauqua and the Societies for Truth and Beauty, and even since the eruption of disorderly conduct provoked by the Armory Show in 1913. An understanding of what is happening to taste in our own time is impossible without at least a cursory look at today's Art World—the people who run museums and those who work in them, the dealers who sell art, the collectors and, almost incidentally, the artists.

The Art World is international. That is not to say that there is any very strong international amity in the arts, for national artistic prides are strong and jealousies are sometimes bitter. Ideas and information, however, circulate through the open channels and through the various undergrounds of the Art World in ways that tie together not only the official echelons, such as museums, but also those who trade in art, the dealers, and those who make it, the artists. For more than a century Paris has been the acknowledged headquarters of the Art World and to it have flocked not only artists and architects to study in its ateliers or lead the bohemian life of its Left Bank and Montmartre, but also connoisseurs, curators, scholars, and dealers to hear the latest word and bask in an aesthetically congenial atmosphere. Since the war Paris has been losing its position in some respects to Rome where, as in the days of Hiram Powers and Horatio Greenough and John Rogers, American artists are again congregating, but its position as the world's art capital remains reasonably secure. The Art World of America is an almost autonomous branch of the bigger Art World, though the habit of looking to Paris for approbation is deeply ingrained in America's art conscience. In spite of its recent efforts to reassure itself of the eminence of its position, the American Art World still casts its eyes across the Atlantic to see if Europe approves of what it is doing.

But as it casts its eyes inland on its own sphere of influence it is bothered by no such misgivings about the importance of its mission or about the position that it occupies in the cultural life of the nation. Its mission is twofold: first, to be the custodian of the accumulated treasures that more than a century of avid collecting have made the property of the public, and second, to educate the public taste. The first of these offers no problems other than the expensive ones of housing, display, care and protection, which absorb the income of hundreds of millions of dollars in endowments and a good deal of tax money besides. The second, however, is full of pitfalls, for the public taste is a volatile and capricious monster that defies being trained and tamed. On the one hand the public looks to the Art World to tell it what it should like and by what standards it should make judgments in matters of taste; on the other hand, it insists on its own right to have opinions on matters of art, or, if it feels that way, to have no opinions at all. It is often resentful of the fact that even those who pose as experts on such matters cannot agree among themselves and seem constantly to be changing their minds. As a result the Art World is a peculiarly touchy group of people, frustrated because they are not listened to as attentively as they believe they should be, frightened that their dirty linen may be washed in public, and fearful lest their fallibility in matters of taste may be exposed by the Philistines. Without the authoritative exercise of taste there could be no Art World, and with it its members can never know peace.

The American Art World is loosely organized in a vast bureaucracy, hydra-headed and munificently financed. It is often shaken by open and acrimonious splits on matters of artistic policy, such as the running battle between the traditionalists and the modernists, but on one count there is unanimity: the public must be made art conscious. The top echelon of the Art World is far more likely to be found in marble palaces than in ivory towers—that is, among museum directors rather than among scholars. America's investment in museum marble, real estate, endowments, and collections of art, history, and science was estimated by the director of the Metropolitan a few years ago to be between three and four billion dollars. This opulence is a far cry from the days when Jarves and his supporters in Boston could raise only $5,000 toward purchasing his distinguished collection of Italian primitives. Today there are more than two thousand museums in America in which are housed a fair share of the artistic treasures that once belonged to great collectors and patrons of Europe and Asia. The invasion of Europe that the *Burlington Magazine* of London complained about so bitterly in 1904 has not only made the Metropolitan Museum "the richest treasure house in the Western Hemisphere" but has been the basis of the National Gallery in Washington, of such distinguished collections as those in the museums of Cleveland, Chicago, St. Louis, Toledo, Detroit, Kansas City, Los Angeles, and San Francisco, and of many once private museums such as Mr. Frick's in New York and Mr. Phillips' in Washington, which are now the property of the people. The custodians of this wealth, the museum directors, are potentially the most important tastemakers in the Art World because they hold the strings to the largest purses; they stand at the top of the art bureaucracy.

By training the museum director considers himself primarily a man of taste. He has been schooled in connoisseurship at the Fogg Museum of Harvard University, or as a medievalist at Princeton, or in the *Kunsthistorische* atmosphere of New York University's Institute of Fine Arts, to which so many celebrated German art historians were brought from Hitler's clutches in the 1930's. He has written his thesis on Catalonian altar frontals, or on Byzantine ivories, or on the Master of the Female Half-length, so he is a scholar as well. He has been trained to believe in the inherent good of masses of accumulated art-historical data, in the historical relevance of the second-rate work of the minor master, and in the miracle of the masterpiece. He knows that his reputation among his colleagues depends on the quality of the exhibitions he stages and the collections he amasses, but that his reputation with his board of trustees is directly related to his ability to raise money and to the magic of the door count. He knows that no matter what his attitude toward contemporary painting may be, three-quarters of the artists in his vicinity are going to consider him a mortal enemy and a stuffed shirt, for to the artist he smacks of officialdom. He is torn, almost inevitably, among his functions as a man of taste and scholarship (who is a patron of the arts), his duties as an administrator, and his calling as a barker for culture.

So he is likely, simultaneously, to indulge in the intensely private pleasures of public collecting and to reach out in an effort to scoop in the public with a gesture of bringing the heathen into the warm fold of taste and culture. The palace that he inhabits is usually an awkward relic of another generation's concept of grandeur, but the ideas of the relation of museums to the public have changed radically in the past twenty-five years and with them methods of displaying art. The great hall of art which was popular in the days when Richard Morris Hunt did over the Metropolitan in the nineties is now being scaled down to more intimate, low-ceilinged, and artificially lighted galleries. Museum aloofness is giving way to a spirit of public service, and the air of the holy sanctuary to that of the palace of entertainment. It is no longer considered by museum directors enough to give the public a "touchstone of taste"; the touchstone in which the founders had such confidence in the 1870's did not seem to solve the problem of the public sensibilities. Museum directors have consequently shifted to a policy of courting "Mr. Citizen," who, according to the *Art News* a few years ago, "has not yet grasped the fact that he has a say in regard to the riches which once belonged to princes."

There is considerable difference of opinion in the Art World about how best to court Mr. Citizen. Some say that he is more enticed by the mysterious riches that once belonged to princes than by art and that there is no reason to explain too much to him. Those who hold this view stick to the old *à la carte* method of display—a number of expensive items with impressive names strung along in a row from which the museum goer is expected to pick his own menu. "When I walk into a museum," Heywood Broun complained of this method, "the most important information I get is longevity statistics—Fra Lippo Lippi, 1360?–1410?"* There are museum directors who agree with this complaint, and consequently there is a tendency now to use (when feasible) the *table d'hôte* method of display; pictures, sculpture, furniture, and *objets d'art* of a period are grouped together, their relationships explained by elaborate (if usually unread) labels, in order to provide a balanced and supposedly digestible meal. This approach is under severe attack from those who consider the masterpiece more important than what it means to the uninitiated, and by those who like their aesthetic stimulants straight.

The museum director uses all sorts of bait to attract the public—cafeteria lunches, children's museums, lectures, tea in the sculpture court. He experiments, as San Francisco and Boston have been doing recently, with television and the prospect of flashing masterpieces into

*Actually his name was Fra Filippo Lippi and his longevity statistics are 1406?-1469.

millions of living rooms. If he is in a large metropolitan center, he sends portable exhibitions, easily installed, into the hinterland (in much the same way and spirit that the Central Art Association did in the nineties) for hanging at the Thursday Morning Club or the high school auditorium. He may set up a "Clinic of Good Taste," as the Chicago Art Institute did a few years ago, or he may put a group of pictures into a trailer truck remodeled to be a little ambulatory gallery and send them on a prolonged tour around the state, as the museum in Richmond, Virginia, has been doing. Supported by a small but steadfast and effective force of curators, assistants, lecturers, librarians, docents, guards, maintenance men, and miscellaneous young women, he wages constant battle against the indifference and Philistinism of the community.

As a result the "Philistines" swarm into the museums, catching at culture as catch can. Museum attendance has been climbing steadily since the end of the war until now the figure has reached about 55,000,000 a year for all museums—about the number that go to the movies each week. Francis Henry Taylor, the director of the Metropolitan, who calls his museum "a gymnasium in which the visitor may develop the muscles of the eye," has explained the growing museum attendance as follows: "A generation of philanthropy in the fine arts is beginning to pay off. A hell of a lot of money, you know, has been poured into institutions like this one, and we're beginning to collect the dividends. People are beginning to realize the social value of what they can get and carry away from a place like this. . . . We're growing up in this country, and the public is beginning to want to know something about the brave new world it is paying for." Each year for the past five years attendance at the Metropolitan has averaged around 2,000,000, and on a single Sunday as many as 30,000 people will traipse through its galleries, peering at mummies and fragments of classic pottery, at armor and sculpture, and jewels, and glass, at period furniture and prints, and at gallery after gallery of paintings. At the far smaller but livelier Museum of Modern Art attendance is a crushing problem. "Frequently the crowds are so great," the museum complained a few years ago when it was trying to raise $3,000,000 for expansion, "that it is impossible to see the exhibition."

In many respects the Museum of Modern Art has been the most

provocative art institution of the past twenty years and has had the greatest influence on taste. It has also made more enemies and been the butt of more jokes and ribaldry than any other museum, largely because it has seemed to many to look upon itself as a crusader in whose hands is entrusted the sword of contemporary aesthetic truth. The museum started in a few rooms in an office building on Fifth Avenue (the Heckscher Building) with an exhibition of Cézanne, Gauguin, Seurat and Van Gogh in the autumn of 1929. None of the painters in its first show were unfamiliar to those who followed exhibitions in New York, and they had all been represented sixteen years earlier in the Armory Show. But, as Alfred H. Barr, Jr., said in the foreword of the catalogue, ". . . so revolutionary are certain aspects of their work that it is still subject to misunderstanding and, for a recalcitrant few, battleground for controversy." Mr. Barr underestimated how many were recalcitrant; it was certainly not a few. The Museum of Modern Art, however, played a strong hand in making these artists and many others accepted in America as "old masters," and through the publication of many catalogues and books, through traveling exhibitions, color reproductions, loan exhibitions and competitions they have made "Modern" not only palatable but a cause, and a genuine delight to a great many thousands of people.

They have also made it *chic.* Since it first opened its doors there has been a special social cachet about the Museum of Modern Art. Its "openings" have been festivals that those who were or professed to be interested in the arts and progressive in their attitudes scarcely dared not to attend. In the thirties the openings were occasions for the fashionable world to dress up in its most elaborate finery and rub elbows with members of Bohemia. So great were the crowds at these openings that no one expected to be able to see the exhibition, but they did expect to be seen themselves and to be known as patrons of the advanced arts. The Rockefellers and the Blisses and the Whitneys contributed not only money but prestige to the museum's efforts to make the public sympathetic with the Modern movement, and in the course of ten years the museum had moved from the Heckscher Building to a private house on Fifty-third Street and finally into its own permanent building and had, according to its own estimate, "come of age—a precocious accomplishment."

Its interests had spread from painting and sculpture to architecture and industrial design. It had added a department devoted to the history of the movies and had developed a collection of films that it showed in its own auditorium and rented to the public. It collected a library devoted to the modern movement and it had bought many pictures for its "permanent collection." Its ingenuity and dramatization in methods of display set a pattern that museums all over the country have tried to copy. But not only that, it has set an example that has been followed in store interiors and window displays, and it has had its effects on magazine and advertising layout. It has made many fads, and sent the prices of many artists soaring; it has infuriated a great many collectors, painters, and scholars, and confused as well as enlightened a great many well-meaning members of the public.

Like most crusading movements that originate in revolutionary zeal it has often given the impression of being both doctrinaire and touchy. In its early days it was an organization run by young men in their twenties and early thirties, full of ardor, eager to experiment, and engaged in a battle that was almost exclusively theirs to fight. In many respects their battle has been won. Now the men who run it are in their fifties, the little outpost has become an established, wealthy, and elaborately organized institution and a vested interest, and it is jealous of its position. When the Institute of Modern Art in Boston, a quasi-official stepchild of the Museum of Modern Art, decided to change its name to the Institute of Contemporary Art an explosion took place. The Institute issued a document called *"Modern Art" and the American Public* in which it said, among other things, that "modern art failed to speak clearly," that "there emerged a general cult of bewilderment," and that "the gap between the artist and the public . . . became an attractive playground for double-talk, opportunism, and chicanery at the public expense." This was heresy. The part of the Art World that deals with the past chuckled, but the Museum of Modern Art was not amused. "No statement," it said to the press at first, "and no comment." But presently the Museum of Modern Art, the Boston Institute, and the Whitney Museum of American Art issued a joint statement "clarifying" their position. It was dignified, it asserted the "urgent need for general objectivity and openmindedness towards the art of our time" and, though it left a good many wounded feelings behind museum walls, it presented to the public a façade of solidarity. There is no question of the power of the Museum of Modern Art in the art world, though its mannerisms sometimes seem like those of a woman of fifty who wants to be treated with the respect due her age—at the same time that she tries to act and dress as though she were still only twenty.

The Museum of Modern Art is alone among the major art museums of the country in its exclusive concern with what it calls a "movement." For the most part America's art museums try to be all things to all tastes so long as those tastes are "serious." They defend and display the cultural past; they try to give all manner of contemporary arts a hearing or a viewing, whether they are traditional or modern, whether they are the work of cartoonists or designers, painters or sculptors, handicrafters or makers of machine products. So far as the contemporary arts are concerned the museums' first concern is with interest and vitality, their second with quality. The mentors of taste have so often been caught with the wrong goods that most museum directors today believe in showing all kinds of goods so long as they can be called *art* and so long as they bring the public in off the streets to have a look. The constant clicking of museum turnstiles testifies to the soundness, so far as the public is concerned, of this approach to taste and to the arts.

The museums (and the philanthropists who have founded and largely supported them) cannot take all the credit for the current interest in art. If art had been a charity patient, it would have withered away by this time in peaceful seclusion. But art has paid its way; the dealers have been on hand to see that it did. It is a tribute to the hardihood of the muse, however, that she should have weathered, even thrived on, the confusion and connivance of the art business.

Compared with the number of people who, out of a sense of duty, solace, pleasure, or curiosity, spend a few hours in an art museum, the number who go to dealers' galleries is minute. It rarely, if ever, occurs to any but a few of those who thoroughly enjoy an afternoon spent looking at the public collections that they might without embarrassment or the slightest intention of buying a picture drop into a commercial art gallery. In most cities even the eager art lover will find no commercial gallery to visit, except, perhaps, a shop that sells a few original pictures, a good many color reproductions, and a selection of frames. Many department stores have picture departments where they sell selections of reproductions (along with mirrors) that include a little of everything from Picasso, Matisse, and Rouault of the École de Paris to old masters and a plethora of Impressionist and Neo-Impressionist landscapes of Venice and Paris, the hills of Vermont, and the peaks of the Cascades at sunrise. The shop that sells only paintings, sculpture, drawings, and prints (etchings, lithographs, dry points) is rare indeed even in such cultural centers as Philadelphia, Washington, Chicago, and Boston. New York, however, has several hundred such art galleries whose sole business is selling the works of contemporary artists, recent artists, and what pass for (and sometimes are) old masters. In the course of a single "season" (which runs from September to June) these galleries will present more than twelve hundred different exhibitions. Some of them are "one-man shows," some are "group shows," some are of painters whose work has never been exhibited before, some are the stand-bys of the art market, and some are very special selections of old masters in the grander establishments exhibited "for the benefit" of charitable organizations. Except in the case of the "benefits," the public may wander in and out free of charge, and in New York quite a few people do; quite a few others, however, are frightened away by the aura that surrounds the strange trade of art dealing. The number of people who go to dealers' galleries is no measure of the influence they exert on taste in general.

Art dealing is free enterprise in one of its most lively dog-eat-dog manifestations. The only noticeable solidarity among dealers in America is geographical; more than ninety per cent of our important art merchants cluster on or near Fifty-seventh Street in New York. Fifty-seventh Street is not notable for its *bonhomie*. Unlike other kinds of merchants, art dealers have no general association to look out for their interests, to adjudicate their differences, and to keep a self-protecting eye on their practices. They are more like the members of an Oriental bazaar than like American merchants. The delicacy of their relationships, the suspicion, rivalry, and secrecy among them are such that

The Taste of Business

The room above is not, as you might think, in the American Wing of the Metropolitan; it is on the eleventh floor of the Graybar Building in New York, the executive dining room of J. Walter Thompson, Inc., advertising. It was installed in the twenties at the height of the antiques craze. Below is business in another mood—Radio City Music Hall displays a perfect example of "modernistic" (of the thirties) in its men's "lounge room."

When Old Style Was Good Style

The room above, a set for the movie "Susan and God" (1940) was designed by Cedric Gibbons as "a modernized early American home," an example of the movies' inclination to reflect taste, not to lead it. The little bit of France below, left, is in Highland Park, Illinois, a product of the panic year of 1929. The Tudor and Spanish mission houses might be in any suburb from Newton, Massachusetts, to Pasadena, California, but they are actually in New Jersey.

Education in Search of a Tradition
The thoroughly unacademic anachronisms on this page are both at Yale; they are in fact the same building. The Gothic stone façade above is the York Street wall of Davenport College. The Georgian courtyard is what one enters through the Gothic portal—a quick transition from the age of the moat to the age of the minuet. The building was built in the early 1930's.

Trying to Outguess the Public

The post-World War II building boom looked to the tastemakers like a golden opportunity. Buckminster Fuller's "Dymaxion" house, top left, was going to be mass-produced by Beech Aircraft; it never was. The *Ladies' Home Journal* put its bets on such houses as the one by Philip Johnson, center above. But *Good Housekeeping* picked the "Western Style" house. If there is any question who was right, look at a portion of Levittown, Pennsylvania (16,000 ranch houses), below.

The Ranch House Takes Over

The area on the right side of the air view on the opposite page (where there are a few tall trees) seems to be the street illustrated above. The ranch houses in Levittown cost about $10,000 for the small ones, nearly $17,000 for the large ones. Levitt came to the ranch house recently, as two of his earlier houses (1929 and 1947) above show. The ranch house below (next to an earlier suburban fad, the inflated Cape Cod cottage) would cost about $60,000 to build today.

MUSEUM OF MODERN ART

MACHINE ART

The Marriage of Art and Industry

When the Museum of Modern Art staged its first Machine Art exhibition in 1934, it gave industry the aesthetic nod. An earlier nod was made at the Centennial Exposition in 1876, which produced the chandelier above. By the 1930's the marriage of art and industry had a new best man—the industrial designer. Below is a bathroom by Crane before and after one of them, Henry Dreyfuss, had at it.

Business Patronizes the Arts

The Glass Center of the Corning Glass Works, above, holds an exhibition of genuine and fake works of art for its employees and visitors. (The painting on the extreme right is the Van Meegeren fake "Vermeer" that Hermann Goering bought for more than half a million dollars.) Below are examples of corporation use of "fine artists." Pierre Roy painted the picture at the left for Dole Pineapple; Charles Howard did the advertisement at the right for the Container Corporation of America.

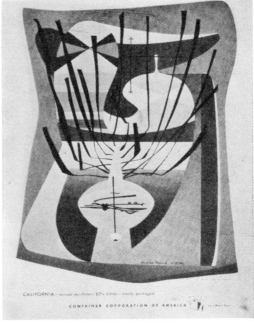

When Scandal Shakes the Art World

Han Van Meegeren precipitated the greatest recent art scandal with his fake "Vermeers." Above is a genuine Vermeer, "A Woman Weighing Gold," from the Widener Collection in the National Gallery, Washington. Below is Van Meegeren's "Supper at Emmaeus" that brought $378,000. In retrospect it is hard to see how the experts were fooled.

any sort of co-operative organization is unthinkable. Before the last war common understandings, unwritten and unspoken, acted to protect the prices of some kinds of pictures, and dealers had some reticence about stealing one another's artists; and the artists, for their part, were likely to stick by dealers to whom they owed discovery. But strange things have happened to the art market in the past ten years.

Wealthy collectors in high income brackets are said to be financing dealers so that they can not only buy pictures cheaply but write off gallery losses on their income taxes. (In spite of the boom, it takes no special talent to operate a gallery at a loss.) Ever since the war old masters which used to be the mainstay of the art market in this country have been bringing much higher prices in London and Paris and Rome than in New York; Europeans are accustomed to purchasing art as a reliable hedge against inflation. European dealers now come to the auctions at Parke-Bernet in New York for bargains to take back to their customers at home, and they can afford to pay higher prices than the local dealers. Partly as a result of these pressures on the market, partly because of the prominence given to American artists by museums since the beginning of the war, and partly because of a newly awakened interest in American culture that has come with our expanding world power, the sale of paintings and sculptures by American artists has been steadily climbing in the last decade. The "adventurous" collectors are no longer those who buy the latest thing from Paris but those who try to pick the best of our own crop. The members of the American Society of Painters and Sculptors, who were so disgusted by the way the Armory Show had flooded the American market with pictures by foreigners, would be pleased by the turn that things have taken.

That is not to say that the market for old and European art has dried up in this country. The Parke-Bernet Galleries, by all odds the most important art auctioneers in America, have maintained, according to the *New York Times*, "an average yearly total of over four million dollars for the past five years." Over their auction block go collections of furniture and rugs, armor and *objets d'art*, paintings and sculpture by "old masters" and miscellaneous artifacts, drawings and prints and rare books. Long-established dealers such as

Knoedler's and Wildenstein's and Duveen's and Durlacher's still traffic heavily in the art of the past as a major part of their business. But Knoedler's and Durlacher's in the last few years have been devoting more and more of their exhibitions to contemporary American painters, and the advertisements in the *Art News*, the quasi-official publication of the Art World, show a far higher percentage of dealers in contemporary American pictures than they did fifteen years ago.

Whatever the shifts in the goods in which they deal, whatever the feuds in which they indulge, and however violently their tastes differ, the dealers present a reasonably unbroken façade of expensive dignity to the outsider. Many of the dealers in American art have maintained a rather open and relaxed attitude toward their customers, much as any merchant does, but in general snobbery, both intellectual and social, is basic to the techniques of art salesmanship.

A very small proportion of those who go to private art galleries to look at pictures have any intention of buying, and a still smaller proportion ever get into the little back rooms with the heavy curtains where the serious work is done. There the prospective client sits in a deep armchair while the dealer has his minion bring in pictures from the stockroom, one at a time, to be propped on a velvet-covered easel. In this atmosphere of intimate luxury the seduction goes on, prices and attributions are discussed, artistic assignations are arranged.

The name of the painter is likely to be the first consideration of both the seller and the buyer. In the old-master market, attributions* become all important (artists' signatures on old pictures are always open to suspicion) and documents of authentication and provenance† take on considerable cash value. The words of the scholar or other "expert" can make a difference of thousands of dollars in the price of a picture or piece of sculpture. A painting attributed to Stefan Lochner will bring about ten thousand dollars more than it will if it is "expertised" as a work by the Master of the Paradise Garden. A Rubens brings a great deal more than a Snyders, though in some cases it takes an expert in seventeenth-century Flemish painting to decide which master painted a disputed picture. There is more than a little basis for saying that there are dealers who will pay a consulting

---

*Informed guesses as to who painted it.

†As many documents as come to hand that say who has owned it and when.

expert more if he attributes a picture to Rubens than if he says it is a Snyders, though neither the dealers nor the "experts" are ever attacked by name in print for fear of libel. Even such august critics as Bernard Berenson, one of the greatest authorities on Italian painting, at one period in his life worked closely with the most spectacularly successful, entertaining, and flamboyant of all dealers, Sir Joseph Duveen. But expert opinion vs. expert opinion on matters of attribution commonly leads the dealer and ultimately the purchaser to accept the attribution which pleases him most.

There are also dealers who purchase badly damaged pictures or merely fragmentary remains of pictures and have them almost completely repainted. These they sell as authentic works, though there may be only the faintest whisper of truth in their claims to authenticity. The Metropolitan in New York has an impressive Raphael in excellent condition which is said to have been so badly cracked and peeling three hundred years ago that it was refused by Christina of Sweden to whom it was then offered for sale. Obviously age has not improved it. The process by which it miraculously recovered is the science known as "restoration," and a sharp distinction is properly made between restoration, no matter how extensive, and outright frauds or fakes. Reputable dealers do not intentionally deal in fakes (though an occasional one may creep in), and the best of them will tell the buyer what has been restored. It is a rare museum that hasn't a few fakes tucked away in its basement or a few almost completely repainted pictures hanging proudly on its walls. In general the tendency in museums today is to clean off extensive restoration and repainting on pictures, get them down to what is left of the original, and then apply the minimum of retouching and resurfacing necessary for protection.

Conscience draws a fine line in the art business. There are many dealers who would never stoop to selling known fakes or to paying an expert for a favorable attribution, but who do not hesitate to accept the attribution which assures the best price. The conscientious buyer can assume, though, that most dealers will not buy unless they are sure of what they are getting, that they are experts in the goods in which they trade, and therefore the client has reasonable security when he buys from a dealer of accepted reputation and long standing.

The same is true of experts. The reputable ones are fiercely jealous of the integrity of their profession.

Only once in a great while does a first-class scandal break in the Art World that sends dealers and experts, collectors and museum curators into a paroxysm of self-pity and self-examination. Such moments shake the Art World to its roots and vastly entertain a public that always enjoys the sight of an expert who is caught with his acumen down.

There has been one such scandal since the last war, though the American Art World was only very peripherally involved in it. It was the case of Han van Meegeren, "a Dutch painter," as someone said after the fact, "of no originality and of less than routine competence in the technical elements of his profession." He decided to revenge himself upon the Art World for having ignored him, and his revenge was sweet, indeed, if ultimately tragic. He studied the works and mannerisms of the seventeenth-century "little Dutch master" Vermeer, whose pictures have brought as much as half a million dollars apiece in America and who, like van Meegeren, lived in Delft. For four years he experimented with methods of reproducing Vermeer's glasslike surface and illusive brushwork, and he finally concocted a formula of solubles and oils and pigments which, when baked in an oven, produced an effect indistinguishable from the master's. Then he painted a picture, "Christ at Emmaus," in a manner and kind of subject matter (Vermeer did very few religious paintings) that was familiar to scholars but not too familiar. He took the painting to a top-flight restorer in Paris, had it slightly touched up to give it an added semblance of authenticity as an old and repaired picture, and then offered it through an agent to the Art World as a forgotten masterpiece from the estate of an ancient French family.

The picture sold for $378,000 to the Boymans Museum in Rotterdam, where it hung for seven years and where it was declared by experts who examined it with excitement and care to be "one of the greatest Vermeers in existence." Van Meegeren haunted the gallery, where the picture was hung in a specially draped room, drinking in the awed and almost religious praise that was lavished on it. But he had made $200,000 out of this first effort, and he went on to make more—five in all, the last one of which was bought by Field Marshal

Goering during the German occupation of Holland. The prices of these afterthoughts varied from $264,000 to more than three quarters of a million. It was through no fault of the experts that the fraud was exposed. Van Meegeren was arrested after the war as a collaborator; he had, the authorities said, sold a Vermeer to Goering, and in the course of the trial it was he, himself, who told how he had duped the Marshal. No one would believe his preposterous claim until in the presence of the court and a panel of experts he painted another "Vermeer." What then was his offense? He was sentenced to a year in prison for forging the master's name, but before his incarceration was to start, he died of a heart attack.

It is stories such as this that make the experts of the Art World toss in their sleep, for none of them is immune to being duped. Fortunately no van Meegeren "Vermeers" were sold in this country, though they were reproduced in American art publications with fanfare and without question of their authenticity. There had, however, been a similar scandal that, not so many years before, had cost American museums and collectors a great deal of money and had profoundly embarrassed a number of scholars, curators, museum directors, and dealers. In that instance it was sculpture and not painting that had caused the trouble, and it pretended to be not the work of a single master but of a variety of masters.

This was the case of Alceo Dossena, the "aristocrat of forgers." His name is known to the Art World with both respect and distaste, and though the case was broken nearly thirty years ago and ultimately reflects credit on the astuteness and detective work of the Art World, it is still a skeleton that the Art World prefers to keep locked fast in its cupboard. The story is a complicated one involving dealers, both savory and unsavory, scholars who could be bought and those of impeccable honesty, as well as Italian politicians and a variety of claims and counterclaims that may very well never be disentangled. Very briefly the outline of the story is this.

Dossena was by early training a stonecutter, and as a boy he became an expert in repairing the columns in ancient churches and the balustrades on palaces, and he worked in the vicinity of Cremona where he was born in the late 1870's. When the First World War engulfed Italy he was drafted into the army, and, while he was still in uniform shortly after the war, he was sitting on Christmas Eve in a café called Felicetto's in Rome with a little piece of sculpture, a Madonna, that he had made in the manner of the Renaissance artist Donatello. He showed it to the tavernkeeper who called a friend named Alberto Fasoli, a fashionable jeweler and something of an art expert. Fasoli was impressed with the piece, about which Dossena explained, "It isn't mine. It's my uncle's and I know nothing about it." Fasoli gave him 100 lire (then about $12) for it, and a few days later he was after the young man for more such pieces. Dossena went into production. He installed himself in a studio with assistants and began to turn out not only Renaissance sculpture but "archaic Greek" and Medieval pieces and even imitations of sculpture as late as the seventeenth century. Fasoli and another dealer named Romano Pallesi undertook to market the pieces and to invent provenances for them. The sculpture was made with the greatest care and was antiqued in ingenious ways—by burying in compost, by dipping in vats of acid, by breaking. Whenever possible, pieces of stone that had been naturally weathered were used, but the quality that distinguished Dossena from nearly all other art forgers was that he never copied an authentic piece. His sculpture was done "in the manner" of a sculptor or the sculptors of a period and as nearly in their spirit as possible. He left their "attribution" to the dealers and the scholars. Fasoli and Pallesi passed off most of the Medieval and Renaissance pieces as coming from a deserted and ruined monastery; the Greek pieces required more elaborate stories of discovery, but a little at a time the sculptures wormed their way into the hands of reputable dealers and from them into public and private collections.

About a million and a half dollars' worth of Dossenas were bought in America alone. A piece of medieval wooden sculpture attributed to Pisano showed up in Cleveland. The Metropolitan Museum bought an "archaic Greek maiden" (it can still be seen in the Museum's collection of fakes). The Boston Museum of Fine Arts spent $100,000 on a tomb said to be by Mino da Fiesole, over which there has been a great deal of expert dispute even though Dossena did not deny that it was his work. The Frick Collection bought two pieces, a Virgin and an Announcing Angel that were attributed to the Sienese painter, Simone Martini, though he was never known to have been a sculptor;

Martini was as close as the experts could get to an attribution on the basis of style.

Who first smelled a rat is by no means clear. A German scholar says he spotted one of the pieces as a fake as early as 1921. Evidently in America it was the Metropolitan, on the advice of one of its purchasing agents in Italy, that first got the wind up over some fragments presumed to be Greek. Another account says that it was a New York dealer named Piero Tozzi who first went to Italy to identify the fraud with Dossena. But the distinction of having traced the forgeries to Dossena's studio is an honor that many art sleuths want to claim, and many do. The most convincing story of the initial detection of the fraud is one that tells of a tempest in the Art World that boiled up in Bologna. A scholar noticed that an inscription on a jewel set into a supposedly fourteenth-century wooden sculpture was copied from an inscription on a Visigothic sculpture in the Bologna museum that was already known to be a fake. At this point the lines to Dossena's studio become vague, and even now members of the Art World who were involved in the scandal, however innocently, are reluctant to talk about it.

It was not until November, 1928, that the story became public knowledge—several years after it was known to the inner circles of museum officials and dealers, and it was Dossena himself who broke the story. He threatened to sue Fasoli and Pallesi, insisting that for all the millions of dollars' worth of sculpture by his hand that they had sold, he had got only $34,200 and that they owed him $65,800 more in accordance with their agreement. Fasoli, thinking to get rid of Dossena, accused him of anti-Fascist activities, but Dossena insisted he was a good Fascist and engaged the sympathy and services of Farinacci, then the Number 2 Fascist in Rome. The Fascist dignitary was glad to take the case as Dossena had become something of a popular hero for having pulled the wool over so many expert eyes. Farinacci got him off. Fasoli disappeared into oblivion, Dossena after a period of very fashionable acclaim drank himself to death, and Farinacci was eventually to be hanged by his heels by partisans in a Milan gas station along with Mussolini and his mistress.

There are few stories of art forgeries as dramatic as this one or as embarrassing to the Art World, but while it reflects discredit on the perpetrators of the fraud, the unraveling of the mystery is a tribute to scholarly acumen. In no business are so many traps laid for the unwary purchaser by so many extremely clever men. There have been art forgeries just as long as there has been an art market, and even Aristotle in the fourth century B.C. counseled young men to study works of art carefully lest they be fooled by fakes. Michelangelo when he was a young man first brought himself to the attention of the Renaissance Art World by making a statue of "Cupid Asleep." He buried it in order to give it an antique patina, and it was sold in Rome in 1496 as a piece of classical sculpture. It is an old profession, and if not an honorable one, it is one of the most exacting. Even in the market for modern pictures one has to be wary. There are many fake Van Goghs (indeed there is a catalogue of some of them) and many so-called Utrillo paintings and Maillol drawings. There have been developed in recent years elaborate laboratory techniques involving paint chemistry, X-ray, and violet-ray photography, and microscopy, that are now commonly used by museums to detect frauds. These are not, unfortunately, available to the private buyer.

For all the millions of dollars spent each year in America on original works of art by confirmed and occasional collectors, for all the efforts on the part of museums to try to improve the public taste in what they buy, the pictures that are most popular with the public have little to do with what the Art World could dignify with the name Art. Recently I asked the executive in charge of buying pictures (as well as "gifts" and lamps) for Sears, Roebuck in Chicago which pictures sold best in the tremendous market that Sears, as the biggest retailer in the world, serves. "Rembrandt, Renoir, and Van Gogh," he said, "don't sell. I wish they did." (He was, of course, talking about reproductions.) "Our best seller is called 'Fiery Peaks.' It's a picture of the Cascade Mountains either at sunset or sunrise, you can't tell which, and the sky is bright orange." I asked him who his most popular artist was. "Huldah," he said. "She paints pictures of Parisian women with big black eyes and frilly things around their necks and we sell them in very fancy Edwardian frames. We also sell a great many small pictures that can be grouped together to make an arrangement, flower prints and Audubons." A trip to a department-store picture department will confirm this general taste. There you will find women buying landscapes to ornament their living-room walls, selecting pictures on the basis that they contain colors that will match curtains and carpets. (The art collector works the other way around, if at all; he will try to make the decoration of his room sympathetic to the pictures.)

That is not to say that there is no market for reproductions of old masters. The Metropolitan Museum, working hand in glove with the Book-of-the-Month Club, sells hundreds of thousands of what they call "miniatures," little color plates of famous pictures suitable for pasting in an album. "When the talk turns to art . . . must you be silent?" asks an advertisement for the miniatures. Newspapers have used reproductions of old masters as premiums for selling subscriptions and found them successful, and the general quality of color plates that are "suitable for framing" has improved considerably both technically and in breadth of selection in the last quarter of a century. It is almost as easy now to find a reproduction of an abstraction as it is of a conventional portrait or still life, but as the buyer for Sears said to me, "Our experience shows that people like realism."

Art has also made its way into many people's lives through quite other, different channels. There has been a wave of art teaching in primary schools in order to give children a chance to "express themselves," and the pictures of the very young often have a boldness and primitive appeal that sits well with those who like the boldness and primitive appeal of much serious modern painting. Many parents have been misled by this into thinking that they have spawned a genius. Art is used as therapy in hospitals, especially mental hospitals, to help engage the interest of those who seem to have lost interest in life or to help others "get outside themselves." The New York Hospital has an annual budget of $10,000 (given anonymously) for the purchase of paintings in order to meet "the needs of the inner man" of the outer man who lies in a hospital bed. In the past seven years the hospital has bought eight hundred pictures. Mass magazines, and notably *Life*, have devoted page after page to the reproduction of paintings, many of them the very latest works of the *avant garde*, so that when an exhibition goes to any city or town, however small, though some things may displease, nothing surprises.

Since the beginning of the war there has been a rapidly growing number of amateur painters. The gas shortage that kept people at home then may well have had something to do with this growth as it did with the prosperity that magazine and book publishers enjoyed at the same time. The shorter work week and consequent great increase in leisure time have also contributed to it. Arthur Brown, the proprietor of the biggest art supply company in New York, says that "The WPA art project should have full credit. Murals in post offices, exhibits— they jumped art appreciation no end." To meet and to keep ahead of the more than 300,000 amateur painters that the *Art News* now estimates spend their spare time at easels or with their hands sticky with clay, the art suppliers have created some remarkable gadgets. Canvases with pictures printed in outline and then covered with numbers which are keyed to the oil colors that are sold with them provide adults with a modern version of the children's coloring book. A material called "Sculpstone" that looks like real stone (it comes in imitation of various sorts) can be carved into sculpture with a penknife. The *Art News* now holds an annual competition for amateurs and gives medals to the winners. Instead of being pleased by this evidence of growing interest in art, many professional painters resent it. They reason that if people paint their own pictures they won't buy pictures by professionals, and instead of creating a body of informed dilettantes who might become eager and intelligent collectors the amateurs merely become a lot of half-baked, self-satisfied artists.

In general, however, one would think that the Art World was in a peculiarly happy state—new collectors, a boom in the market for the work of American artists, ever-increasing attendance at museums, more and more attention paid to art in magazines (if not in most newspapers, where art news is likely to be coupled with social notes), hundreds of thousands of business and professional men and housewives painting in their spare time. It looks as though the intensive efforts of the Art World, which inevitably includes the art critics and teachers, had brought a rich harvest. But all is not as happy as this would seem to show.

There are only a handful of American artists, not in the commercial fields, who can make a living out of selling their art. Most painters and sculptors in order to live must also teach, some in art schools and some in colleges, where they help to train more and more artists who will have an even harder time trying to make a living. Many artists today, and especially the younger ones, feel that the world owes them a living because they are, or think they are, artists. The truth of the matter was summed up by Walt Kuhn, whose attitude was entirely professional. "No one ever asked me to be a painter," he said, and he meant that he painted because he wanted to, and if nobody wanted what he painted, it was nobody's fault but his own. But the real troubles that the arts of painting and sculpture have in our time go deeper than the romantic notion that the world owes the unwanted as well as the wanted artist a living. It is the split between the commercial artist and the fine artist. There was a time when there were good artists and less good artists, and the latter often worked in the studios of the former, but in the nineteenth century, when art for industry grew with such leaps and bounds, a schism appeared in the Art World; the artist had to decide whether he was going to paint for industry or for himself and whatever patrons he could find. Some artists became known as "serious" and some became known as "hacks," and while the rift is being healed in some ways, it is still a wide and dark chasm.

The other trouble is the two-way split among the "serious" artists themselves—between the "modernists" and the "traditionalists"—a situation that leads not merely to artistic disputes but to political name calling. The right and left wings of art have been plastered with political connotations, first by the artists themselves and then by politicians who have wanted to make capital out of them. In 1951 when the Metropolitan Museum held a large exhibition of contemporary American sculpture, the National Sculpture Society, which represents the more conservative branch of the art, let fly with epithets at the modernists (who walked off with the prizes) and at the museum. Not only were modern tendencies dangerous but, they said, they were "left wing" work. Several politicians, but most prominently Congressman Dondero, Republican, of Illinois, have attacked many "modern" painters as identified with political radicalism and communism. In some instances the men they have named have been identified with left-wing organizations, many they have named have not, but the attack on the modernists is a blanket attack. Most of the Art World has little patience with such attacks and has taken a strong stand against anyone who wants to be dogmatic about what art is good and what is not, what art is good for people and what is against the public interest.

This is a new kind of "Philistinism" for the Art World to fight— a Philistinism that works both from within and without—but it is a sign of growth. When any pressure group in this country grows large, no matter how good its will, it finds itself with battles on its hands which it never expected. As its influence grows, and the number of its friends and supporters increases, so inevitably will the numbers of those who question its position, its authority, and its rights. The Art World's case against the new Philistinism is briefly this—that wherever there have been movements to curb what is advanced in art, as in Germany under Hitler and in Russia, there has followed totalitarian despotism. The Art World is fighting for the freedom of the artist— a good thing. It is also fighting for its right to say what is art and what is not. This is ground that has long shaken, Jello-like, under its feet. It shows no sign of becoming a steady, comfortable place to stand.

CHAPTER XVI

Taste—Tax Deductible

"It looks as though never have so many been
dependent on so few for their own surroundings."

CHARLES E. ODEGAARD, at the
Herald Tribune Forum, 1953

George Washington Hill, the head of the American Tobacco Company, was one of the last of the old-style, terrible-tempered,
table-thumping tycoons left over from the era when a corporation's affairs were "nobody else's damn business." One day, so runs a story
that amused the Art World about a decade ago, the advertising
agency that handled the Lucky Strike account needed Hill's approval
of an ambitious and expensive new campaign that it hoped would sell
cigarettes. It also hoped that the campaign would cast a slight glow
of culture and an aura of public benefaction around the corporation.
In the early forties a fad was sweeping through the advertising world
that had cultural overtones; agency art directors were promoting the
use of "fine artists," as they called them, to paint pictures that were
supposed to promote good will for the manufacturers of everything
from diamonds to pills to Pepsi-Cola. The agency's plan for Lucky
Strike was to commission a number of well-known American artists
to depict scenes of the tobacco country. They featured, as you may
remember, "a golden leaf." The agency got together samples of paintings by the various men ("America's foremost artists," it called them)
whose work it hoped to use, and hung the pictures around the walls
of a room. Hill was invited to have a look; he glanced around the
room briefly. "I like this man," he said. "Hire him."

The story may be apocryphal, but the campaign was not; it was launched and ran for several years. It was one of the most expensive, if not the most artistically successful, of the many hopeful and well-meaning incursions that the world of business made into the world of art in the 1940's.

By now there are many large business organizations that have got their feet wet in the stream of culture and taste. The corporation has, in fact, become one of the most powerful and conscientious art patrons of our day, and has established itself not only as a purveyor of tasteful objects but as an arbiter of taste as well. The marriage of business and the arts, while it displays some of the antics of puppy love and some of the endearing inconsistencies of a romance, is essentially an uneasy *mariage de convenance*.

Art and industry have had a very long, but scarcely passionate courtship, full of ups and downs. When Prince Albert launched the great London exposition in the Crystal Palace in 1851, he hoped to bring art and industry together in happy communion. In Philadelphia in 1876 there was, you will remember, proud acclaim over the advances that industry had made in the century since the founding of the Republic, and there were ardent efforts at that time to consummate a closer relationship between the artist and the products that flowed in such quantities from American factories. Even before the Centennial, manufacturers in New England had inspired the teaching of design in the public schools in hopes that artists might be developed who could glorify factory-made objects with their skill and taste. To the modern industrial designer these were fumbling efforts indeed, but they were efforts made in days of more rough-and-tumble industrial competition than we know now. Capitalism is not the same free-for-all it was in the last century, and the men who head our modern corporations are not the same princes of industry and finance who lived in marble palaces surrounded by artistic plunder and were a law unto themselves. The modern corporation has a conscience, or if it hasn't, the laws of the land and the new folklore see to it that it behaves as though it had.

It took disaster to throw business and culture finally into each other's arms. Indeed, it took two disasters in rapid succession—the Great Depression of the thirties and the Second World War. But it was a new science (or an old art with a new scientific name) that was at the bottom of the marriage. It was the science of Public Relations.

During the second half of the nineteenth century business expansion in America had been meteoric in its speed and brilliance, and Americans were both proud and troubled. To most tycoons of the day every means of competition, fair or foul, was justified so long as it was conducted in the name of business. No one bowed his head more devoutly in church on Sunday or sang hymns more lustily or stood more rigidly for family morality than many a businessman who fought his commercial battles with any weapon that came to hand—however deceitful or inhumane. The public welfare was no concern of his. It was a time when business could buy editorial space in the press, and as late as 1898 the Jennings Agency, which handled the advertising for the Standard Oil Company, according to an investigating attorney general of Ohio, "distributed articles to the newspapers and paid for them on condition that they appeared as news or editorials." The tycoon's attitude of the day had been summed up all too succinctly in 1879 by William Henry Vanderbilt in a newspaper interview on the subject of why he had taken an extra-fare mail train off the New York Central run between New York and Chicago. "The public be damned," he said.

The public, however, had no intention of being damned, and business eventually realized that it could not run its affairs entirely to suit itself. Reform movements were in the air; so were stones and rifle bullets. The lines between labor and capital were taut and strikes were bloody. The tension was not eased when George F. Baer in 1920, faced with a strike of anthracite miners, declared that "God in his infinite wisdom has given control of the property interests of the country" to such men as himself. It was a publicity man named Ivy Ledbetter Lee who convinced some business leaders that they had better adopt a new policy—"the public be informed."

This was in 1906. By 1908 the term "public relations" was coined by Theodore Newton Vail, the president of the American Telephone and Telegraph Company, to supplant the older term "publicity." It was not until 1922 that Edward L. Bernays swathed the ancient trade of press agentry in a cloak of professionalism by describing himself to the press at the time of his wedding as a "counsel on public relations." The old art of ballyhoo of which Phineas T. Barnum had been the greatest practitioner became a science called, among other things, "the engineering of consent." Surveys, polls, studies of the "dynamics of public opinion" and other sociological tools supplanted the free-wheeling, individual inspiration of the press agent—the kind of "brass and gas" by which John Rogers had launched his plaster groups in Chicago in the 1850's. "I don't care what they call me so long as they mention my name" may have been a sound enough slogan for the actor George M. Cohan, but it was not good enough for business. Men such as Bernays busied themselves and their little armies of researchers and writers with campaigns that were meant to identify the corporations for which they worked with the public welfare. There was nothing hit-or-miss about the new profession; it not only interpreted corporation policies to the public, but in many instances where the policies beggared justification, the public relations counselors were able to bring about changes in the policies themselves. Today every corporation of any size has its own public relations department whose function is not only to put the corporations best public foot forward but to keep top management informed of the public temper. Public relations, says Bernays, is a "two-way street."

The position of public relations in the corporation scheme of things has assumed an almost mystical loftiness. There is a story told of a Princeton undergraduate who had become concerned about religious doctrine in his sophomore year and who was wrestling with the difficult concept of the Trinity. He took his problem to a clergyman. "I understand about God the Father, and God the Son," he said, "but the Holy Ghost doesn't make sense to me." "Look at it this way," the divine said to him. "Think of it as a corporation. God the Father is the Chairman of the Board. God the Son is the President, and the Holy Ghost is the Vice-President in charge of Public Relations." The public relations department, as the justifier of the ways of the corporate gods to the common man (usually referred to as "the consumer") is also the custodian of the corporate conscience, and this is reflected in all kinds of public pronouncements, including advertising.

All through the nineteenth century and through the first three decades of the twentieth, advertising had been aimed almost exclusively at the sale of goods and services. In the thirties, under the aegis of the public relations counselors, it began to assume a new function. Institutional advertising, as it is called, was introduced into our national folklore for the purpose of encouraging public good will toward the corporation. It was a time when big businessmen, and especially bankers, were at the nadir of their popularity. Unemployment was high, bread lines were long, and apple sellers were a commonplace in the neighborhood of Wall Street. The National Association of Manufacturers ran a series of advertisements in defense of business and aimed them at those who would "strive to pit class against class." So did the United States Steel Corporation. Business felt an urgent need to woo back the public's confidence, which had taken such a calamitous nose dive when people all over the nation had suddenly waked up to discover that their life savings had unaccountably vanished overnight in the crash of 1929.

It was inevitable that sooner or later business, in its efforts to reestablish itself in the confidence of the public, would embrace culture. And this it began to do in earnest in the early 1940's while the war was on.

The great patrons of the arts in America, like the Medici in Florence during the Renaissance, had been businessmen or their scions ever since the days when the industrial revolution had turned the system topsy-turvy. Luman Reed, the wholesale grocer from upstate New York, had retired from his business to become an art patron in the 1830's, and it was he who set a pattern for such men as A. T. Stewart, the department-store magnate whose collection was one of the wonders (for its expensiveness) and one of the horrors (for its quality) of its day, and for later collectors who ignored the present to plunder the past—such men as J. Pierpont Morgan, William Randolph Hearst, P. A. B. Widener, and Andrew Mellon. Patronage of the arts, especially in the collecting sense, was identified in the minds of most Americans with the successful merchant, manufacturer, and financier.

The depression of the thirties all but put a stop to that; the Government, through the Works Progress Administration, suddenly found itself embarked on a program for patronizing the arts on a scale unheard of before in America. It not only took over the responsibilities that the private patron could not afford to exercise, but a good many that he had not thought were any of his business. Thousands of painters and sculptors and woodcarvers were kept busy with the decoration of post offices, courthouses, and city halls. Actors and directors experimented at the public expense with plays like T. S. Eliot's *Murder in the Cathedral* which would have had hard sledding on commercial Broadway. Writers produced guidebooks of every state in the Union, some of them models of informational writing and admirable contributions to historical research. Artists and writers collaborated on an *Index of American Design* that has preserved a great deal of our folk art that might otherwise have disappeared into oblivion. The WPA arts program was the target of much abuse. It was classified with leaf raking and called "boondoggling." Much of it undoubtedly was useless work of inferior quality, but the program was an emergency measure in an era when art was heavily overlaid with "social consciousness," and artists, like factory workers and brokers and clerks, were down and almost out. And anyhow it set a pattern. It was, in a sense, the first large-scale corporate example of patronage that Americans had ever seen; it demonstrated that the artist had some practical social usefulness after all.

The depression not only marked the passing of the old-style flamboyant tycoon but also the approach of what Frederick Lewis Allen has called "the professionalization of business." The leaders of the corporations were overshadowed by the size of the corporations themselves. Their names were less well-known to the public than those of the old tycoons, and their social status and private lives were less a matter of public curiosity. At the same time that Hollywood was building up the glamour of its individual stars and supplanting the old Horatio Alger formula of the businessman's rise from rags to riches with the new formula of the universal sweetheart, business was building down the individual in favor of the business as a whole. It was no longer considered politic for the chairman of the board to make a splash of his wealth; the new concept of the corporation emphasized the fact that it was owned by many thousands of small stockholders, and it represented the chairman of the board and the president and the vice president in charge of public relations as being, like the stockholders, "just folks." The corporation itself, however, stood for power and glamour and public benefaction, and the patronage of the arts passed from the hands of the tycoon to the corporation itself.

It would be misleading to imply that corporation concern with culture is the general rule, for it is not. It is extensive all the same and it is growing, and in its effect on the public taste it is by no means an insignificant force.

If we are to understand this influence of the corporation on the taste of our time, there are three ways in which the corporation must be looked at—as a consumer of the arts, in its role as patron; as a purveyor of the arts, in its role as the manufacturer or dispenser of the objects with which we surround ourselves; and finally as a new kind of society in which taste has a new kind of significance.

To the businessman, as an advertising executive has said, "a sales curve bending upward is one of the world's most beautiful pictures." As a backdrop to the patronage that the corporation has given the artist there has always been, as there should be, this picture and the conviction that the corporation's main business is business. Altruism has not been the motive that has prompted diamond merchants, steamship lines, brewers, phonograph and pharmaceutical manufacturers, cigarette makers, and soft-drink bottlers to become large-scale art collectors and benefactors of artists. The motive, no matter how indirectly expressed, has been profit.

Industry's use of the fine artist in advertising is nothing new, though the pose of the corporation as an art patron is. Pierce Arrow and Steinway both employed "serious" painters early in this century. Pears Soap used a painting by Sir John Millais in its advertising in England in the 1880's. The International Business Machines company has been a collector of paintings (of a very conservative nature) for some years and exhibited its collection at the New York World's Fair of 1939. But the phase of art patronage by business with which we are now concerned started about 1939. The sale of cut and uncut diamonds had dropped during the thirties and the advertising firm of N. W. Ayer & Son, Inc., was selected by DeBeers Diamonds to see what could be done to give the American market a lift. Charles T. Coiner, a vice president at Ayer who is a painter and a collector, took charge of the account, and with one eye on the market and one on the muse of painting, he started the first successful campaign in which an advertiser was conscientiously billed as a collector and patron of the arts.

Coiner's plan was by no means haphazard or capricious. Since all good advertising campaigns start with a survey, Coiner set out to discover just what it was that made people buy diamonds, and his researches revealed that the principal motivating forces were sentiment, fashion, pride of possession, pride of family, beauty, and, of course, permanence of value as an investment. The parallels with the main reasons why people buy works of art were obvious, and since Coiner is a man of imagination, he took the not-so-obvious next step. He decided to sell diamonds by identifying the jewels with the fine arts and the diamond merchant with the art patron. He selected an imposing list of artists and commissioned them to make drawings and paintings— Maillol, Derain, Dame Laura Knight, Pierre Roy, Eugène Berman, Marie Laurencin, and others. The first advertisements were printed in two colors, and were laid out with a lavish use of "white space" and an eye to elegance. The drawings were neatly and not overconspicuously accompanied by a line of type which read "Painted for DeBeers." It was a "quality" approach in keeping with a high-priced luxury item.

Within ten months after the first advertisement appeared in March, 1939, the importation of cut and uncut diamonds increased from $24,000,000 to $35,000,000. Whether this was the result of Coiner's campaign or of a generally rising tide of business or of the war in Europe, DeBeers was gratified and increased its advertising appropriation. From drawings Coiner moved to four-color reproductions of paintings. The accompanying line became "Painted especially for the DeBeers collection," and the "collection" began to assume rather imposing proportions.

The formula was too good to confine to a single account. Coiner also tried it on Dole Pineapple, Capehart Phonograph-Radio, and other products. For the most part he found the "fine artists" co-operative. He paid them well and they liked his approach, and on only one occasion did he have difficulty. He sent Georgia O'Keeffe to Hawaii to make a painting for Dole, but she preferred the Hawaiian mock-bird-of-paradise flower to the pineapple and sent back a painting of the flower. Coiner accepted the picture and reproduced just below it a glass of pineapple juice in full color. After Miss O'Keeffe's return he had a budding pineapple flown from Hawaii to New York and convinced her (she likes to paint dried cattle skulls) that it was worthy of her talents. Coiner's idea caught on elsewhere, and soon what had started out as a calculated method of catching the eye of a special public began to take on the proportions of a fad. Art directors of advertising agencies fell to competing with one another for ways to use the fine arts. The overtones were pleasant and for a while, until the novelty wore off, the sales results were gratifying. Lucky Strike, as we have noted, started its series of "paintings of the tobacco country by America's foremost artists." The United Brewers Foundation initiated "a series of typical American scenes painted by America's foremost artists." The scenes were all occasions for drinking beer.

Other businesses used the "fine artist" in different ways. Upjohn Pharmaceutical bought portraits from a variety of well-known painters and ran them in advertisements with captions that indicated that the sitters might be harboring diseases. A somber portrait of a girl by Fletcher Martin, for example, carried under it the caption: "Anemia?" Steamship lines that were refurbishing their ships after the war turned to industrial designers to give them the modern look and the designers decorated the ships' salons and bars and staircases with works by painters and sculptors that one would expect to be represented at the Museum of Modern Art but not on cruise boats. The Container Corporation of America started on a campaign that was the most daring of all. It used abstract paintings in full color for their decorative and shock effect in magazine advertisements. With the pictures was a minimum of copy, just enough to call attention to the company's name and the nature of its business. The effect made the Container Corporation seem up to date and sure of itself, and it has pursued this policy successfully with slight variations for a decade. Pharmaceutical houses have used the fine artists in the elaborate publications that they send to members of the medical profession; and Standard Oil of New Jersey has used them in its magazine *The Lamp*.

The most spectacular excursion by business into the fine arts, however, was made in 1944 by the Pepsi-Cola Company. It was the most ambitious, most pretentious, and the most frankly overt of all corporate attempts up to that time to associate business and the fine arts. Its professed purpose was to demonstrate that industry could play a leading role in the patronage of American art to the credit and profit of both the industry and the artist. It has been called a mere publicity stunt, but (and the distinction may be a fine one) it had the fulsomeness of a grandiose public relations operation. Briefly the story is this.

Emily Genauer, a New York art critic, approached her old friend Walter S. Mack, then president of the Pepsi-Cola Company, with the suggestion that Pepsi-Cola sponsor a nationwide artists' competition. Pepsi-Cola was to put up the funds for prizes, to reap whatever benefits there might be in publicity, and to issue a calendar using a selection of the prize-winning entries. In order to elicit the interest of artists, an organization called Artists for Victory, Inc., was approached. This group, which had sprung up in 1942 as the painters', sculptors', print-makers', and landscape architects' attempt to throw their concerted weight behind the war effort, had just completed a large exhibition at the Metropolitan Museum in New York with record-breaking attendance. Artists for Victory took kindly to Pepsi-Cola's suggestion for two reasons. First, the scheme looked like a new means of support for painters, and second, it offered a possible way to perpetuate the organization as a sort of artists' bloc, pressure group, and clearing house.

In order to give the competition both artistic and public stature, Pepsi-Cola approached the director of the Metropolitan Museum; nothing so lends prestige to an exhibition as does museum sponsorship. The Museum gave the idea its blessing, (since Artists for Victory was a *bona fide* artists' organization) and agreed to show the paintings selected by the competition's jury. Eight other museums across the country also agreed to hang the exhibition.

Five thousand pictures were submitted by 3,216 painters from every state in the Union except Wyoming, and from Alaska, the Canal Zone, and Puerto Rico. The theme of the competition was "Portrait of America"—"the people, the cities, the farms, factories, woods and rivers, the flora and fauna of the land shown in any season of the year." Pepsi-Cola left the selection of the 150 pictures that would be exhibited entirely to a jury of artists, and the prize winners were singled out by another jury of artists, museum directors, and critics. "Our part in the program," Walter S. Mack wrote in the *Magazine of Art* after the show was over, "was simply to award the prizes, pay the expenses, agree to reproduce the pictures, and to distribute at least 500,000 free calendars to the public, as well as pay for the resulting exhibitions at the Metropolitan Museum of Art and eight other leading museums around the country." The first prize was $2,000 and there were twelve prizes in all totaling $11,000—more generous awards than were offered by any other art competition in the country.

The exhibition, from Pepsi-Cola's point of view, was a towering success. The prize money was less than the cost of a single page of advertising in one issue of *Life* at the time, and even though the expenses of shipping and insurance were high, the total outlay was a pittance for the return in column after column of free publicity not only in New York but in each of the cities to which the exhibition traveled and in national magazines and, of course, the art press. The following year (1945) the experiment was repeated with even larger prizes, but something somewhere had gone sour. The artists were disgruntled by the selections of the jurors, and the quarrel between the "traditionalists" and the "modernists" raised its ugly head. Pepsi-Cola tried to solve this problem by having two different juries to which painters might submit their work. The Metropolitan Museum declined to renew its sponsorship; it had come under some rather harsh criticism for being party to what looked like a publicity stunt. Many of the better-known artists who had submitted their work to the first competition declined to do so again, and many others sent what seemed to the critics to be their second-rate work. The artists and some museum people quite plainly distrusted the strong odor of commercialism and disliked being party to publicizing a soft drink.

Pepsi-Cola's efforts on behalf of the arts did not stop there. The competitions were continued for five years under the title "Paintings of the Year" with the support of other museums than the Metropolitan, and press releases continued to be issued by Pepsi-Cola's "Office of Public Information and Community Services." In addition Pepsi-Cola opened an art gallery of its own on Fifty-seventh street. It was called "Opportunity Art Gallery," and its stated purpose was to "help artists in America who had not yet gained recognition, by providing them with a free gallery in which to display their work to the public." But in due course all of Pepsi-Cola's cultural activities, including a program of college scholarships, came a cropper. The corporation and Mr. Mack parted company, and Pepsi-Cola confined itself to bottling.

Pepsi-Cola's ambitious program did not set a pattern for other corporations, but it left its traces. More and more businesses began to light the lamp of culture. Abbott Laboratories, which issues an expensive magazine called *What's New?* that it sends free to doctors, not only has been using paintings by contemporary artists on its covers, but circulates exhibitions of the pictures it has bought. It has, moreover, commissioned poems from such men as Robert Frost and Archibald MacLeish and has published in its pages music especially composed at its behest by such composers as Harold Rome. Walter P. Paepcke, Chairman of the Container Corporation of America, has moved in another and still more ambitious direction. He has established an annual summer festival at Aspen, Colorado, complete with symphony concerts, showing of "art movies," exhibitions, and symposia on industrial design. The Corning Glass Works, of Corning, New York, has combined business with culture in still other ways. In 1951 in celebration of its one hundredth anniversary, it opened a building almost entirely sheathed in glass and designed by Harrison & Abramovitz, the supervising architects of the United Nations building in New York. They call it "The Glass Center" and it is a combination of museum building, recreation center, and factory. Its galleries house a permanent exhibition of the history of glass and a changing exhibition of the latest discoveries in glass technology. It has special galleries for loan exhibitions of paintings and sculpture, which it borrows from collectors, museums, and dealers; it has recreation rooms for employees (including basketball courts and bowling alleys); it has a factory where visitors can watch Steuben glass being blown and etched, and it has a luxurious executives' club decorated in the Modern manner. Not only does it bring culture to Corning through its borrowed exhibitions, its lectures, its concerts, and its summer theater with a "resident company of professional equity actors," but in the first two years that it was open 736,399 visitors came either to use the building, if they were local citizens, or to visit the exhibitions, plays, and concerts if they were tourists. To supervise the Glass Center Corning hired an experienced museum director, James M. Brown, and to inaugurate it the corporation (jointly with the American Council of Learned Societies) held a three-day symposium on "Living in Industrial Civilization" to which it invited writers and scholars and philosophers to sit down with corporation heads to discuss the problems of our culture.

Whether the concern of many corporations with culture stems from a sound public relations program that envisages the future security of business as closely tied to the cultural needs of the community, or whether it merely reflects (as some people think it does) the pressure of the excess profits tax, the fact is that business is playing an increasingly important role in the support of cultural activities. Not only does it contribute to the support of museums* and universities, but it is bringing its employees and customers to the well of taste and encouraging them to drink. It seems likely that what we have seen so far is only a beginning. Business is discovering that the corporation needs men trained in the humanities just as much as it needs men trained in the sciences, lest it become lopsided in its view of the world with which it has to do business. It is also discovering that shorter working hours are transforming the habits of the American people. "Never have so many people," according to *Business Week* in September, 1953, "had so much time on their hands—with pay—as today in the United States." Habitually the corporation has looked upon the concessions it has reluctantly made to its employees in cutting down the number of hours they work each week as lost production and increased labor costs. Now it is beginning to realize that people with time on their hands constitute not only a market but an opportunity to tie the employees closer to the corporation. Men and women with time to spare devote much of it to refurbishing their homes and to developing hobbies that make them potential customers for all sorts of equipment and gadgets. Many of them, moreover, will turn to refresh their spirits in the ways for which Corning's Glass Center has provided; they will seek recreation, whether it be physical in the bowling alley, social in the recreation rooms, or cultural in the art gallery.

Patronage of the arts can never be more than a peripheral concern of the corporation. The main business of manufacture is to make objects that people want to buy; it is not to improve public taste. There

*The Museum of Modern Art, for example, has fifty "Corporate Members" who pay up to $1,000 a year. The list includes such firms as Monsanto Chemical, I.B.M., Yale & Towne, Lord & Taylor, and the Columbia Broadcasting System.

are businessmen like Walter Paepcke of the Container Corporation and Arthur A. Houghton, Jr., of Corning Glass, who are deeply, although it sometimes seems naïvely, concerned with trying to elevate the standards of what they hope is the public's inherent "good taste." But they are a tiny minority. To a great many manufacturers the problem is not how to improve taste but how to keep it fluid so that what looked new and attractive last year will seem old-fashioned this year and downright archaic ten years from now.

It is the manufacturers of those stylish objects that wear out slowly who are most concerned with finding ways to make their products look out of date. It is the men who make and sell refrigerators and rugs, automobiles and baby carriages, furniture and dresses whose sales charts would have a dismal downward inclination to the right unless they managed to redesign their wares in ways that make last year's "latest word" seem today's drab cliché. An "old-fashioned" stove with its oven at a reasonable eye level may be more efficient than a brand-new one that forces the housewife to bend double to see the roast, but the manufacturer will do his best to make her long for a new model because it is more "up to date" and, euphemistically, "better designed." The same is, of course, true of automobiles—even more true. Ever since 1905 the automobile industry has been second only to the women's fashion industry in its insistence on the glamour of "this year's model" compared with "last year's model." In fact, a man clothes himself in his car in much the same spirit that a woman dresses herself in her clothes, and he is subject to the calculated whims of Detroit just as his wife is subject to the equally calculated whims of Paris.

Manufacturers are concerned with markets and markets are made up of people who want to buy and who can afford to. Basic needs for clothing, food, shelter, and transportation make people buy some things, but a complex of desires, ambitions and emulations makes them buy a great many things that they do not need. The function of much advertising is, of course, to create desire where no basic need exists, but it is the job of the designer to add that extra fillip of taste appeal to the product. Sometimes this taste appeal is called "glamour," sometimes it is called "borax" (which is the furniture industry's word for "corn"), sometimes it is called (especially by the Museum of Modern Art, if it happens to like it, and by Sears, Roebuck if it doesn't sell too well) "Good Design." But whatever it is called it is still taste appeal; it is still the province of the designer—rather than the engineer; and it is aimed at making the customer desire something he does not need, or at making him take pleasure in the looks of something he cannot get along without.

Ever since the machine started to turn out useful objects there have been designers who have tried to apply the trappings of taste appeal to them. In the last century the hand-made look was considered the ultimate goal for the machine-made product, and in the iron castings that held up sewing machines, for example, or the lanterns on the fronts of steam engines, the chic curlicues of the day were ever present. A reed organ designed for the parlor in Eastlake's day is a veritable piece of architecture with turrets and balconies and spindle-work ornament to catch the fancy of the purchaser who wanted the latest in good taste. But in recent years the theoreticians of taste have decided that it is dishonest to make a machine-made object look as though it were anything but machine-made. The arguments are strikingly like those that Eastlake used when he talked about "sincerity," and those that Downing used when he enjoined his readers not to try to make a wooden house look as though it were built of stone, and that Woollett used when he applied Viollet le Duc's architectural principles to making old simple homes into new fancy ones.

With the new application of the old moralities of taste to industrial production there has arisen a new profession. Just as a few press agents emerged from the mass of ballyhoo artists to become Public Relations Counselors, so a few taste-appeal artists have risen above their brethren to become Industrial Designers. The analogy between the public relations man and the industrial designer is more than a casual one. If the former puts a good front on the policies of the corporation, the latter puts a good front on its product; if the former is concerned with cloaking the corporation in the garb of public interest, the latter is concerned with endowing the object he manufactures with the garb of what he calls "honest design."

To the casual observer the industrial designer is primarily concerned with "packaging," that is, with putting an attractive slip cover on a practical object, whether it is the chassis of a car or a bathroom scales or a toaster. But the industrial designer will tell you that his function goes a good deal further than this. He is both an engineer (or employs one) and a designer and therefore is concerned with function as well as packaging. But he doesn't stop with the design of the object; he takes over jobs that used to belong to the architect and the interior decorator, and he designs the interiors (and some-times the exteriors as well) of salesrooms and offices, of display coun-ters and signs; he even on occasion goes so far as to design the cos-tumes of the sales personnel. Just as the public relations counselor is concerned with the corporation's psychological warfare, the industrial designer is concerned with the logistics of taste. His function in other words is to fight the corporation's battles on the taste front.

The three best-known American industrial designers today are Walter Dorwin Teague, Raymond Loewy, and Henry Dreyfuss. Teague is the oldest, now in his seventies. He started his professional life as an artist, book designer, and illustrator and was one of the first men to set up in business as an industrial design consultant to indus-try in 1926. He has ranged over a wide field of products and displays —from Kodaks to gas stations, from airplane interiors to periodicals— and he has written a number of books on industrial design. Loewy, who was born in France, began as a fashion illustrator, and after he came to America gradually armed himself with a battery of archi-tects, engineers, statisticians, researchers, photographers, model mak-ers, and other technicians, and has designed products and buildings for more than a hundred corporations. It is he who is responsible for the Studebaker car in its several recent eccentric shapes. Dreyfuss, the most philosophical of the three, was the man who took the bell off the top of the alarm clock and put it inside. His first job was as a stage designer, and he did the sets for *The Last Mile* and *The Cat and the Fiddle*. Since then he has applied his talents and his re-searchers to everything from fly swatters to the interior of the Peri-sphere at the New York World's Fair.

The profession of industrial designer in America is now about three decades old and is the stepchild of Walter Gropius, who founded the Bauhaus in Germany in 1919. Gropius believed that art and in-dustrial society were at loggerheads and badly in need of reconciliation.

When he opened the famous institution, which has had such far-reaching effects on the design of architecture, furniture, textiles, and practically everything else which now comes under the general heading of "modern," he intended to create a "consulting art center for industry and the trades." Furthermore, he set out to train men who not only were artists and craftsmen but who thoroughly understood industrial production. The result was the first group of industrial designers as we know them today—a quite different breed from the artists who designed for industry in the last century. Industrial designers have steadily increased in their importance to industry and in their influence on the public taste, though twist and turn the ideas that originated in the Bauhaus as they might, they have come up with few new ones of their own.

"In our modern industrial society," Arthur A. Houghton, Jr. of Corning Glass said at the *Herald Tribune* Forum of 1953, "it is the professional designer who increasingly is determining the appearance of our physical environment. The individual is less and less able to participate in this determination." As the creature of industry the industrial designer's first concern is to make a product appeal to as many people as possible. Second he must reconcile its looks as closely as he can with his own theories of aesthetics and still keep it marketable, and third he must always be aware that what he does this year must be "improved" next year. Dreyfuss has said that he is always several designs ahead of what the public is willing to accept in, say, the looks of an alarm clock. Dreyfuss is also a strong believer in the questionable fact that in recent years the public taste has greatly improved. "When I was a young man," he said to me several years ago, "you couldn't buy any decent furniture in a department store. Now you can get good modern furniture almost anywhere." Could it be that what he meant was that what he thought was good design when he was young had come to be accepted by more and more people?

I do not know of a corporation that has a Vice President in Charge of Design, though there may be several. There is, however, considerable pressure in some corporations these days to make design, in the language of business, a function of top management. Some of this pressure is from businessmen who believe that the corporation has a public responsibility for producing a better quality of design, and that if you leave the final decisions about how the product shall look to those greedy fellows in the sales department, the public taste will suffer. Conferences such as the ones held at Aspen on the subject of industrial design and the meeting of the American Federation of Arts on the relations of art and industry that was held in 1953 at Corning were aimed at least partially at making the corporation take its design function more seriously as a matter of public welfare.

The simple economics of the matter is, however, that the corporation which is interested in doing a mass business will let the design department have its head only so long as the sales chart holds up. If designers do not like to put splashes and streaks of chromium on cars, and sales figures indicate that people like "bright work," the designer's job is to think up newer and more dashing ways to use chromium. It is also true, however, that there are corporations that are not interested in mass markets and whose business it is to woo a selected market that wants more than anything to be terribly up to date. For this market the designer can indulge the niceties of his craft, and his originality becomes part of the taste appeal that he builds into his product. This is especially true in a segment of the furniture and textile businesses where such designers as Charles Eames, and George Nelson and T. H. Robsjohn-Gibbings and Dorothy Liebes work both the commercial and the cultural sides of the business street. They are, in a sense, pace setters for the furniture world, and their designs are "copied down" and "boraxed up" in much the same way that Paris fashions are copied down and fancied up by the Seventh Avenue dress houses for the popular-priced market.

"The industrial designer of today is not an industrial designer at all," wrote Percy Seitlin in the *Magazine of Art* in January, 1944, "but an advertising man." And then he adds: "The primary concern of the profession of industrial designing, as we have come to know it, is—to use a phrase which the industrial designers and their clients understand well—the enhancement of salability." The industrial designers admit that this is so, but they retort that unless a product is basically sound the public will not be fooled by it for long no matter what it is made to look like. The fact is that the industrial designers must be experts in the clichés of taste. In general it seems that the most successful industrial designers are also the best talkers. The corporation executive likes the man who can give him a lively line of aesthetic abstractions filled with the old moralities of "honest design" and "sincere use of materials" plus the modern clichés of "form and function." It gives him a feeling of participation in the upper reaches of culture. But he only likes it from a man who can also talk in the practical terms of sales, maintenance, and production costs. Top management can eat its cultural cake from the hand of such a man and have it too.

There is no question that the corporation, through the marketing of its products, through its necessity to change models, through the competitive scramble for the attention of the consumer, and through its use of the industrial designer, plays a major role in determining the character of the public taste. But the corporation can only coax, it cannot lead. Changes in style, the fashion experts insist, cannot be forced on the public, and the designer and the manufacturer cannot launch a new style no matter how good it might be for business, until the public is in a frame of mind to accept it.

If there is any business that should know the answers to the mysterious questions of the public taste, it is the fashion business. Compared with any other industry—whether it be furniture or automobiles or lamps or rugs or anything else in which taste plays an important role—the fashion industry's business is almost ninety-five per cent a gamble in taste. Durability of materials and quality of workmanship play only the tiniest roles in the fashion business; taste is everything. Consequently the fashion industry is not like any other. It is highly segmented, fiercely competitive, and whimsical; it is darkened by a high rate of bankruptcies and brightened by romantically fantastic success stories. It is a business with no cultural aspirations, in the usual meaning of the phrase, but it reflects culture, in the broadest sense, as no other business does. The mood and morals and mores of a people are portrayed by their clothes even more readily than by their arts, because clothes are essentially ephemeral and respond easily and quickly to changes in the public temper.

To a lesser degree this is true of all industries. They reflect taste; they do not make it. They can hasten a trend but they cannot start one until the public is ready for it. They can play on the emotions of desire and pride and emulation, but they cannot create desire or pride or ambition any more than they can create taste unless a host of factors over which they have no control are ready to respond to their stimulus.

The corporation as an art patron and as a dispenser of design is very different from the corporation as a group of individuals who are exerting their personal taste for their own personal ends. The contrast is an interesting one and certainly not without significance. It provides a story in which the same cast of characters lines up in a quite different order.

The front that the corporation puts on for the public, the modern streamlined package in which their product is clothed, is quite unlike the genteel tradition in which its executives live and move. The higher up the corporate ladder you climb the more genteel you will find your surroundings. In fact, if you will visit Lever House in New York, the sheer glass box that sits handsomely on Park Avenue to house the offices of Lever Brothers, you will find that the higher the echelon the more old-fashioned the surroundings. The public front is one of daring modernity. The offices of the clerks and department managers are in the functional tradition. But when you reach the offices of top management you will find that there are open fireplaces and chandeliers with an Early American flavor and furniture that might as well be Biedermeier. If you will visit the executive dining room of the J. Walter Thompson Company, one of America's biggest advertising agencies, with its offices in the Graybar Building next to Grand Central Station, you will find yourself in what appears to be a Cape Cod house furnished with Windsor chairs and rag rugs. It has wooden casement windows and, as Richard Kelly wrote in *Flair* in 1950: "Here, on a depressing rainy day, artificial sunlight can warm patches of old pine flooring when a million dollars is at stake." Only a few years ago Dr. Armand Hammer, the President of United Distillers of America, remodeled his office on the seventy-eighth floor of the Empire State Building, which is almost as high as modern science has provided man with floor space. He installed above the clouds, with only a few minor adjustments to make it fit the space, the Treaty Room of Ye Olde Treaty House of Uxbridge, Middlesex, England. It was in Dr. Hammer's office that Charles I and Oliver Cromwell met in 1645 to end Britain's civil war.

If after inspecting such anachronisms as these you will drive out to the suburbs where the corporation's top management lives, you will find yourselves back in the nineteen-twenties and -thirties surrounded by the architecture and furniture of several centuries earlier than that. It is a rare chairman of the board who, no matter how advanced his industrial thinking, how liberal his personnel policies, or how up to date the appearance of his product, lives in surroundings that are not very like those that were loved by the businessman of a generation ago.

If you will then proceed to a "company town," in which a large corporation occupies in some capacity or other the time of most of the city's residents, you will find that the pattern of taste from the levels of top management down to the most junior executives looks something like this. The chairman of the board lives in the largest house, furthest from the railroad tracks, and if there is a hill he will be on the top of it. The house is more than likely to be thirty or so years old, a large, comfortable home that is some relation of an English country house or possibly a small château, or possibly a combination of both. Its lawns and shrubs are carefully tended and its garden is obviously the pride of the chairman's wife, who has a gardener who "helps" her, as she would put it. Inside, the decoration is rich but unpretentious. The furniture is a little bit of everything from Chippendale and Sheraton to Empire, but not much later; there is nothing modern. There are likely to be several wing chairs upholstered in brocade or even possibly needlepoint. The carpets are Oriental, for the most part, though there might be a Savonnerie or an Aubusson in the drawing room, where there are also mirrors in ornamented gilt frames. The lamps are erstwhile vases, some of them Chinese. On the wall are portraits with picture lights over them and (unless the chairman or his wife are collectors) a nineteenth-century landscape or two. On the piano (parlor grand) are photographs in silver frames with initials engraved on them. Upstairs the bedrooms are bright and chintzy, in the spirit if not the image of the days when Elsie de Wolfe was at her peak. The house smells of fresh flowers, except for the chairman's paneled den which smells of cigars. There are hunting prints on the den wall and pictures in easel leather frames on the chairman's desk. These are mostly of his children and grandchildren.

The chairman's wife has a collection of Early American glass which is set on glass shelves in the windows of the dining room.

The picture, as you see, is one of expensive, well-ordered comfort and completely safe taste. The pieces are all good pieces; the textiles are bought to last for years.

But let us now walk down the driveway and from there down the hill to where the president of the corporation lives and just down the street to the houses of the vice presidents. You will notice quite a difference—not in the general level of taste but in scale. The houses are of about the same vintage, but the driveways are shorter, the rooms are smaller, and they sit on less land. Some of the elegance is missing. It is not that the individual pieces of furniture are any less good, but they seem to be striving to be something they are not. They haven't the settled elegance they had in the chairman's house; they look as though they hadn't quite made their peace with their surroundings (especially in the vice presidents' houses). The vice presidents' wives seem a little busier about their housekeeping, a little more patronizing about their own furniture, and a little quicker to point out the really good pieces, and to tell you something about the artist who painted the picture over the mantel. The vice president to whom the design department reports is very likely to have a few modern pieces around, just to show that he knows about such things and also to establish his right to have opinions about what "these designer fellows are up to." If the chairman of the board, incidentally, drives a Fleetwood Cadillac it behooves the president to drive a regular Cadillac and the vice presidents to drive Buicks. It would hardly be tactful of them, even though they could afford it, to have a better car than the big boss; he might think they were trying to put on airs.

There is no need to visit all the houses all the way down the hill or even to stop at each street. When you get into the homes of the lower levels of the "management team" as they call it, you will find that the pattern repeats itself on an increasingly smaller scale. Among the younger executives modern furniture is acceptable and originality in its use is admired. Eccentricity, however, is not admired, and the wife of the executive, as William H. Whyte, Jr., has so graphically pointed out in his essays in *Fortune* on "The Wives of Management" dares not express any oddities in her tastes lest her husband's contemporaries or his boss think that she is different and therefore not a good risk as a company wife. Indeed if she has a private income, she dare not spend it on herself or her house, lest, like the vice president with his Buick, she might seem to be acting above her corporate station.

The part that the corporation plays in American taste has been growing slowly for a long time. It has long been business that has given architects their greatest chances to experiment with new forms of building. It has long been businessmen who have been the most avid picture collectors and the patrons of the Art World. It has long been the practice of men who have made great individual fortunes to use their private wealth to set up foundations for the support of culture, to establish libraries, and to endow universities. But now it is the corporations who are taking over the functions that once belonged to the old tycoons. It is the corporation that has become the most promising patron of the fine arts and supporter of cultural institutions. Corporations have picture collections; they buy paintings to hang in executive offices; they commission fine artists to paint their advertisements, they hold conferences about ways to raise the level of the public taste, they contribute funds to universities for pure research and even for support of the humanities. Nobody can say that they are not at least half trying, though there are a good many artists, college presidents, and highbrows who wish they would try harder—and more intelligently.

These things are obvious, but while the corporation has been growing in maturity as a responsible rather than a predatory element in the public scheme of things, the businessman has been losing glamour. Corporations have grown to tremendous sizes and the practices of business are carefully regulated by government—even by a government of businessmen. The young men entering on business careers hope to get to the top, but they do not hope to get there by daring or eccentricity. They are working for security, not for fortune and fame. The leaders of business are no longer swashbuckling tycoons; they are corporation bureaucrats and engineers and lawyers and graduates of the Harvard Business School. They are neither villains nor heroes. They are ordinary people.

Ordinary people are cautious and sensible about taste. But they work at it.

CHAPTER XVII

Highbrow, Lowbrow, Middlebrow

"It becomes increasingly difficult to tell who
is serious and who is not."

Mᵧ wife's grandmother, the wife of a distinguished lawyer, once
declined to dine with the Cartiers of jewelry fame because
they were, as she put it, "in trade." Life for grandmother, who lived in
a properly elegant but nondescript town house in New York, was
relatively simple where social distinctions were concerned. While
there are still a few people who think and act as she did, the passage
of time has eliminated a great deal of that particular kind of snobbishness from American society. We are replacing it with another kind.
The old structure of the upper class, the middle class, and the lower
class is on the wane. It isn't wealth or family that makes prestige these
days. It's taste and high thinking.

Edith Wharton's theory that if the taste of the rich could be improved the general level of public taste would benefit has turned out
to be a fallacy. The consumers and makers of taste, it appears, cannot be divided according to the conventional social strata. Good taste
and bad taste, adventurous and timid taste, cannot be explained by
wealth or education, by breeding or background. Each of these
plays a part, but there is no longer such a thing as upper-class taste
and lower-class taste as there was once supposed to be. In recent
years a new social structure has emerged in which taste and intellectual pretension and accomplishment plays a major role. What we see
growing around us is a sort of social stratification in which the highbrows are the elite, the middlebrows are the bourgeoisie, and the lowbrows are *hoi polloi*.

For the time being this is perhaps largely an urban phenomenon, and the true middlebrow may readily be mistaken in the small community for a genuine highbrow, but the pattern is emerging with increasing clarity, and the new distinctions do not seem to be based either on money or on breeding. Some lowbrows are as rich as Billy Rose, and as flamboyant, some as poor as Rosie O'Grady and as modest. Some middlebrows run industries; some run the women's auxiliary of the Second Baptist Church. Some highbrows eat caviar with their Proust; some eat hamburger when they can afford it. It is true that most highbrows are in the ill-paid professions, notably the academic, and that most middlebrows are at least reasonably well off. Only the lowbrows can be found in about equal percentages at all financial levels. There may be a time, of course, when the highbrows will be paid in accordance with their own estimate of their worth, but that is not likely to happen in any form of society in which creature comforts are in greater demand than intellectual uplift. Like poets they will have to be content mostly with prestige. The middlebrows are influential today, but neither the highbrows nor the lowbrows like them; and if we ever have intellectual totalitarianism, it may well be the lowbrows and the highbrows who will run things, and the middlebrows who will be exiled in boxcars to a collecting point probably in the vicinity of Independence, Missouri.

While this social shift, which is also a shift in the weight that we give to taste, is still in its early stages, and the dividing lines are still indistinct and the species not yet (if ever) frozen, let us examine the principal categories, with their subdivisions and splinter groups, and see where we ourselves are likely to fetch up.

The highbrows come first. Edgar Wallace, who was certainly not a highbrow himself, was asked by a newspaper reporter in Hollywood some years ago to define one. "What is a highbrow?" he said. "A highbrow is a man who has found something more interesting than women."

Presumably at some time in every man's life there are things he finds more interesting than women; alcohol, for example, or the World Series. Mr. Wallace has only partially defined the highbrow. Brander Matthews came closer when he said that "a highbrow is a person educated beyond his intelligence," and A. P. Herbert came closest of all when he wrote that "a highbrow is the kind of person who looks at a sausage and thinks of Picasso."

It is this association of culture with every aspect of daily life, from the design of his razor to the shape of the bottle that holds his sleeping pills, that distinguishes the highbrow from the middlebrow or the lowbrow. Spiritually and intellectually the highbrow inhabits a precinct well up the slopes of Parnassus, and his view of the cultural scene is from above. His vision pinpoints certain lakes and quarries upon which his special affections are concentrated—a perturbed lake called Rilke or a deserted quarry called Kierkegaard or a meadow of exotic flowers called Henry James—but he believes that he sees them, as he sees the functional design of his razor, always in relation to the broader cultural scene. There is a certain air of omniscience about the highbrow, though that air is in many cases the thin variety encountered on the tops of high mountains from which the view is extensive but the details are lost.

You cannot tell a man that he is a lowbrow any more than you can tell a woman that her clothes are in bad taste, but a highbrow does not mind being called a highbrow. He has worked hard, read widely, traveled far, and listened attentively in order to satisfy his curiosity and establish his squatters' rights in this little corner of intellectualism, and he does not care who knows it. And this is true of both kinds of highbrow—the militant, or crusader, type and the passive, or dilettante, type. These types in general live happily together; the militant highbrow carries the torch of culture, the passive highbrow reads by its light.

The carrier of the torch makes a profession of being a highbrow and lives by his calling. He is most frequently found in university and college towns, a member of the liberal-arts faculty, teaching languages (ancient or modern), the fine arts, or literature. His spare time is often devoted to editing a magazine which is read mainly by other highbrows, ambitious undergraduates, and the editors of middlebrow publications in search of talent. When he writes for the magazine himself (or for another "little" magazine) it is usually criticism or criticism *of* criticism. He leaves the writing of fiction and poetry to others more bent on creation than on what has been created, for the highbrow is primarily a critic and not an artist—a taster, not a cook. He is often more interested in where the arts have been, and where they are going, than in the objects themselves. He is devoted to the proposition that the arts must be pigeonholed, and that their trends should be plotted, or as W. H. Auden puts it—

> Our intellectual marines,
> Landing in Little Magazines,
> Capture a trend.

This gravitation of the highbrows to the universities is fairly recent. In the twenties, when the little magazines were devoted to publishing experimental writing rather than criticism of exhumed experimental writing, the highbrows flocked to Paris, New York, and Chicago. The *transatlantic review, transition,* and the *Little Review,* of the lower-case era of literature, were all published in Paris; BROOM was published in New York; *Poetry* was (and still is) published in Chicago. The principal little magazines now, with the exception of *Partisan Review,* a New York product but written mostly by academics, are published in the colleges—the *Kenyon Review,* the *Sewanee Review,* the *Virginia Quarterly,* and so on—and their flavor reflects this. But this does not mean that highbrows do not prefer the centers in which cultural activities are the most varied and active, and these are still London, Paris, New York, and more recently Rome. Especially in the fine arts, the highbrow has a chance to make a living in the metropolis where museums are centered and where art is bought and sold as well as created. This is also true of commercial publishing, in which many highbrows find suitable, if not entirely congenial, refuge.

But no matter where they may make their homes, all highbrows live in a world which they believe is inhabited almost entirely by Philistines —those who through viciousness or smugness or the worship of materialism gnaw away at the foundations of culture. And the highbrow sees as his real enemy the middlebrow, whom he regards as a pretentious and frivolous man or woman who uses culture to satisfy social or business ambitions; who, to quote Clement Greenberg in *Partisan Review,* is busy "devaluating the precious, infecting the healthy, corrupting the honest, and stultifying the wise."

It takes a man who feels strongly to use such harsh words, but the militant highbrow has no patience with his enemies. He is a serious man who will not tolerate frivolity where the arts are concerned. It is part of his function as a highbrow to protect the arts from the culture mongers, and he spits venom at those he suspects of selling the Muses short.

The fact that nowadays everyone has access to culture through schools and colleges, through the press, radio, and museums, disturbs him deeply; for it tends to blur the distinctions between those who are serious and those who are frivolous. "Culturally what we have," wrote William Phillips in *Horizon* several years ago, "is a democratic free-for-all in which every individual, being as good as every other one, has the right to question any form of intellectual authority." To this Mr. Greenberg adds, "It becomes increasingly difficult to tell who is serious and who not."

The highbrow does not like to be confused, nor does he like to have his authority questioned, except by other highbrows of whose seriousness he is certain. The result is precisely what you would expect: the highbrows believe in, and would establish, an intellectual elite, "a fluid body of intellectuals . . . whose accepted role in society is to perpetuate traditional ideas and values and to create new ones." Such an elite would like to see the middlebrow eliminated, for it regards him as the undesirable element in our, and anybody else's, culture.

"It must be obvious to anyone that the volume and social weight of middlebrow culture," Mr. Greenberg writes, "borne along as it has been by the great recent increase in the American middle class, have multiplied at least tenfold in the past three decades. This culture presents a more serious threat to the genuine article than the old-time pulp dime novel, Tin Pan Alley, *Schund* variety ever has or will. Unlike the latter, which has its social limits clearly marked out for it, middlebrow culture attacks distinctions as such and insinuates itself everywhere. . . . Insidiousness is of its essence, and in recent years its avenues of penetration have become infinitely more difficult to detect and block."

By no means all highbrows take such a strong position as this or are so concerned with the tastes of others. Many of them, the passive ones, are merely consumers totally indifferent to the middlebrows or supercilious about them. Some without a great deal of hope but in ardent good faith expend themselves in endeavor to widen the circle of those who can enjoy the arts in their purest forms. Many museums, colleges, and publishing houses are at least partly staffed by highbrows who exert a more than half-hearted effort to make the arts exciting and important to the public. But they are aware that most of their labors are wasted. In his heart of hearts nearly every highbrow believes with Ortega y Gasset that "the average citizen [is] a creature incapable of receiving the sacrament of art, blind and deaf to pure beauty." When, for example, the Metropolitan Museum planned to expand its facilities a few years ago, an art dealer who can clearly be classified as a highbrow remarked: "All this means is less art for more people."

There are also many highbrows who are not concerned in the least with the arts or with literature, and who do not fret themselves about the upstart state of middlebrow culture. These are the specialized highbrows who toil in the remote corners of science and history, of philology and mathematics. They are concerned with their investigations of fruit flies or Elizabethan taxation or whatever it may be, and they do not talk about them, as the dilettante always talks of the arts, to the first person they can latch onto at a cocktail party. When not in their laboratories or the library, they are often as not thoroughly middlebrow in their attitudes and tastes.

The real highbrow's way of life is as intellectualized as his way of thinking, and as carefully plotted. He is likely to be either extremely self-conscious about his physical surroundings and creature comforts or else sublimely, and rather ostentatiously, indifferent to them. If he affects the former attitude, he will within the limits of his income surround himself with works of art. If he cannot afford paintings he buys drawings. Color reproductions, except as casual reminders tucked in the frame of a mirror or thrown down on a table, are beneath him. The facsimile is no substitute in his mind for the genuine, and he would rather have a slight sketch by a master, Braque or Picasso or even Jackson Pollock, than a fully-realized canvas by an artist he considers not quite first-rate. Drawings by his friends he hangs in the bathroom. His furniture, if it is modern, consists of identifiable pieces by Aalto, or Breuer, or Mies van der Rohe, or Eames; it does not come from department stores. If he finds modern unsympathetic, he will tend to use Biedermeier or the more "entertaining" varieties of Victorian, which he collects piece by piece with an eye to the slightly eccentric. If he has antiques, you may be sure they are not maple; the cult of Early American is offensive to him.

The food that he serves will be planned with the greatest care, either very simple (a perfect French omelette made with sweet butter) or elaborate recipes from *Wine and Food* magazine published in London and edited by André Simon. If he cannot afford a pound of butter with every guinea fowl, he will in all probability resort to the casserole, and peasant cookery with the sparer parts of animals and birds seasoned meticulously with herbs that he gets from a little importer in the wholesale district. His wine is more likely to be a "perfectly adequate little red wine" for eighty-nine cents a half gallon than an imported French vintage. (Anybody with good advice can buy French wines, but the discovery of a good domestic bottle shows perception and educated taste.) He wouldn't dream of washing his salad bowl. His collection of phonograph records is likely to bulk large at the ends and sag in the middle—a predominance of Bach-and-before at one end and Stravinsky, Schönberg, Bartok, and New Orleans jazz at the other. The nineteenth century is represented, perhaps, by Beethoven quartets and late sonatas, and some French "art songs" recorded by Maggie Teyte. His radio, if he has one, is turned on rarely; he wouldn't have a television set in the house.

The highbrow who disregards his creature comforts does it with a will. He lives with whatever furniture happens to come his way in a disorganized conglomeration of Victorian, department store, and Mexican bits and pieces. He takes care of his books in that he knows where each one is no matter in what disorder they may appear. Every other detail of domestic life he leaves to his wife, of whose taste he is largely unaware, and he eats what she gives him without comment. If he is a bachelor, he eats in a cafeteria or drugstore or diner and sometimes spills soup on the open pages of his book. He is oblivious of the man who sits down opposite him, and if Edgar Wallace is right, to the woman who shares his table. He is not a man without passions, but they have their place. Dress is a matter of indifference to him.

The highbrows about whom I have been writing are mainly consumers and not creators—editors, critics, and dilettantes. The creative artists who are generally considered highbrows—such men as T. S. Eliot, E. M. Forster, Picasso, and Stravinsky—seem to me to fall in another category, that of the professional man who, while he may be concerned with communicating with a limited (and perhaps largely highbrow) audience, is primarily a doer and not a done-by. When Eliot or Forster or Picasso or Stravinsky sits down at his work table, I do not know whether he says to himself, "I am going to create Art," but I very much doubt if that is what is in his mind. He is concerned rather with the communication of ideas within the frame of a poem, a novel, a painting, or a ballet suite, and if it turns out to be art (which many think it frequently does) that is to him a by-product of creation, an extra dividend of craftsmanship, intelligence, and sensibility. But when this happens he is taken up by the highbrow consumer and made much of. In fact he may become, whether he likes it or not, a vested interest, and his reputation will be every bit as carefully guarded by the highbrows as a hundred shares of Standard Oil of New Jersey by the middlebrows. He will be sold—at a par decided upon by the highbrows—to the middlebrows, who are natural gamblers in the commodities of culture.

In a sense it is this determination of par that is the particular contribution of the highbrow. Others may quarrel with his evaluations, but the fact remains that unless there were a relatively small group of self-appointed intellectuals who took it upon themselves to ransack the studios of artists, devour the manuscripts of promising writers, and listen at the keyholes of young composers, many talented men and women might pass unnoticed and our culture be the poorer. Their noncommercial attitude toward discovery of talent is useful, though they have an obsession with the evils of the monetary temptations with which America strews the artist's path. They stand as a wavering bulwark against the enticements of Hollywood and the advertising agencies, and they are saddened by the writers and painters who have set out to be serious men, as Hemingway did, and then become popular by being taken up by the middlebrows. They even go so far as to say that a story published in *Partisan Review* is a better story than if it were published in *The New Yorker* or *Harper's Bazaar*, for the reason that "what we have is at once a general raising and lowering of the level, for which the blurring of distinctions new writing tends to become more and more serious and intellectual and less and less bold and extreme. . . ."

This attitude, which is the attitude of the purist, is valuable. It is the sort of statement that James Jackson Jarves might have made a century before, or James Fenimore Cooper even earlier. They were dismayed at the way every man pretended to be a connoisseur— "knowledge or no knowledge; brains or no brains; taste or no taste." The ground in which the arts grow stays fertile only when it is fought over by both artists and consumers, and the phalanx of highbrows in the field, a somewhat impenetrable square of warriors, can be counted on to keep the fray alive.

The highbrow's friend is the lowbrow. The highbrow enjoys and respects the lowbrow's art—jazz for instance—which he is likely to call a spontaneous expression of folk culture. The lowbrow is not interested, as the middlebrow is, in pre-empting any of the highbrow's function or in any way threatening to blur the lines between the serious and the frivolous. In fact he is almost completely oblivious of the highbrow unless he happens to be taken up by him—as many jazz musicians, primitive painters, and ballad writers have been—and then he is likely to be flattered, a little suspicious, and somewhat amused. A creative lowbrow like the jazz musician is a prominent citizen in his own world, and the fact that he is taken up by the highbrows has very little effect on his social standing therein. He is tolerant of the highbrow, whom he regards as somewhat odd and out-of-place in a world in which people do things and enjoy them without analyzing why or worrying about their cultural implications.

The lowbrow doesn't give a hang about art *qua* art. He knows what he likes, and he doesn't care why he likes it—which implies that all children are lowbrows. The word "beautiful," which has long since ceased to mean anything to the highbrow, is a perfectly good word to the lowbrow. Beautiful blues, beautiful sunsets, beautiful women, all things that do something to a man inside without passing through the mind, associations without allusions, illusions without implications. The arts created by the lowbrow are made in the expression of immediate pleasure or grief, like most forms of jazz; or of usefulness, like the manufacturing of a tool or a piece of machinery or even a bridge across the Hudson. The form, to use a highbrow phrase, follows the function. When the lowbrow arts follow this formula (which they don't always do), then the highbrow finds much in them to admire, and he calls it the vernacular. When, however, the lowbrow arts get mixed up with middlebrow ideas of culture, then the highbrow turns away in disgust. Look, for example, at what happened to the circus, a traditional form of lowbrow art. They got in Norman Bel Geddes to fancy it up, and now its special flavor of authenticity is gone—all wrapped up in pink middlebrow sequins. This is not to say that the lowbrow doesn't like it just as much as he ever did. It is the highbrow who is pained.

Part of the highbrow's admiration for the lowbrow stems from the lowbrow's indifference to art. This makes it possible for the highbrow to blame whatever he doesn't like about lowbrow taste on the middlebrow. If the lowbrow reads the comics, the highbrow understands; he is frequently a connoisseur of the comics himself. But if he likes grade-B double features, the highbrow blames that on the corrupting influence of the middlebrow moneybags of Hollywood. If he participates in give-away quiz programs, it is because the radio pollsters have decided that the average mental age of the listening audience is thirteen, and that radio and televison are venal for taking advantage of the adolescent.

The lowbrow consumer, whether he is an engineer of bridges or a bus driver, wants to be comfortable and to enjoy himself without having to worry about whether he has good taste or not. It doesn't make any difference to him that a chair is a bad Grand Rapids copy of an eighteenth-century *fauteuil* as long as he's happy when he sits down in it. He doesn't care whether the movies are art, or the television improving, so long as he has fun while he is giving them his attention and getting a fair return of pleasure from his investment. It wouldn't occur to him to tell a novelist what kind of book he should write, or a movie director what kind of a movie to make. If he doesn't like a book he ignores it; if he doesn't like a movie he says so, whether it is a Martin and Lewis show or *Henry V*. If he likes jive or square dancing, he doesn't worry about whether they are fashionable or not. If other people like the ballet, that's all right with him, so long as ne doesn't have to go himself. In general the lowbrow attitude toward the arts is live and let live. Lowbrows are not Philistines. One has to know enough about the arts to argue about them with highbrows to be a Philistine.

The popular press, and also much of the unpopular press, is run by the middlebrows, and it is against them that the highbrow inveighs.

"The true battle," wrote Virginia Woolf in an essay called "Middle-brow" (she was the first, I believe, to define the species) ". . . lies not between the highbrows and the lowbrows joined together in blood brotherhood but against the bloodless and pernicious pest who comes between. . . . Highbrows and lowbrows must band together to exterminate a pest which is the bane of all thinking and living."

Pushing Mrs. Woolf's definition a step further, the pests divide themselves into two groups: the upper middlebrows and the lower middlebrows. It is the upper middlebrows who are the principal purveyors of highbrow ideas and the lower middlebrows who are the principal consumers of what the upper middlebrows pass along to them.

Many publishers, for example, are upper middlebrows—as are most educators, museum directors, movie producers, art dealers, lecturers, and the editors of most magazines which combine national circulation with an adult vocabulary. These are the men and women who devote themselves professionally to the dissemination of ideas and cultural artifacts and, not in the least incidentally, make a living along the way. They are the cultural do-gooders, and they see their mission clearly and pursue it with determination. Some of them are disappointed highbrows; some of them try to work both sides of the street; nearly all of them straddle the fence between highbrow and middlebrow and enjoy their equivocal position.

The conscientious publisher, for instance, believes in the importance of literature and the dignity of publishing as a profession. He spends a large part of his time on books that will not yield him a decent return on his investment. He searches out writers of promise; he pores over the "little" magazines (or pays other people to); he leafs through hundreds and hundreds of pages of manuscript. He advises writers, encourages them, coaxes them to do their best work; he even advances them money. But he is not able to be a publisher at all (unless he is willing to put his personal fortune at the disposal of financially naïve muses) if he does not publish to make money. In order to publish slender volumes of poetry he must also publish fat volumes of historical romance, and in order to encourage the first novel of a promising young writer he must sell tens of thousands of copies of a book by an old hand who grinds out one best seller a year. He must take the measure of popular taste and cater to it at the same time that he tries to create a taste for new talent. If he is a successful publisher he makes money, lives comfortably, patronizes the other arts, serves on museum boards and committees for the Prevention of This and the Preservation of That, contributes to the symphony, and occasionally buys pictures by contemporary painters.

The highbrow suspects that the publisher does not pace his book-lined office contriving ways to serve the muses and that these same muses have to wait their turn in line until the balance sheet has been served. He believes that the publisher is really happy only when he can sell a couple of hundred thousand copies of a novel about a hussy with a horsewhip or a book on how to look forty when forty-five. To the highbrow he is a tool to be cultivated and used, but not to be trusted.

The museum director, as we have already seen, is in much the same position, caught between the muses and the masses. If he doesn't make a constant effort to swell the door count, his middlebrow trustees want to know why he isn't serving the community; if he does, the high-brows want to know why he is pandering to popular taste and not minding his main business—the service of scholarship and the support of artists currently certified to be "serious." Educators are in the same position, bound to be concerned with mass education often at the expense of the potential scholar, and editors of all magazines except those supported by private angels or cultural institutions know that they must not only enlighten but entertain if they are to have enough readers to pay the bills. To the highbrow this can lead to nothing but compromise and mediocrity.

The upper-middlebrow consumer takes his culture seriously, as seriously as his job allows, for he is gainfully employed. In his leisure hours he reads Toynbee or Osbert Sitwell's serialized memoirs. He goes to museum openings and to the theater and he keeps up on the foreign films. He buys pictures, sometimes old masters if he can afford them, sometimes contemporary works. He has a few etchings and lithographs, and he is not above an occasional color reproduction of a Cézanne or a Lautrec. Writers and painters are his friends and dine at his house; if, however, his own son were to express an interest in being an artist, he would be dismayed ("so few artists ever really pull it off")—though he would keep a stiff upper lip and hope the boy would learn better before it was too late. His house is tastefully decorated, sometimes in the very latest mode, a model of the modern architect's dream of functionalism, in which case he can discourse on the theory of the open plan and the derivations of the International Style with the zest and uncertain vocabulary of a convert. If his house is "traditional" in character, he will not put up with Grand Rapids copies of old pieces; he will have authentic ones, and will settle for Victorian if he cannot afford Empire. He, or his wife, will ransack second-hand shops for entertaining bibelots and lamps or a piece of Brussels carpet from Andrew Jackson Downing's day for the bedroom. He never refers to curtains as "drapes." He talks about television as potentially a new art form, and he watches the Ford Foundation's TV program *Omnibus*. His library contains a few of the more respectable current best sellers which he reads out of "curiosity" rather than interest. There are a few shelves of first editions, some of them autographed by friends who have dined at his house, some of them things (like a presentation copy of *Jurgen*) that he "just happened to pick up" and a sampling of American and British poets. There is also a shelf of paper-bound French novels—most of them by nineteenth-century writers. The magazines on his table span the areas from *Time* and *The New Yorker* to *Harper's* and the *Atlantic*, with an occasional copy of the *Yale* and *Partisan Reviews*, and the *Art News*.

From this it can be seen that he supports the highbrows—buys some of the books they recommend and an occasional picture they have looked upon with favor—and contributes to organized efforts to promote the arts both by serving on boards and shelling out money. In general he is modest about expressing his opinion on cultural matters in the presence of highbrows but takes a slightly lordly tone

A Taste for Conformity

Some Americans like to live in houses just like their neighbors; some can't avoid it. It is nothing new. The "Italian villas," above, were painted in the 1860's. The concrete houses at the left were "poured" in 1917. The ranch houses below are brand new.

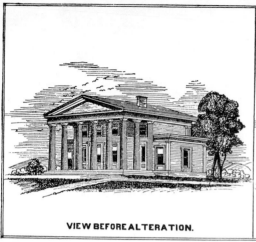

VIEW BEFORE ALTERATION.

VIEW AFTER ALTERATION.

A Taste for the New

In 1878 William M. Woollett in his book *Old Homes Made New* recommended the alterations above as the solution for making an "old" Greek Revival house into a "new" Queen Anne model. In Chicago, below left, a red stone castle home of the 1890's dons a "modern," somewhat International Style, front, and next to it a bank built in 1869 puts on the columns which all banks were supposed to have when it was made new in 1916. This was a throwback to the days of the Greek Revival when gentlemen lived behind columns which were considered a symbol of solidity.

A Taste for the Exotic

A yearning for the exotic runs strong in the veins of American taste. Above left is a cast-in-place concrete castle built in Port Chester, New York, in 1872, and at its right is a Persian villa built in the 1860's for the painter Frederick Church. The gilded temple at the right is the top of a skyscraper (New York Central Building in New York) and the pagoda below is Grauman's Chinese Theater in Hollywood.

1850's-1860's | 1870's-1890's

HIGHBROW

A "Mantegna" from the Bryan Coll.

Whistler's "Arrangement in Gray and Black, No.

MIDDLEBROW

Durand's "Kindred Spirits"

Gérôme's "Pygmalion and Galatea"

LOWBROW

Currier & Ives' "Fourth of July"

Becker's "Custer's Last Fight"

1910's-1920's

Van Gogh's "L'Arlésienne"

Whistler's "Portrait of the Artist's Mother"

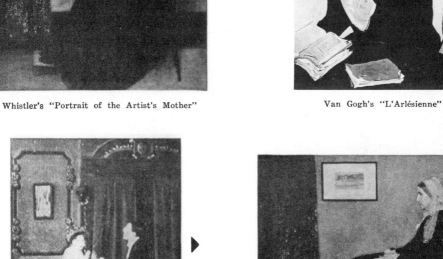

D. W. Griffith in "The Crossroads of Life"

1940's-1950's

"The Crossroads of Life," an early Griffith film

Van Gogh's "L'Arlésienne"

"Whistler's Mother"

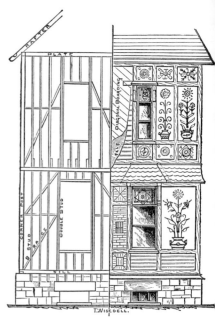

A Taste for Honesty

The moral arguments for architectural styles persist but the looks change. Each of the buildings on this page is an example of the "honest" architecture of its day—the Gothic Revival house, above left, was said to be more honest than Greek Revival. The Queen Anne house, above right, displaced the Gothic for the same reason. Below is today's honest architecture—the entrance hall of Lever House, New York City.

A Taste for Scientific Comfort and Convenience

When Locomobile boasted in 1899 that "No better [horseless carriage] will be made. Time cannot improve it," the automobile manufacturers had not yet learned how to coax the public taste by changing models every year. But manufacturers of all sorts have long understood the American taste for scientific gadgets for comfort and convenience, as the Wilson chair of the 1870's and its modern counterpart, the BarcaLounger, attest.

A Taste for Taste

It is a far cry from the Mississippi River steamer (*City of Hickman*) of a century ago to the brand new restaurant in the Metropolitan Museum in New York, but the gold and white floating palace and the black and gold and white palace of 1954 bespeak the persistence of America's taste for "tastefulness."

when he is talking to other middlebrows. If he discovers a "little" painter or poet, the chances are excellent that the man has already been discovered and promoted by a highbrow or by an upper-middle-brow entrepreneur (art dealer or publisher). Once in a while he will take a flyer on an unknown artist, and hang his picture inconspicuously in the bedroom. He takes his function as a patron of the arts seriously, but he does it for the pleasure it gives him to be part of the cultural scene. If he does it for "money, fame, power, or prestige," as Virginia Woolf says he does, these motives are so obscured by a general sense of well-being and well-meaning that he would be shocked and surprised to be accused of venality.

If the upper middlebrow is unsure of his own tastes, but firm in his belief that taste is extremely important, the lower middlebrow is his counterpart. The lower middlebrow ardently believes that he knows what he likes, and yet his taste is constantly susceptible to the pressures that put him in knickerbockers one year and rust-colored slacks the next. Actually he is unsure about almost everything, especially about what he likes. This may explain his pronouncements on taste, which he considers an effete and questionable virtue, and his resentment of the arts; but it may also explain his strength.

When America and Americans are characterized by foreigners and highbrows, the middlebrows are likely to emerge as the dominant group in our society—a dreadful mass of insensible back-slappers, given to sentimentality as a prime virtue, the willing victims of slogans and the whims of the bosses, both political and economic. The picture painted by middlebrow exploiters of the middlebrow, such as the advertisers of nationally advertised brands, is strikingly similar to that painted by the highbrow; their attitudes and motives are quite different (the highbrow paints with a snarl, the advertiser with a gleam), but they both make the middlebrow out to be much the same kind of creature. The villain of the highbrow and the hero of the advertisers is envisaged as "the typical American family"—happy little women, happy little children, all spotless or sticky in the jam pot, framed against dimity curtains in the windows or decalcomania flowers on the cupboard doors. Lower-middlebrowism is a world pictured without tragedy, a world of new two-door sedans, and Bendix washers, and reproductions of hunting prints over the living-room mantel. It is a world in which the ingenuity and patience of the housewife are equaled only by the fidelity of her husband and his love of home, pipe, and television. It is a world that smells of soap. But it is a world of ambition as well, the constant striving for a better way of life— better furniture, bigger refrigerators, more books in the bookcase, more evenings at the movies. To the advertisers this is Americanism; to the highbrows this is the dead weight around the neck of progress, the gag in the mouth of art.

The lower middlebrows are not like this, of course, and unlike the highbrows and the upper middlebrows, whose numbers are tiny by comparison, they are hard to pin down. They live everywhere, rubbing elbows with lowbrows in apartment houses like vast beehives, in row houses all alike from the outside except for the planting, in large houses at the ends of gravel driveways, in big cities, in medium cities and suburbs, and in small towns, from Boston to San Francisco, from Seattle to Jacksonville. They are the members of the book clubs who read difficult books along with racy and innocuous ones that are sent along by Messrs. Fadiman, Canby, Beecroft *et al.* They are the course takers who swell the enrollments of adult education classes in everything from "The Technique of the Short Story" to "Child Care." They are the people who go to hear the lecturers that swarm out from New York lecture bureaus with tales of travel on the Dark Continent and panaceas for saving the world from a fate worse than capitalism. They eat in tea shoppes and hold barbecues in their back yards. They are hell-bent on improving their minds as well as their fortunes. They decorate their homes under the careful guidance of *Good Housekeeping* and the *Ladies' Home Journal*, or, if they are well off, of *House and Garden*, and are subject to fads in furniture so long as these don't depart too radically from the traditional and the safe, from the copy of Colonial and the reproduction of Sheraton. In matters of taste, the lower-middlebrow world is largely dominated by women. They select the furniture, buy the fabrics, pick out the wallpapers, the pictures, the books, the china. Except in the selection of his personal apparel and the car, it is almost *infra dig* for a man to have taste; it is not considered quite manly for the male to express opinions about things which come under the category of "artistic."

Nonetheless, as a member of the school board or the hospital board he decides which design shall be accepted when a new building goes up. The lower middlebrows are the organizers of the community fund, the members of the legislature, the park commissioners. They pay their taxes and they demand services in return. There are millions of them, conscientious stabilizers of society, slow to change, slow to panic. But they are not as predictable as either the highbrows or the bosses, political or economic, think they are. They can be led, they can be seduced, but they cannot be pushed around.

Highbrow, lowbrow, upper middlebrow, and lower middlebrow— the lines between them are sometimes indistinct, as the lines between upper class, lower class, and middle class have always been in our traditionally fluid society. But gradually they are finding their own levels and confining themselves more and more to the company of their own kind.

The highbrows would apparently like to eliminate the middle-brows and devise a society that would approximate an intellectual feudal system in which the lowbrows do the work and create folk arts, and the highbrows do the thinking and create fine arts. All middlebrows, presumably, would have their televisions taken away, be suspended from society until they had agreed to give up their sub-scriptions to the Book-of-the-Month, turned their color reproductions over to a Commission for the Dissolution of Middlebrow Taste, and renounced their affiliation with all educational and other cultural insti-tutions whatsoever. They would be taxed for the support of all writers, artists, musicians, critics, and critics-of-criticism whose production could be certified "serious"—said writers, artists, musicians, and critics to be selected by representatives of qualified magazines with circula-tions of not more than five thousand copies. Middlebrows, both upper and lower, who persisted in "devaluating the precious, infecting the healthy, corrupting the honest, and stultifying the wise" would be disposed of forthwith.

If life for grandmother, who wouldn't dine with the Cartiers, was simple in its social distinctions, life is becoming equally simple for us. The rungs of the ladder may be different, it may even be a differ-ent ladder, but it's onward and upward just the same. You may not be known by which fork you use for the fish these days, but you will be known by which key you use for your *Finnegans Wake.*

CHAPTER XVIII

Exit the Lawyer's Wife

"Tastes—they depend on the fashion. There
is always a fashionable taste: a taste for
driving the mail—a taste for acting Hamlet
—a taste for philosophical lectures—a taste
for the marvelous—a taste for the simple—
a taste for the brilliant—a taste for the
sombre—a taste for the tender—a taste for
the grim—a taste for banditti—a taste for
ghosts—a taste for the devil—a taste for
French dancers and Italian singers and
German whiskers—a taste for enjoying the
country in November, and wintering in
London till the end of the dog-days—a taste
for making shoes—a taste for picturesque
tours—a taste for taste itself, or for essays
on taste:—but no gentleman would be so
rash as to have a taste of his own, or his last
winter's taste, or any taste, my love, but the
fashionable taste."

THOMAS LOVE PEACOCK,
from *Melincourt,* 1817

The lawyer's wife with whose $7,000 dilemma this book started
was a middlebrow. In her and in many millions of other Americans like her are lodged all of the conflicts and cross-currents that
have shaped the public taste ever since the beginning of the Age of
Public Taste. They have been the quarry of the tastemakers. It is
they who have been told that they must give up the white columns
of the Greek Revival for the somber hues and carved verge boards
of the Gothic cottage. It is they whom Eastlake strove to woo away
from curlicues in hopes that they would embrace his squared-off furni-

334

ture put together with dowels. Edward Bok in the *Ladies' Home Journal* tried to teach them the difference between Good Taste and Bad Taste. Edith Wharton and Elsie de Wolfe lectured them on "suitability" and Emily Post on "personality." They have been subjected to a series of moral sermons. They have been told that each architectural style was more "honest" than the one it displaced— that Gothic was more honest than Greek and that the functional style was more honest than the "adaptations" of the Beaux Arts. At the same time they have been encouraged to express themselves, to create atmosphere, and to keep their eyes raised to the slopes of Parnassus whence the word would come to them.

Surely there has been no shortage of advice on matters of taste and just as surely there has been no lack of response to the advice that has been given. And yet there are a great many people who believe that there is something the matter with American taste, something profoundly the matter.

Whose fault is this, if it is anyone's fault? Just what is the matter with American taste, if anything is the matter with it?

I believe that there is a great deal the matter with it, and the first thing that is the matter is that too many people worry about it. As we have seen, there are thousands and thousands of men and women trying to tell other men and women what their taste ought to be. Taste has become big business and the pressures on us to change our taste, for better or for worse, are never relieved. Some of these pressures are exerted from the highest aesthetic and moral motives; some are just simply commercial; but the fact is that they are unrelenting in their insistence.

The second trouble is that we are constantly told that there is a right thing about taste and a wrong thing, that there is *good* taste and *bad* taste, and that nearly anybody who tries hard enough and is diligent enough can have good taste. But nobody ever tells us what good taste is, for a very good reason. Nobody can define what it is— or at least nobody has. A few years ago Sanford E. Gerard wrote a book called *How Good Is Your Taste?* which was filled with pictures of furniture and lamps and other objects, good and bad, and the reader was supposed to score himself on how many so-called good objects he selected. The reader was given many hints about what to look for and some basic principles of design, but he was not told what good taste is. The same is true of a book by Richard Gump, the head of the famous Gump's store of San Francisco, called *Good Taste Costs No More*. Having explained that one can have good taste for the same price as bad taste, Mr. Gump says: "Any definition of good taste in absolute terms is, of course, an absurdity." This is a little like saying: "I don't know just what it is that you should have that costs no more, but you can have it for the same price."

Yet most Americans are convinced that there is an ultimate right and wrong about taste, and if they were only clever enough or well enough educated they would be able to achieve the indefinable. So they not only worry too much about taste but they worry about what is good taste and what is bad taste, how to achieve one and avoid the other. Sometimes, as my friend's wife did, they worry themselves sick about it.

To these two worries we add still a third. Many people worry about expressing their personalities through their taste. It has long been true that the powerful and would-be powerful men and women of the world have displayed their power or their aspirations by surrounding themselves with the most elegant and expensive trappings that their money, or other people's money, could buy. It has also long been true that emulation of the taste of the successful has played an important role in making men try to seem what they are not. But the emphasis on the idea that a woman's home should express her personality has increased in recent years since the theories of Freud have given wide acceptance to the idea that to suppress one's personality is to deny a basic human need. So the housewife is not only urged to express her personality but to do so with her eye on good taste. Since, if she is normal, she probably has no very clear idea of what her personality is and an even vaguer idea of what good taste is, she is up against a problem with two unknowns. Unable to resolve the equation for herself, she seeks help. She turns to the people who are supposed to know about such matters, the experts on taste. If it were just her personality that was worrying her, she might, if she could afford it, turn to a psychiatrist to tell her who she really is and what she is really like. But she doesn't. She turns to a decorator (or if she can't afford that, to a decorating magazine) who not only makes up a per-

sonality for her but then expresses it according to his private formula
of good taste.

Our troubles with taste go further than merely worrying about it.
There is a moral trouble as well, or perhaps I should say a trouble
that is concerned with morality.

The story of the public taste, the private taste, and the corporate
taste has been filled with moral overtones. Downing was concerned
with truth—the truths of domestic architecture. Eastlake was worried
about sincerity and honesty of construction. We are concerned today
with honesty of design in relation to function. Even the corporation
is worried about its moral responsibilities to culture. Each aesthetic
revolution has been supported by strong moral arguments. It is not
merely the way things look to people that arouses them to such
violent feelings about matters of mere taste. It goes deeper than just
aesthetic appreciation; it touches very basic beliefs. If this were not
so there would be no way to explain the intensity of people's feelings
in the matter.

If we go back again to the middle of the last century from which
came the kind of moralism about taste that is still with us, we encounter John Ruskin, the towering English prophet of reform in the
arts. Taste, he thought, had come to a pretty pass. The new aristocracy
of wealthy industrialists had replaced the old aristocracy and they
had had little training in how to be patrons of the arts. The best they
could do was to imitate the old patrons in display of grandeur. This
display was coupled in Ruskin's mind with the inequities of the way
in which the industrialists ran their factories; it had to do with dark
satanic mills and child labor and sickness. Ruskin's ideas for reform
now seem odd to us. He wanted to return to medieval craftsmanship
and to the simplicities and dignities of the Gothic era. It was an
aesthetic idea deeply immersed in a moral conviction. And in varying
forms every aesthetic revolution that has swept Europe and America
since has had a moral concept somehow attached to it. Sometimes,
as in the Eastlake movement, the moral has seemed specious, as though
a trumped-up morality were being used to sell what was nothing more
than a fad. But if you will read Eastlake you cannot but be impressed
by what seems to have been his honest indignation against faddism.
And so it is with the Modern movement in architecture and design—

a sort of puritan revolt against an overstuffed era in which the stuffing protected the prosperous from the changing realities of the world around them.

One of the reasons, I believe, why the Modern movement has lasted longer than many assaults on the bastion of American taste is quite simply that it appeals to a morality that is deeply imbedded in our history. It seems to be harking back to American puritanism, a morality which stressed the virtues of modesty, clean living, and disdain for what we call vulgar display. Like the Modern movement, puritanism was a revolt against an overelaborated aesthetic. The puritan revolt was against the baroque of the Counter-Reformation; ours is against the baroque of the Industrial Revolution. Furthermore, the Modern movement appeals to another ingrained moral belief which we are pleased to call the pragmatic American philosophy, in which the ultimate question is "Does it work?" Modern architecture, even when it doesn't work—and it often doesn't—looks as though it ought to.

We like to have good, respectable, and rather highflown reasons for changing our taste, even when we suspect, as we often do, that in a great many cases the people who have a new kind of taste to promote make up a morality after they have devised the commodity. Taste, like cigarettes, is often sold on the grounds that it is good for you, rather than on the grounds that you will enjoy it. For some puritan reason, if the sugar pill of taste is dipped in a bitter coating of morality, it is easier for a large segment of the public to swallow.

This brings us to still another consideration of what is the matter with taste in America. It brings us to the uncomfortable question of pleasure.

A great many people enjoy having taste, but too few of them really enjoy the things they have taste about. Or, to put it another way, they are like a man who takes pleasure in his excellent taste in women but takes no pleasure at all in *a* woman. One of the things that is most the matter with American taste is that those who worry hardest about it are not worrying about enjoying the fruits of their taste; they are just worrying about taste itself.

There was a time not so very long ago when we used to hear a great deal about Art for Art's Sake, an argument that burned with a hard, gemlike flame in the nineteenth century and raged for a long while. We hear little about it now. Art, except by artists, is very little thought of for its own sake now. To most consumers it is Art for Taste's Sake. We very rarely find ourselves taking pleasure in other people's pleasure in the art they enjoy. Indeed, we are likely to begrudge them their pleasure unless we happen to share it. We are all too prone to think only about the kind of taste they exhibit, to measure them with a cold and steely eye, and to decide whether we approve of their taste or not. We level this same steely eye on ourselves.

When we stop being concerned with pleasure and understanding and start worrying about the quality of our own and other people's taste, what we have arrived at is not a state of grace, as many people seem to think, but a state of Taste for Taste's Sake.

Our great concern with taste for taste's sake has not increased our enjoyment in the arts; on the contrary it has put a damper on our pleasure. It has directed our attention away from the main issue and has focused it on the side issue of trying to discriminate between what is good taste and bad taste. Taste merely becomes a substitute for understanding and pleasure. It is easy enough, for example, to have architectural good taste in our time merely by following the gospel according to the architects Gropius and Breuer and Wright as it is interpreted for the faithful by the archbishops in the cathedrals of Modern Art. But that is textbook taste, not personal taste, and while it may be safe, it is satisfying only to the unadventurous and the unimaginative.

This book has been concerned from the start with an abstraction called taste, and yet I have not defined it. It is an old trick. No one that I know of who talks about taste defines it, and one of the reasons they do not is that, like the author of *Good Taste Costs No More*, they cannot.

I do not know what *good* taste is. I do know that taste is not constant and that it is a creature of circumstance. I also know that one measure of a man's taste is what he will put up with. Furthermore it seems apparent that not only is one generation's good taste very likely to be the next generation's bad taste, but one individual's ideas about what is good taste and bad taste change as he matures, moves to a different place or a different way of living, and acquires new sets of

values for judging not only his surroundings but what he wants out
of life. It is not easy to pin a definition on anything so fluid or so
elusive.

But it does seem to me that taste is made up of three things that
are common to everyone. One is education, which includes not only
formal but informal education and environment. Another is sensibility, which Webster's defines as "the ability to perceive or receive
sensation." And the third is morality—the kinds of beliefs and principles which direct one's behavior and set a pattern for judging the
behavior of others. Education, sensibility, and morality, all three of
which have been constant themes in this book—these seem to me
to be the components of taste.

Not infrequently one hears that the level of American taste is improving. One heard it in the last century from such men as James
Jackson Jarves, who introduced Italian primitives to America, and
Henry Tuckerman, the critic of the 1860's and 70's. Now one hears
it most often from those who have a stake in selling some special
brand of taste, like the architect or the industrial designer. But rarely
is it from the young that one hears this, or from the old. It is from the
middle-aged, and by it they usually mean that the taste that they considered advanced when they were young has been accepted by more
and more people than they ever thought it would be. To the young
it is already old-fashioned, while to the old it is merely another phase
of taste that is passing across the horizon. In place of the nineteenth
century *what-not* we may have substituted the more functional idea
of *what-for*; for Ruskin's and Downing's brand of aesthetic morality
we have substituted another brand more suitable to our industrial age.
But I doubt that taste has improved. It merely reflects an idea that is
more familiar to the middle-aged among us, and which therefore
seems friendly.

I can see no reason why we should want taste to improve so long
as taste continues to be a set of mannerisms that one learns from a
book of cultural etiquette. We are fortunate in America that we have
so many different ways of satisfying so many different kinds of tastes.
We produce hundreds of movies each year, some of them good by the
most discriminating standards, some of them bad by the least discriminating, and the same may be said of paintings and of architecture

and cookery and probably of circus wagons. The point is that we have a tremendously diversified basis of morality, education, and sensibility and that the frictions among them generate the kind of heat that gives light. It is these conflicts of ideas and tastes that give the arts of our country vitality, and that make the museum and the corner movie houses equally important manifestations of our culture.

Unless I completely misunderstand the real reason for having taste, it is to increase one's faculties for enjoyment. Taste in itself is nothing. It is only what taste leads to that makes any difference in our lives.

AFTERWORD

Taste is just as quixotic, as subject to social pressures, to personal whims and to the pronouncements of tastemakers today as it was a quarter of a century ago when this book was first published. Some of the means by which taste is manipulated, however, and the cultural and social climate in which it is nurtured have changed quite radically. What was new and adventurous in art and architecture then is now merely "historically interesting," and the same is true of the theater, jazz and the movies. 1979 is as different from 1954 as the "Jazz Age" of the 1920s was from the "Gay Nineties," as Hemingway's early stories were from the late works of Henry James.

For one thing we live in a far more crowded world about which we can move, if we move by air, a great deal faster, and, if we move on the ground, a great deal slower. (Jet lag and gas shortages are new contributions to civilization.) There are, quite simply, a lot more of us, so that our cities have grown taller and glassier, our suburbs more sprawling and our countrysides more cluttered. We seem to be constantly moving in herds, treading on each other's toes, sitting thigh to thigh, threatening each other's bumpers, and looking for answers by reading over each other's shoulders. None of us is immune and we seek our different ways of accommodating to these inevitabilities. It is not just a matter of verbal fashion that since this book was published in 1954 the words "lifestyle" and "environment" have become popular clichés. They are both words that, I believe, bespeak anxieties brought on by the pressures that threaten to curtail our freedom of choice and of movement and of privacy and to box us in.

If the social rules have changed to allow for more relaxed and permissive ways of living, the pressures that attempt to control our choices and elevate our taste have intensified. The tastemakers have new weapons at their disposal and new sources of revenue to supply their arsenals. The principal new weapon is television, which was not yet a potent factor in the making of taste in the early fifties, though it existed then in an adolescent state from which much of it has not emerged and is not likely to. The principal source of revenue for improving taste is the government, whether it be directly in the form of federal, state or local grants or indirectly through the remission of taxes. The power of television to exploit "tastefulness" in all its manifestations from lemon-scented floor wax to *Hamlet* is too obvious to examine here. The power of the government dollar in the diffusion of the arts, and hence of taste, is more subtle and less well understood.

During the depression of the 1930s the federal government, as an emergency measure to keep the arts and more particularly the artists from starving, undertook, as we have seen, the role of art patron on a scale unprecedented in the history of our nation. Up to then the only government patronage of the arts had been for self-glorification—the commissioning of government buildings, whether for the capital in Washington or the capitals of states, for county courthouses and city halls. Government also commissioned monuments to heroes, to statesmen and to party bosses, but never to artists or writers or musicians or scholars. It took care of its own, in other words, and the arts were somebody else's business.

Or largely somebody else's business. It has long been government practice to refrain from taxing land and buildings occupied by educational institutions, museums, civic orchestras, and libraries, as well as hospitals, churches, and other organizations operated "not for profit." This has been happily indiscriminate and without prejudice or bias. It has also been the practice of many communities to pick up the tab for the maintenance of certain museums and to pay the salaries of their custodial employees, if not of their intellectual and clerical staffs. How this has worked and still works varies from city to city, state to state, but however it is managed it can reasonably be said to be government patronage of the arts. Since this book was first published, the National Endowments for the Arts and Humanities and the State Arts Councils have been founded, and an infusion of money from Washington into the bloodstream of the arts—musical, visual, theatrical, and literary—has been dribbled. Set against the Niagara of national, state, and municipal budgets it is infinitesimal, but no one can deny that it has been tonic.

So the government has become a tastemaker again along with television, and since it is government bureaucrats who decide who gets the money (after the Congress has decided how much the bureaucrats will get), government (which is known today as "the public sector" to arts administrators and money raisers) is in the business, for better or worse, of being an arbiter of taste. Like any other tastemaker it will decide what is good for us and for itself under pressure from its various constituencies, but unlike most tastemakers its business is not primarily aesthetic or commercial, it is political.

That is not to say that it is evil. Those who contrived the National Foundations for the Arts and Humanities and the state and metropolitan arts councils have done their best to build into them safeguards against political meddling and pressures. But already these safeguards have yielded to the blandishments of congressmen asking for special favors for what the foundations and councils regard as "silly" local programs not for the arts but to keep artistically inclined housewives busy doing handicrafts. I do not mean to pass judgment on a source of support for the arts that so many distinguished arbiters of taste in the arts have so long been struggling to bring about. The funds from the various levels of government have kept symphony orchestras from foundering on the reefs of inflation and local indifference. It has enabled libraries to meet, at least in part, the greatly increased demands on them. It has made it possible for museums to cope with the crowds that wander their halls as they never have before. (At the Metropolitan Museum in New York, for example, a crowd of 30,000 people on a Sunday to see a very special exhibition was rare; now there are 30,000 on every Sunday and twice that many for a special show.) It has also helped institutions like the one in which I write this "Afterword," the American Academy in Rome, to assist artists and scholars, poets and novelists to pursue their elusive and demanding Muses.

I cannot, however, help but be a little sceptical about government as a patron of the arts. If taste is quixotic, politically motivated taste is mercurial. Art and politics are itchy bedfellows. Their marriage was not made in heaven any more than, as we long ago found out, was the marriage of art and industry at which ceremony Prince Albert in the Crystal Palace in London in 1851 was the best man. I hope with all my heart that my scepticism is proved to be unjustified.

Anyone who has sat on the board of a cultural institution in the last twenty years knows only too well that its life depends to an increasing extent on grants not just from the government (they are relatively new) but from what the lingo of philanthropy now calls "the private sector." In general "the private sector" is far grander than those of us who pay our way into museums that used to be free, tuitions to colleges that used to be proud that they charged none, and those of us who join as "members" of public broadcasting stations, and museums and libraries because we believe that if we are going to feed off them we owe them something in return. (Incidentally, this kind of membership support is unknown in Europe.) But when boards of trustees talk about "the private sector" they essentially mean private foundations and corporations which have increasingly lent their support to the arts, to education, to community projects and to noncommercial research. There is scarcely a major corporation these days that hasn't a vice-president whose job it is to give away money to worthy causes. This beneficence is a subdivision of public relations; corporations do not give away money anonymously, any more than J. P. Morgan or Andrew Carnegie did, and for the same reasons which are a combination of pride and conscience with a veneer of benign paternalism.

So far as the arts are concerned, corporations and their foundations and private foundations like the Ford and Mellon have been lavish, though anyone concerned with the support of the arts would contend they have not been lavish enough. They have kept the heads of many institutions above water when drowning threatened them but, as important, they have given "seed money" to pay for new projects and for experiments. Anti-drowning money interests them less than new-project money because it is less showy, and they get less public credit for it. Under the direction of Robert Saudek the Ford Foundation's Radio and Television Workshop, which among other ventures produced the television show *Omnibus* in the fifties and early sixties was something of a paragon of experimentation which opened new vistas to that new medium. Mobil and Exxon have played major roles in providing public television with funds for shows more to the taste of upper-middlebrows than of highbrows, many of whom still will not have a television set in the house. They may, however, listen to the Saturday afternoon radio broadcasts of opera from the Metropolitan in New York which another oil company, Texaco, has been subsidizing for about forty years. By comparison Exxon and Mobil are Johnny-come-latelies.

If there have been several major new patrons of the arts in the last twenty-five years, and they have helped to generate new audiences, they haven't made a dent, or so it seems to me, on what might be called pretentiously the broad spectrum of taste or, disparagingly, the dead level of taste.

Four years before this book was published, Chapter XVII, "Highbrow, Lowbrow, Middlebrow," appeared in *Harper's Magazine,* of which I was then an editor. This chapter was written before any of the rest of the book, but it was written because of it. I thought that if I was going to write about tastemakers, I should define their quarry, and in one of several attempts to write an introductory chapter to the book, I devoted a couple of pages to highbrows, lowbrows, upper-and-lower middlebrows. I showed this draft to Katherine Gauss Jackson, a colleague of mine at *Harper's,* who said, "You've got the essence of a piece here. Why don't you write an article on brows?" So I did, and it appeared as the lead article in the February 1949 issue of *Harper's.* Several weeks later *Life* magazine, which was at the time "the king of the visual media," did an article about my article and published a pictorial chart illustrating the several "brow levels" of American taste at that time. Since then this article (later the chapter only slightly revised) has had an independent life of its own, and though I invented none of them, the words highbrow, lowbrow and middlebrow, with its subdivisions into upper and lower, have become part of the language of taste along with "tastemakers," which was, so far as I know, my coinage.

I can think of no better way to indicate the changes in taste that have occurred in the last quarter of a century than to reproduce here the *Life* chart, in which I had the controlling hand, and to note what has happened in the interim.*

*The following notes come largely from an essay of mine that appeared in the Autumn 1976 issue of *The Wilson Quarterly* and are reprinted with the permission of its editor.

EVERYDAY TASTES FROM HIGH-BROW TO

	CLOTHES		FURNITURE	USEFUL OBJECTS	ENTERTAINMENT	SALADS
HIGH-BROW	TOWN Fuzzy Harris tweed suit, no hat	COUNTRY Fuzzy Harris tweed suit, no hat	Eames chair, Kurt Versen lamp	Decanter and ash tray from chemical supply company	Ballet	Greens, olive oil, wine vinegar, ground salt, ground pepper, garlic, unwashed salad bowl
UPPER MIDDLE-BROW	TOWN Brooks suit, regimental tie, felt hat	COUNTRY Quiet tweed jacket, knitted tie	Empire chair, converted sculpture lamp	Silver cigaret box with wedding ushers' signatures	Theater	Same as high-brow but with tomatoes, avocado, Roquefort cheese added
LOWER MIDDLE-BROW	TOWN Splashy necktie, double-breasted suit	COUNTRY Sport shirt, colored slacks	Grand Rapids Chippendale chair, bridge lamp	His and Hers towels	Musical extravaganza films	Quartered iceberg lettuce and store dressing
LOW-BROW	TOWN Loafer jacket, woven shoes	COUNTRY Old Army clothes	Mail order overstuffed chair, fringed lamp	Balsam-stuffed pillow	Western movies	Coleslaw

LOW-BROW ARE CLASSIFIED ON CHART

DRINKS	READING	SCULPTURE	RECORDS	GAMES	CAUSES
A glass of "adequate little" red wine	"Little magazines," criticism of criticism, avant garde literature	Calder	Bach and before, Ives and after	Go	Art
A very dry Martini with lemon peel	Solid nonfiction, the better novels, quality magazines	Maillol	Symphonies, concertos, operas	The Game	Planned parenthood
Bourbon and ginger ale	Book club selections mass circulation magazines	Front yard sculpture	Light opera, popular favorites	Bridge	P. T. A.
Beer	Pulps, comic books	Parlor sculpture	Jukebox	Craps	The Lodge

Chart reprinted from Life *courtesy Time Inc.*

Since "Highbrow, Lowbrow, Middlebrow" was published, the highbrow has changed his costume and his whiskers several times, the middlebrows have hared off after a succession of "ops" and "pops" and "Art-Decos" (a chic and affectionate new name for what the highbrows used disparagingly to call "modernistic") and *Mary Hartman* (twice), and the lowbrows have found Archie Bunker and CB radios and game shows with which to amuse and identify themselves. The lines of my arbitrary categories have become even more indistinct than they were in 1949. But, I believe, the basic pattern still has some validity, or, if not the pattern, at least the underlying bed of nails which is taste. The adaptation and exercise of taste will, I expect, always be a serious social game as long as taste is regarded as a guide to status and people are convinced that there are durable standards of "good taste" and that "bad taste" is what their inferiors have.

The highbrows in the 1950s had a rather rough time of it. It was the decade of the McCarthy investigations, of Adlai Stevenson's two defeats as a candidate for President, and, perhaps, worst of all, the arrival of television—a symbol of mass middlebrowism. It was, moreover, the era of Sputnik I, the first object put into orbit by the Russians, and the shocked American clamor for more scientific training in order to "catch up." While that incident ultimately gave a good many intellectuals an improved bargaining position, it was not the humanists, the preceptors of taste, who benefited. The Eisenhower years did not supply the highbrows with the opportunities that the election of Kennedy, who flirted ostentatiously with the arts, seemed to offer, if only briefly. And despite Lady Bird Johnson's conscientious efforts to continue to hold high the torch of culture, her husband was barely tolerant of what highbrows considered her well-intentioned gestures to the Muses. It was in the Nixon administration that federal funds were first voted by the Congress for the National Foundation for the Arts, and Nancy Hanks, a woman of remarkable perceptions and the administrative savvy to hold politicians at bay, was put in charge.

During the 1960s it was fashionable to take note of "the cultural explosion." Vastly expensive cultural centers, inspired by Lincoln Center in New York, burgeoned in cities across the land, and it was generally agreed that culture was good for the community and hence

good for business. Culture, you might say, was regarded as civic
Geritol. Community theaters popped up like toadstools, many with the
beneficence of the Ford Foundation, whose cultural and artistic engine
was W. McNeil Lowry. Established art museums were crowded as
never before; new ones appeared by the dozens, and commercial art
galleries multiplied at a rate almost as breathtaking as the prices of the
wares in which they dealt. High in the Berkshires (the home of Tangle-
wood, Music Mountain, Jacob's Pillow) where I was born and which
used to be dairy country, there were suddenly more violinists than
there were cows, or so it seemed.

The highbrows found all this confusing. Obviously they could not
oppose public enthusiasm for the arts, at least not to the point of
wishing to turn off the faucet that dripped gold into their pockets.
They did not want to put a crimp in anything that supported the
avant-garde, though they persisted in passionate disputes about the
problems of mass culture vs. high culture. Moreover they now had to
protect their flanks, not just from the middlebrows, but from the
activist young, the members of the dissident counterculture who
thought that the highbrows were just as responsible for America's sins
as the bankers. Some adult highbrows tried to identify themselves
with the young radicals only to discover that they were not wanted
and not considered trustworthy. And, since everybody now had beards
and refused to dress according to the old rules, how could a poor highbrow tell who were his friends and who were his enemies, who was
serious and who was not?

The upper middlebrows, on the other hand, felt a surge of aesthetic
adrenalin. To serve on the board of the local opera company became
every bit as socially desirable as being on the executive committee of
the Community Chest, and to be engaged in saving the past as a member of the Landmarks Preservation Commission was as creditable as
protecting the future by serving on the hospital board. If anything the
caste (or class) structure of tastefulness that I adumbrated in 1949
became strengthened. In some respects, the line between highbrows
and upper middlebrows became blurred; but the line between upper
and lower middlebrows grew sharper and more social. As a result,
service on boards of artistic institutions made new demands on their

members. They were not only expected to be made of money (or know where to find it) but to be culturally "hip" as well. Keeping up with what's "in" became as socially important as being "in" oneself, and today, when the arts change with a rapidity unknown before, being upper middlebrow involves considerable psychic strain.

As I look at the chart, which a *Life* editor and I concocted over innumerable cups of coffee years ago, it strikes me, as it must you, that what was highbrow then has become distinctly upper middlebrow today. The rate of change, indeed, is about the same as that which is demonstrated in the chart showing what happened between the 1850s and the 1950s (pp. 326–327). Who regards an Eames chair as highbrow now? Or ballet, or an unwashed salad bowl or a Calder stabile? They have all become thoroughly upper middlebrow, and what was upper has become lower. Only the lowbrow line of the chart makes spiritual if not literal sense. Today television would find itself at all levels of the chart in ways, as we have noted, too obvious to define. The "pill" has taken the glamor out of Planned Parenthood as an upper middlebrow cause, and Art and The Environment are now their causes instead . . . and so on. Even if the shapes of the pieces have changed, and the board looks quite different, the basic rules seem to me much the same as they have been since Andrew Jackson Downing set about in the 1840s to make our forebears lead harmonious lives in tasteful surroundings.

RUSSELL LYNES

Rome, April 1979

SOURCES AND
ACKNOWLEDGMENTS

In the fall of 1950 *Harper's Magazine* issued its centennial number to celebrate one hundred years of uninterrupted publication. Frederick Lewis Allen, who was then editor in chief of the magazine, asked me to write for that number a review of what had happened to taste in the visual arts during *Harper's* lifetime; "The Age of Taste," which I produced for the Centennial, was in substance the outline for this book. My first indebtedness, then, is to Mr. Allen for encouraging me to summarize the curious history of our tastes, and, though he is in no way responsible for the shortcomings of the book, my final indebtedness is also to him. On his last day in the editorial rooms of *Harper's* he finished reading and criticizing my manuscript. Mr. Allen was the most skillful editor I have ever known; he was also the most generous and friendly of men, and my debt to him goes far beyond mere literary matters to a sturdy friendship of many years standing.

Some ideas and examples in this book will be familiar to readers who have paid me the compliment of reading my magazine articles, but with the exception of one chapter, "Highbrow, Lowbrow, Middlebrow," the book represents a fresh start and a fresh (to me, anyway) interpretation. "Highbrow, Lowbrow, Middlebrow," which is an attempt to define consumers of taste today, is pretty much as it was published in *Harper's*, where it originally appeared in February, 1949. Its principles seem to me to apply as well today as they did then, and so I include it.

As this book makes no pretensions of being a work of scholarship, it seems to me that to include an exhaustive bibliography of my sources would serve little purpose. The reader will find in the text references to the sources I have used most extensively. I have poked into few documents that other writers have not already investigated, though some of the things they have not thought worth mentioning have interested me most of all. There are, however, a few books and periodicals that the reader who wishes to pursue this subject further will find not only enjoyable but useful.

I have used with pleasure and profit the files of a number of magazines and newspapers which have reflected both the serious and the frivolous attempts to make taste. *Harper's Magazine,* of which, as one of the editors, I have been fortunate to have a file at my elbow, has published not only the serious work of such men as Calvert Vaux and Lewis Mumford but also such entertaining and revealing essays as those by the art auctioneer of the 1850's and Mrs. M. E. W. Sherwood in the seventies. There too Andrew Jackson Downing's friend George William Curtis conducted the column called "The Easy Chair" for many years, and his artistic judgments are revealing of the respectable and in some respects advanced taste of his generation. *Godey's Lady's Book, Leslie's Weekly, Appleton's Journal,* and *Peterson's Magazine* have reflected the popular taste of the mid-century, but they are good reading today only in very small doses. *The Art Journal, The Broadway Journal,* and, of course, *The Atlantic Monthly, Scribner's,* and the *Century* engage one's attention for longer. Just before and just after the turn of the century the *Ladies' Home Journal,* under the editorship of Edward Bok, was (as it is today) full of advice about taste, and *House Beautiful* was busily trying to make the American home more suitable. Current periodicals that deal with taste are as well known to the reader as to me.

There are three books which I would like to mention especially because they were extremely helpful to me and I have drawn largely on them. They are *Art and Life in America* by Oliver Larkin (Rinehart, New York, 1949), which is a comprehensive and successful attempt to set the arts of America against their social and historical background; *Roots of Contemporary American Architecture,* edited and compiled by Lewis Mumford (Reinhold, New York, 1952); and *Made in America* by John A. Kouwenhoven (Doubleday, New York, 1949). Mr. Mumford's book is primarily an anthology of the best architectural writing that has been done in America since the days of Horatio Greenough, Thoreau, and James Jackson Jarves, but it also contains comment of his own. His selection and interpretation seem to me admirable. Mr. Kouwenhoven's book is a reinterpretation of the "vernacular arts" of this country and throws American art into a new perspective. His ideas are provocative and his scholarship constructive. These three books were constantly useful to me throughout the writing of this book. I am greatly indebted to their authors.

Anyone who wants to know about American taste will obviously read the journals of foreigners who have visited America and who have gone home and tried to explain us to their compatriots. No one had a sharper eye for our tastes than Mrs. Trollope and there is no better edition of her book, *Domestic Manners of the Americans,* than Donald Smalley's. Charles Dickens' *American Notes* and David McCrae's *The Americans at Home* contain more revealing comments on taste than the notes of many travelers who were primarily concerned with our social experiment and our frontier society.

This advice to the reader who wishes to pursue the subject is general; to be specific would mean listing several hundred books and magazine articles and newspaper references. I have picked the brains of a great many other writers and scholars, and while I have done so unashamedly I have not done so disrespectfully, and I wish to acknowledge my indebtedness to them and trust that I have done neither their research nor their ideas injustice. Let me list a few reference books and histories that were especially helpful to me:

The Public Taste

Lucius Beebe and Charles Clegg, *Hear the Train Blow,* New York, 1952.

Carl Carmer, *The Hudson,* New York, 1939.

Morton Cronin, "Currier & Ives, a Content Analysis," *American Quarterly,* Winter, 1952, Philadelphia.

C. M. Depew (editor), *One Hundred Years of American Commerce,* New York, 1895.

Garnett L. Eskew, *The Pageant of the Packets,* New York, 1929.

Carl Russell Fish, *The Rise of the Common Man 1830-1850,* New York, 1939.

Roger Gilman (editor), *Romanticism in America,* Baltimore, 1940.

Ralph Nading Hill, *Sidewheeler Saga, a Chronicle of Steamboating,* New York, 1953.

Hotel World Review, "75 Years of Hotel History" (special anniversary number), Chicago, 1950.

Winifred E. Howe, *A History of the Metropolitan Museum of Art,* New York, 1913.

Louis C. Hunter, *Steamboats on the Western Rivers,* Harvard University, 1949.

Joseph Husband, *The Story of the Pullman Car,* Chicago, 1917.

Robert B. Ludy, *Historic Hotels of the World, Past and Present,* Philadelphia, 1927.

Meade Minnegerode, *The Fabulous Forties,* New York, 1924.

Lewis Mumford, *The Brown Decades,* New York, 1931.

Harry T. Peters, *Currier & Ives, Printmakers to the American People,* Garden City, New York, 1942.

Mr. and Mrs. Chitwood Smith, *Rogers Groups, Thought and Wrought by John Rogers,* Boston, 1934.

Francis Steegmuller, *The Two Lives of James Jackson Jarves,* New Haven, 1951.

Jefferson Williamson, *The American Hotel,* New York, 1930.

The Private Taste

Frederick Lewis Allen, *The Great Pierpont Morgan*, New York, 1949.
Wayne Andrews, *The Vanderbilt Legend*, New York, 1941.
——, *Battle for Chicago*, New York, 1946.
Alan Burnham, "The New York Architecture of Richard Morris Hunt," *Journal of the Society of Architectural Historians*, May, 1952.
Edward Bok, *The Americanization of Edward Bok*, New York, 1921.
Victoria Case and Robert Armand Case, *We Called It Culture. The Story of Chautauqua*, Garden City, 1948.
Royal Cortissoz, *American Artists*, New York, 1923.
Elsie de Wolfe (Lady Mendl), *After All*, New York, 1935.
Guy Pène Du Bois, *Artists Say the Silliest Things*, New York, 1940.
Stewart H. Holbrook, *The Age of the Moguls*, New York, 1953.
Walt Kuhn, *Twenty-Five Years After: The Story of the Armory Show*, New York, 1938.
Jerome Melquist, *The Emergence of an American Art*, New York, 1942.
Jerome Myers, *Artists in New York*, New York, 1940.
Walter Pach, *Queer Thing, Painting*, New York, 1938.
Ada Bartlett Taft, *Lorado Taft, Sculptor and Citizen*, Greensboro, N.C., 1946.

The Corporate Taste

Frederick Lewis Allen, *Only Yesterday*, New York, 1932.
——, *The Big Change*, New York, 1952.
Herbert Bayer, Walter Gropius, Ise Gropius, *Bauhaus 1919-1928*, New York, 1938.
Edward L. Bernays, *Public Relations*, University of Oklahoma, 1952.
Lewis Jacobs, *The Rise of the American Film, a Critical History*, New York, 1939.
David Riesman, *The Lonely Crowd*, New Haven, 1950.
Fred J. Ringel (editor), *America as I See It*, New York, 1932.
William H. Whyte, Jr., *Is Anybody Listening?*, New York, 1952.

The libraries in which I have principally worked have been consistently helpful, and I wish to thank the librarians and staff members of the New York Public Library, the New York Historical Society, the New York Society Library, the Metropolitan Museum of Art, the Museum of Modern Art, the Museum of the City of New York, and the Mason Library of Great Barrington, Massachusetts, for their co-operation and, not infrequently, their patience.

So many friends have helped me in so many ways in the preparation of this book that I sometimes think that it is as much theirs as mine. My colleagues at *Harper's Magazine* have not only given me valuable suggestions and criticisms but, by absorbing much of my editorial work, they have made it possible for me to have time to write. I am especially indebted to Katherine Gauss Jackson, who has watched this book from the start with a friendly, sensitive, and encouraging eye and who has helped me with her criticism and advice at every turn. I should also like to thank Eric Larrabee, John Fischer, Catherine Meyer, Anne G. Freedgood, and Ellen Bond, all of *Harper's Magazine,* for their generous help both critical and practical. Others at Harper & Brothers, notably Simon Michael Bessie and Cass Canfield, have ventured far beyond the call of editorial duty to help me, and they know how grateful I am to them.

Without involving them in any responsibility for my results, I want to thank John A. Kouwenhoven and Wayne Andrews for casting the dispassionate but sympathetic eye of scholarship on my manuscript and for their astute observations and helpful suggestions. My brother, George Platt Lynes, has helped me most generously with my photographic problems. James M. Brown, Jr., Carol Cox, Mario Prodan, Elizabeth McKee, Bernard B. Smith, Alister Cameron, Allen Porter, Helen Everitt, Andrew Jackson, Grace M. Mayer, and many others have contributed in various important ways and I wish to thank them for their help.

My greatest debt is to my wife, who is a professional in the history of the arts whereas I am an amateur. She has protected me from interruption, guided me to fascinating sources of material, criticized my manuscript line by line, been patient with my discouragements, and has never lost her sense of humor or let me lose mine. Not easy.

R. L.

INDEX

Aalto, Alvar, 315
Abbott Laboratories, 298
Academy of Design, 41, 73, 196, 221
Adams, Henry, 142, 144
Adams, John, 23
Adaptation, 140, 141, 168, 169, 188, 237, 244, 335
Addams, Jane, 159
Administration Hall, Columbian Exposition, 142
Advertising, in the 1840's, 10-11; fine arts in, 273 (ill.), 287, 293-298, 309; function of, 300; institutional, 291
Albert, Prince, 288
"Albino Lady, The," 19
Allen, Frederick Lewis, 234, 292, 343
Allen, Lewis F., 26-27
Ambassador (steamboat), 91
American Artist Life (Tuckerman), 64
American Art Union, 14-18, 21, 151
American Council of Learned Societies, 298
American Federation of Arts, 152, 304
American Hotel, The (Williamson), 85
American Institute of Architects, 135
Americanization of Edward Bok, The, 175
American Notes (Dickens), 81, 344
American Renaissance, 136, 140, 143, 144, 167, 185, 194
American Renaissance (Dow), 140, 168
Americans at Home, The (McCrae), 344
American Society of Painters and Sculptors, 275
American Woman's Home (Beecher), 66, 70
Andover House, Boston, 158
Andrews, Wayne, 149, 347
Anne, Queen, of Denmark, 32
Antiques, 106, 316
Antiques craze, 186, 238-241
Apartment house, 139, 249, 254
Apollo Gallery, 14
Appleton's Journal, 344; quoted, 79, 105, 107, 113

Architectural Record, quoted, 35-36
Architecture (see also American Renaissance, Bungalow, Classic style, Colonial revival, Georgian architecture, Gothic Revival, Greek Revival, Italian style, Modern architecture, Queen Anne style, Ranch house, and Romanesque style); adaptation in, 140, 141, 168-169, 188, 237, 244, 335; Battle of the Styles, 135, 140, 245; benefits of, 49; bourgeois, 167; castellated, 29; expression of purpose in, 25; and government, 248, 249; hotels, 81-89; landscape, 21-23, 24, 33, 34; morality in, 24-25, 27, 111; palaces for the rich, 121, 122, 131; popular understanding of, 116-117; as a profession, 134, 135; of Richard Morris Hunt, 122, 131, 132, 134-137; rural, 23-27, 28-29, 31, 32-33, 36; for small houses, 176-177; social, 248; suburban, 237-255; teaching of, 135-136
Architecture of Country Houses, The (Downing), 32, 33
Aristocracy, 26, 170, 236; corporation, 236; intellectual, 104, 314; of wealth, 144, 166, 236, 337
Aristotle, 282
Arles, chapel of Saint Gilles at, 122
"L'Arlésienne" (Van Gogh), 327 (ill.)
Armenia (steamer), 34
Armory Show, 198-210, 218 (ill.), 220-222; in Chicago and Boston, 210, 211, 220
Armour, Ogden, 184
Armsmere (Colt's home), 98, 127 (ill.)
"Arrangement in Gray and Black, No. 1" (Whistler), 326 (ill.)
Art(s) (see also Architecture, Painting, and Sculpture); and advertising, 273 (ill.), 287, 293-298, 309; the automobile and, 225, 232-234; as a career, 114, 284-285; carnival, 96; cheap and popular, 65-75, 79-80; contemporary, 262-265 (see also Modern

art); courses in, 155, 156, 159 (*see also* Schools, art in); during the depression, 147, 148, 284, 291-292; early 19th-century, 11-13; enjoyment of, 338-339; European, 197-198, 201, 202-203, 204-205, 207, 220, 236; frauds in, 160, 277, 278-282; and government, 148, 150, 151, 161; historical approach to study of, 61; industrial, 113, 114, 115, 149, 272 (ill.); lectures on history of, 104; lowbrow's indifference to, 319-320; machine, 249, 272 (ill.); mass production of, 66-75, 79-80, 114, 181; movies and, 225, 226-232; patronage of, 13-14, 19-20, 38-64, 137, 138, 148, 151, 234, 330, 331; popular taste in, 282-283; popularization of, 148-162; progressive, 196-197, 198-222; self-expression through, 283; spiritual benefit of, 159; therapy through, 283; values of, 207, 275
Art auctioneering, 45-48, 160 (*see also* Art dealers)
Art Bulletin, quoted, 15
Art congresses, 152, 156
Art dealers, 13, 14, 18, 45-48, 64, 197, 198, 203, 256, 265-282
Art films, 230
Art galleries and museums. *See* Galleries *and* Museums
Art Hints (Jarves), 50
Art Idea, The (Jarves), 61
Art Institute of Chicago, 149-150, 161, 210, 260, 262
Art Journal, 344; quoted, 98, 112
Art and Life in America (Larkin), 344
Art News, 276, 284; quoted, 261
Art Nouveau, 190
Arts for America, 152
Art schools and societies, 148-149, 150, 151-152, 153, 155, 162, 221
Arts and Decorations, 204
Art Studies (Jarves), 50
Art Unions, 14-18, 21, 38, 48, 117, 151, 256
Art Work of Louis C. Tiffany, The (De Kay), 173
Art World, 257-286
Artifacts, 190-191
Artistic craze, 111, 115-117, 147, 165, 190
Artists, commercial and fine, 285; encouragement of, 18, 40, 114; functions of, 38; highbrow, 317; lowbrow, 318-319; modernist and traditional, 285, 297; progressive, 196, 198; relations of, with dealers, 45
Artists for Victory, Inc., 296

"Ash Can School," 196
Association of American Painters and Sculptors, 198-210
Astor, John Jacob, 84, 141
Astor, Mrs. William, 131, 139
Astor Library, New York, 142
Atlantic Monthly, The, 344
Atmosphere, 247
Attribution, 276-277, 280, 281
Auden, W. H., 313
Automobiles, 225, 226, 232-234, 300, 329 (ill.)
Ayer, N. W., & Son, 293

Bachmann, John, 55 (ill.)
Baer, George F., 289
Balloon frame, 109
Bamberger, L., and Company, 238
Barbizon school, 62, 158
BarcaLounger, 329 (ill.)
Barnum, P. T., 19, 20, 99, 290
Baroque style, 338
Barr, Alfred H., Jr., 243-244, 263
Battle for Chicago (Andrews), 149
Battle of the Styles, 135, 140, 245
Bauhaus, 302-303
Bay window, 28
Bazar of Berlin, 77
Beaconsfield, Lord, 101
Beauty, of function, 189; and truth, societies of, 151-162, 221
Beaux-Arts, École des, 133, 143
Becker, Otto, 326 (ill.)
Beecher, Catherine, 66, 67, 70
Beecher, Henry Ward, 73
Bel Geddes, Norman, 319
Bell, Clive, 208, 222
Bellini, Gentile and Giovanni, 198
Bellows, George, 199, 204, 205, 220
Belmont, August, 62
Belmont, O. H. P., 141
Benjamin's House Carpenter, 10
Berenson, Bernard, 277
Berlin, fashion journals of, 76-77
Berman, Eugène, 294
Bernays, Edward L., 289, 290
Bernhardt, Sarah, 227
Bernheim, A. C., 157
Bibelots, 10, 99, 330
Biedermeier, 306, 316
Bierstadt, Albert, 158
Big Change, The (Allen), 234
Bigelow, Erastus B., 9
Biltmore (George Vanderbilt's home), 121-122, 131, 142, 144, 211 (ill.)
Birth of a Nation, The, 228
Blashfield, Edwin, 143

Bliss, Lizzie, 243
Blois, Château de, 131, 139
"Blue Boy, The" (Gainsborough), 197
Bohemianism, 247
Bok, Edward, 96, 172, 175-178, 221, 255, 335, 344
Bookman, quoted, 161
Book-of-the-Month Club, 283
"Boondoggling," 292
"Borax," 300
Bordone, Paris, 56 (ill.)
Borglum, Gutzon, 199, 200
Boston, Andover House, 158; Armory Show in, 219-220; art exhibition for working class in, 158-159; Athenaeum, 59; Institute of Modern (Contemporary) Art, 264; Tremont House, 81-84; Trinity Church, 132; Women's College Settlement, 158
Boucher, François, 198
Bouguereau, Adolphe, 113, 197
Bourdelle, Émile, 205
Bourget, Paul, 137, 138
Bradley, Will, 214 (ill.)
Braque, Georges, 205, 315
Breakers (Cornelius Vanderbilt's home), 142, 144
Breakfast nook, 171
Breuer, Marcel, 315, 339
Bric-a-brac, 106, 115, 165, 170, 238
Broadway Journal, 25, 344
Broadway Tabernacle, 15
Brooks, Van Wyck, 137
BROOM, 313
Brother Jonathan magazine, 29
Broun, Heywood, 261
Brown, Arthur, 284
Brown, Charles Francis, 152, 153, 155
Brown, James M., 298
Browning, Robert and Elizabeth Barrett, 50
Brownstone front houses, 116
Bryan, Thomas Jefferson, 42-44, 48, 56 (ill.), 64, 257
Bryan, William Jennings, 192
Bryan Gallery of Christian Art, 43, 44
Bryant, William Cullen, 14, 33, 40, 64
Building materials, concrete, 193-194, 217 (ill.), 255, 323 (ill.), 325 (ill.); frame, 109; honesty in, 27; steel, 169, 195, 226
Bungalow, 187, 188-189, 194, 217 (ill.), 255
Bungalow Book . . . , The (Wilson), 188, 194
Burlington (steamer), 93

Burlington Magazine, quoted, 198
Burne-Jones, Sir Edward, 115
Burnham, Alan, 139
Burnham, Daniel H., 142, 143, 144, 149
Burr, Ann, 198
Business (*see also* Advertising, Corporations, *and* Industry); and art, 287-288, 291, 292-299; aspirations of, to aristocracy, 167; competition in, 289; and culture, 20, 42, 62-63; professionalization of, 292; and public relations, 289-291, 299
Business Week, quoted, 299
Butler, Governor (of Massachusetts), 150

Calder, Alexander, 230
Canova, Antonio, 71, 73
Capehart Phonograph-Radio, 294
Capitalism, 288
Carnegie, Andrew, 161
Carnival arts, 96
Carpenter Gothic, 35, 55 (ill.)
Carpets, machine-made, 9; in 19th-century parlors, 30; Oriental, 99, 171
Carrère and Hastings, 140, 194
Caruso, Enrico, 207
Cassatt, Mary, 143, 170, 198
Cast-in-place concrete house, 325 (ill.)
Cat and the Fiddle, The, 302
Cathedral of St. John the Divine, 36
Cement, 193-194, 217 (ill.), 255, 323 (ill.), 325 (ill.)
Centennial Exposition of 1876, 97, 112-117, 128 (ill.), 221, 257
Central Art Association, Chicago, 151-152, 153, 155, 156, 262
Central Park, New York, 33
"Central Park, Summer" (Bachmann), 55 (ill.)
Century, 344; quoted, 148
Cézanne, Paul, 74, 201, 202, 204, 207, 263, 330
Chalk talks, 156
"Champions of the Mississippi, The" (Currier & Ives), 125 (ill.)
"Chariot of Phaeton, The" (Reni), 170
Charm, 238
Chase, William Merritt, 158, 196
Chautauqua movement, 153-155
Chautauquan, 154
"Checker Players, The" (Rogers), 72
Chicago, Armory Show in, 210, 219; Art Institute, 149-150, 161, 210, 260, 262; Central Art Association, 151-152, 153, 155, 156, 262; Columbian Exposition in, 142-144, 147, 163, 212

(ill.), 250; Hull House, 159; Palmer House, 87; University of, 242; Woman's Club, 159
Childs restaurants, 241
Chintz, 183
"Christ Healing the Sick in the Temple" (West), 19
Christian Art, Bryan Gallery of, 43, 44
"Chromos" ("Chromolithographs"), 55 (ill.), 70, 79-80
Chrysler Building, 247
Church, Frederick E., 30, 99
Cincinnati, museum and art school in, 148-149, 212 (ill.); Terrace Plaza hotel, 88
Circus, 319
Cities, growth of, 163-164
City of Hickman (steamer), 330 (ill.)
City planning, 248
Clarke, Thomas B., 160
Classic style, in architecture, 135, 143, 144; in sculpture, 71
Clay talks, 156
Clothing, fashion in, *see* Fashion; patterns for making, 76, 77-79; ready-made, 75-76
Cobb, Henry Ives, Jr., 134
Codman, Henry, 142
Codman, Ogden, Jr., 165
Cohan, George M., 290
Coiner, Charles T., 293, 294
Cole, Thomas, 8, 16, 20, 38, 39, 40, 51 (ill.)
Collections, 13, 37-64, 148-150, 155, 157-159, 160, 161, 184, 197-198, 236, 259, 260, 291, 293, 309; antiques, 239-241; classification of, 101; Currier & Ives prints, 67, 69, 239; film, 264; Rogers Groups, 239-240
Collegiate Gothic, 242, 269 (ill.)
Collyer, Dr., 19, 20
Collyer, Thomas, 34, 35
Colonial revival, 140, 169, 214 (ill.), 238-241
Colony Club, New York, 182, 183
Colt, Col. Samuel, 98-99, 236
Columbia Broadcasting System, 299 n.
Columbian Exposition of 1893, 142-144, 147, 163, 212 (ill.), 250
Columbia University, school of architecture at, 136
Commager, Henry Steele, 142
Commercial art, 285
Commercial and industrial building, 148
Commercialism, 45
Company town, 307
Compton, William, 9

Concrete, 193-194, 217 (ill.), 247, 255, 323 (ill.), 325 (ill.)
Concrete House and Its Construction, The, 193
Conley, Colonel, 202
Container Corporation of America, 273 (ill.), 295, 298
Cook, Clarence, 116
Coolidge, Calvin, 74
Cooper, James Fenimore, 7, 12, 40, 318
Cooper Union, 44
Copley, John S., 113
Corcoran, William C., 62
Corning Glass Works, 273 (ill.), 298-299, 328 (ill.)
Corot, J. B. C., 62, 158, 160, 204
Corporations, aristocracy arising from, 236; as art patrons, 166, 288, 292-299; culture and, 337; design functions of, 303-304; public relations and, 290-291, 299
Correspondence courses, 153
"Correy" (Strong), 158
Corset business, 78
Cortissoz, Royal, 206, 207, 220
Cosmopolitan Art Union, 18
Cosmopolitan Bazar, 72
Cottage. *See* Bungalow *and* Ranch house
Cottage Residences (Downing), 24
Country Residences (Downing), 176
Cox, Kenyon, 143
Coxey's army, 147
Craftsman, quoted, 186-187
"Craftsman homes," 188-189
Craftsmanship, 106, 114, 141
Crafts movement, 191, 192, 244
Cram, Ralph Adams, 36, 214 (ill.)
Crane bathroom fixtures, 272 (ill.)
Crayon, quoted, 45, 48, 59
Critic, quoted, 152-153
Crocker, Charles, 98
Crocker, Mrs. William H., 183
Cronin, Morton, 69
"Crossroads of Life, The," 327 (ill.)
"Crucifixion" (Mantegna), 326 (ill.)
"Crucifixion" (Monaco), 56 (ill.)
Crystal Palace exposition, London, 99, 288
Cubism, 204, 205, 208, 219
Culture, business and, 20, 291, 293, 296-297, 298-299, 309; and the corporation, 337; the Chautauqua movement, 153-155; folk, 318; highbrow, lowbrow, and middlebrow, 310-333; march of, in 19th century, 179; mass, 6
Culture clubs, 155-157

Currier, Nathaniel, 68
Currier & Ives, 54 (ill.), 58 (ill.), 66, 67-70, 79, 125 (ill.), 239, 326 (ill.)
Currier & Ives, Printmakers to the American People (Peters), 69
Curtis, Mrs. Cyrus H. K., 175
Curtis, George William, 35, 109-110, 115, 344
"Custer's Last Fight" (Becker), 326 (ill.)

Daily Tribune, New York, quoted, 35, 86
Damrosch, Walter, 154
"Dance at the Spring, The" (Picabia), 210
Dark Victory, 229
Daubigny, Charles, 62, 158, 160
Daumier, Honoré, 204
Davidson, Jo, 199
Davies, Arthur B., 199-200, 201, 202, 203, 205, 208
Davis, Alexander J., 28-30, 31
Davis, Bette, 229
Davis, Harry, 226
Davis, Stuart, 205
Davis, Theo. R., 128 (ill.)
DeBeers Diamonds, 293, 294
Decoration, Bok influence on, 177-178, 221; of business offices, 267 (ill.), 306; in "company towns," 307; with concrete, 194; Early American, 238-241; the Eastlake influence, 97, 106-108, 129 (ill.); in 1840-1860, 9, 10, 27, 30-31; Elsie de Wolfe and, 181-186, 216 (ill.); emphasis on, 252; of Hunt's house, Washington Square, 136; and industrial art, 114, 115 (*see also* Industrial design); of mansions of the rich, 122, 141; Mission, 190, 191, 192; modernistic, 246-247; in the 1890's, 169-171; Oriental, 98, 99, 107, 141, 170-171, 174, 188, 213 (ill.); period, 185, 186; "personality" in, 241, 242; of public buildings, 292; in railroad cars, 95-96; reform in, 165-179; of river and lake steamers, 90-91, 92, 94; "suitability" in, 185-186; of Tiffany flat, 215 (ill.); traditionalism in, 306
Decoration of Houses, The (Wharton and Codman), 165
De Forest, Robert, 240
Degas, Edgar, 174
De Kay, Charles, 173, 174
Delacroix, Eugène, 204
"Delaware Valley" (Inness), 160

DeMille, Cecil B., 225
Democracy, and intellectual authority, 314; and taste, 5, 20
Demorest, W. Jennings, 77
Demorest, Mme. W. Jennings, 77-79
Depression, arts during, 147, 148, 284, 291-292; institutional advertising in, 291; taste during, 248
Derain, André, 294
Description of the Tremont House . . . , A, 83
Design, industrial, 288, 295, 301-304
Design, National Academy of, 41, 73, 196, 221
De Windt, Caroline (Mrs. Andrew Jackson Downing), 23
DeWindt, Mrs. (mother of Caroline), 34
Dewing, Thomas W., 196
De Wolfe, Elsie (Lady Mendl), 107, 180-186, 187, 189, 190, 215 (ill.), 216 (ill.), 253, 307, 335
Dickens, Charles, 81, 93, 344
Dining car, 95, 176
"Distribution of the Art Union Prizes" (Matteson), 51 (ill.)
Documentary films, 229-230
Dole Pineapple, 273 (ill.), 294
Domestic Manners of the Americans (Trollope), 5, 10, 344
Dondero, Congressman, 285
Dossena, Alceo, 279-281
Dow, Joy Wheeler, 7, 140, 167-168, 169
Downing, Andrew Jackson, 21-29, 31-32, 33-36, 37, 48, 49, 53 (ill.), 92, 97, 98, 100, 107, 117, 140, 147, 148, 163, 165, 186, 241, 301, 330, 337
Draper, Dorothy, 251
Dress pattern industry, 76, 77-79
Drew, Daniel, 93, 94
Drew (steamboat), 126 (ill.)
Dreyfuss, Henry, 272 (ill.), 302, 303, 340
Duccio, 198
Duchamp, Marcel, 203, 206, 218 (ill.), 247
Duchamp-Villon, Raymond, 203
Dufy, Raoul, 205
Duke University, 242
Durand, Asher B., 18, 30, 40, 56 (ill.), 326 (ill.)
Durand, John, 18, 40, 41
Dürer, Albrecht, 42, 122
Durlacher Brothers, 276
Duveen, Sir Joseph, 197, 198, 276, 277
"Dymaxion" house, 270 (ill.)

Eakins, Thomas, 113, 162
Eames, Charles, 304, 315
Early American decoration, 186, 238-241, 268 (ill.), 316
Eastlake, Sir Charles, 101
Eastlake, Charles Lock, 97, 100-103, 105, 106, 107, 114, 147, 163, 165, 185, 190, 244, 301, 334, 337
Education, the Chautauqua movement, 153-155; correspondence courses, 153; indiscriminate, 161, 314, 321; as one component of taste, 340, 341; of public taste, 29, 32, 62-63, 153, 221; summer school, 154; universal, 179
"Eight, The," 196
"Eight Bells" (Homer), 160
Elevators, 139, 163
El Greco, 198
Eliot, T. S., 104, 292, 317
Elizabethan style, 23, 97, 108
Elliott, Charles Wyllis, 103, 105-106
Ellsworth, William H., 113
Emerson, Ralph Waldo, 160
Empire State Building, 247, 306
English Gothic, 23 (*see also* Gothic Revival)
Evans, Rudolph, 222
Everett, Edward, 82
Exhibitions of art, 63 (*see also* Galleries *and* Museums); Centennial Exposition, 97, 112-115, 128 (ill.), 221, 257; Columbian Exposition, 142-144, 147, 163, 212 (ill.) 250; traveling, 152, 155, 156, 262, 283; World's Fair, 148, 250, 293, 302
Expositions (*see* Exhibitions of Art)

Farinacci, 281
Farm and Fireside, quoted, 73
Farnum, Dustin, 225
Farwell, Arthur Charles, 219
Fashion, 26, 27, 31, 76-77, 78, 300, 305
Fasoli, Alberto, 280, 281
Favrile glass, 170, 173, 175
Fay, A., 124 (ill.)
Fay, Ruth, 29-30
Fenway Court, 197
Ferry boats, 94
"Fiedler, Mr. and Mrs. Ernest, and Family, 1850," 52 (ill.)
Fiesole, Mino da, 280
Fillmore, Millard, 34
Fisk, Jim, 93, 94
Fitch, James Marsden, 139
Flagler, H. M., 194
Flair, quoted, 306
Fogg Museum, 260

Ford, Henry, 225, 226, 232, 233, 234, 240
Forestry, experimental, 122
Forster, E. M., 317
Forster, Frank J., 238
Forum, quoted, 161
"Four hundred," 167
"Fourth of July" (Currier & Ives), 326 (ill.)
Fowler, O. S., 36
Fragonard, Honoré, 198
Frame buildings, 109
France, modern painters of, 201, 202, 204, 205; motion pictures in, 227
Frauds in painting, 160, 277, 278-282
French, Daniel Chester, 143
French, W. M. R., 219
French flats controversy, 139
French influence, 30, 38, 131, 139, 140, 168, 249, 268 (ill.)
Freud, Sigmund, 336
Frick, Henry C., 184, 198
Frick Collection, 260, 280
"Friend in the Swamp" (Rogers), 74
Frohman, Charles, 180
Frost, Robert, 298
Fruits and Fruit Trees of America, The (Downing), 31
Fry, Roger, 198, 203, 222
Fuller, Buckminster, 250, 270 (ill.)
Fuller, Henry B., 161
Functionalism, 26, 116, 189; in architecture, 111, 244, 245, 248, 249, 330, 335; in furniture, 89, 102-103, 107, 187, 249
Furness, Frank, 136
Furniture, antique, 316; bamboo and wicker, 171; Bok's influence on, 178; Centennial Exposition, 128 (ill.); in "company towns," 307-308; in corporation offices, 306; Early American, 240, 241; Eastlake influence on, 100, 103; 190; factory-made, 9, 10, 99, 186, 187, 190; functionalism in, 89, 102, 103, 107, 187, 249; honest and inexpensive, 106; mail-order, 190, 217 (ill.); Mission, 187, 188, 190, 191, 192, 217 (ill.); modern, 304, 315, 329 (ill.); modernistic, 246-247; morality in, 105; Oriental, 99; parlor, mid-19th century, 27, 30-31
Futurism, 206, 208

Gable, Clark, 229
Gainsborough, Thomas, 197
Galleries, Apollo, 14; Centennial Exposition, 112-115; of Christian Art, 43,

44; Corcoran, 62; early 19th-century, 12, 14-18; Glass Center, 298-299; Jarves Collection at Yale, 57 (ill.), 60; the Louvre, 49; Metropolitan Museum, *see* Metropolitan Museum of Art; Modern Art, *see* Museum of Modern Art; national, efforts to establish, 37, 42, 43, 47, 59, 63-64, 260; New York Gallery of Fine Arts, 40-41; private, 38, 39-40, 45-47, 47-48, 265-277; public, 42, 59, 62, 63; Walters, 62; Whitney Museum, 264

Galton, Douglas, 94
Gambrill, Charles D., 136
Gardner, Mrs. "Jack," 197
Garfield, James A., 154
Garland, Hamlin, 152, 153, 155
Gates, George B., 95
Gauguin, Paul, 201, 204, 263
Genauer, Emily, 296
General Pike (river boat), 90
Georgian architecture, 140, 242, 269 (ill.)
Gerard, Sanford E., 335
Gérôme, Jean Léon, 158, 160, 326 (ill.)
Gerry, Elbridge T., 141
Gifford, Sanford, 113
Gilbert, W. S., 3
Glackens, William, 199, 204, 205
Glamour, 300
Glass, in modern architecture, 243; Favrile, 170, 173, 175, 215 (ill.); Glass Center, 273 (ill.), 298-299, 328 (ill.); stained, 165, 171-172
Gobelin tapestries, 122
Godey's Lady's Book, 10, 13, 176, 344
Goelet, Ogden, 141
Golden Age of Authors, A (Ellsworth), 113
Goldwyn, Sam, 225, 226, 227
Good Housekeeping, 241, 251
Good taste, era of, 165-179, 186
Good Taste Costs No More (Gump), 336
Gothic Revival, 23-24, 26, 27, 28, 29, 31, 35, 36, 53 (ill.), 84, 97, 98, 108, 135, 163, 167, 242, 244, 269 (ill.), 328 (ill.), 334, 335
Goupil, Vibert & Co., 18
Government, and the arts, 148, 150, 151, 161, 284, 291-292; housing projects of, 248, 249; regulation of business by, 309
Goya, Francisco, 198
Graham, Charles, 212 (ill.)
Grand Rapids furniture, 186, 190, 241
Grand Union hotel, Saratoga, 87

Grant, U. S., 154
Grauman's Chinese Theater, Hollywood, 325 (ill.)
Gray and Bowen, 83
"Gray Lowering Day" (Innes), 160
"Great Fight for the Championship, The" (Currier & Ives), 58 (ill.)
Great Republic (river boat), 125 (ill.)
"Great Russian Ball . . . , The" (Homer), 58 (ill.)
Great Train Robbery, The, 227
Greek Revival, 9, 10, 24, 31, 52 (ill.), 84, 92, 111, 244, 334, 335
"Greek Slave, The" (Powers), 19, 51 (ill.), 71
"Green, G. G., Residence & Laboratory" Pfeil & Golz), 127 (ill.)
Greenbelt, Maryland, 248
Greenberg, Clement, 313, 314
Greenough, Horatio, 7, 13, 71, 194
Greenwich Village, 247
Gregg, Frederick James, 204, 208
Griffith, D. W., 327 (ill.)
Gropius, Walter, 244, 302-303, 339
"Gross Clinic, The" (Eakins), 113
Guidebooks, 292
Gump, Richard, 336

Halsey, R. T. H., 240
Hamilton, Gail, 91
Hamlin, Talbot, 143
Hammer, Dr. Armand, 306
Hammond, Dr. W. A., 116
Handicrafts, 103 165, 187 (*see also* Crafts movement)
Hanley, Perkins, 213 (ill.)
Harkness, F. S., 194
Harper, James, 41
Harper's Bazar (Bazaar), 76, 317; quoted, 77, 100, 103, 107-108
Harper's (magazine), 33, 343, 344; quoted, 22, 45, 49-50, 90, 109, 158-159, 251, 252
Harris, John P., 226
Harrison & Abramovitz, 298
Hartley, Marsden, 205
Harvard, Fogg Museum at, 260; Georgian architecture at, 242
Havermeyer, Mrs. O. H., 197-198
Hayes, Rutherford B., 154
Hearst, William Randolph, 291
Hemingway, Ernest, 317
Henderson, Harry, 252
Henri, Robert, 199, 207, 220
Henry Clay (steamer), 34-35
Herald, New York, 17, 145; quoted, 206
Herald Tribune Forum, 287, 303

Herbert, A. P., 312
Herring, James, 13-14
Highbrows, 25, 26, 310, 311-318, 319, 321, 330, 331, 332, 333
Highland Gardens (Downing's home), 23-24, 53 (ill.)
High Renaissance, 148
Hill, George Washington, 287
Hill, Ralph Nading, 93
Hints on Household Taste (Eastlake), 100, 101, 104, 108
Hitchcock, Henry-Russell, 244
Hogarth, William, 73
Holly, H. Hudson, 108, 114
Hollywood, 225
Home for All, A (Fowler), 36
Home Book of Quotations, 191
Home-decorating industries, 9, 10 (*see also* Decoration)
Homer, Winslow, 58 (ill.), 158, 160
Honesty in architecture, 49, 108, 188, 244, 335, 337
Hoovervilles, 248
Hopper, Edward, 205
Horizon, quoted, 314
Horticulturalist, 31
Hotels, 81-89, 247
Hotel World Review, quoted, 88
Houghton, Arthur A., Jr., 300, 303
House Beautiful (magazine), 237, 241, 344; quoted, 193, 194
House Beautiful, The (Cook), 116
House in Good Taste, The (De Wolfe), 184
Household Taste (Smith), 114
Housing, 248, 249, 250
Howard, Charles, 273 (ill.)
Howe, Frank M., 143
How to Furnish a Home (Rodman), 107
How Good Is Your Taste? (Gerard), 335
Hubbard, Elbert, 191-193
Huldah, 282
Hull House, 159
Humphreys, Mary Gay, 171
Hunt, Richard Morris, 122, 131-136, 138-140, 141-143, 144, 145-146, 165, 167, 211 (ill.), 237, 243, 245, 261
Hunt, William Morris, 62, 113, 145
Hunt, Mrs. (mother of Richard and William), 132, 133
Huntington, Henry E., 197
Hutchinson, Charles L., 149
Hutton, Betty, 229

Impressionists, 149-150, 155, 158, 198, 203
Independents, Show of, 197

Index of American Design, 292
Industrial art, 113, 114, 115, 149, 272 (ill.)
Industrial building, 148
Industrial design, 249, 288, 295, 301-304
Industrialism, impact of, on taste, 65-80, 236
Industry, and the arts, 149, 225-234, 287-288, 293-309; new standards for working conditions in, 233-234
Ingres, J. A. D., 204
Inness, George, 160
Institute of Fine Arts, New York University, 260
Institute of Modern (Contemporary) Art, Boston, 264
Interior decoration. *See* Decoration
International Art Union, 18
International Business Machines, 293, 299 n.
International Exhibition of Modern Art (Armory Show), 198-210, 211, 218 (ill.), 220-222
International Style, 243, 244, 245, 330
Intimidation, 185
Intolerance, 229
Iranistan (Barnum's home), 99
Irving, Washington, 40, 74, 99, 181
Italian style in architecture, 26, 29, 31, 35, 36, 54 (ill.), 98, 163, 244, 323 (ill.)
Italian primitive painting, 50, 59-61
It Happened One Night, 229
Ives, James Merritt, 68

Jackson, Andrew, 5, 7, 236
James, Henry, 312
James, William, 154
Jameson, Mrs. Anna, 50
Japanese corner, 171
Japanese decoration, 107, 165
Japanese prints, 170
Jarves, James Jackson, 37-38, 42, 44, 48-62, 56 (ill.), 64, 70, 74-75, 104, 117, 138, 184, 221, 256, 259, 318, 340
Jay, John, 63
Jazz, 318
Jefferson, Thomas, 6, 92
Jennings Agency, 289
"Jeux d'Eau" (Ravel), 219
Johnson, Eastman, 68, 113
Johnson, Philip, 244, 270 (ill.)

Kandinsky, Vasily, 205
Karfiol, Bernard, 205
Keller, Helen, 158
Kelly, Richard, 306

Kenyon Review, 313
Kierkegaard, 312
"Kindred Spirits" (Durand), 326 (ill.)
Knight, Dame Laura, 294
Knoedler's 276
Kobbe, Gustav, 161
Kouwenhoven, John A., 114, 344
Kuhn, Walt, 199, 201, 202, 203, 204, 205, 206, 220, 285
Kuniyoshi, Yasuo, 74

Labor movement, 157, 234, 289
Ladies' Home Journal, 96, 165, 172, 174, 175, 178, 237, 241, 251, 335, 344; quoted, 171
Ladies' Home Journal houses, 176-177, 255, 270 (ill.)
Lady's World of Fashion, The, 10
La Farge, John, 143, 144, 172
Lake steamers, 92-94
Lakewood, California, 251
Lambrequins, 10, 30, 176
"Landing of the Pilgrims," 46-47
Landscape gardening, 21-23, 24, 33, 34
Landscape painting, 12-13, 99
Landseer, Sir Edwin, 73
Larkin, Oliver, 344
Larrabee, Eric, 251
Lasky, Jesse L., 225, 226, 227
Last Mile, The, 302
"Last Supper" (Leonardo), 170
Laurencin, Marie, 205, 294
Le Corbusier, 244, 245
Lee, Ivy Ledbetter, 289
Lefuel, Hector Martin, 133
Léger, Fernand, 205
Lehmbruck, Wilhelm, 203
Leisure, for the masses, 299; for the wealthy, 132
Leonardo da Vinci, 170
Leslie's Weekly Newspaper, 344; quoted, 86-87
Leutze, Emanuel, 31
Lever House, 306
Levitt, William J., 251
Levittown, 251, 270 (ill.), 323 (ill.)
Liebes, Dorothy, 304
Liederer, Baron de, 23
Life, 283
Life classes, 12
"Life Line, The" (Homer), 160
Life on the Mississippi (Twain), 31
Lincoln, Abraham, 74, 95
Lindsay, Lord, 50
Lithographs, Currier & Ives, 54 (ill.), 58 (ill.), 67-68, 69, 70, 125 (ill.), 239, 326 (ill.)

Little Journeys to Homes of Great Men (Hubbard), 191
"Little" magazines, 312-313, 320
Little Review, 313
Lochner, Stefan, 276
Loewy, Raymond, 302
Longworth, Joseph and Nicholas, 148
Lord & Taylor, 299 n.
Lowbrows, 25, 310, 311, 312, 318-320, 333
Lower middlebrows, 320, 331-333
Lucky Strike, 295
Luks, George, 205
Lusitania, 192

McAllister, Ward, 139, 167
McCrae, David, 344
McDougall, Alice Foote, 241-242
Machine art, 249, 272 (ill.)
Machine for living, 245
Mack, Walter S., 296, 298
McKim, Charles F., 131, 132, 144
McKim, Mead, and White, 140, 142, 143, 169, 174
McKinley, William, 154
MacLeish, Archibald, 298
MacMonnies, Frederick, 143, 196
MacRae, Elmer, 199, 205
Macy, R. H., and Company, 251
Made in America (Kouwenhoven), 114, 344
Maillol, Aristide, 205, 282, 294
Magazine of Art, quoted, 296-297, 304
Magazines, in the 1840's, 10; "little," 312-313, 320
Mail-order business, in furniture, 190, 217 (ill.); in patterns, 78
Manet, Edouard, 174, 198
Mansard houses, 98, 99, 244
Mantegna, Andrea, 42, 326 (ill.)
Marbury, Elizabeth, 180, 182
Marquand, John, 239
Marryatt, Frank, 85
Martin, Fletcher, 295
Martini, Simone, 280-281
Massachusetts State Normal Art School, 151
Mass culture, 6
Mass production, 8-11; of art for the home, 66-75, 79-80; of automobiles, 233-234; of clothing, 75-76; of dress patterns, 79; of houses, 246, 250, 252; of "tasteful" objects, 236
Matisse, Henri, 201, 205, 219
Matteson, T. H., 52 (ill.)
Matthews, Brander, 311

Maurer, Alfred, 203
Maxwell House, Nashville, 84
Mead, W. R., 132
Mediocrity, 16-17, 49
Meegeren, Han van, 274 (ill.) 278-279
Meissonier, J. L. E., 63, 160
Melchers, Gari, 143
Mellon, Andrew, 291
Memorial Hall, Centennial Exposition, 112-113
Mendl, Lady (see de Wolfe, Elsie)
"Message to Garcia, A" (Hubbard), 192
Metropolitan Life Insurance Company, 249
Metropolitan Museum of Art, 57 (ill.), 64, 142, 160, 161, 197, 207, 240, 260, 261, 262, 277, 280, 281, 283, 285, 296, 297, 315, 330 (ill.)
Michelangelo, 73, 230, 282
Michigan, University of, 150
Middlebrows, 310, 311, 313, 314, 315, 317, 319, 320-333, 334
Middle class, 236-237, 314
Millais, Sir John, 293
Miller, Lewis, 153
Millet, Jean François, 62
Milligan, Robert J., house, Saratoga Springs, 54 (ill.)
Miniature golf, 256
Minstrel shows, 65
Mission furniture, 187, 188, 190, 191, 192
Mississippi River boats, 89-92, 93, 125 (ill.)
Mock, Elizabeth, 245
Modern architecture, 139, 143, 148, 194, 242-246, 247-248, 337-338; in hotels, 88-89; relation of ranch house to, 189; versus traditional, 245
Modern art, 155, 196-222, 263; and traditional, 285, 297
"Modern Art" and the American Public, 264
Modernistic style, 246-247, 267 (ill.)
Monaco, Lorenzo, 56 (ill.)
Monroe, Harriet, 210
Monet, Claude, 198, 204
Monsanto Chemical, 299 n.
Montclair, 253
Moorish decoration, 141, 171 (see also Oriental influence)
Morality of art and architecture, 24-25, 27, 97, 101, 103, 111, 150-151, 163, 187, 228, 244, 245, 301, 337, 338, 340, 341
Morgan, Anne, 182

Morgan, J. Pierpont, 197, 291
Morris, William, 97, 103, 106, 115, 165, 187, 191, 244
Morse, Mrs. T. Vernette, 152, 155
Morton, J. Sterling, 122
Motion pictures, 225, 226-232; collection of, at Museum of Modern Art, 264
Mount, William Sidney, 40
Mumford, Lewis, 188, 247, 344
Munsell, A. H., 158
Murder in the Cathedral (Eliot), 292
Museum of Fine Arts, Boston, 280
Museum of Modern Art, New York, 102, 152, 243-244, 249, 251, 262-265, 299 n., 300-301
Museums (see also Collections and Galleries); attendance at, 262, 296, 298; directors of, 260-262, 321; early, 12, 19, 117; growth of, 148-150, 155, 157-159, 161, 162, 197-198, 259, 260; influence of, on taste, 262-265
Music after the Civil War, 65; for the movies, 227-228
Myers, Jerome, 199, 207, 220

Nails, machine-made, 109
Nashville, "Art Association," 150; Maxwell House, 84
National Academy of Design, 41, 73, 196, 221
National Association of Manufacturers, 291
National Gallery, Washington, 260
National Sculpture Society, 285
National Theater, Mexico City, 173
"Natural forms," 135
Near-Impressionists, 208
Needlework, 30, 102
Nelson, George, 304
New Place (Crocker home), 183
Newport, Rhode Island, 93, 137, 145
New York, Central Park, 33; Colony Club, 182, 183; Metropolitan Museum, see Metropolitan Museum of Art; Museum of Modern Art, see Museum of Modern Art; Radio City Music Hall, 126 (ill.), 267 (ill.); St. Nicholas Hotel, 86; Tribune Building, 139; University Settlement Society, 157-158; Waldorf-Astoria Hotel, 247
New York Central Building, 325 (ill.)
New Yorker, 317
New York Gallery of Fine Arts, 40-41
New York Historical Society, 41, 44, 59
New York Hospital, 283

New York Illustrated, quoted, 77
New York Public Library, 194
New York Times, quoted, 189, 206, 209, 251, 275
New York University Institute of Fine Arts, 260
New York World's Fair. *See* World's Fair of 1939
Nichols, H. D., 212 (ill.)
Nickelodeon, 226-227
Norton, Charles Eliot, 137
Novelty-seeking, 101-102, 107
"Nude Descending a Staircase" (Duchamp), 203, 206, 218 (ill.)

Odegaard, Charles E., 287
"Oil chromos," 79-80
O'Keeffe, Georgia, 294-295
Olana (Church's home), 99, 325 (ill.)
Old Homes Made New (Woollett), 111
Old masters, 42, 44, 46; reproductions of, 283
Olmsted, Frederick Law, 33, 99, 122, 142
Opportunity Art Gallery, 297
Oriental booth, 170-171, 174, 213 (ill.)
Oriental influence, 98, 99, 107, 141, 170-171, 174, 188
Ortega y Gasset, José, 315
Otis, Elisha Graves, 163
Oud, J. J. P., 244
Outlook, 181; quoted, 179

Pach, Walter, 201, 203, 205, 207, 219, 220
Packaging, 301-302
Paepcke, Walter P., 298, 300
Paff, Michael, 39
Painting (*see also* Art *and* Collections); amateur, 284; at Centennial Exposition, 113; commissioning of, 40; in the 1830's, 12-13; fraudulent, *see* Frauds; Italian primitives, 50, 59-61; landscape, 12-13, 99; modern, 155, 196-222, 263, 285, 297; portrait, 40; value of, 160, 197, 265, 275-282
Palace Hotel, San Francisco, 86-87, 123 (ill.)
Palace hotels, 81-89
Palace ships, 89-94
Pallesi, Romano, 280, 281
Palmer House, Chicago, 87
Palmo's Opera House, New York, 19
Panama Canal, 193
Pape, W. A. C., 212 (ill.)
Paris, as center of fashion, 76-77; Exposition of 1867 in, 99; as headquarters of Art World, 258; Ritz hotel in, 88
Parke-Bernet Galleries, 275
Parker House, San Francisco, 85
Park Forest, Illinois, 251
Parlors, 19th-century, 10, 27, 30-31
Parmly, Dr., 134
Partisan Review, 313, 317
Patience (Gilbert and Sullivan), 3, 116
Patronage of the arts, by corporations, 166, 288, 292-299, 309; by government, 148, 291-292; private, 13-14, 19-20, 38-64, 137, 138, 151, 291; by upper middlebrows, 330, 331; by working class, 234
Pattern (dress) industry, 76, 77-79
Peabody and Stearns, 143
Peale, Charles Willson, 12
Pears Soap, 293
Pène du Bois, Guy, 200, 204, 220
Pepsi-Cola Company, 295-298
Period decoration, 185, 186
Perisphere, 250, 302
Perkins, Charles Callahan, 103, 104, 105
Perrault, Léon, 158
Perry, Admiral, 99
Personality, 247, 335; expressed in decoration, 185, 241; expressed through taste, 336
Personality of a House, The (Post), 241
Peters, Harry T., 69
Peterson's Magazine, 344
Philadelphia, Centennial Exposition at, 97, 112-117, 128 (ill.), 221, 257
Philistine (magazine), 192
Philistinism, 11, 26, 117, 208, 257, 262, 286, 320
Phillips, William, 314
Phillips museum, 260
Picabia, Francis, 205, 209, 210
Picasso, Pablo, 201, 205, 247, 315, 317
Pierce Arrow, 293
Pinchot, Gifford, 122
"Pioneer" (sleeping car), 95
Pisano, 280
Pitkin, Walter B., 246
Plan books, 176-177
Platt, George, 181, 323 (ill.)
Pleasure, 338-339
Plymouth Rock (steamboat), 94
PM, quoted, 250
Poe, Edgar Allan, 25
Poetry, 313
Poetry of Christian Art, The (Rio), 50
"Polish Rider, The" (Rembrandt), 198
Politics, 34, 285
Pollaiuolo, Antonio, 60

Pollock, Jackson, 315
Portland cement, 193-194, 217 (ill.), 255, 323 (ill.), 325 (ill.)
"Portrait of the Artist's Mother" (Whistler), 327 (ill.)
Portrait painting, 40
Post, Emily, 241, 335
Post, George B., 136
Post-Impressionists, 201, 203, 206
Powers, Hiram, 19, 51 (ill.), 71
Pragmatism, 26, 338
Premium selling, 191, 283
Prendergast, Maurice, 210
Princeton University, 36, 242
Provenance, 276, 280
Prudery, 11, 12, 19, 150-151
Pseudo-classicism, 71
Public relations, 289-291, 299
Publishing, 313, 320-321
Pugin, Augustus, 135
Pullman, George Mortimer, 94, 95-96, 226
Pullman Palace Cars, 89, 95, 96, 175
Purism, 318
Puritanism, 338
Puvis de Chavannes, Pierre, 204
"Pygmalion and Galatea" (Gérôme), 326 (ill.)

Quaintness, 238, 240
Queen Anne style in architecture, 97, 108-112, 114, 129 (ill.), 147, 167, 176, 214 (ill.), 244, 328 (ill.)
Quinn, John, 202, 205, 207, 210

Radio City Music Hall, New York, 126 (ill.), 267 (ill.)
Railroad cars, 94-96, 175, 176, 226
Ralph, Julian, 159
Ralston, William C., 87
Ranch house, 187, 188, 189, 251, 253, 270 (ill.), 271 (ill.), 323 (ill.)
Raphael, 277
Ravel, Maurice, 219
Reading room, hotel, 83
Realism, 162, 283
Record Herald, Chicago, quoted, 210
Recreation, 299
Redon, Odilon, 203, 204
Reed, Luman, 38-40, 42, 44, 48, 56 (ill.), 64, 150, 257, 291
Reform movements, 289
Rembrandt, 197, 198, 282
Reni, Guido, 170
Renoir, Auguste, 149, 198, 204, 282
Reproductions of old masters, 283
"Republic, The" (French), 143

"Rest on the Flight into Egypt" (Bordone), 56 (ill.)
Restoration of paintings, 277
Reynolds, Sir Joshua, 73
Rich, increasing wealth of, 117, 166; influence of taste of, 165, 166, 310, 336; mansions for, 121, 122, 131
Richardson, H. H., 132, 140, 142, 144, 243
Rilke, Rainer Maria, 312
Rio, Alexis François, 50
Ritz hotel, Paris, 88
River boats, 89-94, 125 (ill.), 126 (ill.)
Robsjohn-Gibbings, T. H., 304
Rockefeller, Mrs. John D., Jr., 243
Rodman, Ella Church, 107
Roebling, John A., 226
Rogers, Agnes, 236
Rogers, Isaiah, 83-84, 85, 89
Rogers, James Gamble, 242
Rogers, John, 70-75, 79, 290
Rogers Groups, 58 (ill.), 70, 72-75, 239-240
Romanesque style, 122, 140, 149 (*see also* French influence)
Romantics, 162
Rome, Harold, 298
Roosevelt, New Jersey, 248
Roosevelt, Theodore, 154, 208
Root, John Wellborn, 142, 149
Roots of Contemporary American Architecture, 344
Rose, Billy, 311
Rossetti, Dante Gabriel, 115
Rotunda, New York, 41
Rouault, Georges, 205
Round Table, 45
Rousseau, Théodore, 160
Roy, Pierre, 273 (ill.), 294
Roycrofters Inn, 192
Roycroft Press, 191, 192
Rubens, Peter Paul, 197, 276
"Rude Descending a Staircase, The" (Griswold), 218 (ill.)
Rural architecture, 23-27, 28-29, 31, 32-33, 36
Rural Architecture (Allen), 26
Rural Art and Rural Taste, Societies of, 98
Rushmore, Mount, 199
Rushkin, John, 25, 32, 50, 97, 102, 135, 167, 337
Ryder, Albert, 113, 162, 197, 205
Ryerson, Martin A., 149

Sacred and Legendary Art (Jameson), 50

Sage, Mrs. Russell, 240
Saint-Gaudens, Augustus, 143, 144, 150
St. John (steamboat), 94
St. Louis museum, 150, 260
St. Nicholas Hotel, New York, 86
Sandham, Henry, 158
Sandwich Glass Company, 49
San Francisco, museum, 150, 260; Palace Hotel, 86-87, 123 (ill.); Parker House and What Cheer House, 85
Saratoga resort hotels, 87
Sardou, Victorien, 180
Sassetta, Stefano, 60
Saturday Evening Post covers, 70
Schools, of architecture, 136; art in, 159, 283, 288; for decoration, 182; singing taught in, 65; summer, 154; Sunday, 153
Scribner's, 344; quoted, 151
Sculpture, in Armory Show, 203, 205; in the 1840's, 19; in the 1830's, 13; Rogers Groups, 58 (ill.), 70, 72-75, 239-240; traveling exhibitions of, 152
Sears, Roebuck and Company, 190, 217 (ill.), 254, 282, 301
Seitlin, Percy, 304
Seligman, Jacques, 184
Sensibility, 340, 341
Settings, movie and stage, 228-229, 230, 268 (ill.), 302
Seurat, Georges, 263
Sewanee Review, 313
Shakespeare, William, 65
Sharon, William, 87
Shaw's Civil Architecture, 10
Sherman, Captain, 93
Sherwood, Mrs. M. E. W., 103, 104-105, 106, 115, 116, 184, 344
Sherwood, Robert E., 103, 229
Sidewheeler Saga (Hill), 93
Simon, André, 316
Simplicity, 188, 245
Sincerity, 102, 103, 106, 109, 185, 244, 301, 337
Singing, 65
Siple, Allen G., 251, 270 (ill.)
"Sistine Madonna" (Raphael), 170
Sitwell, Osbert, 321
"Six Mark Teapot, The," 130 (ill.)
Sketch Club, 40
Sketches of the History of Christian Art (Lindsay), 50
Skyscraper, 163-164, 169, 226, 246, 247
"Slave Auction, The" (Rogers), 58 (ill.), 72-73
Sleeping car, 94-95
"Sleeping Innocence" (Perrault), 158

Slick, Jonathan, 30
Sloan, John, 199, 205
Slums, 179
Small, Frank O., 212 (ill.)
Smalley, Donald, 344
Smith, Walter, 114
Smithsonian Institution, 33
Snobbishness, aesthetic, 104, 105; in art salesmanship, 276; of hotel clerks, 88; social, 105, 310; in taste, 185
Snyders, Frans, 276
Social competition, 137
Societies of Rural Art and Rural Taste, 98
Society, fluidity of, 138; lessening of income differences in, 234; new structure of, 310; in the 1890's, 165-167
Sonderbund, 202-203
Spanish Colonial style, 188, 268 (ill.)
Spanish Mission style, 189
Spingarn, Joel, 206
Split level house, 253
Squaw Man, The, 225, 226
Stage design, 302
Stained glass, 165, 171-172
Standardization of houses, 252, 253
Standard Oil Company, 289, 295
Stanford, Leland, 87, 137
Starr, Ellen G., 159
Statler Hotel, Washington, 88
Statue of Liberty, 142
Steamboats, 89-94, 125 (ill.), 126 (ill.), 330 (ill.)
Steegmuller, Francis, 49
Steel, 169, 195, 226
Steinway, 293
Stevenson, John J., 109
Stevenson, Robert Louis, 8
Stevenson's *Home Book of Quotations*, quoted, 191
Stewart, A. T., 63, 291
Stickley, Gustav, 186-188, 189, 190, 191
Stieglitz, Alfred, 201
Stillman, James A., 222
Stone, William O., 56 (ill.)
Stowe, Harriet Beecher, 66, 67, 70
Stravinsky, Igor, 317
Streamlining, 243, 249
Street, Julian, 206
Strikes, 289
Strong, Elizabeth, 158
Structure, balloon frame, 109; cement, 193-194, 217 (ill.), 255, 323 (ill.), 325 (ill.); modernism in, 244; steel, 169, 195, 226; of suburban houses, 247
Stuart, Gilbert, 113

Studebaker, 302
Style, architectural, *see* Architecture; Battle of, 135, 140, 245; consistency of, 185; fluidity of, 300, 305; International, 243, 244, 245, 330; regional differences in, 77
Suburbs, 234, 235-255
Suitability, 185-186, 335
Sullivan, Louis, 139, 142, 164, 195, 243
Summer school, 154
Sunday school, 153
"Sunday on the Union Pacific," 124 (ill.)
"Supper at Emmaeus" (Meegeren), 274 (ill.)
Swiss chalet, 35, 169

Tableau vivant, 19, 74
Taft, Lorado, 152, 155, 156, 196
Taft, William Howard, 154
Tales of the Alhambra (Irving), 99
Tampa Bay Hotel, 87-88
Tappan, Lewis, 73
Taste, components of, 340-341; corporate, 7, 225-341; education of, 29, 32, 62-63, 153, 221; expressing personality through, 336; fashionable, 334; fashion and, 305; good, era of, 165-179, 186; impact of industrialism on, 65-80, 236; indefinability of, 339; influence of museums on, 262-265; as major industry, 4, 335; private, 6, 121-222; public, 5-117, 256, 259, 305, 337; rejection of primitives by, 60-61; snobbishness in, 185; taste appeal, 300-301, 304; and wealth, 165, 166, 310, 336
Taylor, Francis Henry, 262
Taylor, Henry Fitch, 199
Taylor, William, 85
Teague, Walter Dorwin, 302
"Temperance but no Maine Law" (Fay), 124 (ill.)
Terrace Plaza hotel, Cincinnati, 88
Teyte, Maggie, 316
Theater, during the depression, 292; revival of, 65-66; settings for, 302
Thermidor (Sardou), 180
Thompson, J. Walter, Inc., 267 (ill.), 306
Tiepolo, G. B., 122
Tiffany, Louis Comfort, 170, 173-175, 190, 191, 215 (ill.)
Tiles, 105, 107, 165
Titian, 197
Toulouse-Lautrec, Henri de, 201, 330
Towle, George Makepeace, 65, 87

Town, Ithiel, 28, 29
Toynbee, Arnold, 321
Toynbee Hall, London, 157
Tozzi, Piero, 281
Traditionalists, 222; versus modernists, 245, 285, 297
Trailer, 250
Trains. *See* Railroad cars
transatlantic review, 313
transition, 313
Tray table, 183
Treatise on the Theory and Practice of Landscape Gardening, A (Downing), 24
Tremont House, Boston, 81-84, 123 (ill.)
Tribune, Chicago, 210
Tribune, New York, quoted, 35, 86
Tribune Building, New York, 139
Trinity Church, Boston, 132
"Triumvirate, the" (Taft, Garland, and Brown), 152-153
Trollope, Mrs. Frances, 5-6, 10, 13, 50, 92, 117, 344
Truman, Harry, 74
Trumbull, John, 68
Truth (*see also* Sincerity); and architecture, 27; and beauty, societies for, 151-162, 221
Trylon, 250
Tuckerman, Henry T., 43, 63, 64, 184, 256, 340
Tudor style, 249, 268 (ill.)
Turcas, Nanette, 209
Turkish corner, 171, 174
Turner, J. M. W., 198
Tuscan villa, 98, 163, 323 (ill.)
Twain, Mark, 31, 89, 92
Two Lives of James Jackson Jarves, The (Steegmuller), 49
"291" gallery, 201

Unemployment, 291
United Brewers Foundation, 295
United Distillers of America, 306
United States Hotel, Saratoga, 87
United States Steel Corporation, 291
University Settlement Society, 157-158
Upholstery, factory-made, 9
Upjohn Pharmaceutical, 295
Upper middlebrows, 320-331, 333
Utrillo, Maurice, 282

Vail, Theodore Newton, 289
Van Brunt, Henry, 132, 135, 136, 143, 146
Vanderbilt, Alva, 139

Vanderbilt, Cornelius, 93, 121
Vanderbilt, Cornelius, II, 121-122, 131
Vanderbilt, George Washington, II, 121-122, 131
Vanderbilt, William H., 121, 289
Vanderbilt, William K., 121, 122, 131, 139, 142, 144
Van der Rohe, Mies, 244, 315
Van Eyck, Jan, 42
Van Gogh, Vincent, 202, 203, 204, 230, 263, 282, 327 (ill.)
Vanity table, 183
Vaudeville, 227
Vaux, Calvert, 32-33, 64, 99, 344
Velásquez, Diego, 42, 198
Veneering, 103
"Venus de Medici," 12
Vermeer, Jan, 274 (ill.), 278
Vernacular art, 319, 344
Vernacular style of building, 109, 244
Victorian era, 164, 316
"Village Smithy, The" (Sandham), 158
Villard, Henry, 140
Villas and Cottages (Vaux), 33
Vincent, John H., 153
Viollet le Duc, Eugène, 301
Virginia Quarterly, 313
Virginibus Puerisque (Stevenson), 8
Vollard, Ambroise, 203
"Voyage of Life" (Cole), 16
Vulgarization, 110

Wagner, Richard, 112
Waldorf-Astoria Hotel, New York, 247
Wallace, Edgar, 311, 316
Wallace, Sir Richard, 184
Waller, Frank, 57 (ill.)
Wall Street Journal, quoted, 240 n.
Walter, Thomas U., 134
Walters, William T., 62
Ware, William R., 136
Washington, D.C., National Gallery, 260; public gardens, 33-34; Statler Hotel, 88
Washington, George, 13
"Washington Crossing the Delaware" (Leutze), 31
Watrous, Henry, 209
Wayside Inn, restoration of, 240
Webster, Daniel, 82
Weir, J. Alden, 143, 199
West, Benjamin, 19, 113
Westminster, Duke of, 197
Wharton, Edith, 107, 165, 167, 172, 180, 182, 310, 335

What Cheer House, San Francisco, 85
Whatnot, 30, 31, 99, 102, 165
What's New? 298
Wheeler, Candace, 179, 181-182, 184
Wheeler, Gervase, 80
Whistler, James McNeill, 170, 174, 326 (ill.), 327 (ill.)
"Whistler's Mother," 327 (ill.)
White, Richard Grant, 43
White, Stanford, 43, 132, 144, 177, 182, 183
"White City," 142-144, 147, 163, 250
White House, landscaping of, 33, 34
Whitney, Gertrude Vanderbilt, 196, 204
Whitney Museum of American Art, 264
Whittier, John G., 112
Whyte, William H., Jr., 308
Wickford Point (Marquand), 239
Widener, P. A. B., 291
Wildenstein's, 276
Williamsburg restoration, 240-241
Williamson, Jefferson, 85
Wilson, Charles, 167
Wilson, Henry L., 188-189, 194, 255
Wilson, Woodrow, 208, 233
Wilson Patent Adjustable Chair, 329 (ill.)
Wine and Food, 316
Woman's Book, 174; quoted, 170, 171
"Woman Weighing Gold, A" (Vermeer), 274 (ill.)
Women's College Settlement, Boston, 158
Woolf, Virginia, 320, 331
Woollett, William M., 111, 301, 324 (ill.)
Working classes, art for, 156-159, 162
Works Progress Administration, 148, 284, 291-292
World's Columbian Exposition of 1893, 142-144, 147, 163, 212 (ill.), 250
World's Fair of 1939, 148, 250, 293, 302
World War II, housing in, 250
"Wounded Scout" (Rogers), 74
Wright, Frank Lloyd, 142, 152, 244, 339
Wurlitzer Juke Box, 213 (ill.)

Yale, architecture at, 242, 269 (ill.); Jarves Collection at, 57 (ill.), 60
Yale & Towne, 299 n.
Young, Mahonri, 199, 205, 220
"Youth" (Cole), 16, 51 (ill.)

Zoning laws, 247